Interactive Curve Modeling

T0214558

M. Sarfraz

Interactive Curve Modeling

With Applications to Computer Graphics, Vision and Image Processing

Springer

M. Sarfraz, BSc, MSc, MSc, Phd
Department of Information Science
Kuwait University
Safat, Kuwait

and

Department of Information and Computer Science
King Fahd University of Petroleum and Minerals
Dhahran, Saudi Arabia

British Library Cataloguing in Publication Data
A catalogue record for this book is available from the British Library

Printed on acid-free paper

ISBN 978-1-84996-663-4   e-ISBN 978-1-84628-871-5

9 8 7 6 5 4 3 2 1

Springer Science+Business Media
springer.com

To the major contributors to my life:

My primary school teacher M. Aslam

My friends Ashfaq and Abid

My father in memoriam

My mother

My wife

My children Ihsan, Humaira, Inam, and Ikram

Preface

Interactive curve modeling techniques and their applications are extremely useful in a number of academic and industrial settings. Specifically, curve modeling plays a significant role in multidisciplinary problem solving. It is extremely useful in various situations like font design, designing objects, CAD/CAM, medical imaging and visualization, scientific data visualization, virtual reality, object recognition, etc. In particular, various problems like iris recognition, fingerprint recognition, signature recognition, etc. can also be intelligently solved and automated using curve techniques. In addition to its critical importance more recently, the curve modeling methods have also proven to be indispensable in a variety of modern industries, including computer vision, robotics, medical imaging, visualization, and even media.

This book aims to provide a valuable source that focuses on interdisciplinary methods and to add up-to-date methodologies in the area. It aims to provide the user community with a variety of techniques, applications, and systems necessary for various real-life problems in the areas such as font design, medical visualization, scientific data visualization, archaeology, toon rendering, virtual reality, body simulation, outline capture of images, object recognition, signature recognition, industrial applications, and many others.

Book Features

It aims to collect and disseminate information in various disciplines including computer graphics, image processing, computer vision, pattern recognition, artificial intelligence, soft computing, shape analysis and description, curve and surface fitting, scientific visualization, shape abstraction and modeling, intelligent CAD systems, computational geometry, reverse engineering, and levels of details for curves and surfaces. The major goal of this book is to stimulate views and provide a source where students, researchers, and practitioners can find the latest developments in the field of interactive curve modeling and its applications. The book provides classical and up-to-date theory and practice to get the problems solved in diverse areas of science and engineering.

All the chapters of the book will contribute toward curve modeling techniques, applications, and systems. The book will have the best possible utility for students, researchers, computer scientists, practicing engineers, and many others who seek classical and state-of-the-art techniques, applications, and systems with curve modeling. It will be an extremely useful book for undergraduate senior students as well as graduate students in the areas of computer science, engineering, and other computational sciences.

Suggested Course Outlines

This book is designed to have around fifteen chapters. These chapters will contribute toward interactive curve modeling techniques, applications, systems, and tools. The book is planned to have the best possible utility for researchers, computer scientists, practicing engineers, and many others who seek classical and state-of-the-art techniques and applications for computer graphics, vision, and imaging. It will also be equally and extremely useful for undergraduate senior students as well as graduate students in the areas of computer science. It is also beneficial to students in other disciplines including computer engineering, electrical engineering, mechanical engineering, and mathematics. The book is equally beneficial to researchers and practitioners in the industry and academia.

The book has been designed as a course book for undergraduate as well as graduate students in the area of computer science in particular. The main audience of the book are the communities related to the field of computer graphics, vision, and imaging. However, it can be useful for students in other disciplines like computer engineering, electrical engineering, mechanical engineering, mathematics, etc. The book is equally beneficial to researchers and practitioners in the industry. The book can formulate at least three courses as follows:

Course I. As an undergraduate course, at senior level, Chaps. 1–3, 8, 9, 11 (any two corner detectors), 12 (any two methods), 13, and 14 (one heuristic approach) will comprise a full length three credit hours course for a semester of 15 weeks. This course can be conducted with practical projects of reasonable weight.

Course II. As a graduate course consisting of Chaps. 1–4, 6–8 (self-study), 9, and 11–14 (one heuristic approach). This course should also have heavy projects for practical applications.

Course III. As a slightly different graduate course, if the undergraduate course described in Course I is considered to be a prerequisite. This course can be designed with Chaps. 4–7, 9 (using other curve schemes in the book but different than those in Chap. 9), 11–13 (just a quick review), 14, and 15. This course design can also consist of some state-of-the-art topics together with good weighted projects.

The researchers and practitioners can utilize the manuscript as a source as well as a reference book. Depending on their needs, they can study on pick and choose basis. They are also advised to study in their leisure time as it may prove to be fruitful to them.

Required Background

As such, it is not required to possess a specific qualification as a prerequisite to any of the undergraduate Course I or graduate courses II or III mentioned above. But, the user of this book is presumed to have some knowledge of computer programming together with some basic mathematical topics including analytic geometry, linear algebra, and calculus.

Acknowledgments

This manuscript has been prepared after a lot of struggle and efforts. Many graduate students and colleagues around the globe have assisted toward its completion. It is worthwhile to mention Asif Masood, Zulfiqar Habib, M. Zawwar Hussain, S. Ali Rizvi, M. Balah, M. Riyazuddin, Humayun Baig, S. Arshad Raza, Murtaza Ali Khan, Faisal AbdulRazzak, and M.A. Siddiqui. The author is thankful to all of them for their valuable efforts and advice. A lot of credit is also due to various experts who reviewed the chapters and provided helpful feedback.

It is not possible to forget my family here without whose help and support I would not have completed this work. Their love, support, and patience were tremendous throughout. In addition to thanking, I should also apologize for having taken much of their time during the conduct of my work.

The author is happy to acknowledge the support of King Fahd University of Petroleum and Minerals (KFUPM) toward the compilation of this book, against the Book Project #ICS/GRAPHICS/306. This book project was a main source of funding to this book. A partial funded support of KFUPM, through another Research Project #ICS/REVERSE ENG./312, also contributed toward a couple of chapters.

M. Sarfraz

Contents

1
Introduction

Abstract. *Interactive curve designing plays an important role not only in the construction and reconstruction of various objects, but also in the description of geological, physical, medical, and different other phenomena. This book presents a description and analysis of a variety of classes of splines for use in CAGD (computer-aided geometric design), CAD (computer-aided design), CAE (computer-aided engineering), CAM (computer-aided manufacturing), computer graphics, computer vision, image processing, and other disciplines. They are useful for the representation of parametric curves in both interpolatory and B-spline-like forms. Scalar function forms will also be discussed occasionally. The specific spline description and the type of continuity constraints between the pieces of the splines can be used to influence, design, and control the shape of the curves. Different parameters in the description of splines can be used for various applications including design in CAD/CAM, font design, image outline capture, multiresolution, description of motion paths for moving objects such as robots, data visualization, reverse engineering, curve or surface editing, object recognition, and so on.*

The book is designed specifically for undergraduate as well as graduate students in the area of computer science. The main audience for the book are the communities related to the fields of computer graphics, vision, and imaging. However, the book can also be useful to students in other disciplines such as computer engineering, electrical engineering, mechanical engineering, mathematics, and so on. The book is equally beneficial for researchers and practitioners.

1.1   Strategy in the Construction of Theory

This book will mainly discuss spline curves in both rational and nonrational forms, although some other curve formulations may also be described occasionally. The spline formulation has manifested itself in various forms including Bézier curves, rational Bézier curves, B-splines, NURBS (nonuniform rational B-splines), beta-splines, rational beta-splines, weighted Nu splines, rational weighted Nu splines, and others. A single function usually does not have enough freedom to represent a given curve. Thus, several segments are joined together to generate a spline curve.

There are at least two methods to visualize the mathematics of a rational curve $p(t)$.

1. The curve p can be thought of as a vector-valued function in R^N, each component of which is a rational function, i.e., the numerator and denominator are polynomial functions.
2. The value p can be thought of as the projection of a vector-valued polynomial function f in R^{N+1} into R^N. The value f is referred to as the *homogeneous* curve associated with p.

Method 2 has the advantage that algorithms for manipulating rational curves such as evaluation, subdivision, degree elevation, etc., can often be obtained by using the corresponding algorithm for polynomial curves. However, this can be a restriction in that the numerator and denominator are assumed to obey the same polynomial spline description. Method 1 is less restrictive and gives us more freedom to develop shape control parameters which behave in a well-defined and well-controlled way. The approach of Method 1 is adopted throughout this book, where ever applicable, to deal with rational splines. Method 1 is also applicable to non-rational (polynomial) splines.

Bézier (rational Bézier) and B-spline (or B-spline-like) curves/surfaces are powerful tools, and are found incorporated into most existing CAD/CAM and computer graphics systems. This book was produced mainly for developing these concepts and using them for a variety of applications in the areas of computer graphics, vision, and imaging.

1.2   Overview

1.2.1   *Splines*

The generation of spline curves [1–48] is a useful and powerful tool in CAGD. Although the splines have many elegant properties discussed in Refs. 1–10, 14–15, 21, 27–28, 36, and 40–42, the curves sometimes exhibit undesirable oscillations. Various methods have been developed to control the shape of a curve, such as those described in Refs. [1–4, 9, 13, 16–18, 22, 28–36, 38–45, 47, 48]. Some methods are well suited for one type of shape control, but not well suited for another. For this reason, a multipurpose system was developed in Refs. 36 and 40, which consists of different spline methods and uses the particular spline that is best suited for the desired type of shape control. Thus, to avoid a multiplicity of methods, one method can suffice that is capable of generating a broad range of interpolating curves, is easy to implement, provides a shape control according to the user's wishes, and is computationally economical. This problem is discussed in Chapters 2–5.

Chapter 2 presents a description and analysis of a cubic spline in both interpolatory as well as B-spline forms. It is actually a weighted Nu spline. Two shape parameters are introduced in the description that provide a variety of shape controls such as point and interval tensions. Similarly, Chapter 3 presents a description and analysis of a rational cubic spline in both interpolatory and B-spline forms. This rational spline provides not only a computationally simple alternative to the exponential based spline under tension, but also provides a C^2 alternative to the well-known existing GC^2 or C^1 methods such as cubic Nu splines of Nielson [31], β-spline representation of such cubics by Barsky and Beatty [2], γ-splines of Boehm [6], and weighted Nu splines [17]. This method is the generalization of the *rational spline with tension* [28]. Two shape parameters are introduced in each interval that provide a variety of shape controls such as biased, point, and interval tensions.

Chapter 4 uses general piecewise rational cubics subject to a general type of continuity constraint between the pieces; we will call them rational σ-splines. These are a generalization of most of the above-mentioned methods and provide economical alternatives to the rest of them. Also, the development of a local support basis for the B-spline-like representation of rational σ-splines can be used to obtain methods in Refs. 1–2, 6–8, 17, and 28. The B-spline-like basis form of the curves can also be used to solve the interpolation problems.

Chapter 5 discusses similar issues to those discussed in Chapter 4. But it also considers linear, quadratic, and cubic splines. Various kinds of continuity constraints are believed to have a more interactive and well-controlled spline formulation. It can enable the user to have a formulation that may be desired to model an object with multiple choice of pieces for designing purposes. Although a local support basis for the B-spline-like representation of such splines was considered, it was not desired and hence is not discussed. A brief discussion of touch-to-surface design (although it is not the main objective of this book) has been also provided in Chapter 5, as an application of curves. These surfaces are based on just curve manipulations and can provide only limited control for designing.

1.2.2 Shape-Preserving Interpolation

Shape-preserving problems [11, 19, 23–25, 27, 40, 50–55] for plane curves are discussed in Chapter 6, which is an extension of the results of Delbourgo and Gregory [11] who developed the rational cubic of Chapter 2 (with one shape parameter in each interval) to solve the problem of shape-preserving interpolation for scalar curves. The spline curves here explore the shape control parameters, which depend on the first derivative data in such a way that the interpolant preserves the monotonic and/or convex shape of the data. Chapters 7 and 8 complement Chapter 6 in the context of scalar shape-preserving curves for the visualization of shaped data. Chapter 7 is related to a rational spline interpolation, while Chapter 8 uses cubic splines. The nature of the data considered may be positive, monotonic, or convex.

1.2.3 Functional Approximation

Chapter 9 is devoted solely to the idea of approximation of curves [56–64] when they result from complex functions or complex data. Two methods [62–64] are

presented as a solution to the problem. One scheme is based on a deterministic approach [62] using quadratic B-splines. The other scheme uses a genetic
algorithm in its formulation [63] where the B-spline can have any order. Both of
the schemes presented in this chapter automatically compute data points to minimize errors.

1.2.4   Spiral Curves

The spiral curves [65–72] are desirable for applications such as highway route
designing, robot path planning, data-fitting problems, shape design, and curve/
surface fairing in geometric modeling. Due to the success of raster displays, scan
conversion algorithms are fundamental in computer graphics. Most of the time,
straight lines and curved primitives are considered for scan conversion, but complicated curve primitives such as spirals are considered less frequently for direct scan
conversion. In Cartesian coordinates they are typically transcendental functions,
which makes the evaluation on Cartesian grids an inefficient process. Chapter 10
describes the issues concerning the scan conversion of Archimedes spiral. A simple algorithm [65–67] based on the piecewise circular approximations has been
reported. Variations of the algorithm to convert other types of spirals has also
been considered.

Chapter 10 also presents an efficient geometric algorithm [72] for visualization
of two-point geometric Hermite conic and arc/conic spiral segments. A comparative study is made of Tschirnhausen cubic spirals.

1.2.5   Corner Detection and Curve Segmentation

Chapter 11 highlights the feature of curve segmentation. This is mainly for digital
curves, which may consist of huge amounts of data. The large data set is subdivided into smaller data sets to overcome the problem on the basis of "divide and
rule." This is done by detecting the points that appeal to the eye visually, as with
a corner point. Corners [73–84] in digital images give important clues for shape
representation and analysis. If the corner points are identified properly, a shape can
be represented in an efficient and compact way with sufficient accuracy in many
shape analysis problem. Shape representation and image interpretation depends
most of the time on how correctly and efficiently the corner points are located.
Specifically, in the area of vectorizing planar images, contour segmentation is very
often managed by locating the exact corner points.

As many as seven techniques [73–84] have been discussed for the corner detection. These techniques have been described, implemented and analyzed. Various
practical examples have been given to test and compare the methods. Merits and
demerits of each method together with the default selection or a variable selection of parameters are stated. Tabular and graphical results are provided for a clear
comparative study so that user can select the best for the need.

1.2.6   *Vectorizing Planar Shapes*

Chapters 12 and 13 are aimed at vectorizing planar images [85–101]. Chapter 12 is devoted to a detailed study of linear or polygonal approximation [102] needed in various applications, including shape recognition, point-based motion estimation, coding methods, and so on, in the areas of computer graphics, imaging, and vision. Some important aspects related to capturing with linear approximation have been addressed. A detailed survey has been made of many methods [85–101] in the current literature. Some commonly discussed algorithms are explained, and their results are demonstrated and compared.

Automatic and efficient algorithms for outline capture of character images, stored as bitmaps, are presented in Chapter 13. A curve methodology [90] based on the Bézier cubic formulation is discussed in detail. Various steps have been described for the completion of the algorithm designed. This method is well suited for characters of non-Roman languages such as Arabic, Japanese, Urdu, Persian, and so on. The process of capturing outlines includes various steps including detection of boundaries, identifying corner points and break points, and fitting the curve. The chapter thoroughly discusss automating the above process and provides optimal results. As an alternate smoother scheme, the Hermite cubic spline curve method [95] is also introduced.

1.2.7   *Reverse Engineering*

Computer-aided reverse engineering (CARE) is an important area of study in the modern age of computers. Multiple solutions in advanced and modern industries are being provided with regard to design and manufacturing [106–108]. In modern designi, scanned digital data leads us to adopt contour styling [98–102], which helps to guide visual acceptance after adopting some curve or surface approximation scheme [103–105].

Various objects including manufactured parts or human body parts are designed and redesigned with complex free-form geometry. This trend is quite popular and can be found in various applications in recent years such as vehicle body design. The wide acceptance of free-form curves and surfaces for component design can also be attributed to the advances in curve and surface modelling and their implementations in CAD/CAM/CAE/CARE systems.

This chapter focuses on CARE. Although reported techniques have been presented for image-based planar objects, they are also extendable to objects in 3D with some modifications. Two nondeterministic evolutionary approaches [98, 108] have been presented. Nonuniform rational B-splines (NURBS) have been utilized as an underlying approximation curve scheme. Simulated annealing and simulated evolution heuristics have both been used as evolutionary methodologies. Optimized NURBS models have been fitted over the contour data of the planar shapes for the ultimate and automatic output. The output results are visually pleasing with respect to the threshold provided by the user.

1.2.8 *Multiresolution Framework*

In the field of geometric modeling, the construction of efficient, intuitive, and interactive editors [109–115] for geometric objects is a fundamental objective. In many freeform geometric modeling systems the users are allowed to work within the framework of a specific data model such as Bézier or nonuniform B-splines. This imposes constraints on the set of geometric manipulation operations that can be performed, the man-machine interface, and the type of objects that can be modeled.

Multiresolution representation [109–115] is a possible solution that allows the user to edit objects at different resolution levels. Both local and global operations can be performed on curves by representing them using multiresolution decomposition. Several approaches have been proposed for multiresolution representation of splines in the case of curves and surfaces. It often requires specific treatment of boundary control points. These approaches depend on the given spline model they manipulate. Chapter 15 presents multiresolution approaches for the uniform B-splines or nonuniform B-splines (NUBS). NUBS are specifically useful because, by manipulating the control points, knot vector, and weights, they facilitate design of a large variety of shapes. They offer a common mathematical form for representing and designing both standard analytic shapes (conics, quadrics) and free-form curves and surfaces. Evaluation is reasonably fast and computationally stable. NUBS have a clear geometric toolkit (knot insertion/deletion, degree elevation, etc.), which can be used to design, analyze, process, and interrogate objects.

1.3 Notation and Conventions

- The symbol R^N will be used to denote the N-dimensional real space.
- Knot partitions will be assumed as

$$\tilde{t}_0 < \tilde{t}_1 < \ldots < \tilde{t}_m, \tag{1.1}$$

$$t_0 < t_1 < \ldots < t_m. \tag{1.2}$$

(1.1) and (1.2) for bivariate case and (1.2) for univariate case.
- For any i the transformations

$$\left. \begin{aligned} \theta \equiv \theta\left(t\right) &= \left(t - t_i\right)/h_i, \\ \tilde{\theta} \equiv \tilde{\theta}\left(\tilde{t}\right) &= \left(\tilde{t} - \tilde{t}_i\right)/\tilde{h}_i, \end{aligned} \right\} \tag{1.3}$$

will be commonly used where

$$h_i = t_{i+1} - t_i, \tilde{h}_j = \tilde{t}_{j+1} - \tilde{t}_j, \tag{1.4}$$

- $F_i, i = 0, 1, \ldots, n$ will denote the interpolatory points and Δ_i will be used for the ratios of the type:

$$\Delta_i = (F_{i+1} - F_i)/h_i. \tag{1.5}$$

P_i can also be used interchangeably with F_i whenever needed. However, f_i will replace F_i whenever the data is in scalar form.

- D_i will be used for the first derivative value at the knot t_i. However, d_i will be used for the first derivative value whenever the spline is in scalar form.
- Given a function such as $p(t)$, we will denote the ith derivative by $p^{(i)}(t)$. In the case of scalar functions, s will replace p.
- Given a function such as $p(\tilde{t}, t)$, we use the notation $p^{\tilde{t}t}(\tilde{t}, t)$ to denote the first partial derivative with respect to $\tilde{t}$ and the first partial derivative with respect to t. That is

$$p^{\tilde{t}t}(\tilde{t}, t) = \frac{\partial^2 p}{\partial \tilde{t} \partial t},$$

and so on.

- For brevity, and when no ambiguity can arise, the independent variables are left off expressions such as $p^{\tilde{t}}(\tilde{t}, t)$ yielding simply $p^{\tilde{t}}$
- We will call a function $p(t)$ σ-*continuous* at $t = t_i$ if it satisfies the following constraints:

$$\begin{bmatrix} p(t_{i+}) \\ p^{(1)}(t_{i+}) \\ p^{(2)}(t_{i+}) \end{bmatrix} = \begin{bmatrix} 1 & 0 & 0 \\ 0 & \sigma_{1,i} & 0 \\ 0 & \sigma_{2,i} & \sigma_{3,i} \end{bmatrix} \begin{bmatrix} p(t_{i-}) \\ p^{(1)}(t_{i-}) \\ p^{(2)}(t_{i-}) \end{bmatrix}, \qquad (1.6)$$

- $p \in C^m[t_0, t_n]$ will mean that each component function of $p \in C^m[t_0, t_n] \to R^N$ is m-times continuously differentiable on $[t_0, t_n]$. Similarly the notations GC^m will be fixed for geometric (reparametrization) continuity.
- We will use $\|\,.\,\|$ to denote the uniform norm, either on $[t_0, t_n]$ or $[t_i, t_{i+1}]$.

1.4   Review of Some Spline Methods

In this section a brief review of some of the existing spline methods is given because these can be considered either as an alternative or as particular cases of the spline methods which are going to be discussed in the theory of the thesis. For each of the splines, we assume the knot partition (1.2) and the values $F_i, i = 0, \ldots, n$ at the knots. Throughout the discussion, we will denote the spline curve by $p(t)$.

1.4.1   *Cubic Spline*

The natural cubic spline [15] is the C^2 piecewise cubic function that minimizes

$$V(f) = \int_{t_0}^{t_n} \left(f^{(2)}(t) \right)^2 dt, \qquad (1.7)$$

over all functions in $H^2[t_0, t_n]$. $H^2[t_0, t_n]$ consists of all functions that have a first derivative that is absolutely continuous and that has a second derivative that belongs to $L^2[t_0, t_n]$.

1.4.2 *Spline Under Tension*

The spline under tension was first introduced by Schweikert [39] and then later discussed by Barsky [3]. The idea was to introduce a new term in equation (1.7) in such a way that some shape control was obtained. Thus, Barsky [3] constructs the spline under tension as the interpolating function in $H^2[t_0, t_n]$ that minimizes

$$V(f) = \int_{t_0}^{(t_n)} (f^{(2)}(t))^2 dt + \sum_{i=0}^{n-1} w_i \int_{t_i}^{t_{i+1}} \left(f^{(1)}(t)\right)^2 dt, \qquad (1.8)$$

where $w_i > 0$, for $i = 0, \ldots, n-1$. The minimizing function is a piecewise exponential and linear function that belongs to C^2. The constants w_i's can be used to control the tension of the curve on the interval $[t_i, t_{i+1}]$ for all i. As w_i increases, the exponential-based spline under tension becomes *tighter* on that interval.

1.4.3 *Weighted Spline*

The weighted spline in Refs 17 and 20 is the interpolating function that minimizes

$$V(f) = \int_{t_0}^{t_n} w(t) \left(f^{(2)}(t)\right)^2 dt, \qquad (1.9)$$

where $w(t)$ is a positive integrable function. The minimizing function belongs to C^1. If $w(t)$ is a piecewise constant function, then the weighted spline is a C^1 piecewise cubic polynomial. If $w(t)$ is large on one interval, relative to bordering intervals, then the weighted spline become *tighter* on that interval in a manner similar to the spline under tension. It should be noted that the spline under tension is C^2, but is computationally more expensive because it is a piecewise exponential, whereas the weighted spline is a piecewise cubic but it only belongs to C^1.

1.4.4 *Nu-spline*

The v-spline in Refs. 32 and 34 is the interpolating function in $H^2[t_0, t_n]$ that minimizes

$$V(f) = \int_{t_0}^{t_n} \left(f^{(2)}(t)\right)^2 dt + \sum_{i=0}^{n} v_i \left(f^{(1)}(t_i)\right)^2 dt, \qquad (1.10)$$

where $v_i \geq 0$, for $i = 0, \ldots, n$. As noted in Ref. 34, the v-spline is a C^1 piecewise cubic function that does not mimic splines in tension well in the functional case. However, in the parametric case the v-spline has geometric continuity of order 2, that is, it is C^2 under an appropriate reparametrization, and as v_i increases, the v-spline curve becomes *tighter* at the ith interpolation point because the magnitude of the tangent vector approaches zero.

1.4.5   *Weighted Nu-spline*

The weighted v-spline [17] is the marriage of the weighted spline and the v-spline. It is the C^1 piecewise cubic interpolatory function $P(t)$ that minimizes

$$V(f) = \sum_{i=0}^{n-1} w_i \int_{t_0}^{t_n} \left(f^{(2)}(t) \right)^2 dt + \sum_{i=0}^{n} v_i \left(f^{(1)}(t_i) \right)^2 dt, \tag{1.11}$$

where $w_i > 0$ for $i = 0, \ldots, n-1$ and $v_i \geq 0$ for $i = 0, \ldots, n$. The v_i are termed as point tension factors because they *tighten* a parametric curve at the ith interval in the same way as they do for the v – spline in Refs. 32 and 34. The w_i are termed interval weights because they tighten the curve on the ith interval in the same way as they do for the weighted splines in Ref. 20. If $v_i = 0$ and all $w_i = c$, where c is some constant value, then the weighted v – spline is the C^2 cubic spline. If all $w_i = c$, then the weighted v – spline equals the v – spline in [32] with tension factors v_i/c. If all $v_i = 0$, then it equals the weighted spline given in [20].

Remark 1.1. It was proven in [17] that if $p(t)$ is any C^1 weighted v – spline that minimizes (1.11), then

$$w^i p^{(2)}(t_{i+}) - w_{i-1} p^{(2)}(t_{i-}) = v_i p^{(1)}(t_i), i = 1, \ldots, n-1. \tag{1.12}$$

This result generalizes the results of Salkauskas [20] that a weighted spline satisfies

$$w_i p^{(2)}(t_{i+}) = w_{i-1} p^{(2)}(t_{i-}) \tag{1.13}$$

and the results of Nielson [32] that a v – spline satisfies

$$p^{(2)}(t_{i+}) - p^{(2)}(t_{i-}) = v_i p^{(1)}(t_i). \tag{1.14}$$

1.4.6   *Beta Splines*

The β – spline [1] is a piecewise cubic function $p(t)$ that satisfies the following derivative constraints:

$$\begin{bmatrix} p(t_{i+}) \\ p^{(1)}(t_{i+}) \\ p^{(2)}(t_{i+}) \end{bmatrix} = \begin{bmatrix} 1 & 0 & 0 \\ 0 & \beta_{1,i} & 0 \\ 0 & \beta_{2,i} & \beta_{1,i}^2 \end{bmatrix} \begin{bmatrix} p(t_{i-}) \\ p^{(1)}(t_{i-}) \\ p^{(2)}(t_{i-}) \end{bmatrix}, \tag{1.15}$$

where $\beta_{1,i} \geq 1, i = 0, \ldots, n-1$ and $\beta_{2,i} \geq 0, i = 0, \ldots, n$. The $\beta_{1,i}$'s are known as biased tension factors because they pull the curve to one side. The parameters $\beta_{2,i}$'s are known as point tension factors because they behave exactly like the v_i in the v – splines. If $\beta_{2,i} = 0$ and $\beta_{1,i} = 1$, then the β – spline is the C^2 cubic spline. If $\beta_{1,i} = 1$, then it equals the v – spline. For parametric curves, the constraints (1.15) mean that the curve is GC^2 (geometric continuity of order 2).

1.4.7 *Sigma* (σ) *Splines*

The σ – spline of Sarfraz [12, 41] is a piecewise cubic function $p(t)$ that satisfies the derivative constraints in Equation (1.6). where $\sigma_{1,i} \geq 1, i = 0, \ldots, n - 1$ and $\sigma_{2,i}, \sigma_{3,i} \geq 0, i = 0, \ldots, n$. The $\sigma_{1,i}$'s are known as biased tension factors because they pull the curve to one side. The parameters $\sigma_{2,i}$'s are known as point tension factors because they behave exactly like the v_i in the v – splines. If $\sigma_{2,i} = 0$, $\sigma_{3,i} = 1$ and $\sigma_{1,i} = 1$, then the σ – spline is the C^2 cubic spline. If $\sigma_{3,i} = 1$ and $\sigma_{1,i} = 1$, then the σ – spline equals the v – spline. Similarly, one can recover the weighted spline, the weighted Nu spline, and various other splines as a result of particular assignments of σ's. For parametric curves, the constraints (1.6) mean that the σ – spline curve is GC^1 (geometric continuity of order 1). But, in most of the special cases, the continuity varies from C^1 to C^2.

1.4.8 *B-Splines*

The recursive function $N_j^k(u)$ given by the equations

$$\left. \begin{array}{l} N_j^1(u) = \begin{cases} 1 \;\; if \;\; u \in [u_j, u_{j+1}) \\ 0 \quad\;\; otherwise \end{cases} \\ N_j^k(u) = \dfrac{u-u_j}{u_{j+k-1}-u_j} N_j^{k-1}(u) + \dfrac{u_{j+k}-u}{u_{j+k}-u_{j+1}} N_{j+1}^{k-1}(u), \end{array} \right\} \tag{1.16}$$

is called the normalized B-spline basis function of order k (degree $k - 1$). The numbers $u_j \leq u_{j+1} \in R$ are called knot values or simply knots, and $0/0 = 0$ by definition.

The curve $s(u)$ defined by

$$p(u) = \sum_{l=0}^{n} N_l^k(u) P_l, \quad u \in [u_{k-1}, u_{n+1}] \tag{1.17}$$

is called the B-spline curve of order k (degree $k - 1$), where $N_l^k(u)$ is the lth normalized B-spline basis function, for the evaluation of which the knots $u_0, u_1, \ldots, u_{n+k}$ are necessary. The points P_i are called control points or de Boor-points, while the polygon formed by these points is called control polygon.

The jth span of the B-spline curve can be written in the form

$$p_j(u) = \sum_{l=j-k+1}^{j} N_l^k(u) P_l, \; u \in [u_j, u_{j+1}). \tag{1.18}$$

Modifying the knot u_i, the point of this span associated with the fixed parameter value $\tilde{u} \in [u_j, u_{j+1})$ will move along the curve.

Nonuniform rational B-spline (NURB) curves are generated from the following formula:

$$\hat{p}(u) = \frac{\displaystyle\sum_{i=0}^{n} w_i P_i N_{i,k}(u)}{\displaystyle\sum_{i=0}^{n} w_i N_{i,k}(u)} \tag{1.19}$$

where $P_i, i = 0, 1, \ldots, n$, are control points, w_i are weights, and $N_{i,k}(u)$ are B-spline basis functions.

1.4.9 Bézier Splines

Given $(n + 1)$ points $P_i : i = 0, 1, 2, \ldots, n$, Bézier curve is defined as follows:

$$P(t) = \sum_{i=0}^{n} P_i B_i(t), \ 0 \le t \le 1, \tag{1.20}$$

where

$$B_i(t) = \binom{n}{i} (1 - t)^{n-i} t^i,$$

are Bernstein polynomials. Here we will refer to $B_i(t)$'s as Bézier blending functions. For example, for $n = 3$, equation (1.20) will reduce to:

$$
\begin{aligned}
P(t) &= \sum_{i=0}^{n} P_i B_i(t), \\
&= P_0 B_0(t) + P_1 B_1(t) + P_2 B_2(t) + P_3 B_3(t), \\
&= \binom{3}{0} (1 - t)^3 P_0 + P_1 \binom{3}{1} (1 - t)^2 t + P_2 \binom{3}{2} (1 - t) t^2 + P_3 t^3, \\
&= (1 - t)^3 P_0 + 3 P_1 (1 - t)^2 t + 3 P_2 (1 - t) t^2 + P_3 t^3. \tag{1.21}
\end{aligned}
$$

The polynomials

$$(1 - t)^3, 3(1 - t)^2 t, 3(1 - t) t^2, t^3,$$

are called Bézier cubic blending functions. The convex hull of points $P_i, i = 0, 1, \ldots, n$ is (roughly speaking) the region surrounded by P_i's. The points P_i's are also known as control points, and the polygon connected by P_i's is called control polygon. There are some interesting properties worth noting:

1. The degree of a Bézier curve is one less than the given control points.
2. The Bézier curve always pass through the first and last points.
3. The Bézier curve always remains within the convex hull of the control polygon.
4. The Bézier curve always satisfies the variation diminishing property. That is, the property that curve does not cross any straight line more than the control polygon crosses.

1.4.10 Hermite Splines

Let

$$P(0) = P_0, \ P(1) = P_3, P^{(1)}(0) = D_0, P^{(1)}(1) = D_1.$$

Then (1.21) becomes like the following:

$$P(t) = (1-t)^3 P_0 + 3t(1-t)^2 \left(P_0 + \frac{D_0}{3}\right) + 3t^2(1-t)\left(P_3 - \frac{D_1}{3}\right) + t^3 P_3.$$

(1.22)

The curve in equation (1.22) is called Hermite cubic curve where $0 \le t \le 1$ can be interchanged with $0 \le \theta \le 1$ without loss of generality. Higher-degree Hermite curves can also be defined in a similar manner. To have a more precise and general notation for a Hermite cubic spline curve, let us adopt the following:

$$P(0) = P_i, \ P(1) = P_{i+1}, \ P^{(1)}(0) = D_i, \ P^{(1)}(1) = D_{i+1}.$$

Then, the Hermite curve takes the following form:

$$P(t) = (1-\theta)^3 P_i + 3\theta(1-\theta)^2 \left(P_i + \frac{h_i D_i}{3}\right)$$
$$+3\theta^2(1-\theta)\left(P_{i+1} - \frac{h_i D_{i+1}}{3}\right) + \theta^3 P_{i+1},$$

(1.23)

where θ and h_i are defined in equations (1.3) and (1.4). If we have the points as follows:

$$P_0, P_1, P_2, \ldots, P_n$$

(1.24)

Then, we can fit Hermite curve pieces between each pair of points for $i = 0, 1, 2, \ldots, n-1$. The curve represented in (1.24) is called a Hermite spline provided the information about the tangents D_i's is given. Let us define D_i's as follows:

$$\left. \begin{array}{l} D_0 = 2(P_1 - P_0) - (P_2 - P_0)/2, \\ D_n = 2(P_n - P_{n-1}) - (P_n - P_{n-2})/2, \\ D_i = a_i(P_i - P_{i-1}) + (1 - a_i)(P_{i+1} - P_i), i = 1, 2, 3, \ldots, n-1, \end{array} \right\}$$

(1.25)

where

$$a_i = \frac{|P_{i+1} - P_i|}{|P_{i+1} - P_i| + |P_i - P_{i-1}|}.$$

Although the tangents provided in equations (1.25) will produce open curves, they can be easily oriented to produce closed curves too.

The Hermite spline $P(t)$ will be called a cardinal spline provided the derivative values D_i's are changed as follows:

$$D_i = \frac{1}{2}(1 - \alpha_i)(P_{i+1} - P_{i-1}),$$

$$D_{i+1} = \frac{1}{2}(1 - \alpha_i)(P_{i+2} - P_i).$$

In this case, we would have the curve segments for $i = 1, 2, \ldots, n-2$. The parameter α_i is called tension parameter because it tightens or loosens the curve when it increases or decreases. When $\alpha_i = 0$, the cardinal spline is called Catmull-Rom spline or Overhauser spline.

The Hermite spline $P(t)$ will be called a Kochanek-Bartels spline provided the derivative values D_i's are changed as follows:

$$D_i = \frac{1}{2}(1 - \alpha_i)\left[(1 + \beta_i)(1 - \gamma_i)(P_i - P_{i-1}) + (1 - \beta_i)(1 + \gamma_i)(P_{i+1} - P_i)\right],$$

$$D_{i+1} = \frac{1}{2}(1 - \alpha_i)\left[(1 + \beta_i)(1 - \gamma_i)(P_{i+1} - P_i) + (1 - \beta_i)(1 + \gamma_i)(P_{i+2} - P_{i+1})\right],$$

where

- α_i is a tension parameter.
- β_i is a biased parameter.
- γ_i is a continuity parameter.

The parameter values $\beta_i = 0 = \gamma_i$ produce the cardinal spline.

1.5 Summary

This chapter provides introductory material that is useful before studying the rest of the book. It provides notation, a summary of spline methods and their history, and a rich bibliography. The chapter also describes who should study the book. Some valuable suggestions have also been made regarding the structure of the book for course work at both the undergraduate and graduate levels.

1.6 Exercises

1. What is this book about?
2. What is a spline?
3. Name at least 10 spline methods in the literature.
4. Write programs to plot the following spline curves:

   (a) Quadratic B-spline
   (b) Cubic B-spline
   (c) Bézier curves of arbitrary degree.
   (d) Cubic Hermite spline
   (e) Cardinal spline
   (f) Kochanek Bartel spline.

5. Name at least 20 applications where a spline can be used.

References

1. Barsky, B.A. (1981), The Beta-spline: a local representation based on shape parameters and fundamental-geometric measure, Ph.D. thesis, University of Utah.
2. Barsky, B.A., and Beatty, J.C. (1983), Local control of bias and tension in beta-splines, *ACM Trans Graphics* 2, 109–134.

3. Barsky, B.A. (1984), Exponential and polynomial methods for applying tension to an interpolating spline curve, *Comput Vision Graph Image Process* 27, 1–18.

4. Bartels, R., and Beatty, J. (1984), Beta-splines with a difference. Technical report CS-83-40, Waterloo Computer Science Department, Waterloo, Ontario, Canada N2L3Gl.

5. Boehm, W., Farin, G., and Kahmann, J. (1984), A survey of curve and surface methods in CAGD, *Comput Aided Geom Des* 1(1), 1–60.

6. Boehm, W. (1985), Curvature continuous curves and surfaces, *Comput Aided Geom Des* 2(2), 313–323.

7. Boehm, W. (1986), Smooth curves and surfaces, in Farin, G.E., ed. *Geometric Modeling*, pp. 175–184.

8. Boehm, W. (1987), Rational geometric splines, *Comput Aided Geom Des* 4, 67–77.

9. Cline, A. (1974), Curve fitting in one and two dimensions using splines under tension, *Comm ACM* 17, 218–223.

10. De Boor, C. (1978), *A Practical Guide to Splines*. Springer-Verlag, New York.

11. Delbourgo, R., and Gregory, J.A. (1985), Shape-preserving piecewise rational interpolation, *SIAM J Stat Comput* 6, 967–976.

12. Sarfraz, M. (1994), Generalized geometric interpolation for rational cubic splines, *Int J Comput Graphics*, Elsevier Science, 18(1), 61–72.

13. Dierckx, P., and Tytgat, B. (1989), Generating the Bézier points of a β-spline curve, *Comput Aided Geom Des* 6, 279–291.

14. Farin, G.E. (1983), Algorithms for rational Bézier curves, *Comput Aided Des* 15, 73–77.

15. Farin, G.E. (1988), *Curves and Surfaces for Computer-Aided Geometric Design,* Academic Press, New York.

16. Foley, T.A. (1986), Local control of interval tension using weighted splines, *Comput Aided Geom Des* 3, 281–294.

17. Foley, T.A. (1987), Interpolation with interval and point tension controls using cubic weighted v-splines, *ACM Trans Math Soft* 13, 68–96.

18. Foley, T.A., and Ely, H.S. (1989), Surface interpolation with tension controls using cardinal bases, *Comput Aided Geom Des* 6, 97–109.

19. Fritsch, F.N., and Carlson, R.E. (1980), Monotone piecewise cubic interpolation, *SIAM J Numer Anal* 17(2), 238–246.

20. Salkauskas, K. (1984), C^1 splines for interpolation of rapidly varying data, *Rocky Mtn J Math* 14, 239–250.

21. Goldman, R.N., and Barsky, B.A. (1989), On beta-continuous functions and their application to the construction of geometrically continuous curves and surfaces, in Lyche, T., and Schumaker, L., eds. *Mathematical Methods in Computer-Aided Geometric Design*, Academic Press, New York.

22. Goodman, T.N.T., and Unsworth, K. (1985), Generation of beta-spline curves using a recursive relation, in R.E. Earnshaw, ed., *Fundamental Algorithms for Computer Graphics*, Springer-Verlag, Berlin, pp. 326–357.

23. Goodman, T.N.T. (1988), Shape-preserving interpolation by parametric rational cubic splines, *Proc Int Conf on Numerical Mathematics, Int Ser Num Math* 86, Birkhauser-Verlag, Basel.

24. Goodman, T.N.T., and Unsworth, K. (1988), Shape-preserving interpolation by parametrically defined curves, *SIAM J Numer Anal* 25, 1–13.

25. Goodman, T.N.T. (1989), Shape-preserving representations, in Lyche, T., and Schumaker, L., eds., *Mathematical Methods in Computer-Aided Geometric Design*, Academic Press, New York.

26. Gordon, W.J. (1971), Blending function methods of bivariate and multivariate interpolation and approximation, *SIAM J Num Anal* 8, 158–177.

27. Gregory, J.A. (1986), Shape-preserving spline interpolation, *Comput Aided Des* 18, 53–57.

28. Gregory, J.A., and Sarfraz, M. (1990), A rational spline with tension, *Comput Aided Geom Des* 7, 1–13.

29. Hohmeyer, M.E., and Barsky, B.A. (1989), Rational continuity, to appear in *Trans Computer Graphics*.

30. Kochanek, D.H., and Bartels R.H. (1984), Interpolating splines with local tension: Continuity and biased control, *Comput Graphics* 18, 33–41.

31. Lewis, J. (1975), "B-spline" bases for splines under tension, nu-splines, and fractional order splines. Presented at the SIAM-SIGNUM Meeting, San Francisco, CA.

32. Nielson, G.M. (1974), Some piecewise polynomial alternatives to splines under tension, in Barnhill, R.F., eds., *Computer-Aided Geometric Design*, Academic Press, New York.

33. Nielson, G.M. (1984), A locally controllable spline with tension for interactive curve design, *Comput Aided Geom Des* 1, 199–205.

34. Nielson, G.M. (1986), Rectangular v-splines. *IEEE Comput Graphics Appl* 6, 35–40.

35. Preuss, S. (1976), Properties of splines in tension, *J Approx Theory* 17, 86–96.

36. Preuss, S. (1979), Alternatives to the exponential spline in tension, *Math. Comp.* 33, 1273–1281

37. Sarfraz M. (1987), Spline curve interpolation with shape control M.Sc. dissertation, Brunel University, U.K.

38. Schoenberg, L. (1981), *Spline Functions: Basic Theory*, John Wiley, New York.

39. Schweikert, D. (1966), An interpolation curve using splines in tension, *J Math Phys* 45, 312–317.

40. Spath, H . (1974), *Spline Algorithms for Curves and Surfaces*, Utilitas Mathematica, Winnipeg.

41. Sarfraz, M. (1990), The representation of curves and surfaces in computer-aided geometric design using rational cubic splines, Ph.D. thesis, Brunel University, UK.

42. Sarfraz, M. (1992), A C^2 rational cubic spline alternative to the NURBS, *Comp & Graph* 16(1), 69–78.

43. Sarfraz, M. (1995), Curves and surfaces for CAD using C^2 rational cubic splines, *Int J Eng Comput*, Springer-Verlag, 11(2), 94–102.

44. Sarfraz, M. (1994), Freeform rational bicubic spline surfaces with tension control, Facta Universitatis (Nis), Series Mathematics and Informatics, Vol. 9, 83–93.

45. Sarfraz, M. (1994), Cubic spline curves with shape control, *Int J Comput Graphics*, Elsevier Science, 18(5), 707–713.

46. Sarfraz, M, (2003), Weighted nu-splines: an alternative to NURBS, in *Advances in Geometric Modeling*, M. Sarfraz, ed., John Wiley, New York, pp. 81–95.

47. Schoenburg, I.J. (1946), Contributions to the problem of approximation of equidistant data by analytic functions, *Appl Math* 4, 45–99.

48. Schweikert, D.G. (1966), An Interpolation curve using a spline in tension, *J Math Phys* 45, 312–317.

49. Sarfraz, M. (2004), Weighted nu-splines with local support basis functions, *Int J Comput Graphics*, Elsevier Science, 28(4), 539–549.

50. Sarfraz, M., Butt, S., and Hussain, M.Z. (2001), Visualization of shaped data by a rational cubic spline interpolation, *Int J Comput Graphics*, Elsevier Science, 25(5), 833–845.

51. Sarfraz, M. (2000), A rational cubic spline for the visualization of monotonic data, *Comput Graphics*, 24(4), 509–516.

52. Sarfraz, M., and Hussain, M.Z. (2006), Data visualization using rational spline interpolation, *Int J Computat Appl Math,* Elsevier Science, 189(1–2), 513–525.

53. Sarfraz, M., Hussain, M.Z., and Chaudhry, F.S. (2005), Shape-preserving cubic spline for data visualization, *Int J Comput Graphics & CAD/CAM,* International Scientific, 1(6), 185–194.

54. Sarfraz, M. (2002), Visualization of positive and convex data by a rational cubic spline, *Int J Infor Sci*, Elsevier Science, 146(1–4), 239–254.

55. Sarfraz, M. (2002), Modelling for the visualization of monotone data, *Int J Modelling Simulation*, ACTA Press, 22(3), 176–185.

56. Hölzle, G.E. (1983), Knot placement for piecewise polynomial approximation of curves. *Comput Aided Des* 15(5), 295–296.

57. Juhász, I., and Hoffmann, M. (2001) The effect of knot modifications on the shape of beta-spline curves. *J Geom Graphics* 5(2), 111–119.

58. Pratt, M., Goult, R., and He, L. (1993), On rational parametric curve approximation. *Comput Aided Geom Des* 10(3/4):363–377.

59. Razdan, A. (1999), *A Knot Placement for B-Spline Curve Approximation.* PRISM Publications.

60. Sarfraz, M., Asim, M.R. and Masood, A. (2004), Capturing outlines using cubic Bézier curves. *Proceedings of 1st IEEE International Conference on Information & Communication Technologies: From Theory to Applications, 2004.*

61. Speer, T., Kuppe, M., and Hoschek., J. (1998), Global reparametrization for curve approximation. *Comput Aided Geom Des* 15, 869–877.

62. Masood, A., Sarfraz, M., and Haq, S.A. (2005), Curve approximation with quadratic B-splines, *Proceedings of IEEE International Conference on Information Visualisation (IV'2005)-UK*, IEEE Computer Society Press, 991–996.

63. Sarfraz, M., and Raza, A. (2002), Visualization of data using genetic algorithm, *Soft Computing and Industry: Recent Applications*, Eds.: R. Roy, M. Koppen, S. Ovaska, T. Furuhashi, and F. Hoffmann, Springer-Verlag, New York, pp. 535–544.

64. Sarfraz, M., and Raza, A., (2002), Visualization of data with spline fitting: a tool with a genetic approach, *The Proc. International Conference on Imaging Science, Systems, and Technology (CISST 2002), Las Vegas, Nevada,* CSREA Press, pp. 99–105.

65. Taponecco, F., and Alexa, M. (2003), Piecewise circular approximation of spirals and polar polynomials, *Proc. of WSCG 2002*, Plzen, Czech. Republic.

66. Taponecco, F., and Alexa, M. (2002), Scan converting spirals, *Proc. of WSCG 2002*, Plzen, Czech. Republic.

67. Rieger, T., and Taponecco, F. (2002), Interactive Information visualization of entity-relationship data, *Proc. of WSCG 2002*, Plzen, Czech. Republic

68. Van Aken, J.R., and Novak, M. (1985), Curve drawing algorithms for raster displays, *ACM Trans. on Graphics*, 4, 147–169.

69. Cook, A.S. (1979), *The Curves of Life: Being an Account of Spiral Formations and Their Application to Growth in Nature, to Science and to Art: with Special Reference to the Manuscripts of Leonardo Da Vinci*, Dover, New York.

70. Habib, Z., and Sakai, M. (2002), T-cubic and arc/T-cubic spirals for web-based visualization of planar data. *The Proceedings of the Fourth IEEE Workshop on Information and Computer Science: Internet Computing (WICS'2002), KFUPM, Saudi Arabia, IEEE Computer Society Chapter*, pp. 267–278.

71. Habib, Z., and Sakai, M. (2005), Conic spiral spline, *International Conference on Geometric Modeling, Visualization & Graphics, JCIS,* pp. 1653–1656.
72. Habib, Z., and Sakai, M. (2005), Web-based Visualization of Conic and Arc/Conic Spirals, *International Journal of Computer Graphics & CAD / CAM,* 1(1), 16–26.
73. Beus, H.L., and Tiu, S.S.H. (1987), An improved corner detection algorithm based on chain coded plane curves, *Pattern Recognition,* 20:291–296.
74. Chetverikov, D., and Szabo, Z. (1999), A simple and efficient algorithm for detection of high curvature points in planner curves, *Proc. of 23rd Workshop of Australian Pattern Recognition Group,* Steyr, pp. 175–184.
75. Davies, E.R. (1988), Application of generalized Hough transform to corner detection, IEE-P(E:135), No. 1, pp. 49–54.
76. Freeman, H., and Davis, L.S. (1977), A corner finding algorithm for chain-coded curves, *IEEE Trans. Computers,* 26:297–303.
77. Liu, H.C., and Srinath, L.S. (1990), Corner detection from chain-code, *Pattern Recognition,* 23:51–68.
78. Rattarangsi, A., and Chin, R.T. (1992), Scale-based detection of corners of planar curves, *Trans. Pattern Analysis and Machine Intelligence,* 14:430–449.
79. Rosenfeld, A., and Weszka, J.S. (1975), An improved method of angle detection on digital curves, *IEEE Trans. Computer,* 24:940–941.
80. Rutkowski, W.S., and Rosenfeld, A. (1978), A comparison of corner-detection techniques for chain-coded curves, TR-623, Computer Science Center, University of Maryland.
81. Sarfraz, M., Asim, M.R., and Masood, A. (2006), *A New Approach to Corner Detection: Computer Vision and Graphics,* Eds.: Konrad Wojciechowski, Bogdan Smolka, Henryk Palus, Ryszard S. Kozera, Wladyslaw Skarbek, Lyle Noakes, Springer-Verlag, New York, pp. 528–533.
82. The, C. and Chin, R. (1990), On the detection of dominant points on digital curves, *IEEE Trans. PAMI* 8:859–873.
83. Wang, H., and Brady, M. (1995), Real-time corner detection algorithm for motion estimation, *Image and Vision Computing,* 13(9), 695–703.
84. Masood, A., and Sarfraz, M. (2006), A novel corner detector approach using sliding rectangles, *The Proceedings of The 4th ACS/IEEE International Conference on Computer Systems and Applications (AICCSA-06), Sharja, UAE,* pp. 621–626, IEEE Computer Society Press.
85. Karow P. *Digital Typefaces: Description and Formats.* Springer-Verlag, Berlin, 1994.
86. Karow P. *Font Technology Methods and Tools.* Springer-Verlag, Berlin, 1994.
87. Cox, M.G. (1971), Curve fitting with piecewise polynomials. *J. Inst. Math Applications* 8, 36–52.
88. Plass, M., and Stone, M. (1983), Curve fitting with piecewise parametric cubics. *Computer Graphics,* 17(3), 229–239.
89. Zhang, S., Li, L., Seah, H.S. (1998), Recursive curve fitting and rendering. *The Visual Computer,* 69–82, 1998.
90. Sarfraz, M. and Khan, M.A. (2004), An automatic algorithm for approximating boundary of bitmap characters, *Future Generation Computer Systems,* Elsevier Science, Vol. 20, 1327–1336.
91. Sarfraz, M. (2004), Some algorithms for curve design and automatic outline capturing of images, *International Journal of Image and Graphics,* World Scientific Publisher, 4(2), 301–324.

92. Sarfraz, M. (2003), Curve fitting for large data using rational cubic splines, *International Journal of Computers and Their Applications*, 10(4), 233–246.

93. Sarfraz, M., and Khan, M.A. (2003), An automatic outline fitting algorithm for Arabic characters, Lecture Notes in Computer Science, Vol. 2669: *Computational Science and Its Applications*, Eds.: V. Kumar, M.L. Gavrilova, C.J.K. Tan, and P. L'Ecuyer, Springer-Verlag, New York, pp. 589–598.

94. Sarfraz, M. (2003), Optimal curve fitting to digital data, *International Journal of WSCG*, 11(1), 128–135.

95. Sarfraz, M., and Razzak, M.F.A., (2003), A web-based system to capture outlines of Arabic fonts, *International Journal of Information Sciences*, Elsevier Science Inc., 150(3–4), 177–193.

96. Sarfraz, M., and Razzak, M.F.A., (2002), An algorithm for automatic capturing of font outlines, *International Journal of Computers & Graphics*, Elsevier Science, 26(5), 795–804.

97. Sarfraz, M., and Khan, M.A. (2002), Automatic outline capture of Arabic fonts, *International Journal of Information Sciences*, Elsevier Science, 140(3–4), 269–281.

98. Sarfraz, M., Riyazuddin, M., and Baig, M.H. (2006), Capturing planar shapes by approximating their outlines, *International Journal of Computational and Applied Mathematics*, Elsevier Science, 189(1–2), 494–512.

99. Sarfraz, M. (2004), Representing shapes by fitting data using an evolutionary approach, *International Journal of Computer-Aided Design & Applications*, 1(1–4), 179–186.

100. Sarfraz, M, and Raza, A. (2002), towards automatic recognition of fonts using a genetic approach, *Recent Advances in Computers, Computing, and Communications*, Eds.: N. Mastorakis and V. Mladenov, WSEAS Press, 290–295.

101. Sarfraz, M. (2003), Outline representation of fonts using a genetic approach, *Advances in Soft Computing: Engineering Design and Manufacturing*, Eds.: Benitez, J.M., Cordon, O., Hoffmann, F., and Roy, R., Springer-Verlag, 109–118.

102. Sarfraz, M., Asim, M.R., and Masood, A. (2004), Piecewise polygonal approximation of digital curves, *The Proceedings of IEEE International Conference on Information Visualisation (IV'2004)-UK,* IEEE Computer Society Press, 991–996.

103. Dierckx, P. (1993), *Curve and Surface Fitting with Splines*. Clarendon Press (1993).

104. Farin, G. (1989), Trends in curves and surface design. *Computer-Aided Design*, 21(5), 293–296.

105. Piegl, L., and Tiller, W. (1991), Curve and surface reconstruction using rational B-splines. *Computer-Aided Design*, 19(9), 485–498.

106. Cho, M-W, Seo, T-I, Kim, J-D, and Kwon, O-Y, (2000), Reverse engineering of compound surfaces using boundary detection method, *Korean Society of Mechanical Engineers International Journal*, 14(10), 1104–1113.

107. Laurent-Gengoux, P., and Mekhilef, M. (1993), Optimization of a NURBS representation, *Computer-Aided Design*, 25(11), 699–710.

108. Sarfraz, M. (2006), Computer-aided reverse engineering using simulated evolution on NURBS, *International Journal of Virtual & Physical Prototyping*, Taylor & Francis, New York, 1(4), 494–512.

109. Gershon, E., and Gotsman, C. (1995), Multiresolution control for nonuniform B-spline curve editing, in *Pacific Graphics '95*.

110. Finkelstein, A., and Salesin, D.H. (1994), Multiresolution curves, in *Proceedings of SIGGRAPH*, pp. 261–268, ACM, New York.

111. Grisoni, L., Schlick C., and Blanc, C. (1997), *An Hermitian Approach for Multiresolution Splines*, Technical Report No. 1192–97, LaBRI.
112. Stollnitz Eric J., DeRose Tony D., and Salesin David H. (1995), Wavelets for computer graphics: a primer, part-1, *IEEE Computer Graphics and Applications*, 15(3), 76–84.
113. Stollnitz E.J., DeRose T.D., and Salesin D.H. (1995), Wavelets for computer graphics: a primer, part-2, *IEEE Computer Graphics and Applications*, 15(4), 75–85.
114. Stollnitz E.J., DeRose T.D., and Salesin D.H. (1996), *Wavelets for Computer Graphics: Theory and Applications*, Morgan Kaufman Publishers, San Francisco.
115. Sarfraz, M., and Siddiqui, M.A. (2004), Development of a multi-resolution framework for NUBS, *International Journal of Information Sciences,* Elsevier Science, 163(4), 239–251.

2
Weighted Nu Splines

Abstract. *Weighted v-splines are the composition of two spline methods, namely, weighted splines and v-splines. These are the generalization of cubic spline method and are highly useful for CAD/CAM and various applications in computer graphics. Both— interpolatory and freeform—schemes are available in the literature. This chapter explains interpolatory weighted v-splines together with a construction of its B-spline-like form. The design curves, constructed through B-spline-like form, possess all the ideal geometric properties such as partition of unity, convex hull, and variation diminishing. The splines provide not only a variety of very interesting shape control such as point and interval tensions but also, as a special case, recover the cubic spline method. In addition, these weighted v-splines also provide, as special cases, the weighted splines and the v-splines. The method for evaluating these splines is suggested by a transformation to Bézier form.*

2.1   Introduction

Designing of curves, especially those curves that are robust and easy to control and compute, has been one of the significant problems of computer graphics and geometric modeling. Specific applications including font designing, capturing hand-drawn images on computer screens, data visualization, and computer-supported cartooning are main motivations toward curve designing. In addition, various other applications in CAD/CAM/CAGD are also a good reason to study this topic. Many authors have worked in this direction. For brevity, the reader is referred to [1–22].

A cubic spline curve method is considered to be a considerably decent approach for designing applications in the area of computer graphics and geometric modeling. However, due to its various limitations, such as lack of freedom in shape control, a designer may not have much help. In this study, the weighted v-spline method has been reviewed. This curve design method, in addition to enjoying the good features of cubic splines, possesses interesting shape design features too. It has two families of shape parameters working in such a way that one family of parameters is associated with intervals and the other with points. These parameters provide a variety of shape control such as point and interval tension. This is an interpolatory curve scheme, which utilizes a piecewise cubic function in its description. However, it is desired to extend this idea to freeform curves, which can enjoy all the ideal properties related to B-spline theory. This work is mainly concerned with developing such a theory.

Weighted splines [7] were discovered as a cubic spline method. The method provides a C^1 computationally simpler alternative to the exponential spline-under-tension [4, 13, 20]. Regarding shape characteristics, it has shape control parameters associated with each interval, which can be used to flatten or tighten the curve locally. Nu-splines [11,12] were discovered as another cubic spline method. It provides a GC^2 computationally simpler alternative to the exponential spline-under-tension [4,13,21]. Regarding shape characteristics, it has shape control parameters associated with each point, which can be used to tighten the curve both locally and globally. The ideas of weighted splines and Nu-splines were married together to formulate another spline called weighted Nu-spline [11, 12, 19, 22]. This curve design method covers the shape features of both of its counter parts and provides a C^1 computationally economical method.

B-splines are a useful and powerful tool for computer graphics and geometric modeling. They can be found frequently in the existing CAD/CAM (computer-aided design/computer -aided manufacturing) systems. They form a basis for the space of n th degree splines of continuity class C^{n-1}. Each B-spline is a non-negative n th-degree spline that is nonzero only on $n + 1$ intervals. The B-splines form a partition of unity, that is, they sum up to one. Curves generated by summing control points multiplied by the B-splines have some very desirable shape properties, including the local convex hull property and variation diminishing property.

It is desirable to generalize the idea of B-spline-like local basis functions for the classes of splines with shape parameters considered in the description of continuity. The first local basis for GC^2 splines was developed by Lewis [10]. In 1981, Barsky [1] generalized B-splines to Beta splines. These splines preserve the geometric smoothness of the design curve while allowing the continuity conditions on the spline functions at the knots to be varied by certain parameters, thus giving greater flexibility. Later, in 1984, Bartels and Beatty [2] developed local bases for Beta spline curves that are equivalent to Boehm's [3] Gamma splines. Foley [7], in 1987, constructed a B-spline-like basis for weighted splines; different weights were built into the basis functions so that the control point curve was a C^1 piecewise cubic with local control of interval tension.

In this work, a constructive approach has been adopted to build B-spline-like basis for cubic spline curves with the same continuity constraints as those for interpolatory weighted v-splines. These are local basis functions with local support which have the property of being positive everywhere. The design curve, constructed through these functions, possesses all the ideal geometric properties like partition of unity, convex hull, and variation diminishing. This curve method provides not only a variety of very interesting shape control such as point and interval tensions, but also, as a special case, recovers the cubic B-spline curve method. In addition, it also provides B-spline-like design curves for weighted splines, v-splines and weighted v-splines. The method for evaluating these splines is suggested by a transformation to Bézier form.

The approach adopted in the construction of local basis for the weighted ν-splines is quite different from those adopted for different spline methods in [1–8, 15]. The way for evaluating the weighted ν-splines representation of a curve is suggested by a transformation to piecewise defined Bézier form. This form will also expedite a proof of the variation diminishing property for the Bézier representation.

This chapter is related the weighted ν-spline method [19, 22] explained in Section 2.2. It studies, in Section 2.3, a B-spline-like local basis for the weighted ν-spline. The design curve in Section 2.4 maintains the C^1 continuity of the weighted ν-splines. This description of freeform weighted ν-spline not only provides a variety of interesting shape control such as point and interval tensions but also, as a special case, recovers the cubic B-spline curve method. In addition, it also provides B-spline like design curves for weighted splines, ν-splines and weighted ν-splines. The method has been extended for the construction of surfaces in Section 2.5. Section 2.6 summarizes the chapter.

2.2   Some Spline Methods

This section gives a brief review of the cubic spline, weighted splines, ν-splines, and weighted ν-splines. Detailed description of the weighted ν-splines is given in Sections 2.3 and 2.4. Assume that we are given knot partition as $t_1 < t_2 < \ldots < t_n$, and set of control points $F_1, F_2, \ldots, F_n$. Let us have the Followings:

$$\left.\begin{array}{ll}\text{Point tension factors: } & \nu_i \geq 0, i = 1, 2, \ldots, n, \\ \text{Interval weights: } & w_i > 0, i = 1, 2, \ldots, n.\end{array}\right\}, \tag{2.1}$$

Consider the piecewise cubic function:

$$p(t) \equiv p_i(t) = F_i(1-\theta)^3 + 3\theta(1-\theta)^2 V_i + 3\theta^2(1-\theta)W_i + F_{i+1}\theta^3, \tag{2.2}$$

where

$$\theta = \frac{t - t_i}{h_i}, \quad h_i = t_{i+1} - t_i, \tag{2.3}$$

and

$$V_i = F_i + \frac{h_i D_i}{3}, \quad W_i = F_{i+1} - \frac{h_i D_{i+1}}{3}. \tag{2.4}$$

It is obvious to see that the piecewise cubic function (2.2) holds the following interpolatory properties:

$$\left.\begin{array}{ll}p(t_i) = F_i, & p(t_{i+1}) = F_{i+1} \\ p^{(1)}(t_i) = D_i, & p^{(1)}(t_{i+1}) = D_{i+1}\end{array}\right\}, \tag{2.5}$$

where $p^{(1)}$ denotes first derivative with respect to t and D_i denote derivative values given at the knots t_i. This leads the piecewise cubic (2.2) to the piecewise Hermite interpolant $p \in C^1[t_1, t_n]$.

2.2.1   *Cubic Splines*

The cubic spline interpolant is a C^2 piecewise cubic function $p(t)$ that minimizes

$$V(f) = \sum_{i=1}^{n-1} \int_{t_i}^{t_{i+1}} \left[f''(t) \right]^2 dt,$$

subject to the interpolation conditions $f(t_i) = F_i$ for $i = 1, 2, \ldots, n$ and one of the following end conditions:

- **Type 1:** First derivative end conditions,
- **Type 2:** Natural end conditions, or
- **Type 3:** Periodic end conditions.

Given F_i and D_i for $i = 1, 2, \ldots, n$, there exists a unique C^2 piecewise cubic function $f(t)$ that satisfies $f(t_i) = F_i$ and $f'(t_i) = D_i$ for $i = 1, 2, \ldots, n$. The unknowns are the first derivative values, D_i, $i = 1, 2, \ldots, n$, and once they are computed, the function $f(t)$ can be easily evaluated using the standard piecewise cubic Hermite form explained in (2.2). Necessary and sufficient conditions for the function $f(t)$ to be the cubic spline interpolant are that its derivatives D_i's satisfy

$$\hat{c}_{i-1} D_{i-1} + \left(2\hat{c}_{i-1} + 2\hat{c}_i \right) D_i + \hat{c}_i D_{i+1} = \hat{b}_i \left(F_{i+1} - F_i \right) + \hat{b}_{i-1} \left(F_i - F_{i-1} \right),$$

for $i = 1, 2, \ldots, n$, where $\hat{c}_i = 1/h_i$, $\hat{b}_i = 3\hat{c}_i/h_i$. The above system of equations provides $(2.n - 2)$ equations for n unknowns, $D_1, \ldots, D_n$, and the additional equations come from the given end conditions. The equations for Type I first derivative end conditions are $D_1 = f'(t_1)$ and $D_n = f'(t_n)$. For Type II natural end conditions they are

$$2\hat{c}_1 D_1 + \hat{c}_1 D_2 = \hat{b}_1 \left(F_2 - F_1 \right),$$

and

$$\hat{c}_{n-1} D_{n-1} + 2\hat{c}_{n-1} D_n = \hat{b}_{n-1}(F_n - F_{n-1}).$$

For Type 3 periodic end conditions, they are

$$\left(2\hat{c}_1 + 2\hat{c}_{n-1} \right) D_1 + \hat{c}_1 D_2 + \hat{c}_{n-1} D_{n-1} = \hat{b}_1(F_2 - F_1) + \hat{b}_{n-1}(F_n - F_{n-1}),$$

and $D_1 = D_n$. The linear system of equations that occurs when Type 1 or 2 end conditions are used is tridiagonal and diagonally dominant; thus it can be solved efficiently by using a standard tridiagonal system solver. Figure 2.1 is a cubic spline curve for a data shown as bullets.

2.2.2   *Weighted Splines*

The weighted spline interpolant is a C^1 piecewise cubic function $p(t)$ that minimizes

$$V(f) = \sum_{i=1}^{n-1} \omega_i \int_{t_i}^{t_{i+1}} \left[f''(t) \right]^2 dt,$$

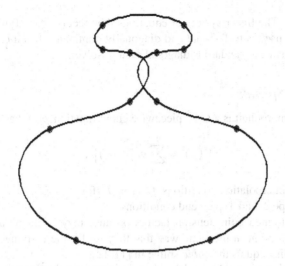

FIGURE 2.1. The default weighted ν-spline with periodic end conditions.

subject to the interpolation conditions $f(t_i) = F_i$ for $i = 1, 2, \ldots, n$ and one of the Type 1, Type 2, and Type 3 end conditions.

The ω_i's are termed as interval weights because they "tighten" the curve on the ith interval in the same way that they do for the weighted splines in [14]. If and all $\omega_i = q$, where q is some constant value, then the weighted spline equals the *cubic spline* as in Section 2.2.1.

The approach taken in [21] uses piecewise cubic Hermite basis functions to represent the weighted splines. Given F_i and D_i for $i = 1, 2, \ldots, n$, there exists a unique C^1 piecewise cubic function $f(t)$ that satisfies $f(t_i) = F_i$ and $f'(t_i) = D_i$ for $i = 1, 2, \ldots, n$. The unknowns are the first derivative values, D_i, $i = 1, 2, \ldots, n$, and once they are computed, the function $f(t)$ can be easily evaluated using the standard piecewise cubic Hermite form. Necessary and sufficient conditions for the function $p(t)$ to be the weighted spline interpolant are that its derivatives D_i satisfy

$$c_{i-1} D_{i-1} + (2c_{i-1} + 2c_i) D_i + c_i D_{i+1} = b_i (F_{i+1} - F_i) + b_{i-1} (F_i - F_{i-1}),$$

for $i = 1, 2, \ldots, n$, where $c_i = \omega_i / h_i$, $b_i = 3c_i / h_i$. The above system of equations provides $(n - 2)$ equations for n unknowns, $D_1, \ldots, D_n$, and the additional equations come from the given end conditions. The equations for Type I first derivative end conditions are $D_1 = f'(t_1)$ and $D_n = f'(t_n)$. For Type II natural end conditions they are

$$2c_1 D_1 + c_1 D_2 = b_1 (F_2 - F_1),$$

and

$$c_{n-1} D_{n-1} + 2c_{n-1} D_n = b_{n-1}(F_n - F_{n-1}).$$

For Type 3 periodic end conditions, they are

$$2c_1 + 2c_{n-1} D_1 + c_1 D_2 + c_{n-1} D_{n-1} = b_1(F_2 - F_1) + b_{n-1}(F_n - F_{n-1}),$$

and $D_1 = D_n$. The linear system of equations that occurs when Type 1 or 2 end conditions are used is tridiagonal and diagonally dominant; thus it can be solved efficiently by using a standard tridiagonal system solver.

2.2.3 Nu Splines

The ν-spline interpolant is a GC^2 piecewise cubic function $p(t)$ that minimizes

$$V(f) = \sum_{i=1}^{n} \nu_i \left[f'(t_i) \right]^2,$$

subject to the interpolation conditions $f(t_i) = F_i$ for $i = 1, 2, \ldots, n$ and one of the Type 1, Type 2, and Type 3 end conditions.

The ν_i are termed point tension factors because they "tighten" a parametric curve at the ith point in the same way that they do for the ν-splines in [11, 12]. If $\nu_i = 0$ ν-spline equals the *cubic* spline in [11, 12].

The approach taken in [11, 12, 19, 21] uses piecewise cubic Hermite basis functions to represent the ν-splines. Given F_i and D_i for $i = 1, 2, \ldots, n$, there exists a unique GC^2 piecewise cubic function $f(t)$ that satisfies $f(t_i) = F_i$ and $f'(t_i) = D_i$ for $i = 1, 2, \ldots, n$. The unknowns are the first derivative values, D_i, $i = 1, 2, \ldots, n$, and once they are computed, the function $f(t)$ can be easily evaluated using the standard piecewise cubic Hermite form. Necessary and sufficient conditions for the function $p(t)$ to be the ν-spline interpolant are that its derivatives D_i satisfy

$$\check{c}_{i-1} D_{i-1} + \left(\frac{1}{2} \nu_i + 2\check{c}_{i-1} + 2\check{c}_i \right) D_i + \check{c}_i D_{i+1} = \check{b}_i \left(F_{i+1} - F_i \right) + \check{b}_{i-1} \left(F_i - F_{i-1} \right),$$

for $i = 1, 2, \ldots, n$, where $\check{c}_i = 1/h_i$, $\check{b}_i = 3\check{c}_i/h_i$. The above system of equations provides $(n-2)$ equations for n unknowns, $D_1, \ldots, D_n$, and the additional equations come from the given end conditions. The equations for Type I first derivative end conditions are $D_1 = f'(t_1)$ and $D_n = f'(t_n)$. For Type II natural end conditions they are

$$\left(\frac{1}{2} \nu_1 + 2c_1 \right) D_1 + c_1 D_2 = b_1 \left(F_2 - F_1 \right),$$

and

$$c_{n-1} D_{n-1} + \left(\frac{1}{2} \nu_n + 2c_{n-1} \right) D_n = b_{n-1} (F_n - F_{n-1}).$$

For Type 3 periodic end conditions, they are

$$\left(\frac{1}{2} \nu_1 + \frac{1}{2} \nu_n + 2c_1 + 2c_{n-1} \right) D_1 + c_1 D_2 + c_{n-1} D_{n-1}$$
$$= b_1 (F_2 - F_1) + b_{n-1} (F_n - F_{n-1}),$$

and $D_1 = D_n$. The linear system of equations that occurs when Type 1 or 2 end conditions are used is tridiagonal and diagonally dominant; thus it can be solved efficiently by using a standard tridiagonal system solver.

2.2.4 *Weighted Nu Splines*

The weighted ν-spline interpolant is a C^1 piecewise cubic function $p(t)$ that minimizes

$$V(f) = \sum_{i=1}^{n-1} \omega_i \int_{t_i}^{t_{i+1}} [f''(t)]^2 dt + \sum_{i=1}^{n} \nu_i [f'(t_i)]^2,$$

subject to the interpolation conditions $f(t_i) = F_i$ for $i = 1, 2, \ldots, n$ and one of the Type 1, Type 2, Type 3 end conditions. This is the marriage of Weighted splines and Nu splines which can be recovered as special cases discussed later in this chapter.

The ν_i are termed point tension factors because they 'tighten' a parametric curve at the ith point in the same way that they do for the ν-splines in [11, 12]. The w_i are termed interval weights because they 'tighten' the curve on the ith interval in the same way that they do for the weighted splines in [14]. If $\nu_i = 0$ and all $\omega_i = q$, where q is some constant value, then the weighted ν-spline equals the ν-spline in [11, 12] with tension factors ν_i/q. If all $\nu_i = 0$, then it equals the weighted spline given in [14].

The approach taken in [8] uses piecewise cubic Hermite basis functions to represent the weighted ν-splines. Given F_i and D_i for $i = 1, 2, \ldots, n$, there exists a unique C^1 piecewise cubic function $f(t)$ that satisfies $f(t_i) = F_i$ and $f'(t_i) = D_i$ for $i = 1, 2, \ldots, n$. The unknowns are the first derivative values, D_i, $i = 1, 2, \ldots, n$, and once they are computed, the function $f(t)$ can be easily evaluated using the standard piecewise cubic Hermite form. Necessary and sufficient conditions for the function $p(t)$ to be the weighted ν-spline interpolant are that its derivatives D_i satisfy

$$c_{i-1} D_{i-1} + \left(\frac{1}{2}\nu_i + 2c_{i-1} + 2c_i \right) D_i + c_i D_{i+1}$$
$$= b_i (F_{i+1} - F_i) + b_{i-1} (F_i - F_{i-1}), \tag{2.6}$$

for $i = 1, 2, \ldots, n$. The above system of equations provides $(n - 2)$ equations for n unknowns, $D_1, \ldots, D_n$, and the additional equations come from the given end conditions. The equations for Type I first derivative end conditions are $D_1 = f'(t_1)$ and $D_n = f'(t_n)$. For Type II natural end conditions they are

$$\left(\frac{1}{2}\nu_1 + 2c_1 \right) D_1 + c_1 D_2 = b_1 (F_2 - F_1),$$

and

$$c_{n-1} D_{n-1} + \left(\frac{1}{2}\nu_n + 2c_{n-1} \right) D_n = b_{n-1}(F_n - F_{n-1}).$$

For Type 3 periodic end conditions, they are

$$\left(\frac{1}{2}\nu_1 + \frac{1}{2}\nu_n + 2c_1 + 2c_{n-1} \right) D_1 + c_1 D_2 + c_{n-1} D_{n-1}$$
$$= b_1(F_2 - F_1) + b_{n-1}(F_n - F_{n-1}),$$

and $D_1 = D_n$. The linear system of equations that occurs when Type 1 or 2 end conditions are used is tridiagonal and diagonally dominant; thus it can be solved efficiently by using a standard tridiagonal system solver.

The weighted ν-spline can be computed by solving for D_i's. This can be done by re-writing the system of equations in (2.10) as follows:

$$c_{i-1}D_{i-1} + \left(\frac{\nu_i}{2} + 2c_{i-1} + 2c_i\right) D_i + c_i D_{i+1} = 3c_i \Delta_i + 3c_{i-1}\Delta_{i-1}, \quad (2.7)$$

where

$$\Delta_i = (F_{i+1} - F_i) / h_i.$$

for $i = 2, \ldots, n - 1$. For given appropriate end conditions (Type 1, Type 2, or Type 3), this system of equations is a tridiagonal linear system. This is also diagonally dominant for the following constraints on the shape parameters as in (2.1), and hence has a unique solution for D_i's. As far as the computation method is concerned, it is much more economical to adopt the LU-decomposition method to solve the tridiagonal system. Therefore, the above discussion can be concluded in the following:

Theorem 2.1. *For the shape parameter constraints (2.1), the spline solution of the weighted ν-spline exists and is unique.*

Remark 2.1. Each component of the parametric weighted ν-spline is a C^1 function in general, but it has second-order geometric continuity at t_i if $\omega_{i-1} = \omega_i$ and the tangent vector at t_i is non zero and it is C^2 at t_i if $\omega_{i-1} = \omega_i$ and $\nu_i = 0$.

2.2.5 Demonstration

Figure 2.1 is the parametric weighted ν-spline interpolant to the points denoted by circles using periodic end conditions. In Figure 2.2, interval weight, ω_i, of 30 is used in the base interval, while point tension factors, ν_i of 10 are used on the four vertices defining the "neck." The rest of the parameters are taken as $\omega_i = 1$ and $\nu_i = 0$.

2.3 Freeform Weighted Nu Spline

This section is devoted to constructing the freeform weighted Nu spline which has inherent properties of B-spline curves. This formulation is possible through the construction of local support basis B_i's to compute the cubic weighted ν-spline $p(t)$ satisfying the following constraints:

$$\begin{bmatrix} p(t_{i+}) \\ p^{(1)}(t_{i+}) \\ p^{(2)}(t_{i+}) \end{bmatrix} = \begin{bmatrix} 1 & 0 & 0 \\ 0 & 1 & 0 \\ 0 & \frac{\nu_i}{\omega_i} & \frac{\omega_{i-1}}{\omega_i} \end{bmatrix} \begin{bmatrix} p(t_{i-}) \\ p^{(1)}(t_{i-}) \\ p^{(2)}(t_{i-}) \end{bmatrix}. \quad (2.8)$$

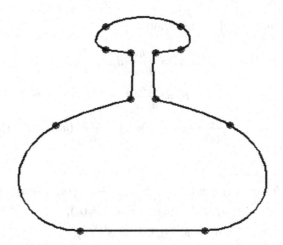

FIGURE 2.2. The weighted ν-spline with periodic end conditions using $\omega_i = 30$ on the base interval, $\omega_i = 1$ otherwise, $\nu_i = 10$ on the four vertices defining the "neck," and $\nu_i = 0$ otherwise.

2.3.1 Local Support Basis

For the purpose of the analysis, let additional knots be introduced outside the knot partition $t_1 < t_2 < \ldots < t_n$ of the interval $[t_1, t_n]$, defined by:

$$t_{-2} < t_{-1} < t_0 < t_1 \text{ and } t_n < t_{n+1} < t_{n+2} < t_{n+3}. \tag{2.9}$$

Let

$$a_i = 1/c_i, \tag{2.10}$$

and ϕ_i be cubic weighted ν-spline:

$$\phi_i(t) = \begin{cases} 0, & t \leq t_{i-2}, \\ 1, & t \geq t_{i+1}. \end{cases} \tag{2.11}$$

Imposing weighted ν-spline constraints (2.8), we have:

$$\phi_i(t_{i-1}) = \frac{h_{i-2}}{3}\phi_i^{(1)}(t_{i-1}),$$

$$\phi_i(t_i) = 1 - \frac{h_i}{3}\phi_i^{(1)}(t_i),$$

$$\phi_i^{(1)}(t_{i-1}) = \frac{A_i}{C_i},$$

and

$$\phi_i^{(1)}(t_i) = \frac{B_i}{C_i},$$

where, if $d_i = \frac{1}{2} a_i a_{i-1} v_i + a_{i-1} + a_i$, then

$$A_i = \frac{3a_{i-2}}{h_{i-1}} d_i,$$

$$B_i = \frac{3a_i}{h_{i-1}} d_{i-1},$$

$$C_i = d_i d_{i-1} + \frac{a_i}{h_{i-1}}(h_{i-1} + h_i)d_{i-1} + \frac{a_{i-2}}{h_{i-1}}(h_{i-1} + h_{i-2})d_i.$$

Let

$$D_i = h_{i-1}d_i d_{i-1} + a_i(h_{i-1} + h_i)d_{i-1} + a_{i-2}(h_{i-1} + h_{i-2})d_i,$$
$$\mu_i = \phi_{i+1}(t_i), \lambda_i = 1 - \phi_i(t_i),$$
$$\hat{\mu}_i = \phi_{i+1}^{(1)}(t_i), \hat{\lambda}_i = \phi_i^{(1)}(t_i),$$

Then

$$\hat{\lambda}_i = \frac{3a_i d_{i-1}}{D_i}, \hat{\mu}_i = \frac{3a_{i-1}d_{i+1}}{D_{i+1}},$$

$$\mu_i = \frac{h_{i-1}}{3}\hat{\mu}_i, \lambda_i = \frac{h_i}{3}\hat{\lambda}_i,$$

and hence

$$0 \leq \mu_i \leq 1, \ 0 \leq \lambda_i \leq 1 \quad \text{and} \quad 0 \leq \mu_i + \lambda_i \leq 1.$$

Now define

$$B_i(t) = \phi_i(t) - \phi_{i+1}(t).$$

Then B_i has the local support (t_{i-2}, t_{i+2}) and an explicit representation of B_j on any interval (t_i, t_{i+1}) (in particular, for $i = j - 2, j - 1, j, j + 1$) can be calculated as:

$$B_j(t) = (1 - \theta)^3 B_j(t_i) + \theta(1 - \theta)^2 (3B_j(t_i)h_i B_j^{(1)}(t_i))$$
$$+ \theta^2(1 - \theta)(3B_j(t_{i+1}) - h_i B_j^{(1)}(t_{i+1})) + \theta^3 B_j(t_{i+1}), \quad (2.12)$$

where

$$B_j(t_i) = B_j^{(1)}(t_i) = 0 \text{ for } i \neq j - 1, j, j + 1,$$

and

$$\left. \begin{array}{ll} B_j(t_{j-1}) = \mu_{j-1}, & B_j^{(1)}(t_{j-1}) = \hat{\mu}_{j-1}, \\ B_j(t_j) \quad = 1 - \lambda_j - \mu_j, & B_j^{(1)}(t_j) \quad = \hat{\lambda}_j - \hat{\mu}_j, \\ B_j(t_{j+1}) = \lambda_{j+1}, & B_j^{(1)}(t_{j+1}) = -\hat{\lambda}_{j+1}. \end{array} \right\} \quad (2.13)$$

Careful examination of the Bézier vertices of $B_j(t)$ in (2.12) shows these to be non-negative for v_i, ω_i satisfying (2.7) and thus $B_j(t) \geq 0, \ \forall t$. This leads to the following:

Proposition 2.1. The local support basis functions (2.12) are such that the following properties hold:

(i) (Local support) $B_j(t) = 0$ for $t \notin (t_{j-2}, t_{j+2})$,

(ii) (Partition of unity) $\sum\limits_{j=-1}^{n+1} B_j(t) = 1$ for $t \in [t_1, t_n]$,

(iii) (Positivity) $B_j(t) \geq 0$ for all t.

2.3.2 Design Curve

Now, we need a convenient method to compute the curve representation. It is desired to apply the above developed local basis functions to develop a freeform weighted v-spline curve as follows:

$$P(t) = \sum_{j=-1}^{n+1} B_j(t) P_j, t \in [t_1, t_n], \tag{2.14}$$

where $P_j \in R^N$, $j = 0, 1, \ldots, n + 1$, define the control points of the representation. By the local support property,

$$P(t) = \sum_{j=i-1}^{i+2} B_j(t) P_j, \ t \in [t_i, t_{i+1}), i = 0, \ldots, n - 1.$$

Substitution of (2.12), $t \in [t_i, t_{i+1})$, then gives the piecewise defined Bézier representation

$$P(t) \equiv P_i(t) = F_i(1 - \theta)^3 + 3\theta(1 - \theta)^2 V_i + 3\theta^2(1 - \theta) W_i + F_{i+1}\theta^3, \tag{2.15}$$

where

$$\left.\begin{array}{rcl}
F_i &=& \lambda_i P_{i-1} + (1 - \lambda_i - \mu_i) P_i + \mu_i P_{i+1}, \\
V_i &=& (1 - \alpha_i) P_i + \alpha_i P_{i+1}, \\
W_i &=& \beta_i P_i + (1 - \beta_i) P_{i+1},
\end{array}\right\} \tag{2.16}$$

with

$$\alpha_i = \mu_i + h_i \hat{\mu}_i/3 = \frac{\hat{\mu}_i}{3}(h_{i-1} + h_i),$$

$$\beta_i = \lambda_{i+1} + h_i \hat{\lambda}_i = \frac{\hat{\lambda}_{i+1}}{3}(h_i + h_{i+1}).$$

This transformation to Bézier form is very convenient for computational purposes and also leads to the following:

Proposition 2.2. (Variation Diminishing Property) The weighted v-spline curve $P(t)$, $t \in [t_0, t_n]$, defined by (2.14), crosses any (hyper) plane of dimension $N - 1$ no more times than it crosses the "control polygon" joining the control points $P_{-1}, P_0, \ldots, P_{n+1}$.

Proof. Following the arguments of positivity in the previous proposition, it is straightforward that $0 \leq \alpha_i \leq 1, 0 \leq \beta_i \leq 1$, and $0 \leq \alpha_i + \beta_i \leq 1$. Thus, V_i and W_i lie on the line segment joining P_i and P_{i+1}, where V_i is before W_i. It can also be simply noted that

$$F_i = (1 - \gamma_i)W_{i-1} + \gamma_i V_i, \tag{2.17}$$

where

$$0 < \gamma_i = \frac{h_{i-1}}{h_{i-1} + h_i} < 1.$$

Thus, the control polygon of the piecewise defined Bézier representation is obtained by corner cutting of the weighted ν-spline control polygon. Since the piecewise defined Bézier representation is variation diminishing, it follows that weighted ν-spline representation is variation diminishing.

2.3.3 *Shape Control*

The shape parameters, defined in (2.7), can be used to control the local or global shape of the design curve. To analyze such behaviors, the explicit form on $(2.t_i, t_{i+1})$ of the weighted ν-spline design curve (2.14) can be expressed as:

$$P(t) = l_i(t) + e_i(t), \tag{2.18}$$

where

$$l_i(t) = (1 - \theta)F_i + \theta F_{i+1}, \tag{2.19}$$

and

$$e_i(t) = \theta(1 - \theta) \left\{ \left[(F_{i+1} - F_i) - h_i P^{(1)}(t_i) \right](\theta - 1) \right.$$
$$\left. + \left[(F_{i+1} - F_i) - h_i P^{(1)}(t_{i+1}) \right]\theta \right\}. \tag{2.20}$$

Proposition 2.3. Let $\omega_i = \omega \geq 1$, and $\nu_i = 0, \forall i$ are all bounded then the weighted ν-spline design curve is straightway the standard cubic spline.

Proof. It follows from the last constraint of relation (2.8).

Proposition 2.4. (Global Tension) Let $\omega_i \geq 1, \forall i$, be bounded and $\nu_i \geq \nu$ then the weighted ν-spline curve (2.14) converges uniformly to the control polygon $P_0, \ldots, P_n$ as $\nu \to \infty$.

Proof. Let $\nu_i = \nu, \forall i$ then from (2.1)

$$\lim_{\nu \to \infty} P^{(1)}(t_i) = 0. \tag{2.21}$$

Moreover

$$\lim_{\nu \to \infty} \hat{\mu}_i = 0 = \lim_{\nu \to \infty} \hat{\lambda}_i, \quad \forall i.$$

This implies the following:

$$\lim_{\nu \to \infty} F_i = P_i, \ \forall i. \tag{2.22}$$

More generally, for $\nu_i \geq \nu \geq 0$, it can be shown that

$$\max_i |\hat{\lambda}_i| \leq r(\nu),$$

and

$$\max_i |\hat{\mu}_i| \leq s(\nu),$$

where

$$\lim_{\nu \to \infty} r(\nu) = 0 = \lim_{\nu \to \infty} s(\nu),$$

and again (2.21) and (2.22) hold. Hence the result.

Proposition 2.5. [Local Tension] Consider an interval $[t_k, t_{k+1}]$ for a fixed k. Then on $[t_k, t_{k+1}]$ weighted ν-spline curve converges uniformly to a line segment of the line $P_k P_{k+1}$ as $w_k \to \infty$ where ω_{k-1} and ν_k are bounded.

Proof. Careful examination shows

$$\lim_{\omega \to \infty} \mu_k = \frac{h_{k-1}}{(3h_k + h_{k-1} + h_{k+1})} = \hat{a}_k (\text{say})$$

$$\lim_{\omega \to \infty} \mu_{k+1} = 0$$

$$\lim_{\omega \to \infty} \lambda_k = 0$$

$$\lim_{\omega \to \infty} \lambda_{k+1} = \frac{h_{k+1}}{(3h_k + h_{k-1} + h_{k+1})} = \hat{\beta}_k (\text{say})$$

This implies the following:

$$\lim_{\omega \to \infty} F_k = \left(1 - \hat{a}_k\right) P_k + \hat{a}_k P_{k+1} = \hat{F}_k (\text{say})$$

and

$$\lim_{\omega \to \infty} F_{k+1} = \hat{\beta}_k P_k + \left(1 - \hat{\beta}_k\right) P_{k+1} = \hat{F}_{k+1} (\text{say})$$

Obviously $\hat{F}_k$ and $\hat{F}_{k+1}$ lie on $\overline{P_k P_{k+1}}$ and $\hat{F}_k$ is before $\hat{F}_{k+1}$ as $\hat{a}_k < (1 - \hat{\beta}_k)$. Also

$$\lim_{\omega \to \infty} (F_{k+1} - F_k) = \lim_{\omega \to \infty} h_k P^{(1)}(t_k) = \lim_{\omega \to \infty} h_k P^{(1)}(t_{k+1}) = \frac{3h_k(P_{k+1} - P_k)}{(3h_k + h_{k-1} + h_{k+1})}$$

Hence from (2.18), (2.19), (2.20) if $P(t) = P_k(t)$ for $t \in (t_k, t_{k+1})$, then

$$\lim_{\omega \to \infty} P_k(t) = (1 - \theta) \hat{F}_k + \theta \hat{F}_k.$$

Proposition 2.6. (Local Tension) Consider an interval as in Proposition 5. Then on $[t_k, t_{k+1}]$, the weighted ν-spline converges uniformly to the linear interpolant $l_i(t)$ as both $\nu_k, \nu_{k+1} \to \infty$, where $\omega_{k-1}, \omega_k, \omega_{k+1}$ are bounded.

Proof. It can be noted that

$$\lim \mu_k = \lim \mu_{k+1} = 0,$$
$$\lim \lambda_k = \lim \lambda_{k+1} = 0,$$

and

$$\lim P^{(1)}(t_k) = \lim P^{(1)}(t_{k+1}) = 0.$$

This gives the desired result.

2.3.4 *Demonstration*

The tension behavior of the weighted ν-spline is illustrated by the following simple examples for data set in R^2. Unless otherwise stated, in all the figures, the parameter ν_i will be assumed as zero $\forall i$ and the parameters ω_i as 1 for all i.

Figure 2.3 is the default curve, which is a cubic spline for $\nu_i = 0$, and $\omega_i = 1$, for all i. The control polygon, together with the control points, is also shown in the figure. Figure 2.4 shows the effect of a progressive increase in the interval tension in the base of the figure. The top, middle, and bottom curves have been demonstrated for $\omega = 1$, 10, and 100, respectively. The effect of the high-tension parameters is clearly seen in the corresponding interval in the base of the figure. Figure 2.5 shows the effect of a progressive increase in point tension behavior locally at two opposite points of the figure. The top, middle, and bottom curves have been demonstrated for $\nu = 0$, 10, and 100, respectively. The effect of the high-tension parameters is clearly seen at the corresponding points in the figure.

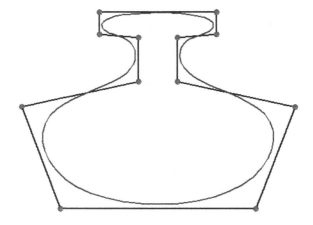

FIGURE 2.3. The default weighted Nu spline.

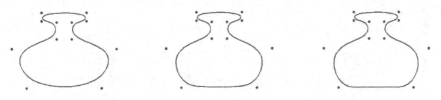

FIGURE 2.4. The weighted Nu spline with interval tension at the base with ω values as 1 (left curve), 10 (middle curve), 100 (right curve).

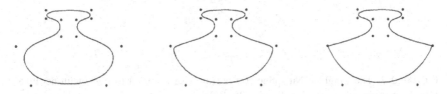

FIGURE 2.5. The weighted Nu spline with corner tension at two opposite points with ν values as 0 (left curve), 10 (middle curve), 100 (right curve).

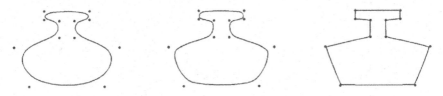

FIGURE 2.6. The weighted Nu spline with global tension $\nu = 1$ (top curve), $\nu = 5$ (middle curve), $\nu = 100$ (bottom curve).

Figures 2.6 illustrates the effect of progressively increasing the values of the point tension parameters ν_i's $= 0, 5$, and 100, for the top, middle, and bottom curves, respectively, at all the points of the figure. This is the global tension effect due to progressive increase.

Figure 2.7 demonstrates an important observation about the negative values of the shape parameters. The global values of the interval shape parameters ω's will not make any effect to the picture. However, the local values do influence the picture. The curve bulges inside for negative values $\omega = 0, -3, -4, -5, -25$, and -100. It can be noted (row-wise from left to right) that lower negative values make the curve bulge more inside, but higher negative values again start making the curve tensed in the interval.

Behavior of the negative ν values can be seen in Figure 2.8. It illustrates the effect of progressive negative increase in the values of the point tension parameters ν_i's $= 0, -1, -5, -25, -100$, and -1000. It can be seen (row-wise from left to right) that Lower negative values make the curve bulge inside so much so the curve starts looping with the negative increase. However, it again starts getting tensed after attaining certain values. Ultimately, higher negative values make the curve tensed to converge to the control polygon.

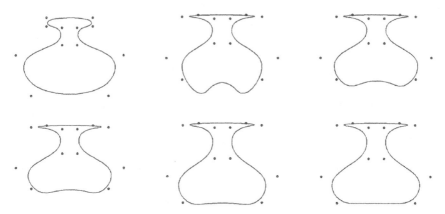

FIGURE 2.7. The weighted Nu spline curves (row vise from left to right) with negative global tension ω values $0, -3, -4, -5, -25, 100$.

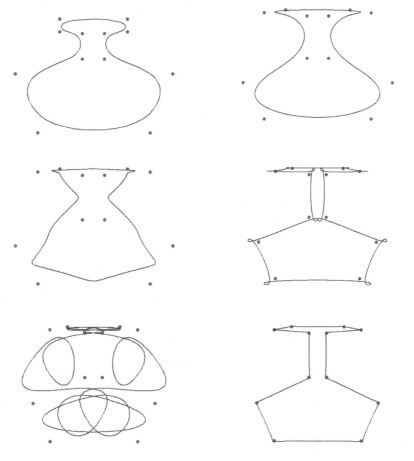

FIGURE 2.8. The weighted Nu spline curves (row vise from left to right) with negative global tension v values $0, -1, -5, -25, 100$, and 1000.

2.3.5 *Advantages and Features*

The method has various advantages and features as follows:

- It enjoys the good features of cubic splines.
- It enjoys all the standard geometric properties of B-splines.
- The method is geometrically smooth.
- It recovers the cubic B-spline method as a special case.
- It recovers the weighted spline method as a special case.
- It recovers the Nu-spline method as a special case.
- It possesses interested shape design features.
- It has two families of shape parameters working in such a way that one family of parameters is associated with intervals and the other with points. These parameters provide a variety of shape controls such as point and interval tension.
- Negative weights can also be utilized for shape design.
- It is computationally economical because it consumes the cubic function only.
- The method of evaluation is suggested by a transformation to Bézier form, which is computable by any well-known recursive method too.
- In addition to direct manipulation, the interpolation method can be computed through B-spline-like formulation too. This point will be discussed in detail somewhere else later.
- The curve method is extendable to surfaces. The direct approach using a tensor product is the simplest one.

2.4 Surfaces

The extension of the curve scheme, to tensor product surface representations:

$$P(\tilde{t}, t) = \sum_{i=-1}^{m+1} \sum_{j=-1}^{n+1} P_{i,j} \tilde{B}_i(\tilde{t}) B_j(t),$$

where $\tilde{t}_{-2} \leq \tilde{t} \leq \tilde{t}_{m+3}, t_{-2} \leq t \leq t_{n+3}$, is immediately apparent. This surface presents a bicubic weighted v-spline surface with shape parameters as:

$$\tilde{v}_i \geq 0, \ i = 1, \ldots, m, \ \tilde{w}_i > 0, \ i = 1, \ldots, m-1,$$
$$v_j \geq 0, j = 1, \ldots, n, \ \omega_j > 0, \ j = 1, \ldots, n-1.$$

Here

$$P_{i,j} \in R^3, i = -1, \ldots, m+1, \ j = -1, \ldots, n+1.$$

are the data points and $\tilde{B}_i, i = -1, \ldots, m+1$ and $B_j, j = -1, \ldots, n+1$ are the local support bases functions for the weighted v-spline in $\tilde{t}$ and t directions, respectively. However, this representation exhibits a problem common to all tensor product descriptions in that the shape control parameters now affect a complete row or column of the tensor product array.

Nielson [12] solves this problem for his cubic ν-spline representation by constructing a Boolean sum, spline-blended, rectangular network of parametric ν-spline curves. Another possibility is to allow the shape parameters to be variable in the orthogonal direction to, for example, the local support basis functions of the tensor product form.

We propose a tensor product like the approach in [16, 17], but actually it is not a tensor product. Instead of step functions, the tension weights are introduced as C^2 continuous cubic B-splines in the description of the tensor product. This produces local control in the construction of surfaces in an independent way. The details of the proposed method are out of the scope of this paper and will be discussed elsewhere.

2.5   Summary

A freeform C^1 weighted Nu spline curve design has been developed through the construction of local support B-spline-like basis functions. This cubic spline method has been developed with a view to its application in computer graphics, geometric modeling, and CAGD. It is quite reasonable to construct a freeform cubic spline method, which involves two families of shape parameters in exactly a similar way as in interpolatory weighted ν-spline. These parameters provide a variety of local and global shape controls such as interval and point shape effects. The visual smoothness of the proposed method is also C^1, which is same as the smoothness of interpolatory weighted ν-spline. The freeform C^1 weighted Nu-spline method can be applied to tensor product surfaces, but unfortunately, in the context of interactive surface design, this tensor product surface is not that useful because any one of the tension parameters controls an entire corresponding interval strip of the surface. Thus, as an application of C^1 spline for the surfaces, a method similar to Nielson's [12] spline blended methods may be attempted. This will produce local shape control, which is quite useful regarding the computer graphics and geometric modeling applications.

2.6   Exercises

1. Write a program to implement the curve design method in Section 2.2.
2. Write a program to implement the curve design method in Section 2.3.
3. Check the difference of shape effects in your programs of Exercise 2.6.1 and 2.6.2 when the schemes are implemented in scalar form.

References

1. Barsky, B.A. (1981), *The Beta-Spline: A Local Representation Based on Shape Parameters and Fundamental Geometric Measure*, Ph.D. Thesis, University of Utah.

2. Bartels, R., and Beatty, J. (1984), Beta-splines with a difference, Technical Report CS-83-40, Computer Science Department, University of Waterloo, Waterloo, Canada.

3. Boehm, W. (1985), Curvature continuous curves and surfaces, *Comp Aided Geom Design* 2(2), 313–323.

4. Cline, A. (1974), Curve fitting in one and dimensions using splines under tension, *Comm ACM* 17, 218–223.

5. Dierckx, P., and Tytgat, B. (1989), Generating the Bézier points of β-spline curve, *Comp Aided Geom Design* 6, 279–291.

6. Farin, G.E. (1996), *Curves and Surfaces for CAGD*, Academic Press, New York.

7. Foley, T.A. (1987), Local control of interval tension using weighted splines. *Comp Aided Geom. Design* 3, 281–294.

8. Foley, T.A. (1987), Interpolation with interval and point tension controls using cubic weighted v-splines, *ACM Trans Math Software* 13, 68–96.

9. Goodman, T.N.T., and Unsworth, K. (1985), Generation of Beta spline curves using a recursive relation. In: *Fundamental Algorithms for Computer Graphics.* R.E. Earnshaw (Ed.), Springer-Verlag, Berlin, pp. 326–357.

10. Lewis, J. (1975), *"B-spline" bases for splines under tension, Nu-splines, and fractional order splines,* Presented at the SIAM-SIGNUM Meeting, San Francisco, CA.

11. Nielson, G.M. (1974), Some piecewise polynomial alternatives to splines under tension, In: *Computer-Aided Geometric Design*, R.F. Barnhill (Ed.), Academic Press. New York.

12. Nielson, G.M. (1986), Rectangular v-splines. *IEEE Comp Graph Appl* 6, 35–40.

13. Pruess, S. (1979), Alternatives to the exponential spline in tension, *Math Comp* 33, 1273–1281.

14. Salkauskas, K. (1984), C^1 splines for interpolation of rapidly varying data, *Rocky Mtn J Math* 14, 239–250.

15. Sarfraz, M. (1992), A C^2 rational cubic spline alternative to the NURBS, *Comp & Graph* 16(1), 69–78.

16. Sarfraz, M. (1995), Curves and surfaces for CAD using C2 rational cubic splines, *Int J Eng Comput*, Springer-Verlag, 11(2), 94–102.

17. Sarfraz, M. (1994), Freeform rational bicubic spline surfaces with tension control, Facta Universitatis (NIS), *Ser Math Informatics*, 9, 83–93.

18. Sarfraz, M. (1994), Cubic spline curves with shape control, *Int J Comput Graphics*, Elsevier Science, 18(5), 707–713.

19. Sarfraz, M, (2003), Weighted Nu splines: an alternative to NURBS, *Advances in Geometric Modeling,* Ed.: M. Sarfraz, John Wiley, pp. 81–95.

20. Schoenburg, I. J. (1946), Contributions to the problem of approximation of equidistant data by analytic functions, *Appl Math* 4, 45–99.

21. Schweikert, D.G. (1966), An interpolation curve using a spline in tension, *J Math Phys* 45, 312–317.

22. Sarfraz, M. (2004), Weighted Nu splines with local support basis functions, *Int J Comput Graphics*, Elsevier Science, 28(4), 539–549.

3
Rational Cubic Spline with Shape Control

Abstract. *Interactive curve design is a basic need for CAD/CAM, computer graphics, vision, imaging and various other disciplines [1–28]. Having a robust, visually pleasant, well controlled, and effective scheme may be a useful solution to many problems in practice. A rational spline with some shape parameters may be a good choice in this regard. This chapter has been devoted to a C^2 rational spline scheme having interesting features. It is also an alternative to various other schemes, in the literature, like weighted spline, ν – spline, weighted Nu spline, and γ – spline, and so on. In addition to the interpolatory version, the spline is also presentable in B-spline-like form to produce freeform curves.*

3.1 Introduction

A rational cubic spline with tension was described and analyzed by Gregory and Sarfraz [23]. It provides a C^2 computationally simpler alternative to the exponential spline-under-tension of Schweikert [24], Cline [25] and Preuss [26] as well as an alternative to C^1 and GC^2 spline methods such as the weighted ν – spline of Foley [8] and γ – spline of Boehm [3], and so on. Regarding shape characteristics, it has a shape control parameter associated with each interval which can be used for flatten or tighten the curve both locally and globally.

This chapter presents a description and analysis of a rational cubic spline that has two shape parameters associated with each interval. The spline can be used in computer graphics, CAGD, and CAD/CAM to represent the parametric curves in interpolatory as well approximation (freeform) form. The rational spline not only recovers the rational cubic spline with tension of Gregory and Sarfraz [23] but also provides a C^2 alternative to most of the existing C^1 and GC^2 spline methods such as the weighted splines of Foley [7], ν – spline of Nielson [11, 12], weighted ν – splines of Foley [8], γ – spline of Boehm [3], rational geometric splines of Boehm [27], and so on.

The shape parameters of the rational spline can be utilized to achieve a variety of shape controls such as biased, point and interval tensions. Since the spline is defined on a nonuniform knot partition, the partition itself provides additional degrees of freedom on the curve. However, the parametrization is normally expected to be defined on a uniform known partition, or by cumulative chord length, or by some other appropriate means.

The rational spline is based on a rational cubic Hermite interpolant which is introduced in Section 3.2. together with some preliminary analysis. Section 3.3 describes the rational spline and analyses of its behavior with respect to one shape parameter in each interval while the generalization to two shape parameters is discussed in Section 3.4. Section 3.5 consists of some illustrative examples about the interpolation spline. The survey of freeform curves is made in Section 3.6 and B-spline-like bases are constructed in Section 3.8. Freeform design curve formulation is made in Section 3.9, whereas Section 3.10 explains the behavior of shape parameters. Freeform curve scheme has been demonstrated in Section 3.11. A brief description of surfaces has been made in Sections 3.12 and 3.13.

3.2 C^1 Piecewise Rational Cubic Hermite Interpolant

A piecewise rational cubic Hermite parametric function $p \in C^1 [t_0, t_n]$, with parameters $v_i, w_i, i = 0, \ldots, n-1$, is defined for $t \in \left[t_i, t_{i+1}\right], i = 0, \ldots, n-1$, by

$$
\begin{aligned}
p(t) &= p_i(t_i; v_i, w_i) \\
&= \frac{(1-\theta)^3 F_i + \theta (1-\theta)^2 (v_i F_i + h_i D_i) + \theta^2 (1-\theta) (w_i F_{i+1} - h_i D_{i+1}) + \theta^3 F_{i+1}}{(1-\theta)^3 + v_i \theta (1-\theta)^2 + w_i \theta^2 (1-\theta) + \theta^3}
\end{aligned}
$$

(3.1)

where the notations $F_i, D_i, t_i, h_i, \theta$ are as mentioned in Section 1.3 and $v_i, w_i \geq 0$.

The function $p(t)$—see Figure 3.1—has the Hermite interpolation properties that

$$p(t_i) = F_i \text{ and } p^{(1)}(t_i) = D_i, i = 0, \ldots, n. \tag{3.2}$$

The v_i and $w_i, i = 0, \ldots, n-1$, will be used as *shape* parameters to control and fine tune the shape of the curve. The case $v_i = w_i = 3, i = 0, \ldots, n-1$ is that of cubic Hermite interpolation and the restriction $v_i, w_i \geq 0$ ensures a positive denominator in Equation (3.1).

For $v_i, w_i \neq 0$, Equation (3.1) can be written in the form:

$$
\begin{aligned}
p_i(t_i; v_i, w_i) &= R_0(\theta; v_i, w_i) F_i + R_1(\theta; v_i, w_i) V_i + R_2(\theta; v_i, w_i) W_i \\
&\quad + R_3(\theta; v_i, w_i) F_{i+1},
\end{aligned}
\tag{3.3}
$$

where

$$V_i = F_i + h_i D_i / v_i, W_i = F_{i+1} - h_i D_{i+1} / w_i, \tag{3.4}$$

and $R_j(\theta; v_i, w_i), j = 0, 1, 2, 3$, are appropriately defined rational functions with

$$\sum_{j=0}^{3} R_j(\theta; v_i, w_i) = 1. \tag{3.5}$$

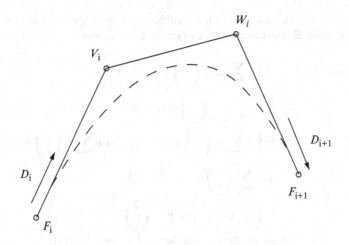

FIGURE 3.1. The rational cubic segment in R^2.

Moreover, these functions are rational Bernstein-Bézier weight functions that are non-negative for $v_i, w_i > 0$. Thus, in $R^N, N > 1$ and for $v_i, w_i > 0$, we have:

Proposition 3.1. (Convex hull property) The curve segment p_i lies in the convex hull of the control points $\{F_i, V_i, W_i, F_{i+1}\}$.

We now consider the variation diminishing property of the rational cubic and for this we require some preliminary analysis. Let

$$p(\theta) = \sum_{i=0}^{3} a_i A_i \binom{3}{i} \theta^i (1-\theta)^{3-i},$$

and

$$q(\theta) = \sum_{i=0}^{3} a_i \binom{3}{i} \theta^i (1-\theta)^{3-i}$$

be scalar curves with $a_i > 0, \forall_i$. Since $p(\theta)$ is a Bézier curve and since $a_i > 0$, we have

$$V(p) \leq V(a_0 A_0, \ldots, a_3 A_3) = V(A_0, \ldots, A_3),$$

where V(.) denotes the number of sign changes of a function or sequence on $[0, 1]$. Also, since $q(\theta) > 0$, we have

$$V\left(\frac{p}{q}\right) = V(p) \leq V(A_0, \ldots, A_3),$$

Let $p(\theta)$ now be considered as planar curve, say, $p(\theta) = (p_1(\theta), p_2(\theta))$ where $A_i = (x_i, y_i) \in R^2$ and let $L \equiv ax + by + c = 0$ be any line. Then the number of times the line L crosses the rational cubic curve $p(\theta)/q(\theta)$ is the same as it crosses the cubic Bézier curve $p(\theta)$, $q(\theta) > 0$. This number is

$$
\begin{aligned}
V(ap_1 + bp_2 + c) &= V\left(a\sum a_i x_i \binom{3}{i}\theta^i(1-\theta)^{3-i}\right. \\
&\quad \left. + b\sum a_i y_i \binom{3}{i}\theta^i(1-\theta)^{3-i} + c\right) \\
&= V\left(a\sum x_i \binom{3}{i}\theta^i(1-\theta)^{3-i} + b\sum y_i \binom{3}{i}\theta^i(1-\theta)^{3-i}\right. \\
&\quad \left. + c\sum \binom{3}{i}\theta^i(1-\theta)^{3-i}\right) \\
&= V\left(\sum (ax_i + by_i + c)\binom{3}{i}\theta^i(1-\theta)^{3-i}\right) \\
&= \text{the number of times the line } L \text{ crosses the polygon } A_0, \ldots, A_3.
\end{aligned}
$$

These arguments can be extended to rational curve of any degree in R^N with any hyper plane of dimension $N - 1$. Thus, we have:

Proposition 3.2. (Variation diminishing property) The curve segment p_i crosses any (hyper) plane of dimension $N - 1$ no more times than it crosses the control polygon joining F_i, V_i, W_i, F_{i+1}.

Remark 3.3. In the scalar case when $v_i, w_i, = r_i$, the convex hull (Proposition 3.1) and variation diminishing (Proposition 3.2) properties apply to the curve segment $(t, p_i(t; r_i, r_i)) \in R^2, t \in (t_i, t_{i+1})$ with control points:

$$
\{(t_i, F_i), (t_i + h_i/r_i, V_i), (t_{i+1} - h_i/r_i, W_i), (t_{i+1}, F_{i+1})\}. \tag{3.6}
$$

This is a consequence of the identity

$$
t \equiv R_0(\theta; r_i)t_i + R_1(\theta; r_i)(t_i + h_i/r_i) + R_2(\theta; r_i)(t_{i+1} - h_i/r_i) + R_3(\theta; r_i)t_{i+1}, \tag{3.7}
$$

where

$$
R_J(\theta; r_i) \equiv R_j(\theta; r_i, r_i), j = 0, \ldots, 3. \tag{3.8}
$$

In fact, $(t, p(t))$ can be considered as an application of the interpolation scheme in R^2 to the values $(t_i, F_i) \in R^2$ and derivatives $(1, D_i) \in R^2, i = 0, \ldots, n$.

3.3   One-Parameter Rational Cubic Spline

For simplicity, in this section, let us assume $v_i = w_i = r_i$ say. The rational cubic in Equation (3.1) can then be expressed in the form:

$$
p_i(t; r_i, r_i) = l_i(t) + e_i(t; r_i), \tag{3.9}
$$

where

$$l_i(t) = (1 - \theta)F_i + \theta F_{i+1}. \tag{3.10}$$

$$e_i(t; r_i) = \frac{h_i\theta(1 - \theta)\{(\Delta_i - D_i)(\theta - 1) + (\Delta_i - D_{i+1})\theta\}}{1 + (r_i - 3)\theta(1 - \theta)}. \tag{3.11}$$

This immediately leads to:

Proposition 3.4. (Interval tension property) For given fixed (or bounded) D_i, D_{i+1} the rational cubic Hermite interpolant in Equation (3.10) converges uniformly to the linear interplant in Equation (3.11) on $[t_i, t_{i+1}]$ as $r_i \to \infty$ i.e.

$$\lim_{r_i \to \infty} ||e_i|| = \lim_{r_i \to \infty} ||p_i - l_i|| = 0. \tag{3.12}$$

Moreover, the component functions of e_i tend to zero monotonically, both uniformly and pointwise on $[t_i, t_{i+1}]$.

Remark 3.5. The interval tension property can also be observed from the behavior of the control points V_i, W_i defined by Equation (3.4), and hence of the Bernstein-Bézier convex hull, as $r_i \to \infty$.

Now we construct a C^2 rational spline interpolant. This requires knowledge of the second derivative which, after some simplifications, is given by:

$$p_i^{(2)}(t; r_i, r_i) = \frac{2\{\alpha_i(1 - \theta)^3 + \beta_i\theta(1 - \theta)^2 + \gamma_i\theta^2(1 - \theta) + \delta_i\theta^3\}}{h_i\{1 + (r_i - 3)\theta(1 - \theta)\}^3}, \tag{3.13a}$$

where

$$\left.\begin{array}{l} \alpha_i = r_i(\Delta_i - D_i) - D_{i+1} + D_i, \\ \beta_i = 3(\Delta_i - D_i), \\ \gamma_i = 3(D_{i+1} - \Delta_i), \\ \delta_i = r_i(D_{i+1} - \Delta_i) - D_{i+1} - D_i. \end{array}\right\} \tag{3.13b}$$

We now follow the familiar procedure of allowing the derivative parameters $D_i, i = 0, \ldots, n$ to be degrees of freedom that are constrained by the imposition of C^2 continuity conditions:

$$p^{(2)}(t_{i+}) = p^{(2)}(t_{i-}), i = 1, \ldots, n - 1. \tag{3.14}$$

These C^2 conditions give, form (3.13a) and (3.13b), the linear system of *consistency equations* as follows:

$$h_i D_{i-1} + \{h_i(r_{i-1} - 1) + h_{i-1}(r_i - 1)\} D_i + h_{i-1}D_{i+1}$$
$$= h_i r_{i-1}\Delta_{i-1} + h_{i-1}r_i\Delta_i, i = 1, \ldots, n - 1, \tag{3.15}$$

with appropriate end conditions D_0 and D_n, Equations (3.15) is a tridiagonal linear system in the unknowns $D_i, i = 1, \ldots, n - 1$. Assume that

$$r_i \geq r > 2, \tag{3.16}$$

then the tridiagonal linear system, in Equations (3.15), is strictly diagonally dominant and hence has a unique solution that can be calculated easily by use of the tridiagonal LU decompositon algorithm. Thus a rational cubic spline interpolant can be constructed with tension parameters r_i, $i = 0, \ldots, n - 1$, where the special case $r_i = 3$, $i = 0, \ldots, n - 1$ corresponds to cubic spline interpolation. We now examine the behavior of the rational spline interpolant with respect to the tension parameters r_i in the following propositions.

Proposition 3.6. (Global tension property) Let $l \in C^0[t_0, t_n]$ denote the piecewise linear interpolant defined for $t \in [t_i, t_{i+1}]$ by $l(t) = l_i(t)$; see Equation (3.11). Suppose that $r_i \geq r > 2$, $i = 0, \ldots, n - 1$, as in Equation (3.16). Then the rational spline interpolant converges uniformly to l as $r \to \infty$, i.e., on $[t_0, t_n]$,

$$\lim_{r \to \infty} ||p - l|| = 0. \tag{3.17}$$

Proof. Suppose $r_i = r$, $i = 0, \ldots, n - 1$, then from Equations (3.15), it follows that

$$\lim_{r \to \infty} D_i = \frac{(h_i \Delta_{i-1} + h_{i-1} \Delta_i)}{h_i + h_{i-1}}, i = 1, \ldots, n - 1. \tag{3.18}$$

More generally, for r_i satisfying (3.16), it can be shown that

$$\max_{1 \leq i \leq n-1} ||D_i||_\infty \leq \max \{||\Delta||_\infty r / (r - 2), ||D_0||, ||D_n||\}, \tag{3.19}$$

where

$$||\Delta|| = \max_{1 \leq i \leq n-1} ||\Delta_i||_\infty. \tag{3.20}$$

Hence the solution D_i, $i = 1, \ldots, n - 1$ of the consistency Equations (3.15) is bounded with respect to r. Now, from Equation (3.12), the tension property in Equation (3.12) of Proposition 3.4 can clearly be extended to the case of bounded r. Thus applying Equation (3.12) on each interval gives the desired result in Equation (3.17). □

Proposition 3.7. (Local tension property) Let $r_i \geq r > 2$, $\forall i$ and consider an interval $[t_k, t_{k+1}]$ for a fixed $k \in \{0, \ldots, n - 1\}$. Then, on $[t_k, t_{k+1}]$ the rational spline interpolant converges uniformly to the line segment l_k as $r_k \to \infty$ i.e.

$$\lim_{r_k \to \infty} ||p_k - l_k|| = 0. \tag{3.21}$$

Proof. The boundedness property in Equation (3.19) holds as in Proposition 3.6 (where we can assume the additional constraints $r_k \geq r > 2$ to the hypotheses currently being imposed. Thus, Equation (3.12) applies for the case $i = k$. □

Remark 3.8. In Proposition 3.7, there is no assumption that the r_i, $i \neq k$ are constant with respect to the limit process. However, in the case of constant r_i, $i \neq k$, an analysis of the linear system in Equation (3.15) shows that

$$\lim_{r_k \to \infty} ||D_k - \Delta_k||_\infty = \lim_{r_k \to \infty} ||D_{k+1} - \Delta_k||_\infty = 0. \tag{3.22}$$

This property reinforces the rate of convergence to zero of $e_k = p_k - l_k$ in Equation (3.21), as can be seen from Equation (3.12) with $i = k$. The following proposition shows that the influence of r_k in this case has an exponential decay away from the interval $[t_k - t_{k+1}]$.

Proposition 3.9. (Exponential decay property) Let $D_i, i = 1, \ldots, n-1$, denote the solution of the consistency equations with tension parameters $r_k \geq r > 2, i = 0, \ldots, n-1$, and let $\hat{D}_i, i = 1, \ldots, n-1$, denote the solution with parameters $\hat{r}_i \geq r > 2, i = 0, \ldots, n-1$, where $\hat{r}_i = r_i$ for $i \neq k$. Consider a knot $t_i, i \in \{0, \ldots, n-1\}$, where $i = k - l$ or $k + 1 + l$, and l is a positive integer. Then

$$||D_i - \hat{D}_i||_\infty \leq \frac{4\gamma^l(1 + 2\gamma)}{1 - \gamma}||\Delta||_\infty, \qquad (3.23a)$$

where $||\Delta||_\infty$ is the constant defined in Equation (3.20) and

$$\gamma = 1/(r - 1) < 1.$$

(Thus, for example, if $r = 3$ then $\gamma = 1/2$.)

Proof. To prove this result, let the consistency equations (3.15) be divided by the coefficient of D_i to give the matrix form

$$(l + F) D = B$$

where $D^T = D_1, \ldots, D_{n-1}$ and the given end conditions D_0 and D_n have been transferred to the right-hand side B. Then F is a tridiagonal matrix such that

$$||F||_\infty \leq \frac{1}{r - 1} = \gamma$$

Also it can be shown that

$$||B||_\infty \leq 2||\Delta||_\infty$$

Similarly, for the perturbed system

$$(1 + \hat{F})\hat{D} = \hat{B}$$

where $\hat{r}_k = r_k + \sigma$, we have

$$||F||_\infty \leq \frac{1}{r - 1} = \gamma \text{ and } ||B||_\infty \leq 2||\Delta||_\infty$$

Now

$$\hat{D} - D = ((1 + \hat{F})^{-1} - (1 + F)^{-1})B + (1 + \hat{F})^{-1}[\hat{B} - B]$$

and we consider each of the terms of the right-hand side separately.

Firstly, $\hat{F}$ and F are tridiagonal matrices that agree in rows $1 \leq i \leq k - 1$ and $k + 2 \leq i \leq n - 1$ (i.e., only the kth and $k + 1$st rows are changed by a perturbation of r_k.) Thus, $\hat{F}^l$ and F^l agree in rows $1 \leq i \leq k - 1$ and $k + 1 + l \leq i \leq n - 1$. Hence

$$\varsigma = ((1 + \hat{F})^{-1} - (1 + F)^{-1})B = \sum_{\vartheta=1}^{\infty} (-1)^\vartheta [\hat{F}^\vartheta - F^\vartheta] B$$

is such that the ith component, for $i = k - l$ or $i = k + l + 1$ satisfies

$$\varsigma_i \leq \sum_{\vartheta=l+1}^{\infty} (\|\hat{F}\|^\vartheta - \|F\|^\vartheta)\|B\| \leq \frac{\gamma^{l+1}}{1 - \gamma} 4\|\Delta\|_\infty \qquad (3.23b)$$

Secondly, we consider

$$E = (1 + \hat{F})^{-1}[\hat{B} - B]$$

and apply an analysis that follows that of [Demko'77] (see his Proposition 3.1). Since $\hat{F}$ is tridiagonal, has bandwidth $2\vartheta + 1$ (i.e., the (i, j) elements are zero for $|i - j| > \vartheta$). Hence for $|i - j| = 1$, the (i, j) element of the series expansion $(1 + \hat{F})^{-1} = \sum (-1)^\vartheta \hat{F}^\vartheta$ is not influenced by $\hat{F}^\vartheta$ for $\vartheta < l$. Thus:

$$\|\hat{f}_{i,j}\| \leq \sum_{\vartheta=l+1}^{\infty} \|\hat{F}\|^\vartheta \leq \frac{\gamma^l}{1 - \gamma} \, for\, |i - j| = l$$

Finally, and B agree in rows $1 \leq i \leq k - 1$ and $k + 1 \leq i \leq n - 1$. Hence the ith component of E satisfies

$$|e_i| = |f_{i,k}(\hat{b}_k - b_k) + f_{i,k+1}(\hat{b}_{k+1} - b_{k+1})| \qquad (3.23c)$$

$$\leq \begin{cases} \frac{\gamma^l}{1-\gamma}(|\hat{b}_k| + |b_k|) + \frac{\gamma^{l+1}}{1-\gamma}(|\hat{b}_{k+1}| + |b_{k+1}|) \\ \frac{\gamma^{l+1}}{1-\gamma}(|\hat{b}_k| + |b_k|) + \frac{\gamma^{l+1}}{1-\gamma}(|\hat{b}_{k+1}| + |b_{k+1}|) \end{cases}$$

$$\leq \left\{ \frac{\gamma^l(1+\gamma)}{1-\gamma} 4 \|\Delta\|_\infty \right.$$

Combination (3.23b) and (3.23c) then gives the desired result (3.23a). $\qquad\square$

Remark 3.10. We note that

(i) the rational spline exists uniquely for $r_i \geq r > 2$
(ii) the case $r_i = 3, i = 0, \ldots, n - 1$ is that of the cubic spline and
(iii) increasing r_i tightens the curve both locally and globally (c.f. Propostions 3.6 and 3.7. For the range $2 < r_i < 3$ the rational spline produces a more flexible, i.e. *looser,* curve than the cubic spline curve, both locally and globally.

3.4   Two-Parameter Rational Cubic Spline

In this section we generalize the curve representation of Section 3.3 and consider the Hermite interpolant in Equation (3.1) of Section 3.2 for rational spline anlaysis and representation. We assume the shape parameters $v_i, w_i > 0$ as

$$v_i = b_i w_i, i = 0, \dots, n - 1, \tag{3.24}$$

where $0 < b_i < \infty$.

Remark 3.11. For given fixed (or bounded) D_i and D_{i+1}, the following observations can be made immediately from the Bernstein-Bézier representation (Equation (3.3)) and the control points V_i, W_i defined by Equation (3.4), that:

(i) if $w_i \to \infty$, then the rational cubic Hermite interpolant (3.1) converges to the rational linear interpolant $L_i(t, b_i)$ where

$$L_i(t, b_i) = \frac{(1 - \theta)b_i F_i + \theta F_{i+1}}{(1 - \theta)b_i + \theta}, \tag{3.25}$$

(ii) if $b_i > 1$, i.e., v_i exceeds w_i, then the curve is pulled towards F_i in the interval $[t_i, t_{i+1}]$.

(iii) if $b_i = 1$, i.e., $v_i = w_i$ then increase in w_i pulls the curve toward F_i and F_{i+1} the interval $[t_i, t_{i+1}]$ (see Proposition 4).

(iv) if $0 < b_i < 1$, i.e., w_i exceeds v_i then the curve is pulled toward F_{i+1} in the interval $[t_i, t_{i+1}]$.

Now we proceed to construct a C^2 rational spline interpolant. For this we are in of the second derivative values of Equation (3.1) at the knots. After some simplifications, we have

$$\left. \begin{aligned} p_i^{(2)}(t_i; v_i, w_i) &= 2\left[w_i \Delta_i - D_{i+1} + (1 - v_i)D_i\right]h_i, \\ p_i^{(2)}(t_{i+1}; v_i, w_i) &= 2\left[-v_i \nabla_i + (w_i - 1)D_{i+1} + D_i\right]h_i. \end{aligned} \right\} \tag{3.26}$$

C^2 continuity condition at the knots $t_i, i = 1, \dots, n - 1$, together with the information in Equation (3.26), lead to the following linear system of *consistency equations* in the unknowns $D_i, i = 0, \dots, n$:

$$h_i D_{i-1} + \{h_i(w_{i-1} - 1) + h_{i-1}(v_i - 1)\} D_i + h_{i-1}D_{i+1}$$
$$= h_i v_{i-1} \nabla_{i-1} + h_{i-1} w_i \nabla_i, i = 1, \dots, n - 1. \tag{3.27}$$

With appropriate end conditions D_0 and D_n and the assumption

$$v_i, w_i > 2, i = 0, \dots, n - 1, \tag{3.28}$$

the system of Equations (3.27) is a strictly diagonally dominant tridiagonal linear system and thus has a unique solution. This system can be solved using tridiagonal LU decomposition algorithm. The shape parameters, in the system, are such that:

A. the case $b_i = 1$, $w_i = 3$, $i = 0, \ldots, n - 1$, corresponds to the cubic spline interpolation and

B. the case $b_i = 1$ is that of rational spline with tension of Section 3.3.

Now we look at the effects of the shape parameters on the rational spline interpolant in the rest of this section.

Proposition 3.12. (Global tension property) Let $L \in C^0 [t_0, t_n]$ denote the piecewise rational linear interpolant defined for $t \in [t_i, t_{i+1}]$ by $L(t) = L_i(t_i b_i)$ in Equation (3.25). Suppose that v_i, w_i satisfy Equations (3.24), (3.28) and $w_i \geq w > 2$. Then the rational spline interpolant converges uniformly to L as $w \to \infty$, i.e. on $[t_0, t_n]$,

$$\lim_{w \to \infty} ||p - L|| = 0. \tag{3.29}$$

Proof. Assume that $b_i = b$ and $w_i = w$, $i = 0, \ldots, n - 1$. Then from Equation (3.27), it follows that

$$\lim_{w \to \infty} D_i = \frac{bh_i \Delta_{i-1} + h_{i-1} \Delta_i}{h_i + bh_{i-1}}, i = 0, \ldots, n - 1. \tag{3.30}$$

More generally, for v_i, w_i satisfying Equations (3.24) and (3.28), the boundedness property

$$\max_{1 \leq i \leq n-1} ||D_i||_\infty \leq \max \left\{ ||\Delta|| \left(\frac{1}{b_i - 2/w} + \frac{b_{i-1}}{1 - 2/w} \right), ||D_0||_\infty, ||D_n||_\infty \right\} \tag{3.31}$$

can be easily shown. Thus application of tension property, in Remark 11(i), in each interval gives the result of Equation (3.29). □

Proposition 3.13. (*Interval tension property*) Let v_i and w_i be as in Equations (3.24) and (3.28) $\forall i$ and consider an interval $[t_k, t_{k+1}]$, for a fixed $k \in \{0, \ldots, n - 1\}$. Then on $[t_k, t_{k+1}]$, with all fixed,

$$\lim_{w_k \to \infty} ||p_k - L_k|| = 0. \tag{3.32}$$

Proof. Gauss elimination without pivoting can be applied to the diagonally dominant tridiagonal system (Equations (3.27)) in both a forward and backward direction, as far as the kth and $(k + 1)$ th equations, respectively, to give

$$\{h_k(w_{k-1} - 1) + h_{k-1}(v_k - 1) - a_k\} D_k + h_{k-1} D_{k+1}$$
$$= h_k v_{k-1} \Delta_{k-1} + h_{k-1} w_k \Delta_k - b_k,$$
$$h_{k+1} D_k + \{h_{K+1}(w_k - 1) + h_k(v_{k+1} - 1) - c_k\} D_{k+1}$$
$$= h_{k+1} v_k \Delta_k + h_k w_{k+1} \Delta_{k+1} - d_k,$$

where the terms a_k, b_k, c_k, d_k are fixed quantities. Taking the limit $w_k \rightarrow \infty$ then gives

$$\left.\begin{aligned} \lim_{w_k \to \infty} D_k &= \nabla_k/b_k, \\ \lim_{w_k \to \infty} D_{k+1} &= b_k \nabla_k, \end{aligned}\right\} \qquad (3.33)$$

This limit property means that the tension result in Equation (3.32) holds for the rational spline on $\left[t_k, t_{k+1}\right]$.   □

Remark 3.14.

(i) Proposition 3.13 also holds for a more general setting, i.e., when $w_i, i \neq k$ are not considered as fixed. In this case, the boundedness property (Equation (3.31)) holds as in Proposition 3.12 (when the additional constraints $w_k \geq w > 2$ can be added in the current assumption). This leads to the tension property in Equation (3.32) in the interval $\left[t_k, t_{k+1}\right]$.

(ii) (*Point tension*) In addition to the assumptions in the previous remark, if we also assume that $w_{k-1} \rightarrow \infty$, then the kth equation of the system of Equations (3.27) results as:

$$\lim_{v_k, w_{k-1} \to \infty} D_k = 0. \qquad (3.34)$$

Thus the curve at the point P_k will appear to have a *corner*.

3.5 Demonstration

The tension behavior of the rational cubic spline interpolants is illustrated by the following simple examples for data sets in R^2. Figure 3.2 shows the effect of a progressive increase in global tension with $r = 3$ (the cubic spline case), 5 and 50. The effect of the high-tension parameter is clearly seen in that the resulting interpolant approaches piecewise linear form.

Figure 3.3 illustrates the effect of progressively increasing the value of the tension parameter as $r_4 = 3, 5$ and 50 in one interval, while elsewhere the tension parameters are fixed equivalent to 3.

Figures 3.4 demonstrate the result of Remark 3.10 (iii) regarding the achievement of a *looser* curve than a cubic spline curve; the second curve of the figure is a cubic spline curve, whereas the first and the last curves show the local and global behavior against the value 2.1 of the corresponding shape parameters.

Figure 3.5 shows the global tension with $w = 2.1, 5$ and 50 where the value of v is assumed as 2.1; Figure 3.6 shows the global tension with $v = 2.1, 3$, and 50 where the value of w is assumed as 2.1.

The effect of the high-tension parameter is clearly seen in that the resulting interpolant approaches piecewise rational linear form. Figure 3.7 illustrates the effect of progressively increasing the value of $w_3 = v_4$ in the order of 3, 4 and 6, for the point tension effect at the knot t_4 while Figure 3.8 shows the biased effect due to progressive decrease in v_4 as 3, 2.5 and 2.1; elsewhere the shape parameters are assumed as 3.

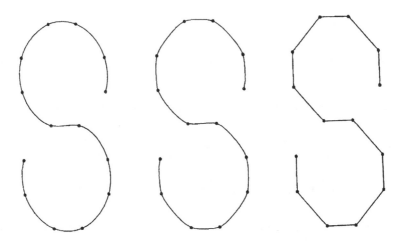

FIGURE 3.2. Interpolatary rational splines with global tension $r_i = r$.

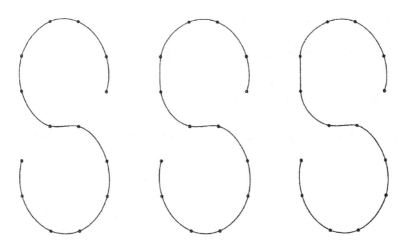

FIGURE 3.3. Interpolatary rational splines with tension r_4 varying.

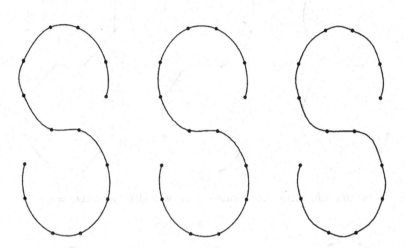

FIGURE 3.4. Interpolatary rational splines can produce looser curves than cubic splines.

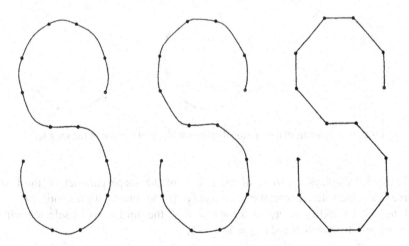

FIGURE 3.5. Interpolatary rational splines with global tension $w_i = w$.

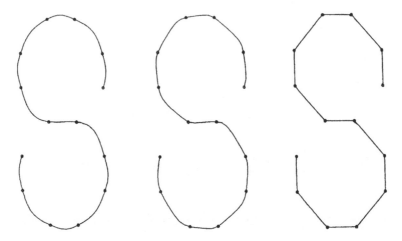

FIGURE 3.6. Interpolatary rational splines with global tension $v_i = v$.

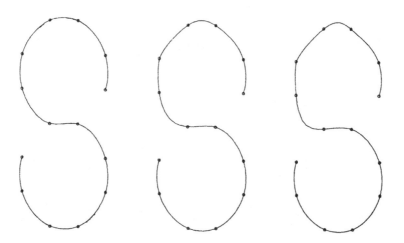

FIGURE 3.7. Interpolatary rational splines with point tension at the knot t_4.

Figure 3.9 displays a variety of the effects of the shape parameters; the first curve is a cubic spline curve; the second curve is fine tuned with the choice $w_3 = 2.1, v_{11} = 2.1$ and $v_i = w_i = 5$ for $i = 8, 9$; the third curve is selected with $v_i = w_i = 5$ for $i = 8, 9$ and $v_{12} = w_{11} = 5$.

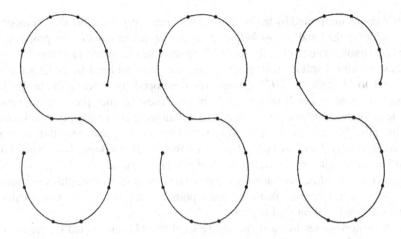

FIGURE 3.8. Interpolatary rational splines with biased effect using v_4.

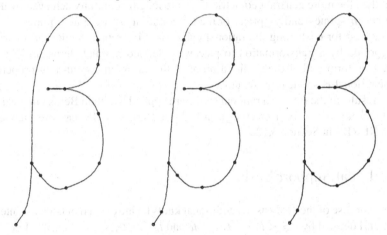

FIGURE 3.9. Interpolatary rational splines with various shape effects.

3.6   Freeform Curves

B-splines were investigated as early as the nineteenth century by Lobachevsky (see Farin [6]); they were constructed as convolutions of a certain probability distribution. In 1946, Schoenberg [28] used B-splines for statistical data smoothing, and his paper started the modern mathematical theory of spline approximation.

B-splines are a useful and powerful tool for CAGD and they can be found frequently in the existing CAD/CAM systems. They form a basis for the space of nth degree splines of continuity class C^{n-1}. Each B-spline is a non-negative nth degree splines that is nonzero only on $n + 1$ intervals. The B-splines form a partition of unity, that is, they sum up to one. Curves generated by summing control points multiplied by the B-splines have some very desirable shape properties, including the local *convex hull* property and *variation diminishing* property.

It is desirable to generalize the idea of B-spline-like local basis functions for the classes of rational splines with shape parameters as considered in the Chapter 2. The first local basis for GC^2 splines was developed by Lewis [10]. In 1981, Barsky [1] generalized B-splines to β-splines. These splines preserve the geometric smoothness of the design curve while allowing the continuity conditions on the spline function at the knots to be varied by certain parameters, thus giving greater flexibility. Later, in 1984. Bartels and Beatty [2] developed local bases for β-spline curves that are equivalent to Boehm's [3] γ-splines. Foley [7], in 1986, constructed a B-spline like basis for weighted splines; different weights were built into the basis functions so that the control point curve was a C^1 piecewise cubic with local control of interval tension.

In the following section, a B-spline-like local basis is constructed for the rational spline of Section 3.2. The design curve maintains the C^2 parametric continuity rather than the more general geometric GC^2 arc length continuity achieved by the v-splines, β-splines, and γ-splines or the C^1 continuity of weighted splines.

A method for evaluating the rational cubic B-spline representation of a curve is suggested by a transformation to piecewise defined rational Bernstein-Bézier form. This form will also expedite a proof of the variation diminishing property for the rational B-spline representation.

The results of the freeform rational spline are applied to obtain Bernstein-Bézier net of tensor product surfaces in Section 3.13 and Bernstein-Bézier representation of the NURBS in Section 3.12.

3.7 Local Support Basis

For the purpose of the analysis, let additional knots be introduced outside the interval $[t_0, t_n]$ defined by $t_{-3} < t_{-2} < t_{-1} < t_0$ and $t_n < t_{n-1} < t_{n-2} < t_{n+3}$. Let

$$v_i, w_i \geq r > 2, i = -3, \ldots, n+2, \tag{3.35}$$

where

$$v_i = b_i w_i \text{ and } 0 < b_i < \infty,$$

are shape parameters defined on this extended partition. Rational cubic spline function $\phi_j, j = 1, \ldots, n+2$, can be constructed (see Figure 3.10) such that

$$\phi_j(t) = \begin{cases} 0 \text{ for } t < t_{j-2}, \\ 1 \text{ for } t > t_{j+1}. \end{cases} \tag{3.36}$$

On the three intervals $[t_i, t_{i+1}], i = j - 2, j - 1, \phi$, will have the rational cubic form:

$$\begin{aligned}
\phi_j(t) = &R_0(\theta; v_i, w_i)\phi_j(t_i) + R_1(\theta; v_i, w_i)(\theta_j(t_i) + h_i\phi_j^{(1)}(t_i)/v_i) \\
&+ R_2(\theta; v_i, w_i)\phi_j(t_{i+1}) - h_i\phi_j^{(1)}(t_{i+1})/w_i \\
&+ R_3(\theta; v_i, w_i)\phi_j(t_{i+1}),
\end{aligned} \tag{3.37}$$

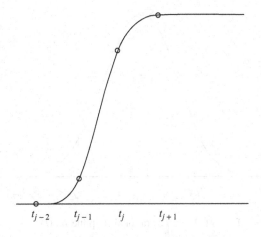

FIGURE 3.10. The rational spline $\phi_j(t)$.

where $R_k(\theta; v_i, w_i)$, $k = 0, 1, 2, 3$ are defined as in Section 3.2, from Equations (3.1) and (3.4). The requirement that $\phi_j \in C^2(-\infty, \infty)$ (in particular, at $t_{j-2}, t_{j-1}, t_j, t_{j+1}$) uniquely determines ϕ_j, since it can then be shown that

$$\left.\begin{aligned}
\phi_j(t_{j-2}) &= \phi_j^{(1)}(t_{j-2}) = 0, \\
\phi_j(t_{j-1}) &= \mu_{j-1}, \phi_j^{(1)}(t_{j-1}) = \mu_{j-1}, \\
\phi_j(t_j) &= 1 - \lambda_j, \phi_j^{(1)} t_j = \lambda_j,
\end{aligned}\right\} \tag{3.38}$$

where

$$\left.\begin{aligned}
\lambda_j &= h_j \lambda_j / v_j, \quad \mu_j = h_{j-1} \mu_j / w_{j-1}, \\
\hat{\lambda}_j &= h_j d_{j-1} / c_j, \quad \hat{\mu}_j = h_{j-1} d_{j+1} / c_{j+1}, \\
c_j &= h_{j-1} d_{j-1} + h_j v_{j-1} d_{j-1} \left(\frac{h_{j-1}}{w_{j-1}} + \frac{h_j}{v_j} \right),
\end{aligned}\right\} \tag{3.39}$$

and

$$d_j = h_j \left(w_{j-1}(w_{j-1} - 1) - v_{j-1} \right) / w_{j-1} + h_{j-1} \left(v_j(v_j - 1) - w_j \right) / v_j.$$

The local support rational cubic B-spline basis is now defined by the difference functions:

$$B_j(t) = \varphi_j(t) - \varphi_{j+1}(t), j = -1, \ldots, n+1. \tag{3.40}$$

Thus, there immediately follows:

Proposition 3.15. (Rational B-spline) The rational spline functions $B_j(t)$, $j = -1, \ldots, n+1$ are such that

$$\text{(Local support)} \quad B_j(t) = 0, \text{ for } t \in (t_{j-2}, t_{j+2}), \tag{3.41}$$

$$\text{(Partition of unity)} \quad \sum_{j=-1}^{n+1} B_j(t) = 1 \text{ for } t \in [t_0, t_n]. \tag{3.42}$$

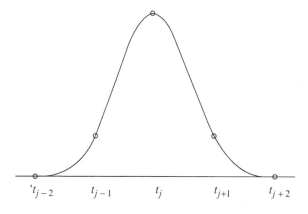

FIGURE 3.11. The rational B-spline $B_j(t)$.

An explicit representation (Figure 3.11) of the rational cubic B-spline B_j on any interval $[t_i, t_{i+1}]$ can be calculated from Equations (3.36)–(3.40) as:

$$
\begin{aligned}
B_j(t) = {} & R_0(\theta; v_i, w_i) B_j(t_i) + R_1(\theta; v_i, w_i) \left(B_j(t_i) + h_i B_j^{(1)}(t_i)/v_i \right) \\
& + R_2(\theta; v_i, w_i) \left(B_j(t_{i+1}) - h_i B_j^{(1)}(t_{i+1})/w_i \right) \\
& + R_3(\theta; v_i, w_i) B_j(t_{i+1}),
\end{aligned} \tag{3.43}
$$

where

$$
B_j(t_i) = B_j^{(1)}(t_i) = 0, \text{ for } i \neq j-1, j, j+1, \tag{3.44}
$$

and

$$
\left.
\begin{aligned}
B_j(t_{j-1}) &= \mu_{j-1}, \quad B_j^{(1)}(t_{j-1}) = \hat{\mu}_{j-1}, \\
B_j(t_j) &= 1 - \lambda_j - \mu_j, \quad B_j^{(1)}(t_j) = 1 - \hat{\lambda}_j - \hat{\mu}_j, \\
B_j(t_{j+1}) &= \lambda_{j+1}, \quad B_j^{(1)}(t_{j+1}) = \hat{\lambda}_{j+1}.
\end{aligned}
\right\} \tag{3.45}
$$

Careful examination of the Bernstein-Bézier vertices of $B_j(t)$ in Equation (3.43) shows these to be non-negative for v_i and w_i satisfying Equation (3.35) and we thus have:

Proposition 3.16. The rational B-spline functions are such that

$$
(\textit{Positivity}) \quad B_j(t) \geq 0, \text{ for all } t. \tag{3.46}
$$

3.8   Design Curve

To apply the rational cubic B-spline as a practical method for curve design, a convenient method for computing the curve representation:

$$
P(t) = \sum_{j=i-1}^{i+2} P_j B_j(t), \, t \in [t_0, t_n], \tag{3.47}
$$

is required, where $P_j \in R^N$ define the control points of the representation. Now, by the local support property,

$$P(t) = \sum_{j=i-1}^{i+2} P_j B_j(t), t \in [t_i, t_{i+1}], i = 0, \ldots, n-1. \qquad (3.48)$$

Substitution of Equation (3.43) then gives the piecewise defined rational Bernstein-Bézier representation:

$$P(t) = R_0(\theta; v_i, w_i) F_i + R_1(\theta; v_i, w_i) V_i + R_2(\theta; v_i, w_i) W_i + R_3(\theta; v_i, w_i) F_{i+1}, \qquad (3.49)$$

where

$$\left.\begin{aligned} F_i &= \lambda_i P_{i-1} + (1 - \lambda_i - \mu_i) P_i + \mu_i P_{i+1}, \\ V_i &= (1 - \alpha_i) P_i + \alpha_i P_{i+1}, \\ W_i &= \beta_i P_i + (1 - \beta_i) P_{i+1}, \end{aligned}\right\} \qquad (3.50)$$

with

$$\left.\begin{aligned} \alpha_i &= \mu_i + h_i \hat{\mu}_i / v_i = \hat{\mu}_i (h_{i-1}/w_{i-1} + h_i/v_i), \\ \beta_i &= \lambda_{i+1} + h_i \hat{\lambda}_{i+1} / w_i = \hat{\lambda}_{i+1} (h_i/w_i + h_{i+1}/v_{i+1}). \end{aligned}\right\} \qquad (3.51)$$

Let

$$X_i = \begin{bmatrix} F_i & V_i & W_i & F_{i+1} \end{bmatrix}^T, Z_i = \begin{bmatrix} P_{i-1} & P_i & P_{i+1} & P_{i+2} \end{bmatrix}^T,$$

and

$$Y_i = \begin{bmatrix} \lambda_i & 1 - \lambda_i - \mu_i & \mu_i \\ & 1 - \alpha_i & \alpha_i \\ & \beta_i & 1 - \beta_i \\ \lambda_{i+1} & 1 - \lambda_{i+1} - \mu_{i+1} & \mu_{i+1} \end{bmatrix},$$

then the transformation in Equation (3.50) can also be represented in matrix notation as:

$$X_i = Y_i Z_i. \qquad (3.52)$$

The transformation to rational Bernstein-Bézier form is very convenient for computational purposes and also leads to:

Proposition 3.17. (Variation diminishing property) The rational B-spline curve $P(t), t \in [t_0, t_n]$, defined by Equation (3.47), crosses any (hyper) plane of dimension $N - 1$ no more times than it crosses the *control polygon P* joining the control points $\{P_j\}_{j=-1}^{n+1}$.

Proof. Examination of the coefficients α_i, β_i in Equation (3.50) shows that

$$\alpha_i \geq 0, \beta_i \geq 0, \alpha_i + \beta_i \leq 1.$$

Thus V_i and W_i lie on the line segment joining P_i and P_{i+1}, where V_i *is before* W_i Also, we can write

$$F_i = (1 - \gamma_i) W_{i+1} + \gamma_i V_i, \qquad (3.53)$$

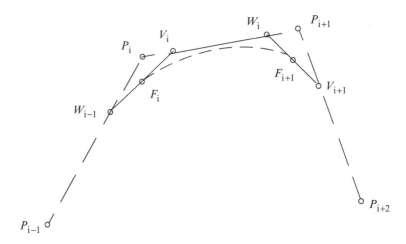

FIGURE 3.12. Corner cutting to obtain Bernstein-Bézier vertices.

where

$$\gamma_i = \frac{(h_{i-1}/w_{i-1})}{(h_{i-1}/w_{i-1} + h_i/v_i)},$$

and hence $0 < \gamma_i < 1$. Thus the control polygon of the piecewise defined Bernstein-Bézier representation is obtained by *corner cutting* of the B-spline control polygon; see Figure 3.12. Since the piecewise defined Bernstein-Bézier representation is variation diminishing, it follows that the B-spline representation is also variation diminishing. □

3.9   Shape Properties

The shape properties of the rational B-spline representation are examined in the following propositions:

Proposition 3.18.   (Linear B-spline tension property) Let $b_i = 1$, i.e., $v_i = w_i = r_i$ (say) $\geq r > 2, i = j - 2, \ldots, j + 1$. Then

$$\lim_{r \to \infty} ||B_j - \phi_j||0, \tag{3.54}$$

where

$$\phi_j = \begin{cases} (t - t_{j-1})h_{j-1}, & t_{j-1} \leq t < t < t_j, \\ (t_{j+1} - t)/h_j, & t_j \leq t < t_{j+1}, \\ 0, & \text{otherwise} \end{cases} \tag{3.55}$$

is the linear polynomial B-spline (see Figure 3.13).

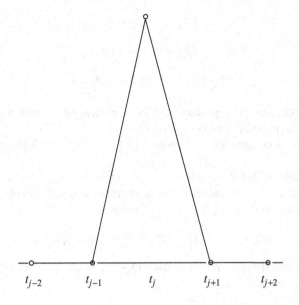

FIGURE 3.13. The linear polynomial B-spline.

Proof. The rational B-spline defined by Equation (3.43) can be expressed for $t \in [t_i, t_{i+1}]$ as:

$$B_j(t) = (1 - \theta)B_j(t_i) + \theta B_j(t_{i+1}) + e_i(t; r_i), \qquad (3.56)$$

where

$$e_i(t; r_i) = \frac{h_i\theta(1 - \theta)\left\{(\Delta_i - B_j^{(1)}(t_i))(\theta - 1) + (\Delta_i B_j^{(1)}(t_{i+1}))\theta\right\}}{1 + (r_i - 3)\theta(1 - \theta)}, \qquad (3.57)$$

and

$$\Delta_i = (B_j(t_{i+1}) - B_j(t_i))/h_i, \qquad (3.58)$$

(cf. (3.10)–(3.12)). Here the $B_j(t_i)$ and $B_j^{(1)}(t_i)$ values are defined by Equations (3.43)–(3.45), where for $i = j - 1, j, j + 1$ they are dependent on $r_i, i = j - 2, \ldots, j + 1$. Examination of the coefficients (3.45) reveals that $\hat{\mu}_j, \hat{\lambda}_j$ and hence the $B_j^{(1)}(t_i)$ are bounded and that

$$\lim_{r_{j-2} \to \infty} B_j(t_{j-1}) = \lim_{r_{j+1} \to \infty} B_j(t_{j+1}) = 0, \quad \lim_{r_{j-1}, r_j \to \infty} B_j(t_j) = 1. \qquad (3.59)$$

It is then a simple matter to show that $\lim \|e_i\| = 0$ and that Equation (3.54) holds. $\qquad \square$

Remark 3.19. From Equation (3.59), there follow the more precise results that

$$\lim_{r_{j+1} \to \infty} \|B_j\| = 0 \text{ on } [t_{j+1}, t_{j+2}],$$

$$\lim_{r_{j-1}, r_j, r_{j+1} \to \infty} \| B_j - \phi_j \| = 0 \text{ on } [t_j, t_{j+2}],$$

$$\lim_{r_{j-2}, r_{j-1}, r_j \to \infty} \| B_j - \phi_j \| = 0 \text{ on } [t_{j-2}, t_j],$$

$$\lim_{r_{j-2} \to \infty} \| B_j \| = 0 \text{ on } [t_{j-2}, t_{j-1}].$$

(Here, and in the proof of Proposition 3.18 the respective rates at which $r_{j-2}, r_{j-1},$ r_j and r_{j+1} tend to infinity are not relevant.)

An immediate consequence of Proposition 3.18 (and Remark 3.19 is:

Corollary 3.20. (*Global tension property*) Let $b_i = 1$, i.e., $v_i, w_i = r_i \geq r > 2, i = -2, \ldots, n+1$, and let $\bar{P}$ denote the rational B-spline control polygon, defined explicitly on $[t_i, t_{i+1}], i = -1, \ldots, n$, by

$$\bar{P}(t) = (1 - \theta)P_i + \theta P_{i+1}, \theta(t) = (t - t_i)/h_i. \tag{3.60}$$

Then the rational B-spline representation (3.47) converges uniformly to $\bar{P}$ on $[t_{-1}, t_{n+1}]$ as $r \to \infty$.

Corollary 3.20 can be proved directly by studying the behavior of the Bernstein-Bézier control points in Equation (3.49) as $r \to \infty$. We follow this approach in the proof of the following proposition.

Proposition 3.21. (Interval tension property) Consider an interval $[t_k, t_{k+1}]$ for a fixed $k \in \{0, \ldots, n - 1\}$ such that $v_k, w_k = r_k$ and let

$$\left. \begin{array}{l} Q_k = (1 - \mu)P_k + \mu P_{k+1}, \\ Q_{k+1} = \lambda P_k + (1 - \lambda)P_{k+1}, \end{array} \right\} \tag{3.61}$$

denote two distinct points on the line segment of the control polygon joining P_k, P_{k+1}, where

$$\left. \begin{array}{l} \lambda = \dfrac{h_{k+1}/v_{k+1}}{h_{k-1}/w_{k-1} + h_{k+1}/v_{k+1} + h_k}, \\[3mm] \mu = \dfrac{h_{k-1}/w_{k-1}}{h_{k-1}/w_{k-1} + h_{k+1}/v_{k+1} + h_k}, \end{array} \right\} \tag{3.62}$$

(Note that Q_k is before Q_{k+1} since $\lambda + \mu < 1$.) Then the rational B-spline representation (see Equation (3.47)) converges uniformly to Q on $[t_k, t_{k+1}]$ as $r \to \infty$. where

$$Q(t) = (1 - \theta)Q_k + \theta Q_{k+1}, \theta(t) = (t - t_k)/h_k. \tag{3.63}$$

Proof. It is a simple matter to show, in Equation (3.39), that

$$\lim_{r_k \to \infty} \lambda_k = \lim_{r_k \to \infty} \mu_{k+1} = 0,$$

$$\lim_{r_k \to \infty} \mu_k = \mu \text{ and } \lim_{r_k \to \infty} \lambda_{k+1} = \lambda.$$

Thus, in the Bernstein-Bézier representation (Equation (3.49)) on $\left[t_k, t_{k+1}\right]$, we have

$$\lim_{r_k \to \infty} F_k = Q_k \text{ and } \lim_{r_k \to \infty} F_{k+1} = Q_{k+1}.$$

Moreover, the Bernstein-Bézier representation can be expressed as

$$p(t) = P_k(t; r_k, r_k) = l_k(t) + e_k(t; r_k, r_k), t \in \left[t_k, t_{k+1}\right]$$

as in Equation (3.10), where it can be shown that

$$\lim_{r_k \to \infty} \|Q_k - l_k\| \le \lim_{r_k \to \infty} \|Q - P\| + \lim_{r_k \to \infty} \|e_k\| = 0 \text{ on } \left[t_k, t_{k+1}\right],$$

which completes the proof.   □

Proposition 3.22. (Point tension property) Let v_i and w_i satisfy Equation (3.35) and $v_k, w_{k-1} \to \infty$ for some k, $1 \le k \le n - 1$. Then the following holds:

$$\lim_{r_k, w_{k-1} \to \infty} P(t) = P_k. \tag{3.64}$$

Proof. From Equations (3.42) and (3.47)

$$P(t_k) - P_k = \sum_{j=-1}^{n+1} \left(P_j - P_k\right) B_j(t_k) = (P_{k-1} - P_k) B_{k-1}(t_k) + (P_{k+1} - P_k) B_{k+1}(t_k)$$

(by local support property)

$$= (P_{k-1} - P_k)\lambda_k + (P_{k+1} - P_k)\mu_k.$$

It can be simply shown that

$$\lim_{r_k, w_{k-1} \to \infty} \lambda_k = \lim_{r_k, w_{k-1} \to \infty} \mu_k = 0,$$

and thus, Equation (3.64) follows straightaway.   □

Remark 3.23. Proposition 3.22 shows that if $v_k, w_{k-1} \to \infty$, then part of the design curve is pulled toward the control point P_k. This can be proved directly by studying the behavior of the Bernstein-Bézier control points in Equation (3.49). We follow this approach to look at the biased behavior in the following:

Remark 3.24. (*Biased tension control*) If $v_k \to \infty$ for any $k \in \{0, \ldots, n - 1\}$, then

$$\lim_{v_k \to \infty} \lambda_k = \lim_{v_k \to \infty} \mu_k = \lim_{v_k \to \infty} \alpha_k = 0,$$

and thus from (3.50)

$$\lim_{v_k \to \infty} F_k = P_k = \lim_{v_k \to \infty} V_k.$$

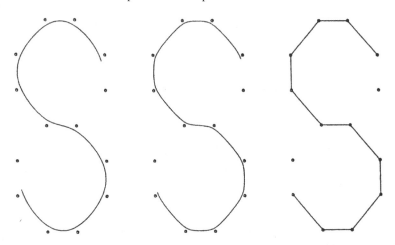

FIGURE 3.14. Rational B-spline curves with global tension $r_i = r$.

This shows that a portion of the design curve, within the interval $[t_k, t_{k+1})$ is pulled towards the control vertex P_k. Similar *biased* behavior can be observed regarding w_k, i.e., if $w_k \to \infty$, then

$$\lim_{w_k \to \infty} \lambda_{k+1} = \lim_{w_k \to \infty} \mu_{k+1} = \lim_{w_k \to \infty} \beta_k = 0$$

and thus from (3.50)

$$\lim_{w_k \to \infty} F_k = P_{k+1} = \lim_{w_k \to \infty} W_k$$

which shows that the part of the design curve controlled by W_k and F_{k+1} is pulled toward the control vertex P_{k+1}.

3.10   Demonstration

Consider the data sets in R^2 identical to that of the interpolatory examples in Section 3.5, where the data now define the control points of the rational B-spline representation. Figures 3.14–3.21 illustrate the corresponding local and global shape effects to Figures 3.2–3.9, respectively, which confirms the analysis done in the previous section regarding interval, point and biased shape effects.

3.11   Nurbs

In this section we give a brief description of another class of rational splines which are commonly known as NURBS (nonuniform rational B-splines). A nonuniform rational cubic B-spline curve, with the same control polygon as that of previously

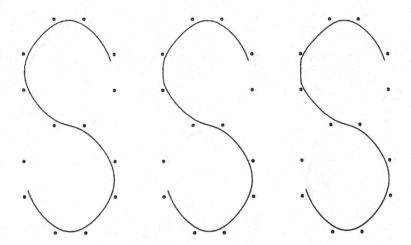

FIGURE 3.15. Rational B-spline curves with tension r_4 varying.

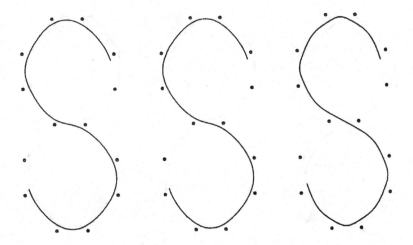

FIGURE 3.16. Freeform rational splines can produce looser curves than cubic B-spline.

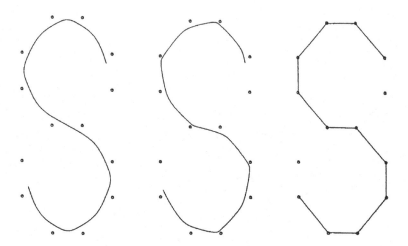

FIGURE 3.17. Rational B-spline curves with global tension $w_i = w$.

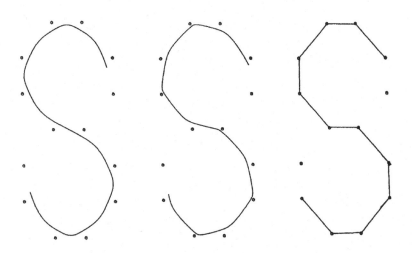

FIGURE 3.18. Rational B-spline curves with global tension $v_i = v$.

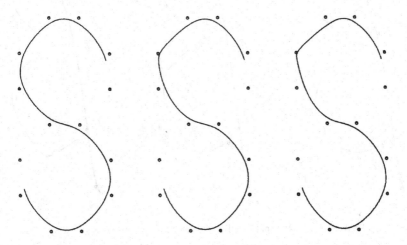

FIGURE 3.19. Rational B-spline curves with point tension at the knot t_4.

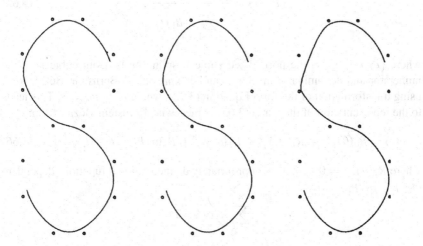

FIGURE 3.20. Interpolatary rational splines with biased effect using v_4.

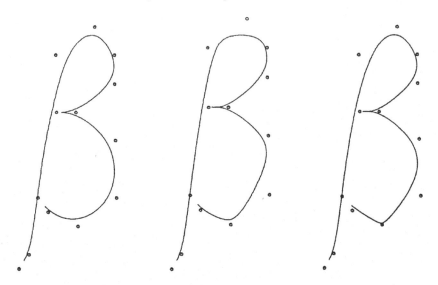

FIGURE 3.21. Rational B-spline curves with various shape effects.

generated rational spline i.e., $[P_i : i = -1, \ldots, n + 1]$ and with corresponding positive weights u_i, is given by:

$$P^*(t) = \frac{\sum\limits_{j=-1}^{n+1} u_i P_i B_i(t)}{\sum\limits_{j=-1}^{n+1} u_i B_i(t)}, \qquad (3.65)$$

where $\{B_i(t)\}_{i=-1}^{n+1}$ is the normalized cubic B-spline basis. Both cubic B-spline numerator and denominator in (3.65) can be expressed in Bernstein-Bézier form using transformation of the form Equation (3.50), where $v_i = w_i = 3$. This leads to the representation of the curve (3.65) in piecewise Bernstein-Bézier form:

$$p(t) = R_0(\theta)F_i^* + R_1(\theta)V_i^* + R_2(\theta)W_i^* + R_3(\theta)F_{i+1}^*, t \in [t_i, t_{i+1}], \quad (3.66)$$

where $R_j(\theta)$, $j = 0, \ldots, 3$ are appropriately defined rational functions dependent on $u_{i-1}, u_i, u_{i+1}, u_{i+2}$ with

$$\sum_{j=0}^{3} R_j(\theta) = 1$$

and

$$\left.\begin{aligned}
F_i &= \lambda_i^* P_{i-1} + (1 - \lambda_i^* - \mu_i^*)P_i + \mu_i^* P_{i+1} = (1 - \gamma_i^*)W_{i-1} + \gamma_i^* V_i, \\
V_i &= (1 - \alpha_i^*)P_i + \alpha_i^* P_{i+1}, \\
W_i &= \beta_i^* P_i + (1 - \beta_i^*)P_{i+1},
\end{aligned}\right\} (3.67)$$

$$\left.\begin{aligned}
\alpha_i^* &= \frac{\bar{\alpha}_i u_{i+1}}{\left[(1 - \bar{\alpha}_i)u_i + \bar{\alpha}_i u_{i+1}\right]}, \\
\beta_i^* &= \frac{(1 - \bar{\beta}_i)u_{i+1}}{\left[(1 - \bar{\beta}_i)u_i + \bar{\beta}_i u_{i+1}\right]},
\end{aligned}\right\} \tag{3.68}$$

$$\gamma_i^* = \frac{h_{i-1}\left[(1 - \bar{\alpha}_i)u_i + \alpha_i u_{i+1}\right]}{h_{i-1}\left[(1 - \bar{\alpha}_i)u_i + \bar{\alpha}_i u_{i+1}\right] + h_i\left[1 - \bar{\beta}_{i-1})u_{i-1} + \bar{\beta}_{i-1}u_i\right]}, \tag{3.69}$$

$$\left.\begin{aligned}
\lambda_i^* &= \frac{\bar{\lambda}_i u_{i-1}}{\bar{\lambda}_i u_{i-1}(1 - \bar{\lambda}_i - \bar{\mu}_i)\mu_i + \bar{\mu}_i u_{i+1}}, \\
\mu_i^* &= \frac{\bar{\mu}_i u_{i+1}}{\bar{\lambda}_i u_{i-1}(1 - \bar{\lambda}_i - \bar{\mu}_i)u_i + \bar{\mu}_i u_{i+1}},
\end{aligned}\right\} \tag{3.70}$$

$$\left.\begin{aligned}
\bar{\alpha}_i &= \frac{h_{i-1}}{h_{i-1} + h_i + h_{i+1}}, \\
\bar{\beta}_i &= \frac{h_{i-1} + h_i}{h_{i-1} + h_i + h_{i+1}},
\end{aligned}\right\} \tag{3.71}$$

$$\left.\begin{aligned}
\bar{\lambda}_i &= \frac{h_i^2}{(h_{i-1} + h_i)(h_{i-2} + h_{i-1} + h_i)}, \\
\bar{\mu}_i &= \frac{h_{i-1}^2}{(h_{i-1} + h_i)(h_{i-1} + h_i + h_{i+1})}.
\end{aligned}\right\} \tag{3.72}$$

Similarly to Equation (3.52), the transformation (in Equation (3.67)) can be represented in matrix notation as:

$$X_i^* = Y_i^* Z_i^*, \tag{3.73}$$

provided *'s are put appropriately. Examination of the coefficients in Equations (3.68)–(3.72) shows that

$$0 \le \alpha_i^*, \beta_i^*, \gamma_i^*, \alpha_i^* + \beta_i^* \le 1. \tag{3.74}$$

Thus, as in the previously generated rational spline, the control polygon of the piecewise defined Bernstein-Bézier representation (Equation (3.66)) can be obtained by *corner cutting* (see Figure 3.12 with the replacement of the Bernstein-Bézier points by the same points with *) of the NURBS control polygon and the NURBS representation is variation diminishing.

Remark 3.25. It can be observed from the algebra of NURBS that if $u_i \to \infty$ then $F_i^* \to P_i$ (for a fixed i) and the design curves sharply toward P_i in the region of $P_{i-2}P_{i-1}P_iP_{i+1}P_{i+2}$. Thus it seems reasonable to assign high weights in regions where the curve is expected to curve sharply. But, as compared to the rational spline (of previous sections), there is not that much freedom for assigning the weights if all of them are very high. This will not have a significant effect on the curve since a common factor in all weights will simply cancel out. For example, if $u_i = u$, $j = i - 1, i, i + 1, i + 2$ and $u \to \infty$, then the curve will be a piece of a cubic spline in the interval $[t_i, t_{i+1}]$ and it will have no effect at all.

3.12   Surfaces

The results of Section 3.8 can be extended for tensor product rational bicubic B-spline surfaces, i.e., surfaces of the form:

$$p(\tilde{t}, t) = \sum_{k=-1}^{m+1} \sum_{l=-1}^{n+1} P_{kl} \tilde{B}_k \left(\tilde{t}\right) B_l(t), t_0 \leq \tilde{t} \leq \tilde{t}_m, t_0 \leq t \leq t_n, \qquad (3.75)$$

with $B_l(t)$ as constructed in Section 3.8 and analogously the $\tilde{B}_k \left(\tilde{t}\right)$ a set of rational cubic B-splines corresponding to a set of knots $t_k, k = -3, \ldots, m + 3 (m \geq 0)$ with shape parameters $\tilde{v}_k, \tilde{w}_k, k = -2, \ldots, m + 2$.

If the representation of a rational spline patch $p\left(t, \tilde{t}\right)$ $t_i \leq t \leq t_{i+1}$, is required as a rational bicubic Bernstein-Bézier patch

$$p_{i,j}\left(\tilde{t}, t\right) = \sum_{k=0}^{3} \sum_{l=0}^{3} X_{k,l}^{i,j} R_l \left(\tilde{\theta}; \tilde{v}_j, \tilde{w}_j\right) R_l \left(\theta; v_j, w_j\right), \qquad (3.76)$$

the Bernstein-Bézier points $X_{k,l}^{i,j}$ can be computed from the rational B-spline vertices $P_{i,j}$ as:

$$X_{i,j} = \tilde{Y}_i Z_{i,j} \left(Y_j\right)^T, \qquad (3.77)$$

where

$$X_{i,j} = \begin{bmatrix} X_{0,0}^{i,j} & X_{0,1}^{i,j} & \cdots & X_{0,3}^{i,j} \\ X_{1,0}^{i,j} & \cdots & & \\ \cdots & & & \\ X_{3,0}^{i,j} & \cdots & & X_{3,3}^{i,j} \end{bmatrix},$$

$$Z_{i,j} = \begin{bmatrix} P_{i-1} & P_{i-1,j} & \cdots & P_{i-1,j+2} \\ P_{i,j-1} & \cdots & & \\ \cdots & & & \\ P_{i+2,j-1} & \cdots & & P_{i+2,j+2} \end{bmatrix},$$

and the matrix Y_i is given as in Equation (3.52) with a corresponding expression for $\tilde{Y}_i$.

Remark 3.26.   There is a drawback with this rational spline surface in that any of the shape parameters influences entire corresponding row or column of the surface.

Similarly, the NURBS construction of Section 3.12 can be extended to surfaces as

$$P^*(t,t) = \frac{\sum\limits_{j=-1}^{m+1}\sum\limits_{i=-1}^{n+1} u_{i,j} P_{i,j} B_i(t) B_j(t)}{\sum\limits_{j=-1}^{m+1}\sum\limits_{i=-1}^{n+1} u_{i,j} B_i(t) B_j(t)}. \tag{3.78}$$

Similar observations, as were made in Remark 3.7 for NURBS, can be made for these kinds of surfaces i.e.sufficiently large $u_{i,j}$ (fixed i and j) gives a pull to the surface toward $P_{i,j}$ in the region $\{P_{k,l}\}_{k=i-2,l=j-2}^{i+2,j+2}$, but there is a limit to the assignment of the weights and they cannot be applied blindly, otherwise there may not be any effect on the surface at all.

3.13   Summary

A C^2 rational cubic spline method has been presented for the objective of designing curves. The spline method is capable of designing interpolation as well as approximation curves to control points. This rational cubic spline method has been developed with a view toward its applications in computer graphics, geometric modeling, and CAGD. It is quite reasonable to construct a spline method, which involves two families of shape parameters in a better way than those in the weighted v-spline of Chapter 2. These parameters provide a variety of local and global shape controls such as biased, interval and point shape effects. The visual smoothness of the proposed method is also C^2, which is better than that in weighted v-spline. The rational spline method can be applied to tensor product surfaces, but unfortunately, in the context of interactive surface design, this tensor product surface is not that useful because any one of the tension parameters controls an entire corresponding interval strip of the surface. Thus, as an effective application to surfaces, a method similar to Nielson's [12] spline blended method or the methods of Sarfraz [16, 17] may be attempted. This will produce local shape control, which is quite useful regarding the computer graphics and geometric modeling applications.

3.14   Exercises

1. Write a program to implement the curve design method in Section 3.2.
2. Write a program to implement the curve design method in Section 3.9.
3. Check the difference of shape effects in your programs of Exercise 3.14.1 and 3.14.2 when the schemes are implemented in scalar form as stated in Remark 3.3.

References

1. Barsky, B.A. (1981), *The Beta-Spline: A Local Representation Based on Shape Parameters and Fundamental Geometric Measure*, Ph.D. Thesis, University of Utah.

2. Bartels, R., and Beatty, J. (1984), *Beta-splines with a difference*, Technical Report CS-83-40, Computer Science Department, University of Waterloo, Waterloo, Canada.

3. Boehm, W. (1985), Curvature continuous curves and surfaces, *Comp Aided Geom Design* 2(2), 313–323.

4. Cline, A. (1974), Curve fitting in one dimension using splines under tension, *Comm ACM* 17, 218–223

5. Dierckx, P., and Tytgat, B. (1989), Generating the Bézier points of β-spline curve, *Comp Aided Geom Design* 6, 279–291.

6. Farin, G.E. (1996), *Curves and Surfaces for CAGD*, Academic Press, New York.

7. Foley, T.A. (1986), Local control of interval tension using weighted splines. *Comp Aided Geom Design* 3, 281–294.

8. Foley, T.A. (1987), Interpolation with interval and point tension controls using cubic weighted Nu-splines, *ACM Trans Math Software* 13, 68–96.

9. Goodman, T.N.T., and Unsworth, K. (1985), Generation of Beta-spline curves using a recursive relation. In: *Fundamental Algorithms for Computer Graphics*. R.E. Earnshaw (Ed.), Springer-Verlag, Berlin, pp. 326–357.

10. Lewis, J. (1975), *"B-spline" bases for splines under tension, Nu-splines, and fractional order splines,* Presented at the SIAM-SIGNUM Meeting, San Francisco, CA.

11. Nielson, G.M. (1974), Some piecewise polynomial alternatives to splines under tension, In: *Computer-Aided Geometric Design*, R.F. Barnhill (Ed.), Academic Press. New York.

12. Nielson, G.M. (1986), Rectangular v-splines. *IEEE Comp Graph Appl* 6, 35–40.

13. Pruess, S. (1979), Alternatives to the exponential spline in tension, *Math Comp* 33, 1273–1281.

14. Salkauskas, K. (1984), C^1 splines for interpolation of rapidly varying data, *Rocky Mtn. J. Math* 14, 239–250.

15. Sarfraz, M. (1992), A C^2 rational cubic spline alternative to the NURBS, *Comp. & Graph* 16(1), 69–78.

16. Sarfraz, M. (1995), Curves and surfaces for CAD using C^2 rational cubic splines, *Int J Eng Comput*, Springer-Verlag, 11(2), 94–102.

17. Sarfraz, M. (1994), Freeform rational bicubic spline surfaces with tension control, Facta Universitatis (NIS), *Ser Math Informatics*, 9, 83–93.

18. Sarfraz, M. (1994), Cubic spline curves with shape control, *Int J Comput & Graphics*, Elsevier Science, 18(5), 707–713.

19. Sarfraz, M, (2003), Weighted Nu-splines: an alternative to NURBS, *Advances in Geometric Modeling*, Ed.: M. Sarfraz, John Wiley, New York, 81–95.

20. Schoenburg, I. J. (1946), Contributions to the problem of approximation of equidistant data by analytic functions, *Appl Math* 4, 45–99.

21. Schweikert, D.G. (1966), An interpolation curve using a spline in tension, *J Math Phys* 45, 312–317.

22. Sarfraz, M. (2004), Weighted Nu-splines with local support basis functions, *Int J Comput & Graphics*, Elsevier Science, 28(4), 539–549.

23. Gregory, J.A., and Sarfraz, M. (1990), A rational spline with tension, *Int J Comput Aided Geom Des*, North-Holland, Elsevier, 7, 1–13.

24. Schweikert, D. (1966), An interpolation curve using splines in tension, *J Math Phys* 45, 312–317.

25. Cline, A. (1974), Curve fitting in one dimension using splines under tension, *Comm ACM* 17, 218–223.

26. Preuss, S. (1979), Alternatives to the exponential spline in tension, *Math Comp* 33, 1273–1281

27. Boehm, W. (1987), Rational geometric splines, *Comput Aided Geom Des* 4, 67–77.

28. Schoenberg, L. (1981), *Spline Functions: Basic Theory*, John Wiley, New York.

4
Rational Sigma (σ) Splines

Abstract. *As interactive curve design is a basic need for CAD/CAM, computer graphics, vision, imaging and various other disciplines. It is desired to have a robust, visually pleasant, well-controlled, and effective scheme that can provide a useful solution to many problems of different kinds at one platform. A rational spline, with some additional shape parameters in its description as well as in the description of its piecewise stitching, may be a good choice in this regard. This chapter has been devoted to a more general rational spline, known as the sigma (σ) spline. Although, a σ – spline is a GC^1 rational spline as far as its theoretical smoothness is concerned, in most practical cases, it provides a C^1, GC^2 or C^2 solution. It is the most generalized spline in the literature and recovers, as a special case, most of the existing methods in the literature. These methods include weighted spline, v – spline, weighted Nu-spline, γ – spline, and so on.*

4.1 Introduction

This chapter discusses the rational splines of Chapters 2 and 3 and presents a generalized description of rational cubics with σ-continuity (c.f. 1.6). The most general description of rational cubics and σ-continuity constraints provides a variety of shape control parameters which can be sufficient and highly useful for any kind of shape influence such as interval tension, point tension, local tension, global tension, or biased tensions. Interpolatory and freeform structures of the rational σ-splines can manage to recover a large number of well-known useful methods [1–28] including weighted splines, v-splines, weighted v-splines, gamma-splines, beta-splines, rational β-splines, rational splines of Chapter 2 and 3, and the rational geometric splines of Boehm.

The approaches adopted in the construction of rational σ-splines are quite analogous to those in Chapters 2 and 3. Section 4.2 discusses the most general form of a rational cubic. The interpolatory and the freeform descriptions of rational σ-splines are made in Section 4.3 and 4.4, respectively. Some special cases and examples are discussed at the end of both of theses sections.

4.2   Generalized Rational Cubic Interpolant

Let $F_i \in R^N$ be given values at knots t_i, $i = 0, \ldots, n-1$, where $t_0 < t_1 < \ldots < t_n$ and let V_i, $W_i \in R^N$, $i = 0, \ldots, n-1$. The most general form of a rational cubic, which interpolates at the knot, is given by:

$$p_i(t) = \frac{(1-\theta)^3 q_i F_i + \theta(1-\theta)^2 v_i V_i + \theta^2(1-\theta)w_i W_i + \theta^3 u_i F_{i+1}}{(1-\theta)^3 q_i + \theta(1-\theta)^2 v_i + \theta^2(1-\theta)w_i + \theta^3 u_i}, \quad (4.1)$$

where $0 \le \theta \le 1$, and we assume $q_i, v_i, w_i, u_i > 0$. Then use of the bilinear transformation

$$\theta \mapsto \frac{\theta}{k_i(1-\theta) + \theta}$$

leads Equation (4.1) to:

$$p_i(t) = \frac{(1-\theta)^3 F_i + \theta(1-\theta)^2 v_i V_i + \theta^2(1-\theta)w_i W_i + \theta^3 F_{i+1}}{(1-\theta)^3 + v_i \theta(1-\theta)^2 + w_i \theta^2(1-\theta) + \theta^3}, \quad (4.2a)$$

where

$$k_i^3 = u_i/q_i., \quad v_i := k_i^2 r_i/u_i, \quad w_i := k_i s_i/u_i. \quad (4.2b)$$

This can be further expressed as:

$$p_i(t_i) = R_0(\theta)F_i + R_1(\theta)V_i + R_2(\theta)W_i + R_3(\theta)F_{i+1}, \quad (4.3)$$

where the basis functions $R_1(\theta)$, $j = 0, \ldots, 3$ are Bernstein-Bézier weight functions that depend on v_i and w_i. The following can be noted:

(i) The curve segment in Equation (4.2) lies in the convex hull of the control points $\{F_i, V_i, W_i, F_{i+1}\}$ (see Proposition 2.1).

(ii) The curve segment (4.3) satisfies the variation diminishing property (see Proposition 2.2).

(iii) If the pieces $P_i(t)$, $i = 0, \ldots, n-1$, are joined together with any kind of continuity, then the composed rational curve

$$p(t) = p_i(t), \quad i = 0, \ldots, n-1,$$

is at least C^0.

(iv) The equivalent Hermite representation of (4.2) is obtained when

$$V_i = F_i + h_i D_i^+/v_i, \quad W_i = F_{i+1} - h_i D_{i+1}^-/w_i, \quad (4.4)$$

where

$$\left. \begin{array}{l} p^{(1)}\left(t_i^+\right) = D_i^+, \\ p^{(1)}\left(t_{i+1}^-\right) = D_{i+1}^- \end{array} \right\} \quad (4.5)$$

(v) The second derivatives of Equation (4.2) at the knots t_i and t_{i+1}, are obtained as:

$$\left. \begin{array}{l} p_i^{(2)}(t_i) = 2\left\{\left(v_i^2 - v_i - w_i\right)F_i - \left(v_i^2 - v_i\right)V_i + w_i W_i\right\}/h_i^2, \\ p_i^{(2)}(t_{i+1}) = 2\left\{\left(w_i^2 - w_i - v_i\right)F_{i+1} - \left(w_i^2 - w_i\right)W_i + v_i V_i\right\}/h_i^2. \end{array} \right\} \quad (4.6)$$

4.3   Interpolatory Rational σ-Splines

Now, we use a generalized form of continuity, i.e., σ-continuity (c.f. Equation (1.6)) to connect the pieces of the generalized rational cubic in Equation (4.2). The second and third equations of the σ-continuity constraints (Equation (1.6)) together with Equations (4.4), (4.5) and (4.6) lead to the system of consistency equations:

$$h_i \sigma_{1,i-1} \sigma_{3,i} D_{i-1}^- + \left\{ \frac{h_i h_{i-1}}{2} \sigma_{2,i} + h_i \sigma_{3,i} (w_{i-1} - 1) + h_{i-1} \sigma_{1,i} (v_i - 1) \right\} D_i^-$$

$$+ h_{i-1} D_{i+1}^- = h_i \sigma_{3,i} v_{i-1} \Delta_{i-1} + h_{i-1} w_i \Delta_i, \, i = 1, \ldots, n-1. \tag{4.7}$$

in unknowns D_i^-, $i = 0, 1, \ldots, n$. Hence for appropriate end conditions D_0^- and D_n^- and the constraints:

$$\sigma_{1,i} = 1, \quad \sigma_{3,i} \geq 0, \sigma_{2,i} \geq 0, v_i > 2, w_i > 2, \forall i, \tag{4.8}$$

the system of Equations (4.7) defines a diagonally dominant tridiagonal linear system that can be solved easily using the LU decomposition algorithm. Thus, a unique rational cubic interpolatory spline is obtained that is at least C^1. (Since $\sigma_{1,i} = 1$, we have $D_i^- = D_i^+$.)

4.3.1   *Shape Control*

Now we look at the effects of the shape parameters on the rational spline interpolant in the rest of this section.

(i) Let us vary v_i and w_i where the rest of the shape parameters are fixed (for simplicity, we can assume $\sigma_{2,i} = 0, \sigma_{3,i} = 1$); this is discussed in detail in Chapter 2.

(ii) If we vary the $\sigma_{2,i}$'s and keep the others fixed according to constraints (4.8), then

   (a) (*Point tension*) for fixed $i = k$ if we assume $\sigma_{2,i} \to \infty$, then the kth Equation of the system of Equations (4.7) results as:

$$\lim_{\sigma_{2,k} \to \infty} D_k = 0. \tag{4.9}$$

   Thus the curve at the point P_k will appear to have a corner

   (b) (*Interval tension*) Similarly as above large values of $\sigma_{2,k}$ and $\sigma_{2,k+1}$ cause D_k and D_{k+1} to approach zero. This behavior tightens the curve in the interval $[t_k, t_{k+1}]$.

   (c) (*Global tension*) Following in the same way as above, $\sigma_{2,j} \to \infty$ for all i, then

$$\lim_{\sigma_{2,k} \to \infty} D_k = 0, \text{ for } i = 1, \ldots, n-1.$$

   Thus the curve is globally tightened in $[t_1, t_{n-1}]$

(iii) (*Biased behavior*) If we vary the $\sigma_{3,i}$'s and keep the other shape parameters fixed according to (4.8), then for any I if $\sigma_{3,i} \to \infty$, the following relationship is obtained from the system of Equations (4.7):

$$D_i = \frac{v_{i-1} \Delta_{i-1} - D_{i-1}}{w_{i-1} - 1}.$$

This shows a biased behavior, i.e., the curve is inclined toward a side of the interval $[t_i, t_{i+1}]$. A similar behavior can be observed when $\sigma_{2,i}, \sigma_{3,i} \to \infty$.

4.3.2 Some Special Cases

A number of spline methods can be obtained as a result of distinct replacements of the parameters involved in the above construction. For example

A. The case
B.
$$\sigma_{1,i} = 1 = \sigma_{3,i}, \quad \sigma_{2,i} = 0, v_i = 3 = w_i,$$

corresponds to the cubic spline interpolation.

C. The case
$$\sigma_{1,i} = 1 = \sigma_{3,i}, \quad \sigma_{2,i} = 0, v_i = w_i > 2,$$

is that of the rational spline method of Chapter 2. This case also recovers the rational spline with tension [23].

D. The weighted spline [14] can be obtained by the following replacement:

$$\sigma_{1,i} = 1, \sigma_{2,i} = 0, \sigma_{3,i} = \frac{\omega_{i-1}}{\omega_i}, \text{ and } v_i = 3 = w_i.$$

E. The Nu-spline [11] can be obtained with the following choice:

$$\sigma_{1,i} = 1 = \sigma_{3,i}, \sigma_{2,i} = v_i \geq 0, \text{ and } v_i = w_i = 3.$$

F. The replacement

$$\sigma_{1,i} = 1, \sigma_{2,i} = \frac{v_i}{\omega_i}, \sigma_{3,i} = \frac{\omega_{i-1}}{\omega_i}, \text{ and } v_i = 3 = w_i.$$

where $v_i \geq 0, \omega_i \geq 0, \forall i$, gives weighted Nu-spline interpolation method of Foley [7]. This also covers the cases C and D.

4.3.3 Examples

The shape control of the rational cubic σ-spline interpolants is illustrated by the following examples for the data sets in R^2 similar to that in Chapter 2. Unless otherwise stated we will assume $\sigma_{1,i} = 1, \sigma_{2,i} = 0, \sigma_{3,i} = 1$, and $v_i = 3 = w_i$ in all the examples.

Interval tension, point tension and biased behavior of the shape parameters v_i and w_i are shown in Figures 3.2–3.9.

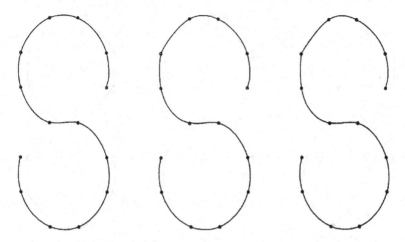

FIGURE 4.1. Interpolatory rational σ-splines with $\sigma_{2,4}$ varying for point tension.

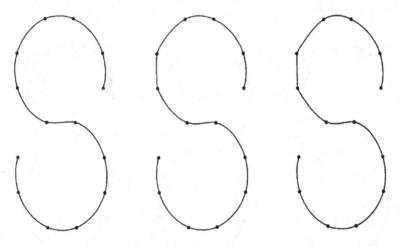

FIGURE 4.2. Interpolatory rational σ-splines with $\sigma_{2,4}$ and $\sigma_{2,5}$ varying for interval tension.

Figure 4.1 illustrates the effect of progressively increasing the value of the point tension parameter $\sigma_{2,4}$ at the knot t_4, while Figure 4.2 shows the interval tension effect due to progressive increases in $\sigma_{2,4}$ and $\sigma_{2,5}$. Figure 4.3 displays the global tension effect due to progressive increase in $\sigma_{2,i}$. The values of the varying parameters, in each curve of the Figures 4.1, 4.2, and 4.3, are taken as 0, 5 and 50, respectively.

Figure 4.4 demonstrates the result of Remark 4.4(iii) regarding local and global biased behavior; the shape parameter σ_3 is chosen as 1 and 50 in the first and third curves, respectively, whereas $\sigma_{3,i}$ is 50 for $i = 4$, and 1 else where in the second curve.

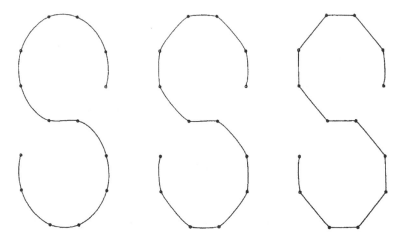

FIGURE 4.3. Interpolatary rational σ-splines with global tension using the shape parameter $\sigma_{2,i}$.

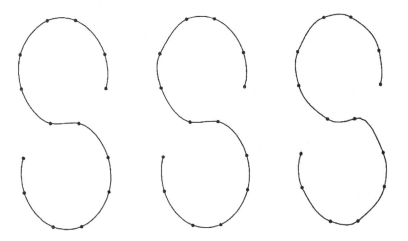

FIGURE 4.4. Interpolatary rational σ-splines with local and global biased behavior using the shape parameter $\sigma_{3,i}$.

Figure 4.5 displays a multishape parameter effect; the first curve is a cubic spline curve; the second curve is fine tuned with the choice $\sigma_{3,3} = 50, \sigma_{2,12} = 5$, $v_i = w_i = 5$ for $i = 7, 8$ and $v_{11} = w_{11} = 2.1$; the third curve is selected with $v_i = w_i = 5$ for $i = 7, 8$ and $v_{12} = w_{11} = 5$.

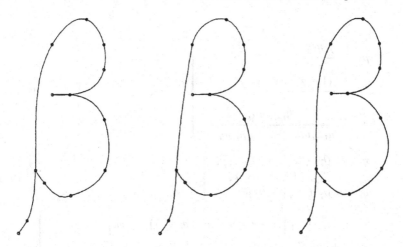

FIGURE 4.5. Interpolatory rational σ-splines fine tuned using multishape parameter effect.

4.4   Freeform Rational σ-Splines

In this section, we present a method for the computation of freeform rational cubic σ-splines by a transformation to piecewise Bernstein-Bézier form. We adopt the same strategy and notations in this construction as was adopted for the rational splines in Chapter 3 except that the piecewise representation of the rational cubic in each interval is assumed in Bernstein-Bézier form instead of Hermite form. We consider the most general rational cubic (4.1) and the most general continuity constraints for our purposes. At the end of this section the σ-spline representation will also be used to discuss the interpolation problem; this will be in a more general setting and with more general shape parameter constraints than the previous section. Let us assume that

$$\sigma_{1,i}, \sigma_{3,i} > 0, \quad \sigma_{2,i} \geq 0, \quad v_i > 3q_i - 2, \quad w_i > 3u_i - 2. \tag{4.10}$$

Now, for the construction of the local support basis functions, let $\phi_j, j = -1, \ldots, n+2$ be the rational σ-spline functions as defined in Equation (4.2) (see Figure 4.1) with the piecewise representation

$$\phi_j(t) = R_0(\theta)\hat{F}_{j,i} + R_1(\theta)\hat{V}_{j,i} + R_2(\theta)\hat{W}_{j,i} + R_3(\theta)\hat{F}_{j,i}, \tag{4.11}$$

in each interval $[t_i, t_{i+1}]$, where $R_k(\theta), k = 0, \ldots, 3$ are defined as in Section 4.3 but are now dependent on $q, v, w,$ and u. The requirement that ϕ_j be a rational σ-spline uniquely determines the following:

$$\left. \begin{array}{l} \hat{F}_{i,i-2} = 0, \ \hat{F}_{i,i-1} = \mu_{i-1}, \ \hat{F}_{i,i} = 1 - \lambda_i, \\[2mm] \hat{V}_{i,i-2} = 0, \ \hat{V}_{i,i-1} = \frac{\mu_{i-1}}{\gamma_{i-1}}, \ \hat{V}_{i,i} = 1, \\[2mm] \hat{W}_{i,i-2} = 0, \ \hat{W}_{i,i-1} = \frac{\lambda_i}{1-\gamma_i}, \ \hat{W}_{i,i} = 1, \end{array} \right\} \tag{4.12}$$

where

$$
\left.\begin{aligned}
\mu_i &= \frac{\gamma_i\, \eta_{1,i}}{\eta_i}, \\
\lambda_i &= \frac{(1-\lambda_i)\, \eta_{2,i-1}}{\eta_{i-1}}, \\
\gamma_i &= \frac{h_{i-1} v_i u_i}{h_{i-1} v_i u_i + h_i \sigma_{1,i} q_i w_{i-1}},
\end{aligned}\right\} \tag{4.13a}
$$

$$
\left.\begin{aligned}
\eta_{1,i} &= \theta_{2,i}\left(\theta_{3,i+1} - \theta_{4,i+1}\right), \\
\eta_{2,i} &= \theta_{4,i+1}\left(\theta_{1,i} - \theta_{2,i}\right), \\
\eta_i &= \theta_{1,i}\theta_{3,i+1} - \theta_{2,i}\theta_{4,i+1},
\end{aligned}\right\} \tag{4.13b}
$$

$$
\left.\begin{aligned}
\theta_{1,i} &= 2h_{i-1}^2 u_{i-1}^2 \left\{(1-\gamma_i)\left(v_i^2 - v_i\left(3q_i - 2\right)\right) + \gamma_i w_i\right\} \\
&\quad + 2h_{i-2}h_i^2 \sigma_{2,i}\gamma_i q_i^2 w_{i-1} u_{i-1} \\
&\quad + 2h_i^2 q_i^2 \sigma_{3,i}\left\{\gamma_i\left(w_{i-1}^2 - w_{i-1}\left(3u_{i-1} - 2\right) - v_{i-1}\right)\right\}, \\
\theta_{2,i} &= 2h_{i-1}^2 w_i u_{i-1}^2, \\
\theta_{3,i} &= 2h_{i-1}^2 u_{i-1}^2\left(1-\gamma_i\right)\left(v_i^2 - v_i\left(3q_i - 2\right) - w_i\right) \\
&\quad + 2h_{i-1}h_i^2 \sigma_{2,i}\gamma_i q_i^2 w_{i-1} u_{i-1} \\
&\quad + 2h_i^2 q_i^2 \sigma_{3,i}\left\{\gamma_i\left(w_{i-1}^2 - w_{i-1}\left(3u_{i-1} - 2\right)\right) + (1-\gamma_i) v_{i-1}\right\}, \\
\theta_{4,i} &= 2h_i^2 \sigma_{3,i} q_i^2 v_{i-1}.
\end{aligned}\right\} \tag{4.13c}
$$

The local support rational σ-B-spline basis is now defined by the difference function $B_j(t)$ as in Equation (3.6). Thus if in any interval $[t_i, t_{i+1}]$,

$$
B_j(t) = R_0(\theta) F_{j,i} + R_1(\theta) V_{j,i} + R_2(\theta) W_{j,i} + R_3(\theta) F_{j,i}, \tag{4.14}
$$

then we have:

$$
\left.\begin{aligned}
&F_{j,i-2} = 0,\; i-1 \geq j \geq i+2,\; F_{i,i-1} = \mu_{i-1},\; F_{i,i} = 1 - \lambda_i - \mu_i,\; F_{i,i+1} = \lambda_{i+1}, \\
&V_{j,i-2} = 0,\, i-2 \geq j \geq i+1,\; V_{i,i-1} = \frac{\mu_{i-1}}{\gamma_{i-1}},\; V_{i,i} = 1 - \frac{\mu_i}{\gamma_i}, \\
&W_{j,i-2} = 0,\, i-2 \geq j \geq i+1,\; W_{i,i-1} = 1 - \frac{\lambda_i}{1-\gamma_i},\; W_{i,i} = \frac{\lambda_{i+1}}{1-\gamma_{i+1}}.
\end{aligned}\right\} \tag{4.15}
$$

Proposition 4.2. The rational σ-spline functions $B_j(t)$, $j = -1, \ldots, n+l$, are such that

$$
(Local\ support) \qquad B_j(t) = 0 \text{ for } t \in \left(t_{j-2}, t_{j+2}\right), \tag{4.16}
$$

$$
(Partition\ of\ unity) \sum_{j=-1}^{n+1} B_j(t) = 0 \text{ for } t \in \left(t_{j-2}, t_{j+2}\right), \tag{4.17}
$$

$$
(Positively) \qquad B_j(t) = 0 \text{ for all } t. \tag{4.18}
$$

Proof. The local support and the partition of unity properties follow immediately from the definition and the construction of the basis functions. For the positively property (4.18), it can be noted immediately that for the parameters defined in (4.10),

$$\gamma_j, \theta_{i,j} > 0, \text{ for all } j \text{ and } i = 2, 4. \tag{4.19}$$

Moreover

$$\theta_{1,j} - \theta_{2,j} = \theta_{3,j} - \theta_{4,j}, \tag{4.20a}$$

where

$$\theta_{1,j} - \theta_{2,j} = 2\left\{h_{j-1}^2 u_{j-1}^2 \left\{(1 - \gamma_j)\left(v_j^2 - v_j(3q_j - 2)\right) + \gamma_j w_j\right\}\right.$$
$$+ \frac{h_{j-2}h_j^2}{2}\sigma_{2,j}\gamma_j q_j^2 w_{j-1} u_{j-1}$$
$$+ \left.h_j^2 q_j^2 \sigma_{3,j}\left\{\gamma_j\left(w_{j-1}^2 - w_{j-1}(3u_{j-1} - 2)\right) - v_{j-1}\right\}\right\}, \tag{4.20b}$$

is also positive. Therefore, the quantities $\eta_{1,j}$, $\eta_{2,j}$ and hence

$$\eta_j = \eta_{1,j} + \eta_{2,j} + 2\left(\theta_{1,j} - \theta_{2,j}\right)\left(\theta_{3,j+1} - \theta_{4,j+1}\right), \tag{4.21}$$

are positive. The above imply that all nonzero terms in Equation (4.15) are positive and thus Equation (4.18) follows.

To apply the rational cubic B-spline as a practical method for curve design, a convenient method for computing the curve representation

$$p(t) = \sum_{j=i-1}^{i+2} P_j B_j(t), \, t \in [t_0, t_n], \tag{4.22}$$

is required, where $P_j \in R^N$ define the control points of the representation. Now, by the local support property,

$$p(t) = \sum_{j=i-1}^{i+2} P_j B_j(t), \, t \in [t_i, t_{i+1}], \, i = 0, 1, \ldots, n - 1. \tag{4.23}$$

Substitution of (3.10) then gives the piecewise defined rational Berstein-Bézier representation

$$p(t) = R_0(\theta) F_i + R_1(\theta) V_i + R_2(\theta) W_i + R_3(\theta) F_{i+1}, \tag{4.24}$$

where

$$\left.\begin{array}{l} F_i = \lambda_i P_{i-1} + (1 - \lambda_i - \mu_i) P_i + \mu_i P_{i+1}, \\ V_i = (1 - \alpha_i) P_i + \alpha_i P_{i+1}, \\ W_i = \beta_i P_i + (1 - \beta_i) P_{i+1}, \end{array}\right\} \tag{4.25}$$

with

$$\alpha_i = \frac{\eta_{1,i}}{\eta_i}, \beta_i = \frac{\eta_{2,i}}{\eta_i}, \tag{4.26}$$

The transformation to rational Bernstein-Bézier form is very convenient for computational purposes and also leads to the following:

Proposition 4.3. (*Variation diminishing property*) The rational σ-B-spline curve $p(t)$, $t \in [t_0, t_n]$, defined by Equation (4.22), crosses any (hyper) plane of dimension $N - 1$ no more times than it crosses the *control polygon P* joining the control points $\{P_j\}_{j=-1}^{n+1}$.

Proof. Following the arguments in Equations (4.19)–(4.21), for positivity, in the previous proposition, it is straightforward that the coefficients α_i, β_i in Equation (4.25) satisfy

$$\alpha_i \geq 0, \ \beta_i \geq 0, \ \alpha_i + \beta_i \leq 1.$$

Thus V_i and W_i lie on the line segment joining P_i and P_{i+1}, where V_i is before W_i. Also, we write

$$F_i = (1 - \gamma_i) W_i + \gamma_i V_i, \tag{4.27}$$

where we already know that $0 < \gamma_i < 1$. Thus the control polygon of the piecewise defined Bernstein-Bézier representation is obtained by *corner cutting* of the σ-B-spline control polygon; see Figure 4.3. Since the piecewise defined Bernstein-Bézier representation is variation diminishing, it follows that the σ-B-spline representation is also variation diminishing.

Remark 4.4. Using the rational σ-B-spline, the interpolation problem of the rational σ-splines can be tackled through

$$\sum_{j=-1}^{n+1} P_j B_j (t_i) = F_i, \ \forall i. \tag{4.28}$$

where the matrix of the $B_j(t_i)$ is tridiagonal matrix. Since $0 < \mu_i, \lambda_i < 1/2$, the tridiagonal system of Equations (4.28) is diagonally dominant. Thus a unique interpolatory rational σ-spline exits with more general shape constraints (4.10) than (4.8) in Section 4.3.

4.4.1 *Shape Control*

The parameters defined in Equation (4.10) can be used to control the local or global shape of the curve:

(i) Since the shape constraints $v_i > 3q_i - 2$ and $w_i > 3u_i - 2$ must be satisfied, then increase or decrease in q_i and u_i corresponds to increase or decrease in v_i and w_i, respectively. Keeping q_i and u_i fixed (say, $q_i = u_i = 1$, for simplicity) and varying v_i and w_i is discussed in detail in Chapter 3 where the interval, point and the biased behaviors were observed by using these parameters.

(ii) It is a simple matter to see that, for any i when $\sigma_{2,i}$ is increased (and other shape parameters are kept fixed), $\lambda_i, \mu_i \to 0$ which implies $p(t_i) \to P_i$. Thus the curve is pulled toward the control point P_i. If we also let $\sigma_{2,i} \to \infty$, then we shall have $p(t_{i+1}) \to P_{i+1}$ and it follows that for any $t \in [t_i, t_{i+1}]$, $p(t)$ must converge to a point on the straight line from P_i to P_{i+1}. Thus, the behavior of $\sigma_{2,i}$ can be used to achieve the point and interval tensions both locally and globally.

(iii) The shape parameter $\sigma_{1,i}$ also produces a similar shape behavior as that of $\sigma_{2,i}$ in a different way. The increase in $\sigma_{1,i}$ for any i, (while the other shape parameters are kept fixed) makes the curve approaching the point

$$P = \lambda P_{i-1} + (1 - \lambda)P_i, \quad \text{where} \quad 0 < \lambda = \lim_{\sigma_{1,i} \to \infty} \lambda_i.$$

This shows that the curve is not only pulled toward a point on the line from P_{i-1} to P_i, but also shifts backward. Similarly, if $\sigma_{1,i+1}$ is also increased sufficiently large, this will make the curve tighten between two points P and Q which lie on the lines from P_{i-1} to P_i and P_i to P_{i+1}, respectively.

(iv) Another interesting shape characteristic can be achieved by the variation of the shape parameters $\sigma_{1,i}$ and $\sigma_{3,i}$. If they are assumed large enough (and other shape parameters supposed to be fixed; for simplicity, let $v_i = 3 = w_i$ and $\sigma_{2,i} = 0$) then λ_i and μ_i decrease and increase monotonically towards 0 and 1, respectively. This shows that the curve at t_i is pulled and shifted completely to the control point P_{i-1}. In the case when $\sigma_{1,i+1}$ and $\sigma_{3,i+1}$ are also increased, the curve is shifted and pulled to the line segment $P_{i-1}P_i$.

4.4.2   Some Special Cases

A number of spline methods can be obtained as the result of distinct replacements of the parameters involved in the above construction. For example

A. The case

$$\sigma_{1,i} = \sigma_{3,i} = 1, \quad \sigma_{2,i} = 0, q_i = u_i = 1, \quad v_i = w_i = 3,$$

corresponds to the cubic spline representation.

B. The case

$$\sigma_{1,i} = \sigma_{3,i} = 1, \quad \sigma_{2,i} = 0, q_i = u_i = 1, \quad v_i = w_i > 2,$$

is that of a rational spline with tension [23].

C. The weighted spline [14] can be obtained by the following replacement:

$$\sigma_{1,i} = 1, \sigma_{2,i} = 0, \sigma_{3,i} = \frac{\omega_{i-1}}{\omega_i}, \omega_i > 0, q_i = u_i = 1, v_i = w_i = 3.$$

D. The Nu-spline [11] can be obtained with the following choice:

$$\sigma_{1,i} = 1 = \sigma_{3,i} = 0, \ \sigma_{2,i} = v_i \geq 0, \ q_i = u_i = 1, \ v_i = w_i = 3.$$

E. The replacement

$$\sigma_{1,i} = 1, \ \sigma_{2,i} = \frac{v_i}{\omega_i}, \ \sigma_{3,i} = \frac{\omega_{i-1}}{\omega_i}, \ q_i = u_i = 1, \ v_i = w_i = 3,$$

where $v_i \geq 0$, $\omega_i > 0$, $\forall i$, gives weighted Nu-spline method of Foley [7]. This also covers the cases C and D.

F. The special case

$$\sigma_{1,i} = \beta_{1,i}, \ \sigma_{2,i} = \beta_{2,i}, \ \sigma_{3,i} = \beta_{1,i}^2, \ q_i = u_i = 1, \ v_i = w_i = 3,$$

where $\beta_{1,i} > 1, \beta_{2,i} > 0$, corresponds to the β-splines method.

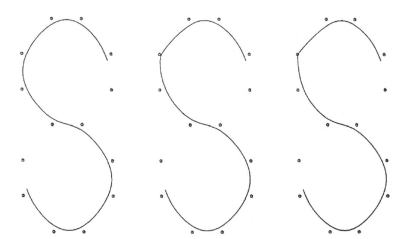

FIGURE 4.6. Freeform rational σ-splines with $\sigma_{2,4}$ varying for point tension control.

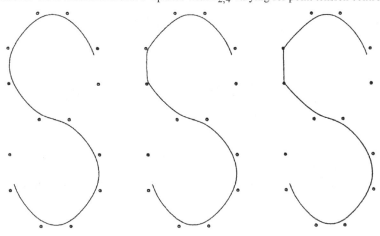

FIGURE 4.7. Freeform rational σ-splines with $\sigma_{2,4}$ and $\sigma_{2,5}$ varying for interval tension.

G. The rational geometric splines of Boehm [27] can also be recovered. The relationship of our $\sigma_{2,i}$ and the tension factors *(Boehm's γ_i)* used by Boehm for his curvature continuous rational cubic splines is derived here from our Bernstein Bézier representation as:

$$(\text{Boehm's}\gamma_i) = \frac{6h_{i-1}h_iu_{i-1}^2}{\theta_{1,i} - \theta_{2,i}},$$

where $\sigma_{1,i} = \sigma_{3,i} = 1$. It can be easily noticed that the behavior of $1/(Boehm's\gamma_i)$ is the same as that of $\sigma_{2,i}$.

4.4.3 *Examples*

The same data sets in R^2 are considered for this section as the interpolatory examples in the last section, where the data now define the control points of the rational σ-B-spline representation.

The shape effects of the parameters, mentioned in (i) of Subsection 4.4.1 are demonstrated in Figures 4.5–4.12.

Figures 4.6–4.10 correspond to the shape parameters of the examples demonstrated in Figures 4.1–4.5, respectively.

Figures 4.11, 4.12 and 4.13 display the results in (iii) of Subsection 4.4.1. The first, second and third curve:

(a) of the Figure 4.11, respectively, correspond to the values 1, 5 and 50 of $\sigma_{1,5}$,
(b) of the Figure 4.12, respectively, correspond to the values $\sigma_{1,4} = \sigma_{1,5} = 1, 5$ and 50,
(c) of the Figure 4.13, respectively, correspond to the values 1, 5 and 50 of $\sigma_{1,i}$, $\forall i$.

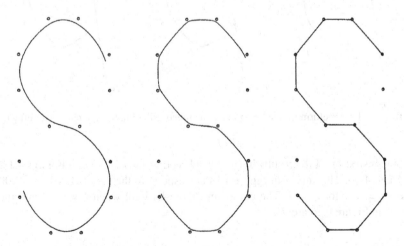

FIGURE 4.8. Freeform rational σ-splines with global tension using the shape parameter $\sigma_{2,i}$.

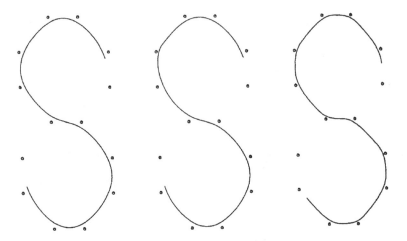

FIGURE 4.9. Freeform rational σ-splines with local and global biased behavior using the shape parameter $\sigma_{3,i}$.

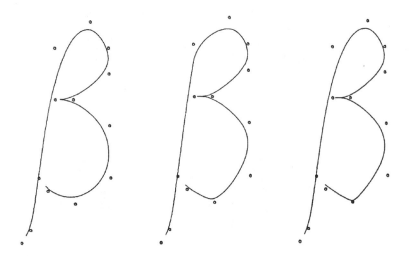

FIGURE 4.10. Freeform rational σ-splines fine tuned using multishape parameter effect.

Demonstration of the results in (iv) of Subsection 4.4.1 is done in Figures 4.14, 4.15 and 4.16. The curves in Figure 4.14 correspond to the values 1, 10 and 1000 of $\sigma_{1,i} = \sigma_{3,i}$ for $i = 4$. The curves in Figure 4.15 are when $i = 4, 5$ and the curves in Figure 4.16 are $\forall i$.

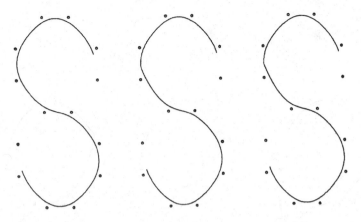

FIGURE 4.11. Freeform rational σ-splines with $\sigma_{1,4}$ varying for appearing a corner in the middle of the interval.

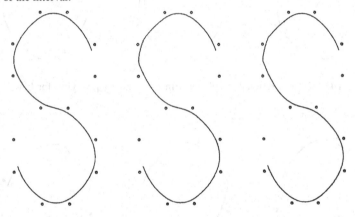

FIGURE 4.12. Freeform rational σ-splines with $\sigma_{1,4}$ and $\sigma_{1,5}$ varying to tighten the curve across the line segments P_3P_4 and P_4P_5.

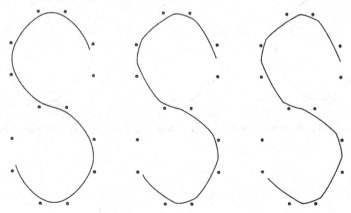

FIGURE 4.13. Freeform rational σ-splines with global tension using the shape parameter $\sigma_{1,i}$.

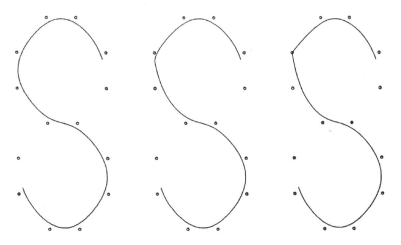

FIGURE 4.14. Freeform rational σ-splines with $\sigma_{1,4}$ and $\sigma_{3,4}$ varying for biased point tension.

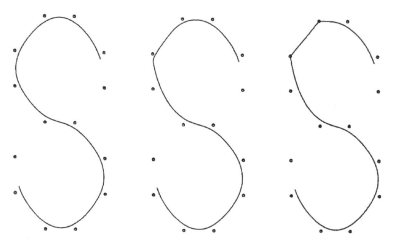

FIGURE 4.15. Freeform rational σ-splines with $\sigma_{1,i}$ and $\sigma_{3,i}$ varying for biased interval tension.

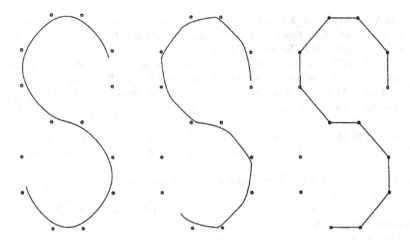

FIGURE 4.16. Freeform rational σ-splines with $\sigma_{1,i}$ and $\sigma_{3,i}$ varying for biased global tension.

4.5   Exercises

1. Write programs to implement the curve design methods in Section 4.3.2.
2. Write programs to implement the curve design methods in Section 4.4.2.
3. Check the difference of shape effects in your programs of Exercise 4.5.1 and 4.5.2.
4. Check the difference of shape effects in your programs of Exercise 4.5.1 and 4.5.2 when the schemes are implemented in scalar form as stated in Remark 3.

References

1. Barsky, B.A. (1981), *The Beta-Spline: A Local Representation Based on Shape Parameters and Fundamental Geometric Measure*, Ph.D. Thesis, University of Utah.
2. Bartels, R., and Beatty, J. (1984), Beta-splines with a difference, Technical Report CS-83-40, Computer Science Department, University of Waterloo, Waterloo, Canada.
3. Boehm, W. (1985), Curvature continuous curves and surfaces, *Comp Aided Geom Design* 2(2), 313–323.
4. Cline, A. (1974), Curve fitting in one and dimensions using splines under tension, *Comm ACM* 17, 218–223
5. Dierckx, P., and Tytgat, B. (1989), Generating the Bézier points of β-spline curve, *Comput Aided Geom Design* 6, 279–291.
6. Farin, G.E. (1996), *Curves and Surfaces for CAGD*, Academic Press, New York.
7. Foley, T.A. (1986), Local control of interval tension using weighted splines. *Comp Aided Geom Design* 3, 281–294.
8. Foley, T.A. (1987), Interpolation with interval and point tension controls using cubic weighted Nu-splines, *ACM Trans Math Software* 13, 68–96.

9. Goodman, T.N.T., and Unsworth, K. (1985), Generation of beta spline curves using a recursive relation. In: *Fundamental Algorithms for Computer Graphics*. R.E. Earnshaw (Ed.), Springer-Verlag, Berlin, pp. 326–357.

10. Lewis, J. (1975), *"B-spline" bases for splines under tension, Nu-splines, and fractional order splines*, Presented at the SIAM-SIGNUM Meeting, San Francisco, CA.

11. Nielson, G.M. (1974), Some piecewise polynomial alternatives to splines under tension, In: *Computer-Aided Geometric Design*, R.F. Barnhill (Ed.), Academic Press. New York.

12. Nielson, G.M. (1986), Rectangular ν-splines. *IEEE Comp Graph Appl* 6, 35–40.

13. Pruess, S. (1979), Alternatives to the exponential spline in tension, *Math Comp* 33, 1273–1281.

14. Salkauskas, K. (1984), C^1 splines for interpolation of rapidly varying data, *Rocky Mtn J Math* 14, 239–250.

15. Sarfraz, M. (1992), A C^2 rational cubic spline alternative to the NURBS, *Comp & Graph* 16(1), 69–78.

16. Sarfraz, M. (1995), Curves and surfaces for CAD using C^2 rational cubic splines, *Int J Eng Comput*, Springer-Verlag, 11(2), 94–102.

17. Sarfraz, M. (1994), Freeform rational bicubic spline surfaces with tension control, Facta Universitatis (NIS), *Ser. Mathematics and Informatics*, 9, 83–93.

18. Sarfraz, M. (1994), Cubic spline curves with shape control, *Int J Comput Graphics*, Elsevier Science, 18(5), 707–713.

19. Sarfraz, M, (2003), Weighted Nu-splines: an alternative to NURBS, *Advances in Geometric Modeling*, Ed.: M. Sarfraz, John Wiley, New York, pp. 81–95.

20. Schoenburg, I. J. (1946), Contributions to the problem of approximation of equidistant data by analytic functions, *Appl Math* 4, 45–99.

21. Schweikert, D.G. (1966), An interpolation curve using a spline in tension, *J Math Phys* 45, 312–317.

22. Sarfraz, M. (2004), Weighted Nu-splines with local support basis functions, *Int J Comput Graphics*, Elsevier Science, 28(4), 539–549.

23. Gregory, J.A., and Sarfraz, M. (1990), A rational spline with tension, *Int J Comput Aided Geom Des*, North-Holland, Elsevier, 7, 1–13.

24. Schweikert, D. (1966), An interpolation curve using splines in tension, *J Math and Phys.* **45**, 312–317.

25. Cline, A. (1974), Curve fitting in one and dimensions using splines under tension, *Comm ACM* 17, 218–223.

26. Preuss, S. (1979), Alternatives to the exponential spline in tension, *Math Comp* 33, 1273–1281

27. Boehm, W. (1987), Rational geometric splines, *Comput Aided Geom Des* 4, 67–77.

28. Schoenberg, L. (1981), *Spline Functions: Basic Theory*, JohnWiley, New York.

5
Linear, Conic and Rational Cubic Splines

Abstract. *A rational cubic spline has been used with the view to its applications in computer graphics, vision, and image processing. It incorporates linear, conic and parametric cubic curve sections as special cases. The parameters (weights), in the description of the spline curve can be used to modify the shape of the curve, locally and globally. The spline attains parametric smoothness of different degrees depending on different choices of derivative settings and nature of curve segments. However, the stitching of the rational cubic segments preserves C^2 smoothness and stitching of the conic segments preserves visually reasonable C^1 smoothness at the neighboring knots. The curve scheme is interpolatory and can plot parabolic, hyperbolic, elliptic, and circular splines independently as well as bits and pieces of a rational cubic spline. This chapter discusses cases of elliptic arcs in space and also introduces intermediate point interpolation scheme which can force the curve to pass through given point between any segment.*

5.1 Introduction

A common problem, in computer graphics, vision, and imaging is to design a curved outline by stitching small pieces of curves together [1–14]. Piecewise rational cubic spline functions provide powerful tools for designing of curves, surfaces and some analytic primitives such as conic sections that are widely used in engineering design and various other applications. Such applications may include representing a font outline [13], the round corner of an object [3], or a smooth fit to given data [9]. Several segments of curves, to compose a desired curve outline, can have different mathematical descriptions. For example, a font "S" when designed, appears to have straight lines, conics, and cubics as essential parts of its outline. Single mathematical formulation for the precise definition of various types of geometry shapes is one of the major advantages of the rational cubic spline functions. We aim in this chapter to represent a piecewise parametric curve scheme, which has all the design features to produce a desired manipulated curve.

In [2], C^1 rational cubic splines with exact derivatives for control points were used. This chapter introduces a similar interpolant but with a very simple distance-based approximated derivative scheme as well as an exact derivative scheme. Our goal is to achieve results for problems in various applications. This chapter also describes the parametric C^1 and C^2 rational cubic spline representation containing a family of shape control parameters. This family of shape parameters has been used to produce straight-line segments, conics and cubics.

The following features are also a significant addition to the chapter:

- maintaining a reasonable amount of continuity (C^1) between conic and cubic arcs,
- estimated end derivatives,
- conic (circular, elliptical, parabolic and hyperbolic) splines,
- circular arcs for s given radius or center,
- elliptic arc in space and
- intermediate point interpolation

In [2], the end derivatives are based on the assumption of the user, which is not convenient. Moreover, the conics are not discussed at all. This chapter has a description of suitable end derivatives for more pleasing results [14]. In [10], cubic and conic segments are joined with G^1 continuity, which is not reasonable for some practical applications. Intermediate point interpolation scheme and circular arcs, presented in [5], are not practical because the space curves and exact circular arcs are not possible. In [11], intermediate point interpolation scheme with C^0 continuity at neighborhood points was offered. G^1 continuity on constrained guided curve scheme has been introduced in [6] where rational quadratic functions were used. This chapter discusses rational cubic function and offers better continuity. In [4], the rational quadratic spline is used for the circular spline. This chapter uses a very simple technique [10] using a rational cubic spline to achieve the same circular spline.

The curve scheme presented here can generate exact circular, parabolic, hyperbolic, and elliptical arcs. Degree elevation techniques have been applied on rational quadratic splines as mentioned in [7]. Although NURBS (nonuniform rational B-spline) representation of ellipse is given in [7], an improved technique [14] is explained to handle any type of elliptic arcs even in space. In addition, the scheme has the following properties, which may lead to a more useful approach to curve and surface design in CAGD:

- The curve has C^2 continuity between the rational cubic arcs and C^1 continuity between cubic and conic arcs.
- Suitable end derivatives are estimated.
- The scheme is local, i.e., shape control parameters will not significantly affect the adjacent parts of the design curve.
- A distance-based approximated derivative scheme is also used to compute control points. Tangent vectors vary continuously along the curve preserving C^1 continuity.

- Any part of the rational cubic spline can be made conic (with exact circle and ellipse) or straight line using the same interpolant.
- Intermediate point interpolation scheme has been introduced for use in a guided curve.
- The scheme can handle any kind of elliptic arc in space.
- All methods are suitable for space curves and hence can also be generalized to surfaces.

The parametric rational cubic spline scheme is considered in the next section. Analysis of the designing curve is given in Section 5.3. In Section 5.4, there is a scheme to calculate the end derivatives (tangents). The conditions for conics and straight-line segments are discussed in Section 5.5. This section also covers all types of circular, parabolic, hyperbolic and elliptical arcs and introduces a very powerful method for intermediate point interpolation. Examples are discussed in Section 5.6. Finally, the chapter is summarized in Section 5.7.

5.2   The Rational Cubic Spline

The cubic spline is the spline of the lowest degree with C^2 continuity. C^2 continuity meets the needs of most problems arising from engineering and mathematical physics. Rational cubic spline functions of lower degree are numerically simple, stable and are the most fundamental of all rational space curves. Let $F_i \in R^m$, $i = 1, \ldots, n$, be a given set of points at the distinct knots $t_i \in R$, with unit interval spacing. Consider a first-degree parametric piecewise rational function for the straight-line segment between F_i and F_{i+1}:

$$L(t) \equiv L_i(t) = \frac{(1 - \theta) \alpha_i F_i + \theta \beta_i F_{i+1}}{(1 - \theta) \alpha_i + \theta \beta_i}, \tag{5.1}$$

where

$$\theta = (t - t_i)/h_i, \quad h_i = t_{i+1} - t_i.$$

The degree elevation formula [1] can be applied to get the quadratic rational Bézier function:

$$Q(t) \equiv Q_i(t) = \frac{(1 - \theta)^2 \alpha_i F_i + \theta (1 - \theta) \gamma_i U_i + \theta^2 \beta_i F_{i+1}}{(1 - \theta)^2 \alpha_i + \theta (1 - \theta) \gamma_i + \theta^2 \beta_i}, \tag{5.2}$$

where U_i may be taken as the point of intersection of tangents at F_i and F_{i+1} (see Figure 5.1).

Applying degree elevation again, we get the rational cubic Bézier function:

$$P(t) \equiv P_i(t) = \frac{N_1}{N_2}, \tag{5.3}$$

where

$$N_1 = (1 - \theta)^3 \alpha_i F_i + \theta (1 - \theta)^2 (\alpha_i + \gamma_i) V_i + \theta^2 (1 - \theta) (\beta_i + \gamma_i) W_i$$
$$+ \theta^3 \beta_i F_{i+1},$$
$$N_2 = (1 - \theta)^2 \alpha_i + \theta (1 - \theta) \gamma_i + \theta^2 \beta_i,$$

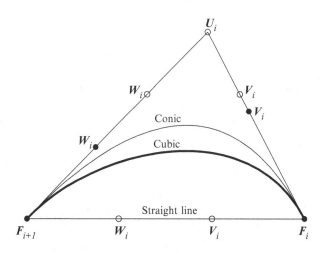

FIGURE 5.1. Plot of $P(t)$ with V_i, W_i from straight line, conic and cubic.

which is a straight-line segment between F_i and F_{i+1} with control points:

$$V_i = \frac{2\alpha_i F_i + \beta_i F_{i+1}}{2\alpha_i + \beta_i}, \ W_i = \frac{\alpha_i F_i + 2\beta_i F_{i+1}}{\alpha_i + 2\beta_i},$$

and weight $\gamma_i = \alpha_i + \beta_i$. Similarly this function (5.3) is a conic curve between F_i and F_{i+1} with following control points:

$$V_i = \frac{\alpha_i F_i + \gamma_i U_i}{\alpha_i + \gamma_i}, \ W_i = \frac{\beta_i F_{i+1} + \gamma_i U_i}{\beta_i + \gamma_i},$$

It is known that only one interpolant (5.3) is enough for a straight-line segment, conic arc, and cubic arc. It is a C^1 Hermite function for:

$$V_i = F_i + \frac{\alpha_i}{\alpha_i + \gamma_i} D_i, \ W_i = F_{i+1} - \frac{\beta_i}{\beta_i + \gamma_i} D_{i+1}.$$

This can be achieved by imposing the Hermite interpolation conditions:

$$P(t_i) = F_i \text{ and } P^{(1)}(t_i) = D_i, \forall_i. \tag{5.4}$$

The interpolant can further be simplified, as targeted, to the interpolant of Section 3.3 with just single shape parameter in its description. This can be achieved by having $\alpha_i = 1$, $\beta_i = 1$ and $\gamma_i = r_i - 1$. Thus, it takes the following form:

$$
\begin{aligned}
P(t) &\equiv P_i(t) \\
&= \frac{(1-\theta)^3 F_i + \theta(1-\theta)^2 (\gamma_i + 1)V_i + \theta^2(1-\theta)(\gamma_i + 1)W_i + \theta^3 F_{i+1}}{(1-\theta)^2 + \theta(1-\theta)\gamma_i + \theta^2}, \\
&\quad i = 1, \ldots, n-1,
\end{aligned}
\tag{5.5}
$$

The following choice of control vertices

$$V_i = F_i + \frac{1}{1 + \gamma_i} D_i, \left.\vphantom{\frac{1}{1}}\right\}$$

$$W_i = F_{i+1} + \frac{1}{1 + \gamma_i} D_{i+1}.$$

leads (5.5) to a C^1 piecewise rational cubic Hermite spline. The choice of parameters $\gamma_i > -1$ ensures a strictly positive denominator in the rational cubic. Thus, from Bernstein-Bezier theory, the curve lies in the convex hull of the control points $\{F_i, V_i, W_i, F_{i+1}\}$ and is variation diminishing.

For the construction of a C^2 rational cubic spline, we need to manipulate the second derivative of (5.5), which is as follows:

$$P_i^{(2)}(t) = \frac{2\left\{A_i\theta^3 + B_i\theta^2(1-\theta) + C_i\theta(1-\theta)^2 + E_i(1-\theta)^3\right\}}{h_i\{1 + (\gamma_i - 2)\theta(1-\theta)\}^3},$$

where

$$A_i = (\gamma_i + 1)(D_{i+1} - \Delta_i) - D_{i+1} + D_i, \left.\vphantom{\frac{1}{1}}\right\}$$
$$B_i = 3(D_{i+1} - \Delta_i),$$
$$C_i = 3(\Delta_i - D_i),$$
$$E_i = (\gamma_i + 1)(\Delta_i - D_i) - D_{i+1} + D_i,$$

and

$$\Delta_i = (F_{i+1} - F_i)/h_i.$$

5.2.1 Estimation of Tangent Vectors

There are different choices of the tangent vectors D_i at F_i, which can be chosen for practical implementation in the computation of a curve with a specific amount of smoothness. For C^1 curve methods, some reasonable tangent approximation method can be used. The distance-based approximations are found to be reasonably good as far as pleasing smoothness is concerned. We now, define the tangent vectors D_i at F_i. For open curves, the end conditions are defined as:

$$D_1 = 2(F_2 - F_1) - (F_3 - F_1)/2, \left.\vphantom{\frac{1}{1}}\right\} \quad (5.6)$$
$$D_n = 2(F_n - F_{n-1}) - (F_n - F_{n-2})/2.$$

This choice will control the direction of the curve properly at the end segments. The tangents at the interior knots, for $i = 2, \ldots, n - 1$, are given by:

$$D_i = a_i(F_i - F_{i-1}) + (1 - a_i)(F_{i+1} - F_i) \quad (5.7)$$

where

$$a_i = \frac{|F_{i+1} - F_i|}{|F_{i+1} - F_i| + |F_i - F_{i-1}|}.$$

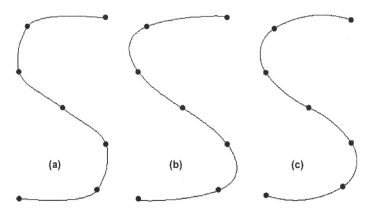

FIGURE 5.2. Spline curves with various end conditions: (a) with distance-based derivatives, (b)–(c) with exact derivatives.

For closed curves, the end conditions are defined as:

$$F_{-1} = F_{n-1}, F_{n+1} = F_1,$$

and the tangents at the interior knots are same as in Equation (5.7) but $i = 1, \ldots, n$.

The experiments have shown that the use of the distance-based approximated derivatives, corresponding to any control polygon (open or closed), provides visually pleasing output. Figure 5.2(a) is the display of this derivative scheme for an "S" shaped data. For further details, the reader is referred to Sarfraz et al. [10].

For a higher continuity than C^1, more complicated constraints are required to be fitted. For example, for a C^2 rational cubic spline, the constraints lead to a tridiagonal linear system of equations. This system is diagonally dominant and hence provides a unique solution. This system can be solved using some tridiagonal linear system solver like the LU decomposition method. Details are as follows:

C^1 constraints

$$P^{(1)}(t_i^+) = P^{(1)}(t_i^-), i = 2, \ldots, n - 1.$$

give

$$D_i = \gamma_{i-1}(F_i - F_{i-1}) - D_{i-1},$$

and C^2 constraints

$$P^{(2)}(t_i^+) = P^{(2)}(t_i^-), i = 2, \ldots, n - 1.$$

lead to the following system of equations:

$$h_i D_i + (h_i (\gamma_{i-1} - 1) + h_{i-1} (\gamma_i - 1)) + h_{i-1} D_{i+1}$$
$$= \gamma_{i-1} \Delta_i + \gamma_i \Delta_{i-1}, i = 2, \ldots, n - 1. \tag{5.8}$$

For the need of graphical results, exact derivatives may be computed from (5.8) together with the end conditions in (5.6). Figure 5.2 (b) is the demonstration for

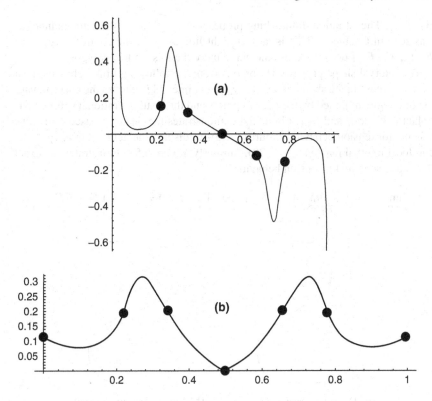

FIGURE 5.3. Curvature plots of spline curves with exact derivatives: (a) with distance-based end derivatives, (b) with conic-compatible end derivatives.

this derivative scheme. The end conditions used here may not be appropriate for the objectives of this chapter. Therefore, a reasonable choice has been made in Section 5.5, which demonstrates the "S" shaped data in Figure 5.2(c). The difference can be seen in Figure 5.3 demonstrating curvature plots of Figures 5.2(b) and 5.2(c) in Figures 5.3(a) and 5.3(b), respectively.

5.3   Design Curve Analysis

The parameters γ_i are mainly meant to be used freely to control the shape of the curve. At the same time, for the convenience of the designer, it is also necessary that the ideal geometric properties of the curve not be lost. The geometric properties, such as variation diminishing, convex hull, and positivity, need to be presented in the description of the design curve.

For the constraints, $\gamma_i > -1, \forall i$, it is very obvious that the rational cubic is characterized as of Bernstein-Bézier form. The case for default values of shape parameters, for $\gamma_i = 2$, is that of cubic Hermite interpolation. Thus, following the Bernstein-Bézier theory, the piece of curve $P_i(t)$ lies in the convex hull of F_i, V_i,

W_i, F_{i+1}. The variation diminishing property also follows in the same manner as was seen in Chapter 3. That is, any straight line crossing the control polygon of F_i, V_i, W_i, F_{i+1} does not cross the curve more than its control polygon.

The interval shape property is obvious from the following limit behavior. That is, the increase in the shape parameter γ_i in any interval i tightens the curve toward the line segment joined by the control points and the resulting rational spline interpolant is C^1 at t_i and t_{i+1}. Figure 5.4 demonstrates the distance-based derivative scheme for tension behavior. Figures 5.4(a)-(c) display the default curve ($\gamma_i = 2$) and local interval tension ($\gamma_2 = 20$). Similarly, Figure 5.5 demonstrates the exact derivative scheme for tension behavior.

$$\lim_{\gamma_i \to \infty} V_i = F_i, \ \lim_{\gamma_i \to \infty} W_i = F_{i+1} \ \text{and} \ \lim_{\gamma_i \to \infty} P_i(t) = (1 - \theta) F_i + \theta F_{i+1}.$$

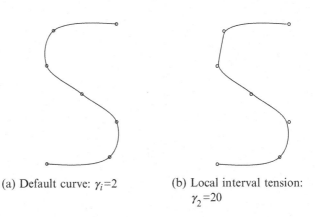

(a) Default curve: $\gamma_i=2$ (b) Local interval tension:
$\gamma_2=20$

FIGURE 5.4. Demonstration of shape parameters using distance-based derivatives (C^1 continuity).

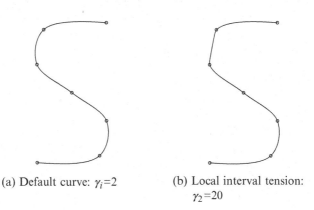

(a) Default curve: $\gamma_i=2$ (b) Local interval tension:
$\gamma_2=20$

FIGURE 5.5. Demonstration of shape parameters using exact derivatives (C^2 continuity).

Applying the interval property above successively, the design curve converges to the control polygon as the derivatives, either being distance-based or computed from the system of equations, are bounded.

5.4   Estimation of End Tangent Vectors

Tangent vectors for end segments are usually supposed, but less fortunately these are not always visually pleasing. To make the end segments more appropriate, a more compatible choice [14] for the curve scheme is presented here. For the tangent at the first point, let θ_1 be the angle between $F_3 - F_1$ and $F_2 - F_1$. Let T_1 be the rotation of F_2 around F_1 by an angle θ_1 on the plane passing through F_1, F_2 and F_3. Now, the tangent vector D_1, at first point, can be derived as follows:

$$\mu_1 = \frac{(F_2 - F_1)^2}{2(F_2 - F_1) \cdot T_1}, U_1 = F_1 + \mu_1 T_1, V_1 = \frac{F_1 + 2U_1}{3}, D_1 = 3(V_1 - F_1),$$
(5.9)

where μ_1 is determined by the condition:

$$|U_1 - F_1| = |U_1 - F_2|.$$
(5.10)

Similarly, for tangent vector D_n at the last point, let θ_n be the angle between $F_{n-2} - F_n$ and $F_{n-1} - F_n$. Let T_n be the rotation of F_{n-1} around F_n by an angle θ_n on the plane passing through F_n, F_{n-1} and F_{n-2}. Then

$$\mu_{n-1} = \frac{(F_{n-1} - F_n)^2}{2(F_{n-1} - F_n) \cdot T_n}, U_{n-1} = F_n + \mu_{n-1} T_n,$$

$$W_{n-1} = \frac{F_n + 2U_{n-1}}{3}, D_n = 3(F_n - W_{n-1}),$$

where μ_{n-1} is determined by the condition:

$$|U_{n-1} - F_n| = |U_{n-1} - F_{n-1}|.$$
(5.11)

Visual difference between different types of end tangent vectors has been demonstrated in Figure 5.6.

5.5   Conic Splines and Straight Line

Conics and straight-lines are the most important parts in designing. These can be achieved through a rational cubic interpolant (5.3). It is interesting to see that one can use the same interpolant for all types of curves. As mentioned before, U_i is the point of intersection of tangents at F_i and F_{i+1}. In case the tangents are

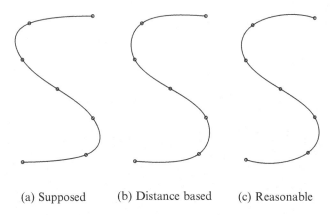

(a) Supposed   (b) Distance based   (c) Reasonable

FIGURE 5.6. Demonstration of end derivatives using exact derivatives (C^2 continuity).

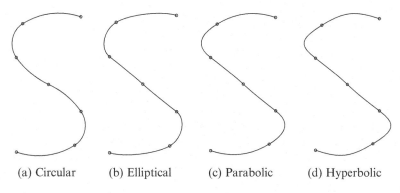

(a) Circular   (b) Elliptical   (c) Parabolic   (d) Hyperbolic

FIGURE 5.7. C^1 Conic spline.

parallel, U_i can be taken as the point where the arc is desired to be divided into two pieces; for example, it may be the inflection or the middle point, and so on.

For conic section properties and choice of shape parameters, various conics are recovered depending upon the nature of weights [8]. Also, readers are referred to [7] and [1] for details. According to [7], the conic shape factor:

$$k = \frac{1}{\gamma_i^2} \tag{5.12}$$

determines the conic if the three weights are changed in such a way that k is not changed. Thus, any two weights can be chosen arbitrarily; the conic is then determined by the third weight. The C^1 conic spline is:

- Elliptic if $-1 < \gamma_i < 2$ (Figure 5.7(b)).
- Parabolic if $\gamma_i = 2$ (Figure 5.7(c)).
- Hyperbolic if $\gamma_i > 2$ (Figure 5.7(d)).

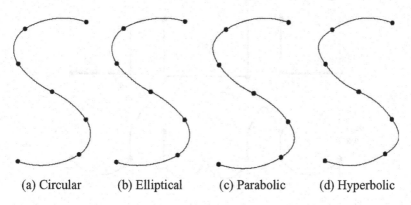

(a) Circular   (b) Elliptical   (c) Parabolic   (d) Hyperbolic

FIGURE 5.8. C^2 conic spline.

Similarly C^2 elliptic, parabolic, and hyperbolic splines are given in Figures 5.8(b), 5.8(c), and 5.8(d), respectively. The corresponding curvature plots of Figures 5.8(b)–(d) are shown in Figures 5.9(b)–(d).

5.5.1 *Conic Arc in Cubic Spline*

Rational cubic interpolant (5.5) can easily adjust conic segments in cubic spline. Cubic segments are already joined by C^2 continuity but there is also a need for some smoothness between conic and cubic segments. C^1 continuity is enough for visually pleasing results. Let the ith segment between F_i and F_{i+1} be a conic curve. If $i > 1$, then for C^1 continuity at F_i, impose the constraints $P^{(1)}(t_i^-) = P^{(1)}(t_i^+)$ to find

$$W_{i-1} = \frac{(2 + \gamma_{i-1} + \gamma_i) F_i - (1 + \gamma_i) V_i}{1 + \gamma_{i-1}}. \qquad (5.13)$$

If $i < n$, then for C^1 continuity at F_{i+1}, impose the constraints $P^{(1)}(t_{i+1}^-) = P^{(1)}(t_{i+1}^+)$ to find

$$V_{i+1} = \frac{(2 + \gamma_i + \gamma_{i+1}) F_{i+1} - (1 + \gamma_i) W_i}{1 + \gamma_{i+1}}. \qquad (5.14)$$

5.5.2 *Circular Spline*

For the G^1 circular spline, see Figure 5.10, consider:

$$\gamma_i = 2\cos\phi, \qquad (5.15)$$

where ϕ is the angle between $F_{i+1} - F_i$ and $U_i - F_i$. Let T_i be the unit vector along D_i, and U_i, the point of intersection of tangent vectors at F_i and F_{i+1}. Then, we have:

$$U_i = F_i + \mu_i T_i, \qquad (5.16)$$

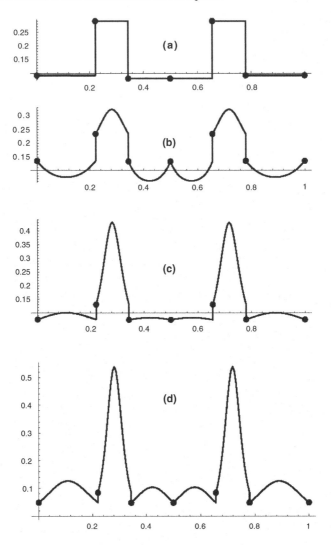

FIGURE 5.9. Curvature plots of Figure 5.8: (a) circular spline, (b) elliptic spline, (c) parabolic spline, (d) hyperbolic spline.

where μ_i is determined by the condition:

$$|U_i - F_i| = |U_i - F_{i+1}|, \tag{5.17}$$

which yields the following:

$$\mu_i = \frac{(F_{i+1} - F_i)^2}{2\,(F_{i+1} - F_i)\cdot T_i}. \tag{5.18}$$

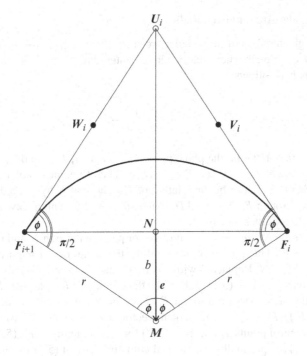

FIGURE 5.10. Bézier points of a circular arc.

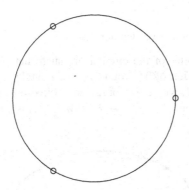

FIGURE 5.11. A three-point circle given in rational cubic Bézier form.

The circular spline, thus obtained, has been shown in Figure 5.7(a). Figure 5.11 shows a three-point exact circle.

5.5.3 Circular Arc

This section is devoted to the construction of a circular arc. The cases for a given radius and given center are discussed independently.

5.5.3.1   Circular Arc for Given Radius

Let r be the given radius of the circular arc such that $r > (|F_{i+1} - F_i|)/2$. Then, the center M can lie anywhere on the circle centered at $N = (F_i + F_{i+1})/2$ and having radius b as follows:

$$b = \sqrt{r^2 - \frac{|F_{i+1} - F_i|^2}{4}}. \tag{5.19}$$

It is preferred that M lie on the plane passing through F_i, F_{i+1} and $\acute{U}_i$, where $\acute{U}_i$ is the intersection of $F_i - D_i$ and $F_{i+1} - D_{i+1}$. Therefore, the circular arc should lie on the side of $\acute{U}_i$. Let e_1 be the rotation of F_{i+1} around N by an angle θ on the plane passing through F_i, F_{i+1} and $\acute{U}_i$, where $\theta = \pi/2$ for anticlockwise rotation and $\theta = -\pi/2$ for clockwise rotation.

Now, $e = (e_1 - N)/|e_1 - N|$ is a unit vector passing through N and perpendicular to $F_{i+1} - F_i$. Then, $M = N + be$ will be the center of our required circular arc. Let $\phi = \angle F_i M N$. Replace ϕ with $-\phi$ if circular arc rotation is anticlockwise. Next, one can find γ_i from (5.15). Let T' be the rotation of F_{i+1} around F_i through angle ϕ on the plane passing through F_i, F_{i+1} and $\acute{U}_i$ from which one can have $T_i = (T' - F_i)/|T' - F_i|$, a unit tangent vector at F_i. Now use (5.16) to find U_i, (5.5) to find control points V_i and W_i, (5.13) for C^1 continuity at F_i, (5.14) for C^1 continuity at F_{i+1} and finally use rational cubic interpolant (5.3) for the required circular arc. In this scheme, the radius r can be used as a shape control parameter demonstrated in Figure 5.12.

5.5.3.2   Circular Arc for a Given Center

Let M be the given center of the circular arc such that $|F_{i+1} - M| = |F_i - M|$. Let M' be the rotation of M around F_i by an angle θ on the plane passing through F_i, F_{i+1} and M, where $\theta = \pi/2$ for clockwise rotation and $\theta = -\pi/2$ for anticlockwise rotation. $T_i = (M' - F_i)/|M' - F_i|$ is a unit tangent vector at

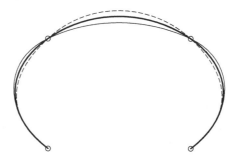

FIGURE 5.12. Rational cubic spline with a mid-interval as a circular arc piece for radius $r = 15$ (dashed), 18 (bold), 24 (normal).

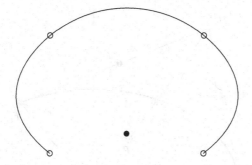

FIGURE 5.13. Rational cubic spline with mid-interval as a circular arc piece for a given center.

F_i. Let ϕ be the angle between $F_{i+1} - F_i$ and T_i. Now use (5.15) to find γ_i, (5.16) to find U_i, (5.5) to find control points V_i and W_i, (5.13) for C^1 continuity at F_i, (5.14) for C^1 continuity at F_{i+1} and finally use rational the cubic interpolant (5.3) for required circular arc. Figure 5.13 shows the plot of C-type rational cubic spline with the mid-segment as a circular arc. The center of this circular arc is shown as small disk where given data is shown as small circles.

5.5.4 Elliptic Arc

This section is devoted to the construction of an elliptic arc in three dimension. Very complicated cases have also been treated, e.g., when the major axis becomes much larger than the minor axis and the required elliptic arc consists of the highest curvature part of the ellipse.

Given a start point F_i, end point F_{i+1}, center M, unit vector along major axis X, unit vector along minor axis Y, semi-major axis a and semi-minor axis b (see Figure 5.14), XMY is a local coordinate system in space. Let $\theta_s = \angle XMF_i$ and $\theta_e = \angle XMF_{i+1}$. If necessary, use the Newton-Raphson method to compute θ_s and θ_e. If $\theta_s > \theta_e$, replace θ_s with $\theta_s - 2\pi$. $S(= M + a\cos\theta X + b\sin\theta Y)$ a point on an elliptic arc, where $\theta = (\theta_s + \theta_e)/2$. Let U_i be the point of intersection of tangents $T_0(= -a\sin\theta_s X + b\cos\theta_s Y)$ and $T_1(= -a\sin\theta_e X + b\cos\theta_e Y)$ at F_i and F_{i+1} respectively. Let R be the point of intersection of $S - U_i$ and $F_{i+1} - F_i$. The quadratic rational Bézier arc (5.2) can be written in the form:

$$Q(u) = \frac{(1-u)^2 F_i + u(1-u)\gamma_i U_i + u^2 F_{i+1}}{(1-u)^2 + u(1-u)\gamma_i + u^2}. \tag{5.20}$$

Now the line $L(u) = [F_i, F_{i+1}]$ is obtained by taking $\gamma_i = 0$. Therefore,

$$L(u) = \frac{(1-u)^2 F_i + u^2 F_{i+1}}{(1-u)^2 + u^2}, \tag{5.21}$$

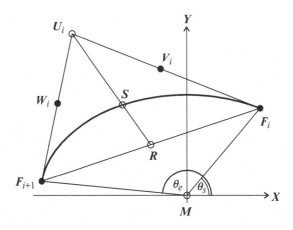

FIGURE 5.14. Bézier points of an elliptic arc.

which is convex combination of F_i and F_{i+1} and

$$\frac{|R - F_i|}{|R - F_{i+1}|} = \frac{u^2}{1 - u^2}. \tag{5.22}$$

Then $u = c/(1 + c)$, where

$$c = \sqrt{\frac{|R - F_i|}{|R - F_{i+1}|}}. \tag{5.23}$$

Therefore, $Q(u) = S$ and from (5.20), we can easily find

$$\gamma_i = \frac{1}{u(1 - u)|U_i - S|} \times \left\{ (1 - u)^2 (S - F_i) + u^2 (S - F_{i+1}) \right\} (U_i - S). \tag{5.24}$$

Now use (5.5) to find control points V_i and W_i and rational cubic interpolant (5.3) for the required elliptic arc. A demonstration of a four-point ellipse is given (see Figure 5.15) in rational cubic Bézier form. Figure 5.16 shows an elliptic arc in space that follows the given information:

$$a = 20, b = 1, M = (0, 0, 2),$$

$$F_i = (18.967819, -2.184863, 3.943775),$$

$$F_{i+1} = (-7.476452, 1.674027, 1.144135),$$

$$X = (0.990033, -0.099335, 2.099833),$$

$$Y = (0.109252, 0.989038, 1.900665).$$

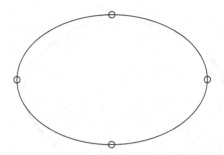

FIGURE 5.15. A four-point ellipse given in rational cubic Bézier form.

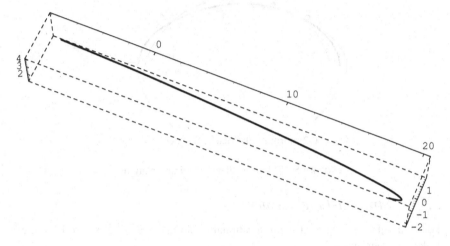

FIGURE 5.16. An elliptic arc in space.

5.5.5 Intermediate Point Interpolation

For the intermediate point interpolation, we need to insert point C between F_i and F_{i+1} while preserving some reasonable continuity (C^1) at F_i and F_{i+1}. Consider:

$$U_i = \frac{1}{u(1-u)\gamma_i} \left[\left\{ (1-u)^2 + u(1-u)\gamma_i + u^2 \right\} C - (1-u)^2 F_i - u^2 F_{i+1} \right],$$

where

$$u = \frac{|F_i - C|}{|F_i - C| + |F_{i+1} - C|}. \tag{5.25}$$

Next, use (5.5) to find control points V_i and W_i, (5.13) for C^1 continuity at F_i, (5.14) for C^1 continuity at F_{i+1}. Finally, use the rational cubic interpolant (5.3) for the required result. Figure 5.17(a) shows an intermediate point interpolation in the middle segment where the curve is forced to pass through different small disks.

The parameter u can also be used as a shape control parameter within the range $0 < u < 1$. For different values of u, one can construct a family of curves interpolating C (small disk) as shown in Figure 5.17(b).

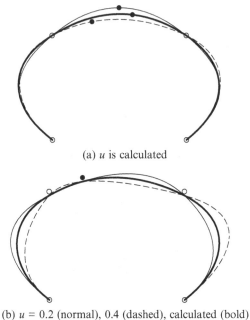

(a) u is calculated

(b) $u = 0.2$ (normal), 0.4 (dashed), calculated (bold)

FIGURE 5.17. Intermediate point interpolation.

5.5.6 Straight-Line Segment

For a straight-line segment using a rational cubic interpolant (5.3), we have the following four methods:

1. Consider $\gamma_i = 0$.
2. Replace U_i with F_i or F_{i+1} and then use (5.5) to find control points V_i and W_i.
3. Use an intermediate point interpolation scheme by inserting point C on the line joining F_i and F_{i+1}.
4. Consider $\gamma_i = \alpha_i + \beta_1$; then find control points V_i and W_i from (5.4).

5.6 Examples

Data taken from a Times New Roman font "S" has been interpolated by a default rational cubic spline in Figure 5.18(a). It is not as desired. Point and interval tension parameters are changed to achieve visually pleasing shape for font "S" in Figure 5.18(b).

Figures 5.19–5.22 illustrate the design of a rational cubic spline used for a surface of revolution that represents a cup, lamp, bowling pin and vase. Figures 5.19(a)–5.22(a), are the default shapes with exact derivatives and use default values of shape parameters, i.e., $\gamma_i = 2$. Figures 5.19(b)–5.21(b), are also exact derivatives, whereas Figure 5.22(b) is plotted with distance-based approximated derivatives.

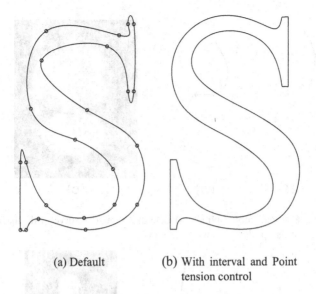

(a) Default

(b) With interval and Point
tension control

FIGURE 5.18. Times New Roman font "S" with rational cubic spline interpolation.

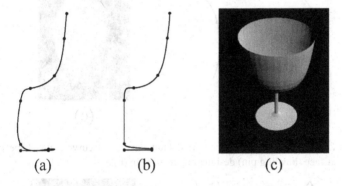

(a)   (b)   (c)

FIGURE 5.19. Rational cubic spline: (a) default curve, (b) curve with shape control, (c)
shaded surface (cup) designed with curve in (b).

To make these figures well-shaped and pleasing, we use shape control parameters
and insert some conic or straight-line segments connected by C^1 continuity with
the neighborhood cubic segments.

   Further details about Figures 5.19–5.22 are as follows. In Figure 5.19(b), $\gamma_1 =$
100, $\gamma_3 = 10$ and $\gamma_4 = 100$ from the bottom. The second segment is a circular
arc. All other segments are cubics connected by C^2 continuity and use default
values of shape parameters. In Figure 5.20(b) (from bottom), $\gamma_1 = 100$, $\gamma_3 =$
100, $\gamma_5 = 100$, $\gamma_6 = 0.1$ and $\gamma_7 = 100$. The second segment is a circular arc
with radius 15. All other segments are cubics connected by C^2 continuity and use
default values of shape parameters. In Figure 5.21(h) (from top), the first segment
is a circular arc with radius 8; the second to last is a conic; and the last one is

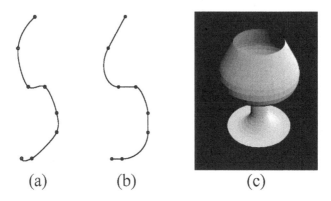

FIGURE 5.20. Rational cubic spline: (a) default curve, (b) curve with shape control, (c) shaded surface (lamp) designed with curve in (b).

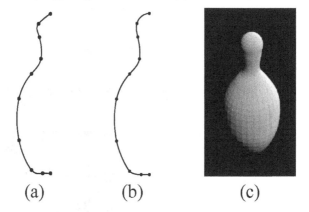

FIGURE 5.21. Rational cubic spline: (a) default curve, (b) curve with shape control, (c) shaded surface (bowling pin) designed with curve in (b).

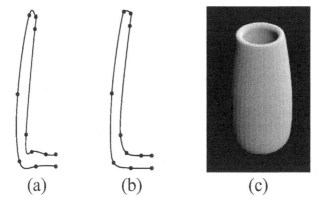

FIGURE 5.22. Rational cubic spline: (a) default curve, (b) curve with shape control, (c) shaded surface (vase) designed with curve in (b).

a straight line. All other segments are cubic connected by C^2 continuity and use default values of shape parameters. Figure 5.22(k) (from bottom) is taken with $\gamma_1 = 200$, $\gamma_7 = 0.01$, $\gamma_{n-1} = 100$. The fifth segment is a circular arc. All other segments are cubics connected by C^1 continuity and use default values of shape parameters.

5.7 Summary

This chapter has described an interval-controlled rational cubic interpolation scheme. The scheme offers a number of possible ways in which the shape of the corresponding curves may be altered by the users. Such a scheme can be a useful addition to an interactive design package, with the user having enough control over the curve segments. The provision of the shape parameters, in the description of the piecewise rational functions, provides the freedom to modify the shape in the desired regions in a stable manner. The rational spline scheme is meant for parametric curves and is capable of designing plane as well as space curves. It is an interpolatory rational spline scheme enjoying all the ideal geometric properties. It has features to produce all types of conic curves in such a way that the whole design curve may be produced as a circular, elliptic, parabolic, or a hyperbolic spline curve. In addition, the desired conic pieces may also be fitted within the rational cubic spline. Overall smoothness of the rational cubic spline is C^2, whereas the conics are stitched with C^1 continuity. Linear segments can also fitted as part of the whole scheme. The curve scheme is extendable to surfaces.

5.8 Exercises

1. Show that, for the constraints, $\alpha_I > 0$, $\beta_I > 0$ and $\gamma_i > -\alpha_i, -\beta_i, \forall i$, the rational cubic (5.3) is characterized as a Bernstein-Bézier form.
2. Prove that the values of shape parameters as $\alpha_i = 1 = \beta_i$ and $\gamma_i = 2$ reduce the rational cubic (5.3) to the standard cubic Hermite form.
3. Prove that, for the constraints, $\alpha_I > 0$, $\beta_I > 0$ and $\gamma_i > -\alpha_i, -\beta_i, \forall i$, the rational cubic (5.3) lies in the convex hull of F_i, V_i, W_i, F_{i+1}.
4. Prove that, for the constraints, $\alpha_I > 0$, $\beta_I > 0$ and $\gamma_i > -\alpha_i, -\beta_i, \forall i$, the rational cubic (5.3) follows the variation diminishing property. That is, any straight line crossing the control polygon of F_i, V_i, W_i, F_{i+1} does not cross the curve more than its control polygon.
5. Write a program to implement the C^2 rational cubic spline scheme with exact derivatives.
6. Write a program to implement the C^1 rational cubic spline scheme with distance-based derivatives.
7. Implement the rational cubic spline in Exercises 5.8.5 and 5.8.6 with unit parameterization as well as chord length parameterization. How different would the two rational cubic curves look? Please test it for at least two example data.

8. Write a program to implement the rational cubic spline scheme with distance-based derivatives but resulting in an elliptic curve.
9. Write a program to implement the rational cubic spline scheme with distance-based derivatives but resulting in a hyperbolic curve.
10. Write a program to implement the rational cubic spline scheme with distance-based derivatives but resulting in a parabolic curve.
11. Write a program to implement the rational cubic spline scheme with distance-based derivatives but resulting in a curve with circular pieces.
12. Write a program for the C^2 rational cubic spline which, in addition to passing through the regular data points, can also pass through another desired data point(s) in some desired piece(s).
13. Derive the tridiagonal linear system of equations by imposing the constraints for C^2 continuity

$$P^{(2)}\left(t_i^-\right) = P^{(2)}\left(t_i^+\right), i = 2, 3, \ldots, n-1$$

on rational cubic function $P(t)$ in (5.3) with control points in (5.5).
14. Write a program to solve the tridiagonal linear system of equations in Exercise 5.8.13 by LU-factorization to find the values of exact derivatives D_i, $i = 2, \ldots, n-1$ by estimation of appropriate end derivatives.
15. Write an algorithm to implement the rational cubic spline scheme for closed data.
16. Find the equation in (5.15) for the quadratic rational function $Q(t)$ to be a circular arc with condition in (5.17).
17. Derive the formula for intermediate point interpolation in Section 5.5 to find the value of U_i.
18. Write a program to implement the elliptic arc in three dimensions by using given data in Section 5.5.
19. Prove the fact that the presented spline scheme, in this chapter, has C^2 continuity between the rational cubic arcs and C^1 continuity between cubic and conic arcs.
20. Show, by practical implementation of Exercise 5.8.5, that the scheme is local, i.e., shape control parameters will not significantly affect the adjacent parts of the design curve.
21. Implement Exercises 5.8.5–5.8.8 to show that all these methods are suitable for space curves and hence can also be generalized to surfaces.

References

1. Farin, G. (1995), *NURB Curves and Surfaces*, A.K. Peters.
2. Gregory, J.A., and Sarfraz, M. (1990), A rational spline with tension, *Comput Aided Geom Design*, 7, 1–13.
3. Habib, Z., and Sarfraz, M. (2001), A rational cubic spline for the visualization of convex data, *The Proceedings of IEEE International Conference on Information Visualization-IV'01-UK*, IEEE Computer Society Press, pp. 744–748.
4. Hoschek, J. (1992), Circular splines, *Comput Aided Design*, 24, 611–618.

5. Jamaludin, M.A., Said, H.B., and Majid, A. (1995), Shape control of parametric cubic curves, *The Proceedings of CAD/Graphics'95*, China, SPIE Proceedings Series, Vol. 2644, pp. 128–133.

6. Meek, D.S., Ong, B., and Walton, D.J. (2003), A constrained guided G^1 continuous spline curve, *Comput Aided Design*, 35, 591–599.

7. Piegl, L., and Tiller, W. (1995), *The NURBS Book*, Springer-Verlag, New York.

8. Sarfraz, M. (1995), Curves and surfaces for CAD using C2 rational cubic splines, *Eng Comput* 11 (2), 94–102.

9. Sarfraz, M. (2003), Optimal curve fitting to digital data, *Int J WSCG*, 11 (1), 128–135.

10. Sarfraz, M., and Habib, Z. (2000), Rational cubic and conic representation: a practical approach, *IIUM Eng J*, Malaysia, 1 (2), 7–15.

11. Sarfraz, M., Habib, Z., and Hussain, M. (1998), Piecewise interpolation for designing of parametric curves, *The Proceedings of IEEE International Conference on Information Visualization-IV'98-UK*, IEEE Computer Society Press, pp. 307–313.

12. Sarfraz, M., Hussain, M., and Habib, Z. (1997), Local convexity preserving rational cubic spline curves, *The Proceedings of IEEE International Conference on Information Visualization-IV'97-UK*, IEEE Computer Society Press, pp. 211–218.

13. Sarfraz, M. and Khan, M. (2002), Automatic outline capture of Arabic fonts, *Int J Information Sci*, Elsevier Science, 140 (3–4), 269–281.

14. Habib, Z., Sakai, M., and Sarfraz, M. (2004), Interactive shape control with rational cubic splines, *Int J Comput Aided Design Appl*, 1(1–4), 709–718.

6

Shape-Preserving Rational Interpolation for Planar Curves

Abstract. *Data visualization is an important issue in information visualization. In specific applications, data may have different shapes when occurring in scientific phenomena or in some other perspective. A simple application may be when data is globally monotone or convex. Representing data in a visually meaningful and computationally efficient way is a significant topic to consider. This chapter deals with such situations using the piecewise rational cubic interpolant of Section 3.3. For simplicity, the shape parameters introduced in each interval have been constrained to solve the problem of shape-preserving interpolation for planer curves. Scalar curves are also considered as a special case, but they are discussed in detail in Chapters 7 and 8.*

6.1 Introduction

Many authors work in the area of representing shape-preserving curves for shaped data. For brevity, the reader is referred to [1–23]. This chapter uses the piecewise rational cubic interpolant of Section 3.3, where only one shape parameter is introduced in each interval, to solve the problem of shape-preserving interpolation for plane curves. The scalar curves are also considered as a special case, but their detailed versions have been discussed in details in Chapters 7 and 8. The results derived here are actually the extensions of the results of Delbourgo and Gregory [4] who developed a C^1 shape-preserving interpolation scheme for scalar curves using the same piecewise rational function. They derived the constraints, on the shape parameters occurring in the rational function under discussion, to make the interpolant preserve the monotonic and/or convex shape of the data.

This chapter begins with some preliminaries about the rational cubic interpolant. The constraints with convex and/or monotonic data are derived in Sections 6.3, 6.4 and 6.5. These constraints depend on the tangent vectors. The description of the tangent vectors, which are consistent and dependent on the given data, is made in Section 6.6. The shape-preserving results are explained with examples in Section 6.7.

6.2   The Rational Cubic Interpolant

Let $F_i \in R^2, i = 0, 1, 2, \ldots, n$ be a given set of data points, where $t_0 < t_1 < \ldots < t_n$. We consider the C^1 piecewise rational cubic interpolant as follows:

$$p(t) = \frac{(1 - \theta) f_i + \theta(1 - \theta)^2 (r_i F_i + h_i D_i) + \theta^2(1 - \theta)(r_i F_{i+1} - h_i D_{i+1}) + \theta^3 F_{i+1}}{1 + (r_i - 3)\theta(1 - \theta)},$$
(6.1)

which was discussed in Section 3.3. We use this to generate an interpolatory planar curve that preserves the shape of the data. Let

$$\left. \begin{array}{l} p(t) = (p_1(t), p_2(t)), \\ F_i = (x_i, y_i), \\ D_i = \left(D_i^x, D_i^y \right), \\ \Delta_i = \left(\Delta_i^x, \Delta_i^y \right), \end{array} \right\}$$
(6.2)

where

$$\Delta_i^x = \frac{(x_{i+1} - x_i)}{h_i}, \ \Delta_i^y = \frac{(y_{i+1} - y_i)}{h_i},$$

and D_i denotes the tangent vector to the curve at the knot t_i. It can be noted that $p(t)$ interpolates the points F_i and the tangent vectors D_i at the knots t_i.

The parameter r_i is to be chosen such that $r_i > -1$, which ensures a strictly positive denominator in the rational cubic. For our purposes r_i, will be chosen to ensure that the interpolant preserves the shape of the data. This choice requires the knowledge of $p^{(1)}(t)$ and $p^{(2)}(t)$ which are as follows.

$$p^1(t) = \frac{(1 - \theta)^4 D_i + \alpha_{1,i}\theta(1 - \theta)^3 + \alpha_{2,i}\theta^2(1 - \theta)^2 + \alpha_{3,i}\theta^3(1 - \theta) + D_{i+1}\theta^4}{\{1 + (r_i - 3)\theta(1 - \theta)\}^2},$$
(6.3)

$$p^2(t) = \frac{2\{\alpha_{4,i}(1 - \theta)^3 + \alpha_{5,i}\theta(1 - \theta)^2 + \alpha_{6,i}\theta^2(1 - \theta) + \alpha_{7,i}\theta^3\}}{h_i\{1 + (r_i - 3)\theta(1 - \theta)\}^3},$$
(6.4)

where

$$\left. \begin{array}{l} \alpha_{1,i} = 2(r_i \Delta_i - D_{i+1}), \\ \alpha_{2,i} = (r_i^2 + 3)\Delta_i - r_i(D_i + D_{i+1}), \\ \alpha_{3,i} = 2(r_i \Delta_i - D_i), \\ \alpha_{4,i} = 2r_i(\Delta_i - D_i) - D_{i+1} + D_i, \\ \alpha_{5,i} = 3(\Delta_i - D_i), \\ \alpha_{6,i} = 3(D_{i+1} - \Delta_i), \\ \alpha_{7,i} = r_i(D_{i+1} - \Delta_i) - D_{i+1} + D_i \end{array} \right\}$$
(6.5)

and we denote

$$\alpha_{j,i} = (\alpha_{j,i}^x, \alpha_{j,i}^y).$$
(6.6)

6.3   Interpolation of Convex Data

We assume a strictly locally convex set of data so that

$$\Delta_i = a_i \Delta_{i-1} + b_i \Delta_{i+1}, i = 1, 2, \ldots, n - 2, \tag{6.7a}$$

or equivalently the vectors

$$\Delta_i \times \Delta_{i+1}, i = 1, 2, \ldots, n - 2, \tag{6.7b}$$

must be in the same directions. To have a convex interpolant $p(t)$ and to avoid the possibility of $p(t)$ having straight line segments, it is necessary that the tangent vectors should satisfy the following constraints:

$$\Delta_i = a_i \Delta_{i-1} + b_i \Delta_i, i = 1, 2, \ldots, n - 1, c_i, d_i > 0, \tag{6.8a}$$

with appropriate end conditions D_0 and D_n. Or, equivalently the following vectors

$$D_i \times \Delta_i, \Delta_i \times D_{i+1}, \Delta_i \times \Delta_{i+1}, \tag{6.8b}$$

must be in the same direction $\forall i$. Thus if

$$\left.\begin{aligned}
\beta_{1,i} &= \Delta_i^x \Delta_{i+1}^y - \Delta_i^y \Delta_{i+1}^x, \\
\beta_{2,i} &= D_i^x \Delta_i^y - D_i^y \Delta_i^x, \\
\beta_{3,i} &= \Delta_i^x D_{i+1}^y - \Delta_i^y D_{i+1}^x, \\
\beta_{4,i} &= D_i^x D_{i+1}^y - D_i^y D_{i+1}^x,
\end{aligned}\right\} \tag{6.9}$$

then we immediately have the following:

Lemma 6.1.   The conditions (6.7) and (6.8) imply that

$$\beta_{j,i}, j = 1, \ldots, 4, i = 0, 1, \ldots, n - 1,$$

must be of the same sign.

Now assume without loss of generality that the data is consistent with a convex curve with positive curvature. Then by, Lemma 6.1, we must have

$$\beta_{j,i} > 0, j = 1, \ldots, 4, i = 0, 1, \ldots, n - 1. \tag{6.10}$$

Moreover, $p(t)$ is convex, with positive curvature if and only if

$$p_1^{(1)}(t) p_2^{(2)}(t) - p_1^{(2)}(t) p_2^{(1)}(t) > 0, \tag{6.11}$$

for all $t \in [t_0, t_n]$ (The case of the negative curvature can be treated in a similar way when the inequality is reversed.) After some simplifications using (6.2)–(6.6), it can be shown that for $t \in [t_i, t_{i+1}]$,

$$p_1^{(1)}(t) p_2^{(2)}(t) - p_1^{(2)}(t) p_2^{(1)}(t) = \frac{2 \sum_{j=1}^{8} \gamma_{j,i}(1 - \theta)^{j-1}\theta^{8-j}}{h_i \{1 + (r_i - 3)\theta(1 - \theta)\}^5}, \tag{6.12}$$

where

$$
\begin{aligned}
\gamma_{1,i} &= (r_i \beta_{3,i} - \beta_{4,i}), \\
\gamma_{2,i} &= 2(r_i - 1)(r_i \beta_{3,i} - \beta_{4,i}) + 3\beta_{3,i}, \\
\gamma_{3,i} &= 3\beta_{2,i} + 6(r_i - 1)\beta_{3,i} + [(r_i - 1)^2 + 2](r_i \beta_{3,i} - \beta_{4,i}), \\
\gamma_{4,i} &= (7r_i - 6)\beta_{2,i} + [r^2_i + 2(r_i - 2)^2 + r_i + 1]\beta_{3,i} + (2r_i - 1)(r_i \beta_{3,i} - \beta_{4,i}), \\
\gamma_{5,i} &= (7r_i - 6)\beta_{3,i} + [r^2_i + 2(r_i - 2)^2 + r_i + 1]\beta_{2,i} + (2r_i - 1)(r_i \beta_{2,i} - \beta_{4,i}), \\
\gamma_{6,i} &= 3\beta_{3,i} + 6(r_i - 1)\beta_{2,i} + [(r_i - 1)^2 + 2](r_i \beta_{2,i} - \beta_{4,i}), \\
\gamma_{7,i} &= 2(r_i - 1)(r_i \beta_{2,i} - \beta_{4,i}) + 3\beta_{2,i}, \\
\gamma_{8,i} &= (r_i \beta_{2,i} - \beta_{4,i}).
\end{aligned}
\tag{6.13}
$$

Thus, from (6.12), necessary conditions for convexity are

$$
\gamma_{1,i} > 0 \quad \text{and} \quad \gamma_{8,i} > 0
\tag{6.14a}
$$

The sufficient conditions for convexity are

$$
\gamma_{j,i} > 0, j = 2, \dots, 7.
\tag{6.14b}
$$

and a sufficient condition for (6.14b) together with conditions (6.14a), is

$$
r_i \geq \max \left\{ 1, \frac{\beta_{4,i}}{\beta_{2,i}}, \frac{\beta_{4,i}}{\beta_{3,i}} \right\}.
\tag{6.15}
$$

A number of choices of r_i can be adopted for graphical demonstration. It has been found that if

$$
M_i = \max \left\{ \frac{\beta_{4,i}}{\beta_{2,i}}, \frac{\beta_{4,i}}{\beta_{3,i}} \right\} \text{ and } m_i = \min \left\{ \frac{\beta_{4,i}}{\beta_{2,i}}, \frac{\beta_{4,i}}{\beta_{3,i}} \right\},
$$

the choice

$$
r_i = 1 + \left(1 + \frac{M_i}{2} \right)^2 + \left(1 + \frac{m_i}{2} \right)^2,
\tag{6.16}
$$

satisfies (6.15) and produces pleasing graphical results.

Remark 6.2.

(a) It follows immediately that the choice of r_i in (6.16) is such that $r_i > 1$.
(b) A strictly convex data set has been assumed so far. Otherwise, if $\Delta_i = \Delta_{i+1}$ for some i, i.e., F_i, F_{i+1} and F_{i+2} are collinear, then $p(t)$ must be linear on $[t_i, t_{i+1}]$. Thus we must have $D_j = D_{j+1} = \Delta_j$ on $[t_j, t_{j+1}], j = i, I+1$ and the rational cubic then reduces to the straight-line segment.

$$
p(t) = (1 - \theta)F_j + \theta F_{j+1}, j = i, I + 1.
$$

6.4   Interpolation of Monotonic Data

Let us assume for simplicity that

$$
\Delta^x_i \neq 0, i = 0, \dots, n - 1,
\tag{6.17}
$$

and that the data is monotonic increasing and arises from a function. Then we must have

$$\frac{\Delta_i^y}{\Delta_i^x} \geq 0, i = 0, \ldots, n - 1, \tag{6.18}$$

i.e., Δ_i^x and Δ_i^y are of the same sign. The case of a monotonic decreasing set of data can be treated in a similar manner when the inequalities are reversed. The necessary conditions for the interpolant $p(t)$ to be monotonic are then the following:

$$\frac{D_i^y}{D_i^x} \geq 0, i = 0, \ldots, n - 1, \tag{6.19}$$

i.e., D_i^x and D_i^y are of the same sign. We also note that D_i^x and D_i^y must have the same sign as Δ_i^x and Δ_i^y, respectively. Thus we have the following:

$$\left.\begin{array}{l} \Delta_i^x \Delta_i^y, D_i^x D_i^y \geq 0, \\ D_i^x \Delta_i^y, D_i^y \Delta_i^x \geq 0, \\ \Delta_i^x D_{i+1}^y, \Delta_i^y D_{i+1}^x \geq 0, \end{array}\right\} \tag{6.20}$$

for $i = 0, \ldots, n - 1$.

Remark 6.3. Let

$$\left.\begin{array}{l} \hat{\beta}_{1,i} = \Delta_i^x \Delta_i^y, \\ \hat{\beta}_{2,i} = D_i^x \Delta_i^y + \Delta_i^x D_i^y, \\ \hat{\beta}_{3,i} = \Delta_i^x D_{i+1}^y + \Delta_i^y D_{i+1}^x, \\ \hat{\beta}_{4,i} = D_i^x D_{i+1}^y + D_i^y D_{i+1}^x, \\ \hat{\beta}_{5,i} = D_i^x D_i^y. \end{array}\right\}, \tag{6.21}$$

Then it follows from (6.20) that

$$\hat{\beta}_{j,i} \geq 0, j = 1, \ldots, 5, i = 0, \ldots, n - 1. \tag{6.22}$$

Now $p(t)$ is monotonic increasing if and only if

$$\frac{p_2^{(1)}(t)}{p_1^{(1)}(t)} \geq 0, \forall t \in [t_0, t_n]. \tag{6.23}$$

i.e., $p_1^{(1)}(t)$ and $p_2^{(1)}(t)$ are of the same sign. Thus, (6.23) can be equivalently written as

$$p_1^{(1)}(t) p_2^{(1)}(t), t \in [t_0, t_n]. \tag{6.24}$$

After some simplifications, using (6.2)–(6.6), it can be shown that for $t \in [t_i, t_{i+1}]$,

$$p_1^{(1)}(t) p_2^{(1)}(t) = \frac{\sum_{j=1}^{9} \hat{\gamma}_{j,1}(1 - \theta)^{9-j}\theta^{j-1}}{\{1 + (r_{i-3})\theta(1 - \theta)\}^4}, \tag{6.25}$$

where

$$
\left.
\begin{aligned}
\hat{\gamma}_{1,i} &= D_i^x D_i^y, \\
\hat{\gamma}_{2,i} &= D_i^x \alpha_{1,i}^y + \alpha_{1,i}^x D_i^y = 2r_i \hat{\beta}_{2,i} - 2\hat{\beta}_{4,i}, \\
\hat{\gamma}_{3,i} &= D_i^x \alpha_{2,i}^y + \alpha_{1,i}^x \alpha_{1,i}^y + \alpha_{2,i}^x D_i^y, \\
\hat{\gamma}_{4,i} &= D_i^x \alpha_{3,i}^y + \alpha_{1,i}^x \alpha_{2,i}^y + \alpha_{2,i}^x \alpha_{1,i}^y + \alpha_{3,i}^x D_i^y, \\
\hat{\gamma}_{5,i} &= D_i^x D_{i+1}^y + \alpha_{1,i}^x \alpha_{3,i}^y + \alpha_{2,i}^x \alpha_{2,i}^y + \alpha_{3,i}^x \alpha_{1,i}^y + D_{i+1}^x D_i^y, \\
\hat{\gamma}_{6,i} &= \alpha_{1,i}^x D_{i+1}^y + \alpha_{2,i}^x \alpha_{3,i}^y + \alpha_{3,i}^x \alpha_{2,i}^y + D_{i+1}^x \alpha_{1,i}^y, \\
\hat{\gamma}_{7,i} &= \alpha_{2,i}^x D_{i+1}^y + \alpha_{3,i}^x \alpha_{3,i}^y + D_{i+1}^x \alpha_{2,i}^y, \\
\hat{\gamma}_{8,i} &= \alpha_{3,i}^x D_{i+1}^y + D_{i+1}^x \alpha_{3,i}^y = 2r_i \hat{\beta}_{3,i} - 2\hat{\beta}_{4,i}, \\
\hat{\gamma}_{9,i} &= D_{i+1}^x D_{i+1}^y.
\end{aligned}
\right\}
\tag{6.26}
$$

The conditions

$$
D_j^x D_j^y \geq 0, \, j = i, i+1,
\tag{6.27}
$$

are necessary for the interpolant to be monotonic increasing on $[t_i, t_{i+1}]$ (see Lemma 6.3) and, assuming these necessary conditions, sufficient conditions are as follows:

$$
\hat{\gamma}_{j,i} \geq 0, \, j = 2, \ldots, 8.
\tag{6.28}
$$

It should be noted that if $\Delta_i^y = 0$, then $D_i^y = D_{i+1}^y = 0$ and hence $\hat{\beta}_{2,i} = \hat{\beta}_{3,i} = 0$. Moreover $p_2(t) = y_i$, $t_i \leq t \leq t_{i+1}$, therefore $p(t)$ is constant on $[t_i, t_{i+1}]$.

If $\Delta_i^y \neq 0$, then a sufficient condition for (6.28) is

$$
r_i \geq \max \left\{ \frac{D_i^x + D_{i+1}^x}{\Delta_i^x}, \frac{D_i^y + D_{i+1}^y}{\Delta_i^y} \right\},
\tag{6.29}
$$

Moreover, since

$$
\max \left\{ \frac{\hat{\beta}_{4,i}}{\hat{\beta}_{2,i}}, \frac{\hat{\beta}_{4,i}}{\hat{\beta}_{3,i}} \right\} \geq \max \left\{ \frac{D_i^x + D_{i+1}^x}{\Delta_i^x}, \frac{D_i^y + D_{i+1}^y}{\Delta_i^y} \right\},
\tag{6.30}
$$

the choice,

$$
r_i = \frac{\hat{\beta}_{4,i}(\hat{\beta}_{2,i} + \hat{\beta}_{3,i})}{\hat{\beta}_{2,i}\hat{\beta}_{3,i}},
\tag{6.31}
$$

satisfies (6.29) and provides nice graphical results.

Remark 6.4. As mentioned in Remark 2.3, the scalar case can be considered as an application of interpolation scheme $(t, p(t))$ in R^2 to the values $(t_i, F_i) \in R^2$ and derivatives $(1, D_i) \in R^2$, $i = 0, 1, \ldots, n$. It can also be noted that $\Delta_i = (1, \Delta_i)$. Therefore the convexity and monotonicity constraints, in this case are, respectively,

$$
r_i \geq \max \left\{ \frac{D_{i+1} - D_i}{\Delta_i - D_i}, \frac{D_{i+1} - D_i}{D_{i+1} - \Delta_i} \right\},
\tag{6.32}
$$

and

$$r_i \geq \max \left\{ 2, \frac{D_{i+1} + D_i}{\Delta_i} \right\},$$ (6.33)

which are same as in [4].

6.5 Interpolation of Convex and Monotonic Data

In this section we consider the possibility that together with a strict convexity condition, the data also satisfy a monotonicity condition. Let us assume for simplicity that the data satisfy (6.17) and the monotonicity condition (6.18). The inequalities

$$0 \leq \frac{D_0^y}{D_0^x} < \frac{\Delta_0^y}{\Delta_0^x} < \frac{D_1^y}{D_1^x} < \cdots < \frac{\Delta_{i-1}^y}{\Delta_{i-1}^x} < \frac{D_i^y}{D_i^x} < \frac{\Delta_i^y}{\Delta_i^x} < \cdots < \frac{D_n^y}{D_n^x},$$ (6.34)

then must be satisfied. Any convex interpolant must then also be monotonic. This result follows since

$$\frac{p_2^{(1)}(t)}{p_1^{(1)}(t)} = \int_{t_o}^{t} \frac{p_1^{(1)}(t) p_2^{(2)}(t) - p_1^{(2)}(t) p_2^{(1)}(t)}{(p_1^{(1)}(t))^2} dt + \frac{p_2^{(1)}(t_0)}{p_1^{(1)}(t_0)}$$

$$= \int_{t_o}^{t} \frac{p_1^{(1)}(t) p_2^{(2)}(t) - p_1^{(2)}(t) p_2^{(1)}(t)}{(p_1^{(1)}(t))^2} dt + \frac{D_0^y}{D_0^x}.$$

Hence $\frac{D_0^y}{D_0^x}$ and the convexity condition (6.11) imply that

$$\frac{p_2^{(1)}(t)}{p_1^{(1)}(t)} \geq 0, \forall t \in [t_0, t_n].$$ (6.35)

Moreover, for the data satisfying (6.34), it can be simply shown that

$$\max \left\{ \frac{\hat{\beta}_{4,i}}{\hat{\beta}_{2,i}}, \frac{\hat{\beta}_{4,i}}{\hat{\beta}_{3,i}} \right\} \geq \max \left\{ \frac{D_i^x + D_{i+1}^x}{\Delta_i^x}, \frac{D_i^y + D_{i+1}^y}{\Delta_i^y} \right\}.$$

Therefore, the convex interpolation method of the Section 6.2 is also suitable for the interpolation of convex and monotonic data, and the convexity condition (6.15) is sufficient to ensure that the monotonicity condition (6.29) is satisfied.

6.6 Choice of Tangent Vectors

In most applications, the tangent vectors D_i are not given and hence must be determined from the data $F_i \in R^2, i = 0, 1, \ldots, n$. Delbourgo and Gregory [4] have described arithmetic and geometric mean derivative choices for their convexity and convexity-/monotonicity-preserving scalar curves. Similar choices of tangent vectors can be defined for plane curves, which satisfy the shape-preserving conditions. The arithmetic mean choice of tangent vectors is

$$D_i = \lambda_i \Delta_{i-1} + (1 - \lambda_i) \Delta_i, i = 0, 1, \ldots, n - 1, \qquad (6.36a)$$

where

$$\lambda_i = \frac{h_i}{(h_{i-1} + h_i)}, \qquad (6.36b)$$

While if $p(t)$ is not closed, the tangents at the endpoints will be given as follows:

$$\left.\begin{aligned} D_0 &= \lambda_0 \Delta_0 + (1 - \lambda_0)\Delta_{2,0}, \\ D_n &= \lambda_n \Delta_{n-1} + (1 - \lambda_n)\Delta_{n,n-2}, \end{aligned}\right\} \qquad (6.36c)$$

where

$$\left.\begin{aligned} \lambda_0 &= 1 + \frac{h_0}{h_1}, \lambda_n = 1 + \frac{h_{n-1}}{h_{n-2}}, \\ \Delta_{2,0} &= \frac{F_2 - F_0}{t_2 - t_0}, \Delta_{n,n-2} = \frac{F_n - F_{n-2}}{t_n - t_{n-2}}. \end{aligned}\right\} \qquad (6.36d)$$

These arithmetic mean approximations are suitable for convex data since they satisfy the necessary conditions for convexity and produce pleasing graphical results.

The geometric means are defined as:

$$D_i = ((\Delta_{i-1}^x)^{\lambda_i}(\Delta_i^x)^{1-\lambda_i}, (\Delta_{i-1}^y)^{\lambda_i}(\Delta_i^y)^{1-\lambda_i}), i = 1, \ldots, n - 1, \qquad (6.37a)$$

with the end conditions

$$\left.\begin{aligned} D_0 &= ((\Delta_0^x)^{\lambda_0}(\Delta_{2,0}^x)^{1-\lambda_0}, (\Delta_0^y)^{\lambda_0}(\Delta_{2,0}^y)^{1-\lambda_i}), \\ D_n &= ((\Delta_{n-1}^x)^{\lambda_n}(\Delta_{n,n-2}^x)^{1-\lambda_n}, (\Delta_{n-1}^y)^{\lambda_n}(\Delta_{n,n-2}^y)^{1-\lambda_i}), \end{aligned}\right\} \qquad (6.37b)$$

where the choice of λ_i's is as given in (6.36b) and (6.36d). These approximations are suitable for the interpolation of the monotonic data. These approximations are also referred in the case when data is both monotonic and convex as they satisfy the corresponding necessary conditions.

6.7 Examples

Figures 6.1 and 6.2 demonstrate the convexity- and monotonicity-preserving results corresponding to the arithmetic and geometric derivative values, respectively; the first and second curves in each of these figures represent the scalar and parametric cubic spline-preserving interpolations. The shape-preserving results for the data, which are both monotonic and convex, are shown in Figure 6.3. Arithmetic derivative values are used in the second and fourth curves; the geometric mean choice of derivative values is considered in the third and sixth curves. The first three curves are scalar and the rest of them are parametric curves.

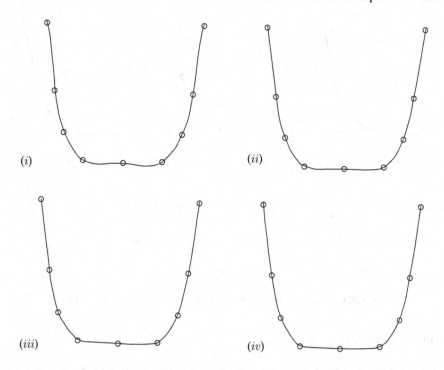

FIGURE 6.1. Convexity-preserving rational cubic interpolation.

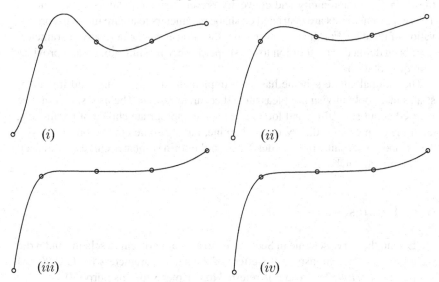

FIGURE 6.2. Monotonicity-preserving rational cubic interpolation.

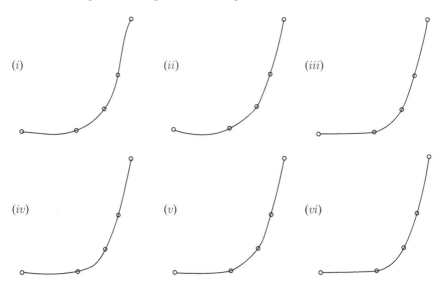

(i) $\qquad$ (ii) $\qquad$ (iii)

(iv) $\qquad$ (v) $\qquad$ (vi)

FIGURE 6.3. Convexity/monotonicity preserving rational cubic interpolation.

6.8   Summary

A rational cubic interpolant, with one family of shape parameters, has been utilized to obtain C^1 monotonicity and convexity-preserving interpolatory spline curves. The shape constraints are restricted on shape parameters to assure the shape preservation of the data. For the C^1 interpolant, the choices on the derivative parameters have been defined. The solution to the shape-preserving spline exists and provides a unique solution.

The rational spline scheme has been implemented successfully and it demonstrates nice looking visually pleasant and accurate results. The user should not be worried about struggling and looking for some appropriate choice of parameters, as in the case of an ordinary rational spline, having some control on the curves. The shape-preserving spline is described in the form of planer curves where as it is also implementable in the scalar case.

6.9   Exercises

1. Extend the curve scheme in Section 6.2 to a parametric curve scheme and write a program to demonstrate the effect of the shape parameters for CAD/CAM purposes. (*Hint*: The reader is referred to Chapter 3 for this purpose)
2. Extend the curve scheme in Section 6.2 to a parametric curve scheme such that it preserves the positive data.
3. Extend the curve scheme in Section 6.2 to a parametric curve scheme such that it preserves the positive and monotone data.

4. Extend the curve scheme in Section 6.2 to a parametric curve scheme such that it preserves the positive and convex data.

5. Extend the curve scheme in Section 6.2 to a parametric curve scheme such that it preserves the positive, monotone and convex data.

6. Write programs to visualize the results of the schemes in Exercises 6.9.1–6.9.5.

7. Extend the curve scheme in Section 6.2 to a C^2 curve scheme.

8. Extend the curve scheme in Section 6.3 to a C^2 curve scheme.

9. Extend the curve scheme in Section 6.4 to a C^2 curve scheme.

10. Extend the curve scheme in Section 6.5 to a C^2 curve scheme.

References

1. McAllister, D.F. and Roulier, J.A. (1981), An algorithm for computing a shape-preserving osculatory quadratic spline, *ACM Trans Math Software* 7, 331–347.

2. Passow, E., and Roulier, J.A. (1977), Monotone and convex spline interpolation. *SIAM J Num Anal* 14, 904–909.

3. Fritsch, F.N., and Carlson, R.E. (1980), Monotone piecewise cubic interpolation, *SIAM J Num Anal* 17, 238–246.

4. Gregory, J.A. (1986), Shape-preserving spline interpolation, *Computer-Aided Design*, 18(1), 53–57.

5. Fritsch, F.N., and Butland, J. (1984), A method for constructing local monotone piecewise cubic interpolants, *SIAM J Sc Stat Comput* 5, 303–304.

6. Schumaker, L.L. (1983), On shape-preserving quadratic spline interpolation, *SIAM J Num Anal* 20, 854–864.

7. Brodlie, K.W., and Butt, S. (1991), Preserving convexity using piecewise cubic interpolation, *Comput Graphics* 15, 15–23.

8. Butt, S., and Brodlie, K.W. (1993), Preserving positivity using piecewise cubic interpolation, *Comput Graphics* 17(1), 55–64.

9. Sarfraz, M. (1992), Convexity preserving piecewise rational interpolation for planar curves, *Bull Korean Math Soc* 29(2), 193–200.

10. Sarfraz, M. (1997), Preserving monotone shape of the data using piecewise rational cubic functions, *Comput Graphics* 21(1), 5–14.

11. Brodlie, K.W. (1985), Methods for drawing curves. In: *Fundamental Algorithm for Computer Graphics*, ed. R.A. Earnshaw, Springer-Verlag, Berlin, pp. 303–323.

12. DeVore, A., and Yan, Z. (1986), Error analysis for piecewise quadratic curve fitting algorithms, *Comp Aided Geom Design* 3, 205–215.

13. Greiner, K. (1991), A survey on univariate data interpolation and approximation by splines of given shape, *Math Comp Mod* 15, 97–106.

14. Constantini, P. (1997), boundary-valued shape preserving interpolating splines, *ACM Transactions on Mathematical Software*, 23(2), 229–251.

15. Lahtinen, A. (1996), Monotone interpolation with application to estimation of taper curves, *Ann Numer Math* 3, 151–161.

16. Sarfraz, M. (1992), Interpolatory rational cubic spline with biased, point and interval tension, *ComputGraphics*, 16(4), 427–430.

17. Moreton, H.P., and Sequin, C.H. (1995), *Minimum Variation Curves and Surfaces for Computer-Aided Geometric Design, Designing Fair Curves and Surfaces*, Nick Sapidis, ed., Proceedings of SIAM'94 Conference, pp, 123–159.

18. Sarfraz, M., Butt, S., and Hussain, M. Z. (2001), Visualization of shaped data by a rational cubic spline interpolation, *Int J Comput Graphics*, Elsevier Science, 25(5), 833–845.

19. Sarfraz, M. (2000), A rational cubic spline for the visualization of monotonic data, *Comput Graphics* 24(4), 509–516.

20. Sarfraz, M., and Hussain, M.Z. (2006), Data visualization using rational spline interpolation, *Int J Computational Appl Math*, Elsevier Science, 189(1–2), 513–525.

21. Sarfraz, M., Hussain, M.Z., and Chaudhry, F.S. (2005), shape-preserving cubic spline for data visualization, *Int J Comput Graphics CAD/CAM*, International Scientific, 1(6), 185–194.

22. Sarfraz, M. (2002), Visualization of positive and convex data by a rational cubic spline, *Int J Information Sci*, Elsevier Science, 146(1–4), 239–254.

23. Sarfraz, M. (2002), Modelling for the visualization of monotone data, *Int J Modelling Simulation*, ACTA Press, 22(3), 176–185.

7
Visualization of Shaped Data by a Rational Cubic Spline

Abstract. *A smooth curve interpolation scheme for positive, monotonic and convex data is described. This scheme uses piecewise rational cubic functions. The two families of parameters, in the description of the rational interpolant have been constrained to preserve the shape of the data. The rational spline scheme has a unique representation. In addition to preserving the shape of positive, monotonic and convex data sets, it also possesses extra features to modify the shape of the design curve when desired. The degree of smoothness attained is C^1.*

7.1 Introduction

Smooth curve representation, to visualize the scientific data, is of great significance in the area of computer graphics and in particular data visualization. Particularly, when the data is obtained from some complex function or from some scientific phenomena, it becomes crucial to incorporate the inherited features of the data. Moreover, smoothness is also one of the very important requirements for a pleasing visual display. Ordinary spline schemes, although smoother, are not helpful for the interpolation of the shaped data. Extremely misguided results, violating the inherited features of the data, can be seen when undesired oscillations occur. For example, for the positive data set in Table 7.1, the corresponding curve in Figure 7.1 is not as may be desired by the user for a positive data. The user would be interested in visualizing it as it is displayed in Figure 7.2. Thus, unwanted oscillations that completely destroy the data features need to be controlled. Another example is the monotonically increasing data set in Table 7.2. The corresponding traditional spline curve is shown in Figure 7.3, which has destroyed the features of monotonicity as may be desired corresponding to Figure 7.4. Similarly, a traditional spline curve in Figure 7.13 is not displaying the convex data in Table 7.10 such that the curve is also convex.

Interpolation is a fundamental process in scientific visualization. Smooth curve representation, to visualize the scientific data, is of great significance in various areas of scientific research including scientific visualization, computer graphics,

TABLE 7.1. Oxygen levels in the gas.

i	1	2	3	4	5	6	7
x_i	0	2	4	10	28	30	32
y_i	20.8	8.8	4.2	0.5	3.9	6.2	9.6

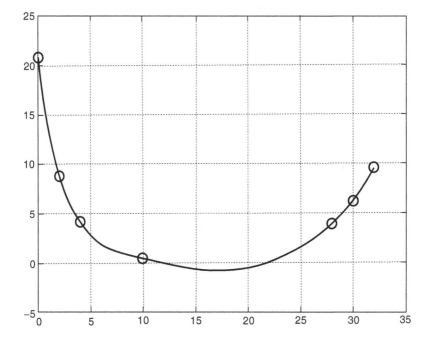

FIGURE 7.1. The default rational cubic spline for the positive data in Table 7.1.

geometric modeling, numerical analysis, approximation theory, and so on. Especially when the data arises from some complex function or from some scientific phenomena, it becomes crucial to incorporate the inherited features of the data. It gives an insight and guide to understanding some physical phenomenon pertaining to the data, which one would otherwise only have partial information about. It is an effective way of communication because it helps to represent the numeric data in a quickly understandable pictorial display.

If smoothness is one of the very important requirements for pleasing visual display of the data on one hand, the computational efficiency and accuracy are not less significant on the other hand. Ordinary spline schemes, although smoother, are not helpful for the interpolation of the shaped data. Severely misguided results, violating the inherited features of the data, are seen when undesired oscillations occur. Thus, unwanted oscillations, which may completely destroy the data features must be controlled.

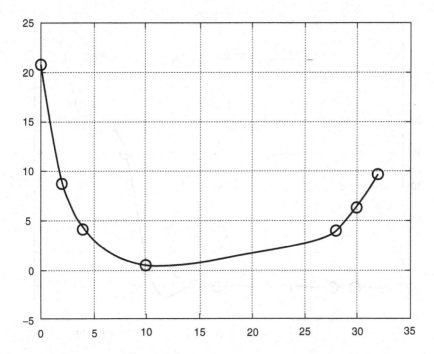

FIGURE 7.2. The default shape-preserving spline for the positive data in Table 7.1.

TABLE 7.2. Akima's data set.

i	1	2	3	4	5	6	7	8	9	10	11
x_i	0	2	3	5	6	8	9	11	12	14	15
y_i	10	10	10	10	10	10	10.5	15	30	60	85

This chapter examines the problem of shape preservation of data $(x_i, f_i), i = 1, 2, \ldots, n$, where x_i represents the data site and f_i is the data value at site x_i. Positivity, monotony and convexity are the basic and fundamental shapes, which normally arise in everyday scientific phenomena. These shapes are the targeted features here. As a first step, we generate an empirical model of the data to be visualized. As a second step, we construct a model curve that matches the data values at the location allowing no deviations. Afterwards, the model curve will be constrained to reflect a continuous visual display of the data.

Various authors have worked in the area of shape preservation [1–23]. In this chapter, the shape-preserving interpolation has been studied for positive, monotonic and convex data, using rational cubic splines. The motivation to this work is due to the past work of many authors, e.g., quadratic interpolation methodology has been adopted in [1, 15] for the shape-preserving curves. Fritsch and Carlson [3] and Fritsch and Butland [5] have discussed the piecewise cubic interpolation to monotonic data. Also, Passow and Roulier [2] considered the

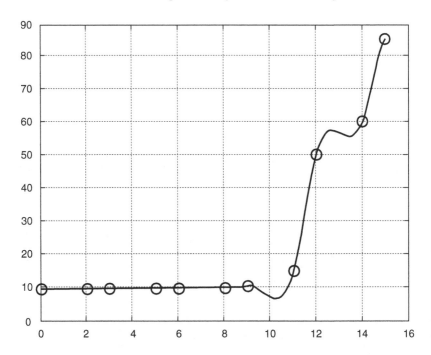

FIGURE 7.3. The default rational cubic spline for the monotonic data in Table 7.2.

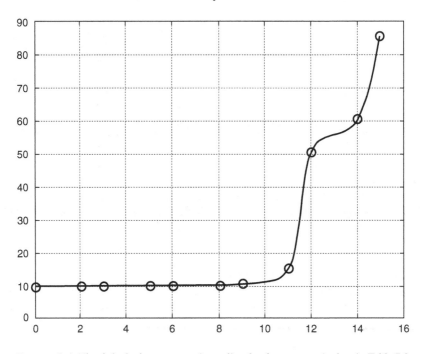

FIGURE 7.4. The default shape-preserving spline for the monotonic data in Table 7.2.

piecewise polynomial interpolation to monotonic and convex data. In particular, an algorithm for quadratic spline interpolation is given in McAllister and Roulier [1]. An alternative to the use of polynomials for the interpolation of monotonic and convex data is the application of piecewise rational quadratic and cubic functions by Gregory [4]. Rational functions have been discussed by Sarfraz [9] in a parametric context. Scalar representations of rational functions, in a more generalized and effective way, have been made in [18–23]. These representations mainly deal with the shape-preserving data visualization and are the main objective of the chapter.

The theory of methods, in this chapter, has a number of advantageous features. It produces C^1 interpolant. No additional points (knots) are needed. In contrast, the quadratic spline methods of Schumaker [6] and the cubic interpolation method of Brodlie and Butt [7] require the introduction of additional knots when used as shape-preserving methods. The interpolant is not concerned with an arbitrary degree as in [4]. It is a rational cubic with cubic numerator and cubic denominator. The rational spline curve representation is bounded and unique in its solution.

The chapter begins with a definition of the rational function in Section 7.2 where the description of rational cubic spline, which does not preserve the shape of positive and/or monotonic data, is made. Although this rational spline was discussed in Sarfraz [16], it was in the parametric context that it was useful for design applications. This section reviews it for the scalar representation so that it can be utilized to preserve the scalar-valued data. The positivity problem is discussed in Section 7.3 for the generation of a C^1 spline which can preserve the shape of a positive data. The sufficient constraints on the shape parameters have been derived to preserve and control the positive interpolant. The monotonicity problem is discussed in Section 7.4 for the generation of a C^1 spline which can preserve the shape of monotonic data. The sufficient constraints, in this section, lead to a monotonic spline solution. Section 7.5 discusses the scheme when a data set has convexity features. Section 7.6 concludes the chapter.

7.2   Rational Cubic Spline with Shape Control

Let $(x_i, f_i), i = 1, 2, \ldots, n$, be a given set of data points, where $x_1 < x_2 < \ldots < x_n$. Let

$$h_i = x_{i+1} - x_i, \quad \Delta_i = \frac{f_{i+1} - f_i}{h_i}, i = 1, 2, \ldots, n - 1. \qquad (7.1)$$

Consider the following piecewise rational cubic function:

$$s(x) \equiv s_i(x) = \frac{U_i(1 - \theta)^3 + v_i V_i \theta(1 - \theta)^2 + w_i W_i \theta^2(1 - \theta) + Z_i \theta^3}{(1 - \theta)^3 + v_i \theta(1 - \theta)^2 + w_i \theta^2(1 - \theta) + \theta^3}, \qquad (7.2)$$

where

$$\theta = \frac{x - x_i}{h_i}. \qquad (7.3)$$

To make the rational function (7.2) C^1, one needs to impose the following interpolatory properties:

$$s(x_i) = f_i, \quad s(x_{i+1}) = f_{i+1} \atop s^{(1)}(x_i) = d_i, \quad s^{(1)}(x_{i+1}) = d_{i+1} \Bigg\},$$ (7.4)

which provide the following manipulations:

$$U_i = f_i, \qquad Z_i = f_{i+1} \atop V_i = f_i + \dfrac{h_i d_i}{v_i}, \quad W_i = f_{i+1} - \dfrac{h_i d_{i+1}}{w_i} \Bigg\},$$ (7.5)

where $s^{(1)}$ denotes derivative with respect to x and d_i denotes derivative value given at the knot x_i. This leads the piecewise rational cubic (7.2) to the following piecewise Hermite interpolant $s \in C^1[x_1, x_n]$:

$$s(x) \equiv s_i(x) = \frac{P_i(\theta)}{Q_i(\theta)},$$ (7.6)

where

$$P_i(\theta) = f_i(1 - \theta)^3 + v_i V_i \theta(1 - \theta)^2 + w_i W_i \theta^2(1 - \theta) + f_{i+1}\theta^3,$$
$$Q_i(\theta) = (1 - \theta)^3 + v_i \theta(1 - \theta)^2 + w_i \theta^2(1 - \theta) + \theta^3.$$

The parameters v_i's, w_i's, and the derivatives d_i's are to be chosen such that the monotonic shape is preserved by the interpolant (7.6). One can note that when $v_i = w_i = 3$, the rational function obviously becomes the standard cubic Hermite polynomial. Variation for the values of v_i's and w_i's control (tighten or loosen) the curve in different pieces of the curve. This behavior can be seen in the following subsection.

7.2.1 Shape Control Analysis

The parameters v_i's and w_i's can be utilized properly to modify the shape of the curve according to the desire of the user. Their effectiveness, for the shape control at knot points, can be seen that if v_i, $w_{i-1} \to \infty$, then the curve is pulled toward the point (x_i, f_i) in the neighborhood of the knot position x_i. This shape behavior can be observed by looking at $s_i(x)$ in Equation (7.6). This form is similar to that of a Bernstein-Bezier formulation. One can observe that when v_i, $w_{i-1} \to \infty$, then V_i and $W_{i-1} \to f_i$.

The interval shape control behavior can be observed by rewriting $s_i(x)$ in Equation (7.6) to the following simplified form:

$$s(x) = f_i(1 - \theta) + f_{i+1}\theta$$
$$+ \frac{\left[(1 - \theta)(d_i - \Delta_i) + \theta(\Delta_i - d_{i+1}) + \theta(1 - \theta)\Delta_i(w_i - v_i)\right]h_i\theta(1 - \theta)}{Q_i(\theta)}.$$

(7.7)

When both v_i and $w_i \to \infty$, it is simple to see the convergence to the following linear interpolant:

$$s(x) = f_i(1 - \theta) + f_{i+1}\theta. \tag{7.8}$$

It should be noted that the shape control analysis is valid only if the bounded derivative values are assumed. A description of appropriate choices for such derivative values is made in the following subsection.

7.2.2 Determination of Derivatives

In most applications, the derivative parameters $\{d_i\}$ are not given and hence must be determined either from the given data $(x_i, f_i), i = 1, 2, \ldots, n$, or by some other means. In this article, they are computed from the given data in such a way that the C^1 smoothness of the interpolant (7.6) is maintained. These methods are the approximations based on various mathematical theories. The descriptions of such approximations are as follows:

7.2.2.1 Derivative Method I

The arithmetic mean method is the three-point difference approximation method based on arithmetic manipulation. It is defined as follows:

$$d_i = \begin{cases} 0, \text{ if } \Delta_{i-1} = 0 \text{ or } \Delta_i = 0, \\ (h_i \Delta_{i-1} + h_{i-1}\Delta_i) / (h_i + h_{i-1}), \text{ otherwise}, \ i = 2, 3, \ldots, n-1. \end{cases} \tag{7.9}$$

The end conditions are given as:

$$d_1 = \begin{cases} 0, \text{ if } \Delta_1 = 0 \text{ or sgn } (d_1^*) \neq \text{sgn}(\Delta_1), \\ d_1^* = \Delta_1 + (\Delta_1 - \Delta_2)h_1 / (h_1 + h_2), \text{ otherwise}. \end{cases} \tag{7.10}$$

$$d_n = \begin{cases} 0, \text{ if } \Delta_{n-1} = 0 \text{ or sgn } (d_n^*) \neq \text{sgn}(\Delta_{n-1}), \\ d_n^* = \Delta_{n-1} + (\Delta_{n-1} - \Delta_{n-2})h_{n-1} / (h_{n-1} + h_{n-2}), \text{ otherwise}. \end{cases} \tag{7.11}$$

7.2.2.2 Derivative Method II

The geometric mean method provides the non-linear approximations which are defined as follows:

$$d_i = \begin{cases} 0, \text{ if } \Delta_{i-1} = 0 \text{ or } \Delta_i = 0, \\ \Delta_{i-1}^{h_i/(h_{i-1}+h_i)} \Delta_i^{h_{i-1}/(h_{i-1}+h_i)} \text{ otherwise}, \ i = 2, 3, \ldots \ldots, n-1. \end{cases} \tag{7.12}$$

The end conditions are given as:

$$d_i = \begin{cases} 0, \text{ if } \Delta_1 = 0 \text{ or } \Delta_{3,1} = 0 \\ \Delta_1 \{\Delta_1/\Delta_{3,1}\}^{h_1/h_2}, \text{ otherwise}. \end{cases} \tag{7.13}$$

$$d_i = \begin{cases} 0, \text{ if } \Delta_{n-1} = 0 \text{ or } \Delta_{n,n-2} = 0 \\ \Delta_{n-1} \{\Delta_{n-1}/\Delta_{n,n-2}\}^{h_{n-1}/h_{n-2}}, \text{ otherwise}. \end{cases} \tag{7.14}$$

where

$$\left.\begin{array}{l} \Delta_{3,1} = (f_3 - f_1) / (x_3 - x_1), \\ \Delta_{n,n-2} = (f_n - f_{n-2}) / (x_n - x_{n-2}). \end{array}\right\} \qquad (7.15)$$

7.2.2.3 Derivative Method III

Another nonlinear choice of derivative values is the following:

$$d_i = \begin{cases} 0 \text{ if } f_{i+1} - f_{i-1} = 0, \\ \Delta_{i-1}\Delta_i / \left[(f_{i+1} - f_{i-1}) / (x_{i+1} - x_{i-1})\right] \text{ otherwise, } i = 2, 3, \ldots, n-1 \end{cases}$$

with end conditions

$$d_1 = \begin{cases} 0 \text{ if } f_3 - f_1 = 0, \\ \Delta_1^2 / \Delta_{3,1} \text{ otherwise,} \end{cases}$$

$$d_n = \begin{cases} 0 \text{ if } f_n - f_{n-2} = 0, \\ \Delta_{n-1}^2 / \Delta_{n,n-2} \text{ otherwise} \end{cases}$$

For given bounded data, the derivative approximations in Subsections 7.2.2.1, 7.2.2.2 and 7.2.2.3 are bounded. Hence, for bounded values of the appropriate shape parameters:

$$v_i, w_i, i = 1, 2, \ldots n - 1, \qquad (7.16)$$

the interpolant is bounded and unique. Therefore, we can conclude the above discussion in the following:

Theorem 7.1. For bounded v_i, w_i, $\forall i$, and the derivative approximations in Subsections 7.2.2.1, 7.2.2.2 and 7.2.2.3, the spline solution of the interpolant (7.6) exists and is unique.

7.2.3 *Examples and Discussion*

For the demonstration of a C^1 rational cubic curve scheme, the derivatives are computed from the Subsections 7.2.2.1. We choose the following choice of shape parameters:

$$v_i = 3 = w_i, \qquad (7.17)$$

to generate the initial default curves. This initial default curve is actually the same as a cubic spline curve. Further modification can be made by changing these parameters interactively.

Figures 7.1 and 7.3 are the default curves for the positive and monotonically increasing data in Table 7.1 and Table 7.2, respectively. The data in Table 7.1 has been taken from an experiment showing oxygen levels in the flue gas (see [7]) and the data in Table 7.2 is another scientific data (Akima's data) discussed in [3]. It can be seen that the ordinary spline curves do not guarantee to preserve the shape of the data.

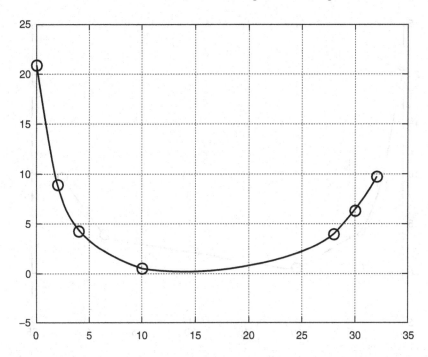

FIGURE 7.5. The rational cubic spline with global shape control having $v_i = 25 = w_i$, $\forall i$.

Figures 7.5 and 7.6 are for the demonstration of global shape control $v_i = w_i = 25, 500$, $\forall i$, respectively. One can see that the increasing global values of the shape parameters gradually pull the curve toward the control polygon, and hence the default curve moves toward the data-preserved curve. But, this way the curve is getting tightened everywhere which may be undesired.

Another alternate is the allocation of values to the shape parameters according to the nature of the curve behavior over various intervals. For example, the curves in Figures 7.7 and 7.8 are for the shape parameter values in Tables 7.3 and 7.4, respectively. These curves seem to visually satisfy the shapes preserved. That is, one can note that the curves seem to preserve the inherent features of the data in Tables 7.1 and 7.2. But these shapes were achieved after making a couple of experiments for different values of parameters, which is very time consuming and not very accurate and, therefore, is not recommended for practical applications too.

The problems, mentioned in the above paragraphs, are the basic motivation for the discussion in this chapter. These problems are to be removed and an automated solution is to be found out. Some constructive approaches have been adopted in the coming sections. The user has been provided facility to visualize positive and monotonic data sets in an automated way. Moreover, some extra degree of freedom has also been provided in case of further modification in the visualization of automated shaped design curve.

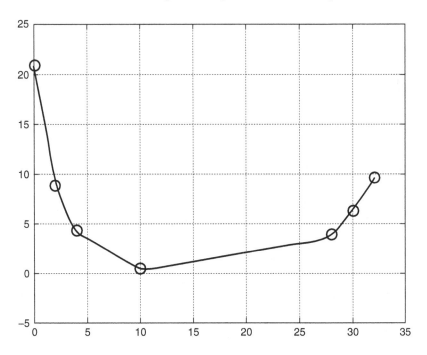

FIGURE 7.6. The rational cubic spline with global shape control having $v_i = 500 = w_i, \forall i$.

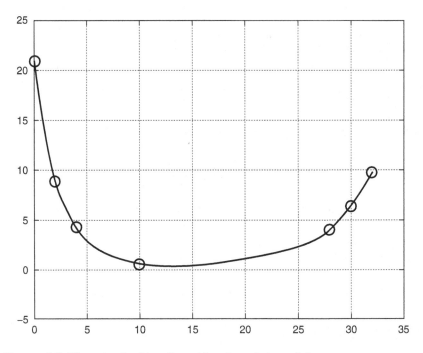

FIGURE 7.7. The rational cubic spline with various choices of shape parameters as mentioned in Table 7.3.

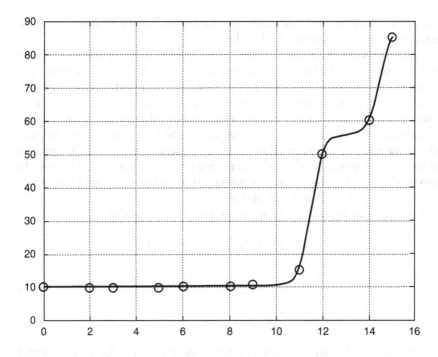

FIGURE 7.8. The rational cubic spline with various choices of shape parametrs as mentioned in Table 7.4.

TABLE 7.3. Suitable shape parameters for data set in Table 7.1.

i	1	2	3	4	5	6
v_i	3	3	5	10	3	3
w_i	3	3	3	12	3	3

TABLE 7.4. Suitable shape parameters for Akima's data set.

i	1	2	3	4	5	6	7	8	9	10
v_i	3	3	3	3	3	3	9	3	8	3
w_i	3	3	3	3	3	3	9	3	8	3

7.3 Positive Spline Interpolation

The rational spline method, described in the previous section, has deficiencies as far as the positivity-preserving issue is concerned. For example, the rational cubic in Section 7.2 does not preserve the shape of the positive data (see Figure 7.1). Very clearly, this curve does not preserve the shape of the data. It is necessary to assign appropriate values to the shape parameters so that it generates a data-preserved shape. Thus, it looks as if ordinary spline schemes do not provide the desired shape features, and hence some further treatment is required to achieve a shape-preserving spline for positive data.

One way, for the above spline method, to achieve the positivity preserving interpolant is to play with shape parameters v_i's and w_i's, on trial and error basis, in those regions of the curve where the shape violations are found. This strategy may result in a required display as can be seen in the previous section. But this is not a comfortable and accurate way to manipulate the desired shape preserving curve.

Another way, which is more effective, useful and is the objective of this article, is the automated generation of positivity-preserving curve. This requires an automated computation of suitable shape parameters and derivative values. To proceed with this strategy, some mathematical treatment is required which will be explained in the following paragraphs.

For simplicity of presentation, let us assume positive set of data:

$$(x_1, f_1), (x_2, f_2), \ldots, (x_n, f_n)$$

so that

$$x_1 < x_2 < \ldots < x_n, \tag{7.18}$$

and

$$f_1 > 0, f_2 > 0, \ldots, f_n > 0, \tag{7.19}$$

It is required to develop sufficient conditions on piecewise rational cubics under which C^1 positive interpolation is preserved. The key idea, to preserve positivity using $s(x)$, is to assign suitable automated values to v_i, w_i in each interval.

As v_i, $w_i > 0$ guarantee strictly positive denominator $Q_i(\theta)$, so initial conditions on v_i, w_i are:

$$v_i > 0, w_i > 0 (v_i < 0, w_i < 0, \text{ for positive data}), i = 1, 2, \ldots, n - 1. \tag{7.20}$$

Since $Q_i(\theta) > 0$ for all v_i, $w_i > 0$, so the positivity of the interpolant (7.6) depends on the positivity of the cubic polynomial $P_i(\theta)$. Thus, the problem reduces to the determination of appropriate values of v_i, w_i for which the polynomial $P_i(\theta)$ is positive. Now, $P_i(\theta)$ can be expressed as follows:

$$P_i(t) = \alpha_i \theta^3 + \beta_i \theta^2 + \gamma_i \theta + \delta_i, \tag{7.21}$$

where

$$\left.\begin{aligned}
\alpha_i &= (1 - w_i)f_{i+1} - (1 - v_i)f_i + (d_{i+1} + d_i)h_i, \\
\beta_i &= w_i f_{i+1} - (3 - 2v_i)f_i - (d_{i+1} + d_i)h_i, \\
\gamma_i &= d_i h_i - (3 - v_i)f_i, \\
\delta_i &= f_i.
\end{aligned}\right\} \tag{7.22}$$

For the strict inequality (for positive data) in (7.6), according to Butt and Brodlie [8], $P_i(\theta) > 0$ if and only if

$$(P_i'(0), P_i'(1)) \in R_1 U R_2. \tag{7.23}$$

where

$$R_1 = \left\{ (a, b) : a > \frac{-3f_i}{h_i}, b < \frac{3f_{i+1}}{h_i} \right\}, \tag{7.24}$$

$$R_2 = \left\{ (a, b) : 36 f_i f_{i+1}(a^2 + b^2 + ab - 3\Delta_i(a + b) + 3\Delta_i^2) + \\ 3(f_{i+1}a - f_i b)(2h_i ab - 3f_{i+1}a + 3f_i b) + \\ 4h_i(f_{i+1}a^3 - f_i b^3) - h_i^2 a^2 b^2 > 0 \right\}. \tag{7.25}$$

We have

$$P_i'(0) = \frac{f_i}{h_i}(v_i - 3) + d_i,$$

$$P_i'(1) = d_{i+1} - \frac{f_{i+1}}{h_i}(w_i - 3).$$

Now (7.23) is true when

$$(P_i'(0), P_i'(1)) \in R_1,$$

$$P_i'(0) > \frac{-3f_i}{h_i}, \quad P_i'(1) < \frac{3f_{i+1}}{h_i}.$$

This leads to the following constraints:

$$v_i > m_i, \quad w_i > M_i. \tag{7.26}$$

where

$$m_i = Max\left\{ 0, \frac{-h_i d_i}{f_i} \right\}, \quad M_i = Max\left\{ 0, \frac{h_i d_{i+1}}{f_{i+1}} \right\}. \tag{7.27}$$

Further

$$(P_i'(0), P_i'(1)) \in R_2$$

if

$$36 f_i f_{i+1}[\phi_1^2(r_i, u_i) + \phi_2^2(w_i) + \phi_1(v_i)\phi_2(w_i) - 3\Delta_i(\phi_1(v_i) + \phi_2(w_i)) + 3\Delta_i^2] + \\ 3[f_{i+1}\phi_1(v_i) - y_i\phi_2(w_i)][2h_i\phi_1(v_i)\phi_2(w_i) - 3f_{i+1}\phi_1(v_i) + 3f_i\phi_2(w_i)] + \\ 4h_i[f_{i+1}\phi_1^3(v_i) - y_i\phi_2^3(w_i)] - h_i^2\phi_1^2(v_i)\phi_2^2(w_i) > 0 \tag{7.28}$$

where

$$\phi_1(v_i) = P_i'(0), \\ \phi_2(w_i) = P_i'(1). \tag{7.29}$$

This leads to the following:

Theorem 7.2. For a strictly positive data, the rational cubic interpolant (7.6) preserves positivity if and only if either (7.26) or (7.28) is satisfied.

Remark 7.1. The constraints (7.27) can be further modified to incorporate both shape-preserving and shape control features. Without loss of generality, one can find parameters r_i and q_i satisfying

$$r_i, q_i \geq 1. \tag{7.30}$$

such that the constraints (7.26) and (7.27) lead to the following sufficient conditions for the freedom over the choice of r_i and q_i:

$$v_i = (1 + m_i) r_i, \, w_i = (1 + M_i) q_i. \tag{7.31}$$

One can make the choice of r_i and q_i to be the greatest lower bound as follows:

$$r_i = 1, \, q_i = 1. \tag{7.32}$$

This choice satisfies (7.26) and it also provides visually very pleasant results. Some more practical sufficient conditions, which satisfy (7.26) too, are the following:

$$v_i = w_i = 1 + \max(m_i r_i, M_i q_i). \tag{7.33}$$

Although, these conditions appear to be stronger than (7.31) but their use has shown quite pleasing results. For more practical and better results, however, we will utilize the constraints in (7.31) as can be seen in the demonstration Subsection 7.3.1.

Remark 7.2. Although v_i and w_i satisfying (7.28) can be determined, it requires a lot of computations. The alternate choice, in Remark 7.1, provides efficient and reasonably attractive results as can be seen in the following subsection.

Remark 7.3. This curve-plotting method can be used in both cases when either d_i's are particularly specified or estimated by some method.

7.3.1   *Examples and Discussion*

We will assume the derivative approximations as mentioned in Subsection 7.2.2.1. These approximations are computationally more economical. However, one can use the derivative choice in Subsection 7.2.2.1, too. The scheme has been implemented on the data set of Table 7.1. Figure 7.1 is the default rational cubic spline curve for the choice of parameters in (7.17), whereas the Figure 7.2 is its corresponding shape-preserving spline curve for the automatic choice of parameters in (7.31) and (7.32). The corresponding automatic outputs of the derivative and shape parameters, for the shape preserving curves in Figure 7.2 is given in Table 7.5. The pleasing visualization of the data set (see Figure 7.2) is apparent from its counterpart rational cubic spline default curve; see Figure 7.1. Another example of the shape-preserving spline for the positivity is shown in Figure 7.9. This is for the data set in Table 7.6 (the cubic spline version of this data is shown in Figure 7.13.) The automated values of the shape parameters and the computed derivative values are shown in Table 7.7.

Further modification in the default positive curve, in Figure 7.2, is also possible. This can be achieved by assigning appropriate values to r_i's and q_i's in the desired

TABLE 7.5. Computed derivatives and shape parameters for the data in Table 7.1.

i	1	2	3	4	5	6	7
d_i	−7.8500	−4.1500	−1.8792	−0.4153	1.0539	1.4250	1.6000
$v_i = w_i$	1.7548	1.9432	3.6845	15.9500	1.4597	1.3333	–

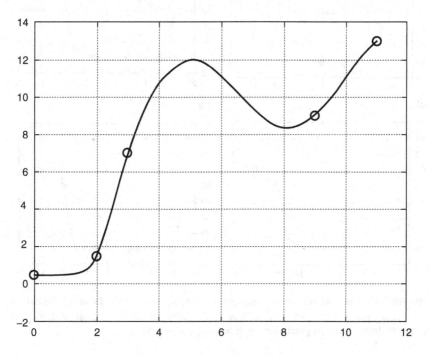

FIGURE 7.9. The positivity-preserving spline for the positive data in Table 7.6.

TABLE 7.6. A positive dataset.

i	1	2	3	4	5
x_i	0	2	3	9	11
y_i	0.5	1.5	7	9	13

TABLE 7.7. Computed derivatives and shape parameters for the data in Table 7.6.

i	1	2	3	4	5
d_i	0.4167	3.8333	4.7619	1.5833	1.5000
$v_i = w_i$	6.1111	1.6803	2.0556	1.2308	1.1333

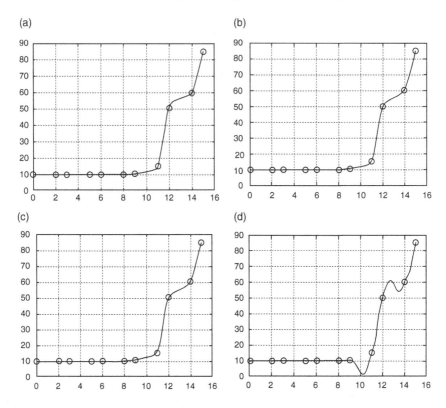

FIGURE 7.10. The positivity preserving spline for the positive data in Table 7.1: (a) having $r_i = 1, q_i = 2, \forall i.$; (b) having $r_i = 2, q_i = 2, \forall i.$; (c) having $r_i = 5, q_i = 5, \forall i.$; (d) having violation of shape parameters as $r_i = -3, q_i = -3, \forall i$.

regions. Figures 7.10(a)–(d) are for the data set in Table 7.1 for various global values of r_i's and q_i's. For Figure 7.10(a), these values are assumed to be $r_i = 1$ and $q_i = 2$. Figure 7.10(b) is the demonstration for the values $r_i = 2$ and $q_i = 2$. Figure 7.10(c) is plotted for $r_i = 5$ and $q_i = 5$. It can be observed that the gradual uniform increase in the values of r_i's and q_i's is tightening the curve gradually. Infinitely large values will result to the control polygon. The violation of the constraints (7.30) on the parameters r_i's and q_i's will result in a curve that may not preserve the shape. This is displayed in Figure 7.10(d) for $r_i = -3$ and $q_i = -3$. Figures 7.10(a)–(d) are for global values of r_i's and q_i's.

Similarly, the user has freedom to play with values individually when desired. For example, the curve in Figure 7.9 can be redisplayed, after modification in the third interval of the curve, as shown in Figure 7.11. This is done for the parameter values in Table 7.8 and displays a much more natural behavior as compared to Figure 7.9.

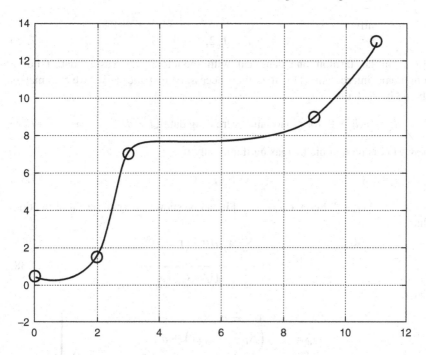

FIGURE 7.11. The positivity-preserving spline for the positive data in Table 7.1, having shape parameters as in Table 7.8.

TABLE 7.8. Suitable shape parameters for data set in Table 7.6.

i	1	2	3	4	5
r_i	1	1	10	1	–
q_i	1	1	5	1	–

7.4 Monotone Spline Interpolation

The rational cubic in Section 7.2 does not preserve the shape of the monotonic data (see Figure 7.3). Thus, it looks as if ordinary spline schemes do not provide the desired shape features, and hence some further treatment is required to achieve a shape preserving spline for monotonic data. This requires an automated computation of suitable shape parameters and derivative values. To proceed with this strategy, some mathematical treatment is required which will be explained in the following paragraphs.

For simplicity of presentation, let us assume monotonic increasing set of data so that

$$f_1 \leq f_2 \leq \ldots \leq f_n, \tag{7.34}$$

or equivalently

$$\Delta_i \geq 0, i = 1, 2, \ldots, n-1. \tag{7.35}$$

(In a similar fashion one can deal with monotonic decreasing data.) For a monotonic interpolant $s(x)$, it is then necessary that the derivative parameters should be such that

$$d_i \geq 0(d_i \leq 0, \text{ for monotonic decreasing data}), i = 1, 2, \ldots, n. \tag{7.36}$$

Now $s(x)$ is monotonic increasing if and only if

$$s^{(1)}(x) \geq 0 \tag{7.37}$$

for all $x \in [x_1, x_n]$. For $x \in [x_i, x_{i+1}]$ it can be shown, after some simplification, that

$$s^{(1)}(x) = \frac{\sum_{j=1}^{6} A_{ji} \theta^{j-1} (1-\theta)^{6-j}}{[Q_i(x)]^2}, \tag{7.38}$$

where

$$\left. \begin{array}{l}
A_{1,i} = d_i, \\
A_{2,i} = 2w_i \left(\Delta_i - \frac{1}{w_i} d_{i+1} \right) + d_i, \\
A_{3,i} = 3\Delta_i + 2w_i \left(\Delta_i - \frac{1}{w_i} d_{i+1} \right) + v_i w_i \left(\Delta_i - \frac{1}{v_i} d_i - \frac{1}{w_i} d_{i+1} \right) \\
A_{4,i} = 3\Delta_i + 2v_i \left(\Delta_i - \frac{1}{v_i} d_i \right) + v_i w_i \left(\Delta_i - \frac{1}{v_i} d_i - \frac{1}{w_i} d_{i+1} \right) \\
A_{5,i} = 2v_i \left(\Delta_i - \frac{1}{v_i} d_i \right) + d_{i+1}, \\
A_{6,i} = d_{i+1}.
\end{array} \right\} \tag{7.39}$$

The denominator in (7.38), being a squared quantity, is positive; therefore, the sufficient conditions for monotonicity on $[x_i, x_{i+1}]$ are:

$$A_{j,i} \geq 0, j = 1, 2, \ldots, 6, \tag{7.40}$$

where the necessary conditions

$$d_i \geq 0 \text{ and } d_{i+1} \geq 0 \tag{7.41}$$

are assumed.

If $\Delta_i > 0$ (strict inequality) then following are sufficient conditions for (7.40):

$$\left. \begin{array}{l}
\Delta_i - \frac{1}{v_i} d_i \geq 0 \\
\Delta_i - \frac{1}{w_i} d_{i+1} \geq 0, \text{ and} \\
\Delta_i - \frac{1}{v_i} d_i - \frac{1}{w_i} d_{i+1} \geq 0.
\end{array} \right\} . \tag{7.42}$$

which lead to the following constraints:

$$v_i = \frac{l_i d_i}{\Delta_i}, \quad w_i = \frac{k_i d_{i+1}}{\Delta_i}. \tag{7.43}$$

where l_i and k_i are positive quantities satisfying

$$\frac{1}{l_i} + \frac{1}{k_i} \leq 1. \tag{7.44}$$

This, together with (7.43) leads to the following sufficient conditions for the freedom over the choice of r_i and q_i:

$$l_i \geq 1 + \frac{d_{i+1}}{d_i}, \quad k_i \geq 1 + \frac{d_i}{d_{i+1}}. \tag{7.45}$$

One can make the choice of r_i and q_i to be the greatest lower bound as follows:

$$l_i = 1 + \frac{d_{i+1}}{d_i}, \quad k_i = 1 + \frac{d_i}{d_{i+1}}. \tag{7.46}$$

This choice satisfies (7.44). Further simplification of (7.43) and (7.46) leads to the following sufficient conditions for monotonicity:

$$v_i = \frac{d_i + d_{i+1}}{\Delta_i}, \quad w_i = \frac{d_i + d_{i+1}}{\Delta_i}. \tag{7.47}$$

This choice satisfies (7.44) and it also provides visually very pleasant results, as can be seen in Subsection 7.4.1. However, one can find some positive quantities r_i and q_i such that (7.45) can be rewritten as:

$$l_i = \left(1 + \frac{d_{i+1}}{d_i}\right) r_i, \quad k_i = \left(1 + \frac{d_i}{d_{i+1}}\right) q_i. \tag{7.48}$$

where

$$r_i, q_i \geq 1. \tag{7.49}$$

Substitution of parameters in (7.47) into (7.43) yields the sufficient condition to the following:

$$v_i = \left(\frac{d_i + d_{i+1}}{\Delta_i}\right) r_i, \quad w_i = \left(\frac{d_i + d_{i+1}}{\Delta_i}\right) q_i. \tag{7.50}$$

The parameters r_i and q_i will help out the user in a further modification of the automated monotone curve.

It should be noted that if $\Delta_i = 0$, then it is necessary to set $d_i = d_{i+1} = 0$, and thus

$$s(x) = f_i = f_{i+1} \tag{7.51}$$

is a constant on $[x_i, x_{i+1}]$. Hence the interpolant (7.6) is monotonic increasing together with the conditions (7.41) and (7.47). For the case where the data is monotonic but not strictly monotonic (i.e., when some $\Delta_i = 0$), it would be necessary to divide the data into strictly monotonic parts. If we set $d_i = d_{i+1} = 0$ whenever $\Delta_i = 0$, then the resulting interpolant will be C^0 at break points. The above discussion can be summarized as:

Theorem 7.3. Given the conditions (7.36) on the derivative parameters, (7.47) and (7.50) are sufficient conditions for the interpolant (7.6) to be monotonic increasing.

TABLE 7.9. Computed derivatives and shape parameters for the data in Table 7.2.

i	1 2 3 4 5	6	7	8	9	10	11
d_i	0 0 0 0 0	0		1.0833	24.0833	25.0000	18.3333	12.5000
$v_i = w_i$	– – – – –	–	2.1667	11.1852	1.4024	8.6667	0.2333	–

7.4.1 *Examples and Discussion*

As in Section 7.3, we will assume the derivative approximations as mentioned in Subsection 7.2.2.1. The scheme has been implemented on the data set of Table 7.2. Figure 7.3 is the default rational cubic spline curve for the choice of parameters in (7.17), whereas Figure 7.4 is its corresponding shape-preserving spline curve for the automatic choice of parameters in (7.47). The corresponding automatic outputs of the derivative and shape parameters, for the shape-preserving curves in Figure 7.4 is given in Table 7.9. The pleasing visualization of the data set (see Figure 7.4) is apparent from its counterpart rational cubic spline default curve; see Figure 7.3.

Further modification in the default monotonic curve, in Figure 7.4, is also possible. This can be achieved by assigning appropriate values to r_i's and q_i's in the desired regions. Figures 7.12(a)–(d) are for the data set in Table 7.2 for various global values of r_i's and q_i's. For Figure 7.12(a), these values are assumed to be $r_i = 1$ and $q_i = 2$. Figure 7.12(b) is the demonstration for the values $r_i = 2$ and $q_i = 2$. Figure 7.12(c) is plotted for $r_i = 5$ and $q_i = 5$. It can be observed that the gradual uniform increase in the values of r_i's and q_i's is tightening the curve gradually. Infinitely large values will result to the control polygon. The violation of the constraints (7.30) on the parameters r_i's and q_i's will result in a curve that may not preserve the shape. This is displayed in Figure 7.12(d) for $r_i = 0.1$ and $q_i = 0.1$. Figures 7.12(a)–(d) are for global values of r_i's and q_i's. Similarly, the user has freedom to play with values individually when desired.

7.5   Convex Spline Interpolation

Figures 7.1 and 7.13 are the default curves to the positive and convex data in Table 7.1 and Table 7.10, respectively. The data in Table 7.10 is data from a function $f(x) = 10/x^2$. It can be seen that the ordinary spline curves do not guarantee to preserve the shape.

As was seen in Section 7.2, Figures 7.5 and 7.6, for the data in Table 7.1, are for the demonstration of global shape control $v_i = w_i = 25, 500, \forall i$, respectively. One can see that the increasing global values of the shape parameters gradually pull the curve toward the control polygon and hence the default curve moves toward the data-preserved curve. But, this way the curve is getting tightened everywhere, which may not be desired.

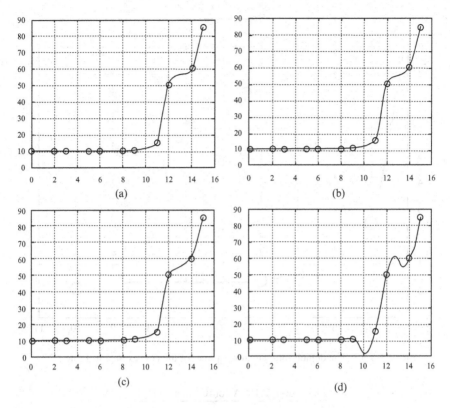

FIGURE 7.12. The monotonicity-preserving spline for the positive data in Table 7.2: (a) having $r_i = 1, q_i = 2, \forall i$.; (b) having $r_i = 2, q_i = 2, \forall i$.; (c) having $r_i = 5, q_i = 5, \forall i$.; (d) having violation of shape parameters as $r_i = 0.1, q_i = 0.1, \forall i$.

Another alternate is the allocation of values to the shape parameters according to the nature of the curve behavior over various intervals. For example, the curves in Figures 7.7 and 7.14 are for the shape parameter values in Tables 7.3 and 7.11 (corresponding to the data in Tables 7.1 and 7.10), respectively. These curves seem to visually satisfy the shapes preserved. That is, one can note that the curves seem to preserve the inherent features of the data in Tables 7.1 and 7.10. But these shapes were achieved after making various experiments for different values of parameters, which is really time consuming and not very accurate and, therefore, is not recommended for practical applications too.

The problems, mentioned in the above paragraphs, are the basic motivation for this section. These problems will be removed and an automated solution will be presented. Some constructive approaches are adopted in the coming sections. The user will visualize convex data sets in an automated way.

The rational cubic, in Section 7.2, does not preserve the shape of the convex data. Thus, it looks as if ordinary spline schemes do not provide the desired shape features, and hence some further treatment is required to achieve a

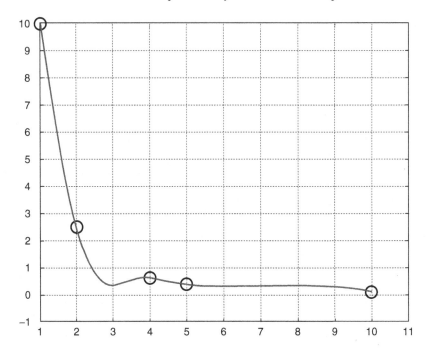

FIGURE 7.13. The default rational cubic spline for the convex data in Table 7.2.

TABLE 7.10. A convex data set.

i	1	2	3	4	5
x_i	1	2	4	5	10
f_i	10	2.5	0.625	0.4	0.1

shape-preserving spline for convex data. This requires an automated computation of suitable shape parameters and derivative values. To proceed with this strategy, some mathematical treatment is required that will be explained in the following paragraphs.

For simplicity of presentation, let us assume a strictly convex set of data so that

$$\Delta_1 < \Delta_2 < \ldots < \Delta_{n-1}. \tag{7.52}$$

In a similar fashion, one can deal with a concave data so that

$$\Delta_1 > \Delta_2 > \ldots > \Delta_{n-1}. \tag{7.53}$$

For a convex interpolant $s(x)$, it is then necessary that the derivative parameters should be such that

$$d_1 < \Delta_1 < \ldots < \Delta_{i-1} < d_i < \Delta_i < \ldots < \Delta_{n-1} < d_n, \tag{7.54}$$

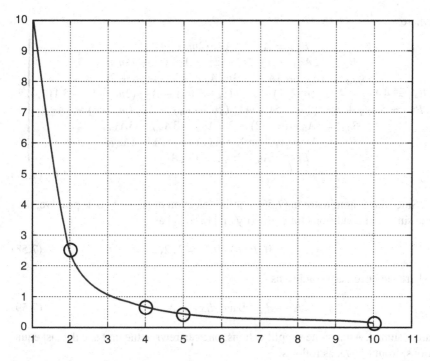

FIGURE 7.14. The rational cubic spline with various choices of shape parameters as mentioned in Table 7.11.

TABLE 7.11. Suitable shape parameters for Akima's data set.

i	1	2	3	4
v_i	3	10	3	12
w_i	3	13	3	20

and

$$d_1 > \Delta_1 > \ldots > \Delta_{i-1} > d_i > \Delta_i > \ldots > \Delta_{n-1} > d_n, \text{ for concave data.}$$

Now $s(x)$ is convex if and only if

$$s^{(2)}(x) \geq 0, \tag{7.55}$$

for all $x \in [x_1, x_n]$. For $x \in [x_i, x_{i+1}]$ it can be shown, after some simplification, that

$$s^{(2)}(x) = \sum_{j=1}^{8} \frac{B_{j,i}\theta^{j-1}(1-\theta)^{8-j}}{h_i[Q_i(x)]^3}, \tag{7.56}$$

where

$$
\left.\begin{array}{c}
B_{1,i} = A_{2,i} - A_{1,i}\,(2v_i - 1)\,, \\
B_{2,i} = 2A_{3,i} - A_{2,i}\,(v_i - 2) - A_{1,i}\,(v_i + 4w_i)\,, \\
B_{3,i} = 3A_{4,i} + 3A_{3,i} - 3w_i A_{2,i} - 3A_{1,i}\,(w_i + 2)\,, \\
B_{4,i} = 4A_{5,i} + 4A_{4,i}\,(v_i + 1) + A_{3,i}\,(v_i - 2w_i) - A_{2,i}\,(2w_i + 5) - 5A_{1,i}\,, \\
B_{5,i} = 5A_{6,i} + A_{5,i}\,(2v_i + 5) + A_{4,i}\,(2v_i - w_i) - A_{3,i}\,(w_i - 4) - 4A_{2,i}\,, \\
B_{6,i} = 3A_{6,i}\,(v_i + 2) + 3v_i A_{5,i} - 3A_{4,i} - 3A_{3,i}\,, \\
B_{7,i} = A_{6,i}\,(4v_i + w_i) + A_{5,i}\,(w_i - 2) - 2A_{4,i}\,, \\
B_{8,i} = A_{6,i}\,(2w_i - 1) - A_{5,i}\,,
\end{array}\right\}
$$

$$(7.57)$$

Since the denominator in (7.56), for the selection of v_i, $w_i > 0$, is positive, then the sufficient conditions for convexity on $[x_i, x_{i+1}]$ are:

$$v_i, w_i > 0,\ B_{j,i} \geq 0,\ j = 1, 2, \ldots, 8, \tag{7.58}$$

where the necessary conditions

$$\Delta_i - d_i \geq 0 \text{ and } d_{i+1} - \Delta_i \geq 0 \tag{7.59}$$

are assumed. After some simplifications, one can rewrite the first and the last equations, from (7.57), as follows:

$$
\left.\begin{array}{l}
B_{1,i} = 2\{(w_i - v_i)\,\Delta_i + v_i\,(\Delta_i - d_i) - (d_{i+1} - d_i)\}\,, \\
B_{8,i} = 2\{(w_i - v_i)\,\Delta_i + w_i\,(d_{i+1} - \Delta_i) - (d_{i+1} - d_i)\}\,.
\end{array}\right\}
$$

$$(7.60)$$

If $\Delta_i - d_i > 0$ and $d_{i+1} - \Delta_i > 0$ (strict inequalities), then the following are sufficient conditions for (7.60):

$$
\left.\begin{array}{c}
v_i = w_i\,, \\
v_i\,(\Delta_i - d_i) - (d_{i+1} - d_i) \geq 0, \\
w_i\,(d_{i+1} - \Delta_i) - (d_{i+1} - d_i) \geq 0.
\end{array}\right\}
$$

$$(7.61)$$

These are equivalent to the followings constraints:

$$v_i = w_i = l_i + \max\left(\frac{d_{i+1} - d_i}{\Delta_i - d_i}, \frac{d_{i+1} - d_i}{d_{i+1} - \Delta_i}\right), \tag{7.62}$$

where l_i are non-negative quantities satisfying

$$l_i \geq 0. \tag{7.63}$$

After some manipulations, it is trivial to show that the sufficient conditions (7.58), for (7.56), are also sufficient for (7.54). Since

$$\frac{d_{i+1} - \Delta_i}{\Delta_i - d_i} + \frac{\Delta_i - d_i}{d_{i+1} - \Delta_i} \geq \max\left(\frac{d_{i+1} - d_i}{\Delta_i - d_i}, \frac{d_{i+1} - d_i}{d_{i+1} - \Delta_i}\right). \tag{7.64}$$

Therefore, the sufficient conditions (7.62) for convexity take the following form:

$$v_i = w_i = l_i + \frac{d_{i+1} - \Delta_i}{\Delta_i - d_i} + \frac{\Delta_i - d_i}{d_{i+1} - \Delta_i}, l_i \geq 0. \qquad (7.65)$$

However, the following choice of parameters

$$v_i = w_i = l_i + \max \left(\frac{d_{i+1} - d_i}{\Delta_i - d_i}, \frac{d_{i+1} - d_i}{d_{i+1} - \Delta_i} \right), l_i = 0, \qquad (7.66)$$

will be considered for practical implementation of default curve design. This choice satisfies (7.62) and it also provides acceptable results.

Remark 7.4. The default value of the parameters l_i, being taken as zero, leads to the default constraints:

$$v_i = w_i = \max \left(\frac{d_{i+1} - d_i}{\Delta_i - d_i}, \frac{d_{i+1} - d_i}{d_{i+1} - \Delta_i} \right), \qquad (7.67)$$

provides visually pleasing results and produces automated curve interpolation. Further modification is achieved by taking other positive values in various intervals.

Remark 7.5. It should be noted that if $\Delta_i - d_i = 0$ or $d_{i+1} - \Delta_i = 0$, then it is necessary to set $d_i = d_{i+1} = \Delta_i$. The interpolant then will be linear in that region, i.e.,

$$s(x) = (1 - \theta) f_i + \theta f_{i+1}. \qquad (7.68)$$

It should also be noted that if $\Delta_i = 0$, then it is necessary to set $d_i = d_{i+1} = 0$, and thus

$$s(x) = f_i = f_{i+1} \qquad (7.69)$$

is a constant on $[x_i, x_{i+1}]$. Hence the interpolant (7.6) is convex together with the conditions (7.65). For the case, where the data is convex but not strictly convex, it would be necessary to divide the data into strictly convex parts. If we set $d_i = d_{i+1} = 0$ whenever $\Delta_i = 0$, then the resulting interpolant will be C^0 at break points.

The above discussion can be summarized as follows:

Theorem 7.4. Given the conditions (7.54) on the derivative parameters and the data, the constraints (7.65) are the sufficient conditions for the interpolant (7.6) to be convex.

7.5.1 Demonstration

We will assume the derivative approximations as mentioned in Subsection 7.2.2.2. The scheme has been implemented on the data set of Table 7.10. Figure 7.13 is the default rational cubic spline curve for the choice of parameters in (7.17), whereas Figure 7.15 is its corresponding shape-preserving spline curve for the automatic choice of parameters in (7.67).

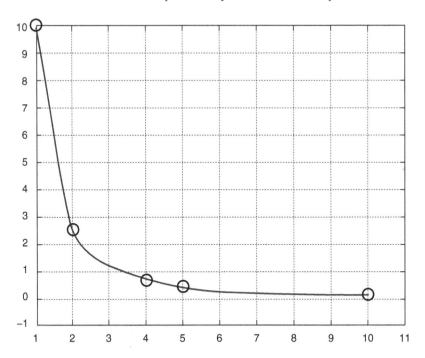

FIGURE 7.15. The default shape-preserving spline for the convex data in Table 7.10.

7.6   Summary

A rational cubic interpolant with two families of shape parameters has been utilized to obtain C^1 positivity-, monotonicity- and convexity-preserving interpolatory spline curves. The shape constraints are restricted on shape parameters to assure the shape preservation of the data. For the C^1 interpolant, the choices on the derivative parameters have been defined. The solution to the shape-preserving spline exists and provides a unique solution.

In addition to the default curve choices, extra degree of freedoms have been provided to the users. This will help for further satisfaction of the default design curves.

The rational spline scheme has been implemented successfully and it demonstrates visually pleasant and accurate results. The user is not worried about struggling and looking for some appropriate choice of parameters as in the case of an ordinary rational spline having some control on the curves.

7.7   Exercises

1. Extend the curve scheme in Section 7.2 to a parametric curve scheme and write a program to demonstrate the effect of the shape parameters for CAD/CAM purposes. (*Hint*: The reader is referred to Chapter 3 for this purpose)

2. Extend the curve scheme in Section 7.3 to a parametric curve scheme such that it preserves the positive data.
3. Extend the curve scheme in Section 7.4 to a parametric curve scheme such that it preserves the monotonic data.
4. Extend the curve scheme in Section 7.5 to a parametric curve scheme such that it preserves the convex data.
5. Write program to visualize the results of the scheme in Exercises 2–4.
6. Extend the curve scheme in Section 7.2 to a C^2 curve scheme.
7. Extend the curve scheme in Section 7.3 to a C^2 curve scheme.
8. Extend the curve scheme in Section 7.4 to a C^2 curve scheme.
9. Extend the curve scheme in Section 7.5 to a C^2 curve scheme.

References

1. McAllister, D.F., and Roulier, J.A. (1981), An algorithm for computing a shape-preserving osculatory quadratic spline, *ACM Trans Math Software* 7, 331–347.
2. Passow, E., and Roulier, J.A. (1977), Monotone and convex spline interpolation. *SIAM J Num Anal* 14, 904–909.
3. Fritsch, F.N., and Carlson, R.E. (1980), Monotone piecewise cubic interpolation, *SIAM J Num Anal* 17, 238–246.
4. Gregory, J.A. (1986), Shape-preserving spline interpolation, *Comput Aided Design*, 18(1), 53–57.
5. Fritsch, F.N., and Butland, J. (1984), A method for constructing local monotone piecewise cubic interpolants, *SIAM J Sci Stat Comput* 5, 303–304.
6. Schumaker, L.L. (1983), On shape-preserving quadratic spline interpolation, *SIAM J Num Anal* 20, 854–864.
7. Brodlie, K.W., and Butt, S. (1991), Preserving convexity using piecewise cubic interpolation, *Comput Graphics*, 15, 15–23.
8. Butt, S., and Brodlie, K.W. (1993), Preserving positivity using piecewise cubic interpolation, *Comput Graphics*, 17(1), 55–64.
9. Sarfraz, M. (1992), Convexity-preserving piecewise rational interpolation for planar curves, *Bull Korean Math Soc* 29(2), 193–200.
10. Sarfraz, M. (1997), Preserving monotone shape of the data using piecewise rational cubic functions, *Comput Graphics*, 21(1), 5–14.
11. Brodlie, K.W. (1985), Methods for drawing curves. In: *Fundamenal Algorithm for Computer Graphics*, ed. R.A. Earnshaw, Springer-Verlag, Berlin, pp. 303–323.
12. DeVore, A., and Yan, Z. (1986), Error analysis for piecewise quadratic curve-fitting algorithms, *Comp Aided Geom Design* 3, 205–215.
13. Greiner, K. (1991), A survey on univariate data interpolation and approximation by splines of given shape, *Math Comp Mod* 15, 97–106.
14. Constantini, P. (1997), Boundary-valued shape preserving interpolating splines, ACM *Trans Math Software*, 23(2), 229–251.
15. Lahtinen, A. (1996), Monotone interpolation with application to estimation of taper curves, *Ann Numer Math* 3, 151–161.
16. Sarfraz, M. (1992), Interpolatory rational cubic spline with biased, point and interval tension, *Comput Graphics* 16(4), 427–430.

17. Moreton H.P., and Sequin, C.H. (1995), Minimum variation curves and surfaces for computer-aided geometric design, *Designing Fair Curves and Surfaces*, Nick Sapidis ed., Proc. of SIAM'94 Conference, pp. 123–159.

18. Sarfraz, M., Butt, S., and Hussain, M.Z. (2001), Visualization of shaped data by a rational cubic spline interpolation, *Int J Comput Graphics*, Elsevier Science, 25(5), 833–845.

19. Sarfraz, M. (2000), A rational cubic spline for the visualization of monotonic data, *Comput Graphics*, 24(4), 509–516.

20. Sarfraz, M., and Hussain, M.Z. (2006), Data visualization using rational spline interpolation, *Int Computational Appl Math*, Elsevier Science, 189(1–2), 513–525.

21. Sarfraz, M., Hussain, M.Z., and Chaudhry, F.S. (2005), Shape-preserving cubic spline for data visualization, *Int J Comput Graphics CAD/CAM*, International Scientific, 1(6), 185–194.

22. Sarfraz, M. (2002), Visualization of positive and convex data by a rational cubic spline, *Int J Infor Sci*, Elsevier Science,146(1–4), 239–254.

23. Sarfraz, M. (2002), Modelling for the visualization of monotone data, *Int J Modelling Simulation*, ACTA Press, 22(3), 176–185.

8
Visualization of Shaped Data by Cubic Spline Interpolation

Abstract. *This chapter reiterates the subject of the previous chapter. Instead of a rational cubic model, a polynomial cubic spline has been presented here for the same objective. A piecewise cubic spline has been introduced to preserve the shape of the data when it is convex, monotone or positive. The spline representation is interpolatory and applicable to the scalar valued data. The shape parameters, in the description of the cubic, have been constrained in such a way that they control the shape of the curve to avoid any noise. As far as visual smoothness is concerned, the curve scheme under discussion is GC^1. Thus the continuity constraints have been relaxed from C^1 to GC^1.*

8.1 Introduction

This chapter is a continuation of the previous chapter. The difference arises mainly in two ways: (i) the interpolant used is a piecewise cubic polynomial, and (ii) visual smoothness is of the curve scheme under discussion, which is GC^1. Thus, the continuity constraints have been relaxed from C^1 to GC^1 to obtain a shape-preserving cubic spline.

The early work in this chapter was reported in [17] and further extension of the preliminary work was achieved in [18]. The shape-preserving techniques presented here are an economical alternative to their counterparts in the previous chapter as well as in [1–16]. The methods under consideration in this chapter have the following important and advantageous features that no additional points (knots) need to be supplied. In contrast, the cubic interpolation method of Brodlie and Butt [1, 2] requires the introduction of additional knots when used as shape-preserving methods. Moreover, existing algorithms such as the de Castlejau algorithm can be used for rapid computations.

The chapter is organized so that Section 8.2 describes the Hermite-like cubic interpolation. An introduction to shape-preserving is provided in Section 8.3. The problems of convexity, monotonicity and positivity are discussed in Sections 8.4, 8.5 and 8.6, respectively. Section 8.7 is devoted to the extension of positivity when a data is above an arbitrary line. Section 8.8 summarizes the chapter.

8.2   Cubic Interpolant

Let (x_i, f_i), $i = 1, 2, \ldots, n$, be a given set of data points, where $x_1 < x_2 < \cdots < x_n$. Let

$$h_i = x_{i+1} - x_i, \quad \Delta_i = \frac{f_{i+1} - f_i}{h_i}, i = 1, 2, \ldots, n - 1. \qquad (8.1)$$

Consider the following piecewise cubic function:

$$S(x) \equiv S_i(x) = U_i(1 - \theta)^3 + 3V_i\theta(1 - \theta)^2 + 3W_i\theta^2(1 - \theta) + Z_i\theta^3, \quad (8.2)$$

where

$$\theta = \frac{x - x_i}{h_i}. \qquad (8.3)$$

To make the function (8.2) GC^1, one needs to impose the following interpolatory properties:

$$S(x_i) = f_i, \text{ and } S(x_{i+1}) = f_{i+1}, \; S^{(1)}(x_i) = \frac{d_i}{r_i}, \text{ and } S^{(1)}(x_{i+1}) = \frac{d_{i+1}}{r_i}, \qquad (8.4)$$

which provide the following manipulations:

$$U_i = f_i, \quad Z_i = f_{i+1}, \quad V_i = f_i + \frac{h_i d_i}{3r_i}, \text{ and } W_i = f_{i+1} - \frac{h_i d_{i+1}}{3r_i}, \qquad (8.5)$$

where $S^{(1)}(x)$ denotes derivative with respect to x and d_i denotes derivative value given at the knot x_i. This leads the piecewise cubic (8.2) to the following piecewise Hermite-like interpolant $S \in C^1[x_1, x_n]$:

$$S(x) \equiv S_i(x), \qquad (8.6)$$

where

$$S_i(x) = f_i(1 - \theta)^3 + 3V_i\theta(1 - \theta)^2 + 3W_i\theta^2(1 - \theta) + f_{i+1}\theta^3. \qquad (8.7)$$

The parameters r_i's, and the derivatives d_i's are to be chosen such that the shape of the data is preserved by the interpolant (8.6). One can note that when $r_i = 1$, the cubic function obviously becomes the standard cubic Hermite polynomial. Variation for the values of r_i's control (tighten or loosen) the curve in different pieces of the curve. When $r_i \to 0$, it is simple to see that the curve gets tightened in the corresponding interval. This interval shape control behavior is desired as a constraint so that the interpolant automatically becomes convex to the convex data, monotone to monotone data and positive to positive data.

It should be noted that the shape control analysis is valid only if the bounded derivative values are assumed. In most applications, the derivative parameters $\{d_i\}$ are not given and hence must be determined either from the given data (x_i, f_i), $i = 1, 2, \ldots, n$, or by some other means. In this chapter, they are computed exactly in the same way as in Section 8.8.2 of the previous chapter. The smoothness of the interpolant (8.6), hence would be GC^1.

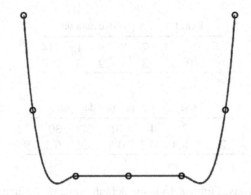

FIGURE 8.1. Cubic Hermite spline curve to the data in Table 8.1.

TABLE 8.1. A convex data set.

x	−4	−3.5	−2	0	2	3.5	4
y	5	0	−3.5	−3.5	−3.5	0	5

TABLE 8.2. A convex data set.

x	−9	−8	−4	0	4	8	9
y	7	5	3.5	3.25	3.5	5	7

TABLE 8.3. A monotone data set.

x	0	6	10	29.5	30
y	0	15	15	25	30

TABLE 8.4. A monotone data set.

x	0.0	1.0	1.7	1.8
y	0.25	1.00	11.10	25

8.2.1 Demonstration

For the demonstration of this GC^1 Hermite-like cubic spline scheme, we choose the following choice of shape parameters as the default value:

$$r_i = 1. \tag{8.8}$$

However, other values of shape parameters can also be allocated for the achievement of a controlled curve. Figures 8.1 and 8.3 are the default curves to the convex data in Table 8.1 and Table 8.2, respectively. Figures 8.5 and 8.7 are the default curves to the monotone data in Table 8.3 and Table 8.4, respectively. Figures 8.9 and 8.11 are the default curves to the positive data in Table 8.5 and

TABLE 8.5. A positive data set.

x	2	3	7	8	9	13	14
y	10	2	3	7	2	3	10

TABLE 8.6. A positive data set.

x	0	2	4	10	28	30	32
y	20.8	8.8	4.2	0.5	3.9	6.2	9.6

Table 8.6, respectively. Figure 8.13 is the default curve to the data that lie above a line $f = \frac{x}{2} + 1$. It can be seen that the ordinary spline curve does not guarantee to preserve the shape. Some odd behavior (noise) can be seen in the presentation of the curve.

8.3   Shape-Preserving Interpolation

The cubic spline method, described in the previous Section 8., has deficiencies as far as the shape-preserving issue is concerned. For example, the cubic in Section 8.2 does not preserve the shape of the data (see Figures 8.1, 8.3, 8.5, 8.7, 8.10, 8.12 and 8.14). Very clearly, these curves do not preserve the shape of the data. It is necessary to assign appropriate values to the shape parameters so that they generate a data-preserved shape. Thus, it looks as if ordinary spline schemes do not provide the desired shape features. Some further treatment is required to achieve a shape-preserving spline for shape-preserving data.

The proposed method, which is effective, useful and is the focus of this chapter, is the automated generation of shape-preserving curves. This requires automated computation of suitable shape parameters. To proceed with this strategy, some mathematical treatment is needed, which is explained in the following Section 8.

8.4   Convex Cubic Spline

For given points:
$$(x_1, f_1), (x_2, f_2), \ldots, (x_n, f_n)$$
with
$$x_1 < x_2 < \cdots < x_n,$$
let us assume convex set of data so that
$$\Delta_1 \leq \Delta_2 \leq \cdots \leq \Delta_{n-1}. \tag{8.9}$$
Similarly, one can assume concave data so that
$$\Delta_1 \geq \Delta_2 \geq \cdots \geq \Delta_{n-1}.$$

In this chapter we develop necessary and sufficient conditions on piecewise cubics under which GC^1 convex interpolation is preserved. We describe the cubic spline S on the grid $x_1 < x_2 < \cdots < x_n$. The key idea to preserve convexity using $S(x)$, is to assign suitable values to r_i in each interval. But, first of all, we determine conditions for r_i, which guarantee convexity.

For a convex interpolant $S(x)$, it is then necessary that the derivative parameters should be

$$d_1 \leq \Delta_1 \leq d_2 \leq \Delta_2 \leq \cdots \leq \Delta_{n-1} \leq d_n. \tag{8.10}$$

$(d_1 \geq \Delta_1 \geq d_2 \geq \Delta_2 \geq \cdots \geq \Delta_{n-1} \geq d_n$, for concave data).

Now $S(x)$ is convex if and only if

$$S^{(2)}(x) \geq 0, \quad x_1 \leq x \leq x_n. \tag{8.11}$$

For $x \in [x_1, x_n]$, it can be shown, after some simplification, that

$$S^{(1)}(x) = \sum_{j=1}^{3} A_{j,i} (1 - \theta)^{3-j} \theta^{j-1},$$

where

$$\left. \begin{array}{l} A_{1,i} = \frac{d_i}{r_i}, \\ A_{2,i} = 3\Delta_i - \left(\frac{d_i}{r_i} + \frac{d_{i+1}}{r_i} \right), \\ A_{3,i} = \frac{d_{i+1}}{r_i}. \end{array} \right\} \tag{8.12}$$

and

$$S^{(2)}(x) = \sum_{j=1}^{2} B_{j,i} (1 - \theta)^{2-j} \theta^{j-1},$$

where

$$B_{1,i} = \left[6\Delta_i - 2 \left(\frac{2d_i}{r_i} + \frac{d_{i+1}}{r_i} \right) \right] / h_i, \tag{8.13}$$

$$B_{2,i} = \left[2 \left(\frac{d_i}{r_i} + \frac{2d_{i+1}}{r_i} \right) - 6\Delta_i \right] / h_i \tag{8.14}$$

The sufficient conditions for convexity on $[x_1, x_n]$ are:

$$B_{j,i} \geq 0, \quad j = 1, 2,$$

where the necessary conditions (8.10) are assumed.

If $\Delta_i > 0$ (strict inequality) then following are sufficient conditions for (8.13) and (8.14):

$$r_i = \frac{2(d_i + d_{i+1})}{3\Delta_i}, \tag{8.15}$$

We will consider this as the default automatic choice. This choice satisfies (8.11) and produces pleasing results.

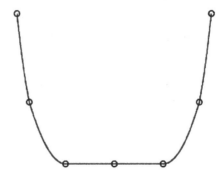

FIGURE 8.2. Shape-preserving cubic spline curve to the data in Table 8.1.

It should be noted that if $\Delta_i = 0$, then it is necessary to set $d_i = 0 = d_{i+1}$, and thus

$$S(x) = f_i = f_{i+1}$$

is a constant on $[x_1, x_n]$. Hence the interpolant (8.7) is convex together with the conditions (8.10) and (8.15). For the case where the data is convex but not strictly convex (i.e., when some $\Delta_i = 0$) it would be necessary to divide the data into strictly convex parts. If we set $d_i = 0 = d_{i+1}$ whenever $\Delta_i = 0$, then the resulting interpolant will be C^0 at break points. This leads to the following:

Theorem 8.1. The cubic polynomial (8.7) preserves convexity if and only if (8.15) is satisfied.

8.4.1 *Demonstration*

The first example is that of data given in Table 8.1. Application of the Hermite cubic spline method (see Section 8.2) produces the curve in Figure 8.1. This curve shows noise, which is misguiding. We now apply piecewise cubic of Section 8.3 to the same data. Figure 8.2 is produced by the default settings of the parameters r_i satisfying the convex conditions derived in Section 8.4. One can see that the convexity nature of the data is preserved in a pleasing way.

The second example regards data taken at random. The curve in Figure 8.3 is due to the Hermite cubic spline method (see Section 8.2). This is not a desired display as some unnecessary oscillations on the curve are also noticed in a certain time limit. Figure 8.4 is produced by the default settings of the parameters r_i satisfying the convex conditions derived in Section 8.4. One can observe that the curve is convex and visually pleasing.

8.5   Monotone Cubic Spline

For given points:

$$(x_1, f_1), (x_2, f_2), \ldots, (x_n, f_n)$$

FIGURE 8.3. Cubic Hermite spline curve to the data in Table 8.2.

FIGURE 8.4. Shape preserving cubic spline curve to the data in Table 8.2.

with
$$x_1 < x_2 < \cdots < x_n,$$

Let us assume monotonic increasing set of data so that
$$f_1 \leq f_2 \leq \cdots \leq f_n$$

or equivalently
$$\Delta_i \geq 0, i = 1, 2, \ldots, n - 1.$$

In a similar fashion, one can deal with a monotonic decreasing data.

In this section we develop necessary and sufficient conditions on piecewise cubics $S(x)$ to assign suitable values to r_i in each interval under which GC^1 monotone interpolation is preserved. For a monotone interpolant $S(x)$, it is then necessary that derivative parameters should be such that

$$d_i \geq 0, \quad i = 1, 2, \ldots, n \text{ for monotonic increasing data,}$$

$d_i \leq 0, \quad i = 1, 2, \ldots, n$ for monotonic decreasing data. Now $S(x)$ is monotonic increasing if and only if

$$S^{(1)}(x) \geq 0, \quad x_1 \leq x \leq x_n.$$

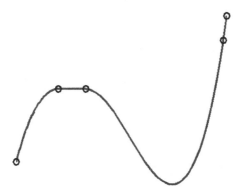

FIGURE 8.5. Cubic Hermite spline curve to the data in Table 8.3.

The sufficient conditions for monotonic on $[x_1, x_n]$ are

$$A_{j,i} \geq 0, \quad j = 1, 2, 3.$$

where the necessary conditions

$$d_i \geq 0 \text{ and } d_{i+1} \geq 0,$$

are assumed. If $\Delta_i > 0$, then the following are the sufficient conditions for (8.12):

$$r_i > \frac{d_i + d_{i+1}}{3\Delta_i}. \tag{8.16}$$

Theorem 8.2. The cubic polynomial (8.7) preserves monotonicity if and only if (8.16) is satisfied.

8.5.1 *Demonstration*

Let us take the example of monotone data as in Table 8.3. Figure 8.5 is produced by applying the Hermite cubic spline method on this monotone data, which loses the monotonicity. Figure 8.6 shows the monotone curve through monotone data in Table 8.3 using the monotone cubic function of Section 8.5.

Secondly, we consider a monotone set of data from Sakai and Schmidt [10] in Table 8.4.

Figure 8.7 is produced by applying the Hermite cubic spline method which loses monotonicity. Figure 8.8 is produced using the monotone cubic function of Section 8.5 that preserves the shape of data in Table 8.4.

8.6 Positive Cubic Spline

The problem of positive interpolation can be described as follows: For given data points

$$(x_1, f_1), (x_2, f_2), \ldots, (x_n, f_n)$$

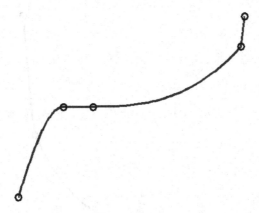

FIGURE 8.6. Shape-preserving cubic spline curve to the data in Table 8.3.

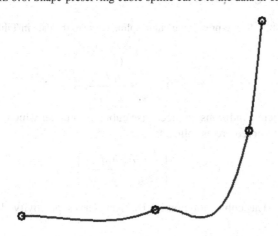

FIGURE 8.7. Cubic Hermite spline curve to the data in Table 8.4.

with
$$x_1 < x_2 < \cdots < x_n,$$
and
$$f_1 > 0, f_2 > 0, \ldots, f_n > 0,$$
construct an interpolant $S(x)$ which is positive on the whole interval $[x_1, x_n]$, that is,
$$S(x) > 0, x_1 \le x \le x_n.$$

The key idea to preserve positivity using $S(x)$ is to assign suitable values to r_i's in each interval. We would like to determine conditions for r_i which guarantee positivity. Since $S(x) > 0$ for all $V_i, W_i > 0$, so we have the following:
$$V_i > 0 \text{ if } r_i > \frac{-h_i d_i}{3 f_i},$$

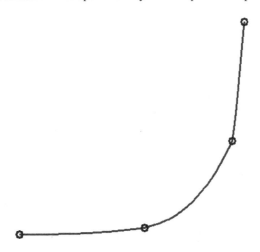

FIGURE 8.8. Shape-preserving cubic spline curve to the data in Table 8.4.

and

$$W_i > 0 \text{ if } r_i > \frac{h_i d_{i+1}}{3 f_{i+1}}.$$

Thus, the sufficient conditions on piecewise cubic $S(x)$ under which GC^1 positive interpolant is preserved are as follows:

$$r_i > \max \left\{ \frac{-h_i d_i}{3 f_i}, \frac{h_i d_{i+1}}{3 f_{i+1}} \right\}. \tag{8.17}$$

Theorem 8.3. The cubic polynomial (8.7) preserves positivity if and only if (8.17) is satisfied.

8.6.1 *Demonstration*

For this demonstration, consider the positive data in Table 8.4. This data has come from the known volume of NaOH taken in a beaker and its conductivity was determined. An HCL solution was added from the burette in steps, drop by drop. After each addition, the volume of HCL(x) was stirred by gentle shaking, and conductance (y) was determined as shown in Table 8.4. Application of the Hermite cubic spline method produces the curve in Figure 8.7. This curve shows the negative value of conductance, which is ridiculous. This flaw is recovered nicely in Figure 8.9 using the positivity-preserving cubic scheme of Section 8.6.

Other positive data (W shaped) is shown in Table 8.5. Application of the Hermite cubic spline method produces the curve in Figure 8.10. This curve shows the negative value of conductance, which is ridiculous. This flaw is recovered nicely in Figure 8.11 using the positivity-preserving cubic scheme of Section 8.6.

We consider another positive set of data from Butt and Brodlie [2] in Table 8.6. Figure 8.12 is produced by applying the Hermite cubic spline method, which loses

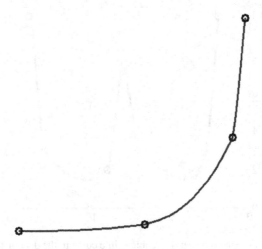

FIGURE 8.9. Positivity-preserving cubic spline curve to the data in Table 8.4.

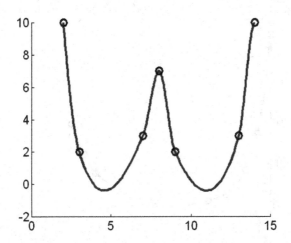

FIGURE 8.10. Cubic Hermite spline curve to the data in Table 8.5.

the shape of data in Table 8.6. Figure 8.13 shows the positive curve through positive data in Table 8.6 using positive interpolation of Section 8.6.

8.7 Extension of Positive Cubic Spline

Let $(x_i, f_i), i = 1, 2, \ldots, n$ be the given data points that lie above any straight line $f(x) = mx + c$, that is $f_i > mx_i + c$ for all $i = 1, 2, \ldots, n$. We require

$$S(x) \equiv S_i(x) > mx_i + c.$$

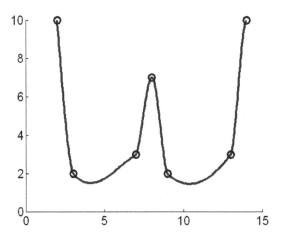

FIGURE 8.11. Shape-preserving cubic spline curve to the data in Table 8.5.

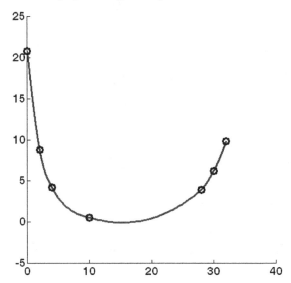

FIGURE 8.12. Cubic Hermite spline curve to the data in Table 8.6.

We assume that $m > 0$. The case $m < 0$ can be handled in a similar way. In each interval $mx + c$ can be expressed as:

$$a_i (1 - \theta) + b_i \theta$$

where

$$a_i = mx_i + c, \quad b_i = mx_{i+1} + c.$$

We thus require

$$S_i(x) > a_i(1 - \theta) + b_i\theta, \quad i = 1, 2, \ldots, n.$$

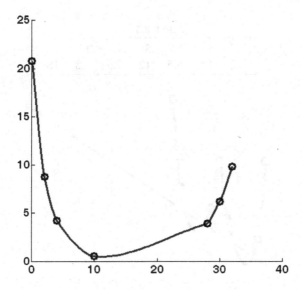

FIGURE 8.13. Shape-preserving cubic spline curve to the data in Table 8.6.

So we require

$$U_i = f_i(1-\theta)^3 + 3V_i\theta(1-\theta)^2 + 3W_i\theta^2(1-\theta) + f_{i+1}\theta^3 - \{a_i(1-\theta) + b_i\theta\} > 0. \tag{8.18}$$

It can be expressed as

$$U_i = (f_i - a_i)(1-\theta)^3 + (3V_i - 2a_i - b_i)\theta(1-\theta)^2$$
$$+ (3W_i - a_i + 2b_i)\theta^2(1-\theta) + (f_{i+1} - b_i)\theta^3 > 0.$$

Since

$$f_i - a_i > 0 \text{ and } f_{i+1} - b_i > 0,$$

so $U_i > 0$ if and only if

$$3V_i - 2a_i - b_i > 0 \text{ and } 3W_i - a_i - 2b_i > 0.$$

$3V_i - 2a_i - b_i > 0$ if

$$r_i > \frac{-h_i d_i}{3f_i - 2a_i - b_i}$$

and $3W_i - a_i - 2b_i > 0$ if

$$r_i > \frac{h_i d_{i+1}}{3f_{i+1} - a_i - 2b_i}.$$

The above discussion leads to the following theorem.

Theorem 8.4. The polynomial (8.7) lies above the given straight line if and only if

$$r_i > \max\left\{\frac{-h_i d_i}{3f_i - 2a_1 - b_i}, \frac{h_i d_{i+1}}{3f_{i+1} - a_i - 2b_i}\right\}.$$

TABLE 8.7.

x	2	3	7	8	9	13	14
f	12	4.5	6.5	12	7.5	9.5	18

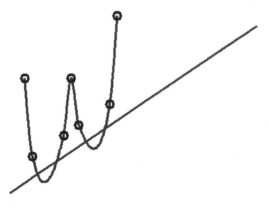

FIGURE 8.14. Cubic Hermite spline curve to the data in Table 8.7.

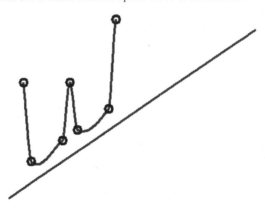

FIGURE 8.15. Shape-preserving cubic spline curve to the data in Table 8.7.

8.7.1 *Demonstration*

We finally consider the data in the Table 8.7 where f-values lie above the line

$$f = \frac{x}{2} + 1.$$

Figure 8.14 is produced using the cubic Hermite spline. This curve does not lie above the line $f = \frac{x}{2} + 1$. This flaw is recovered nicely in Figure 8.15 using the scheme of Section 8.7.

Remark 8.1. These methods can be used in both cases when either d_i's are particularly specified or estimated by some method. We propose the arithmetic mean approximation method [3] for the practical implementation in this chapter.

8.8 Summary

A piecewise cubic interpolant, in a generalized form, has been utilized to obtain a GC^1 convexity-, monotonicity- and positivity-preserving curve methods. Data-dependent shape constraints are derived on shape parameters to assure the shape preservation of the data. Choice of the derivative parameters is considered to be the approximation through arithmetic choice.

The proposed curve schemes are visually smooth enough and present reasonably acceptable demonstrations of the shape of the data, but a higher degree of smoothness, while stitching the pieces of curves, may enhance the visual display.

8.9 Exercises

1. Extend the curve scheme in Section 8.2 to a parametric curve scheme and write a program to demonstrate the effect of the shape parameters for CAD/CAM purposes.
2. Extend the curve scheme in Section 8.4 to a parametric curve scheme such that it preserves the convex data.
3. Extend the curve scheme in Section 8.5 to a parametric curve scheme such that it preserves the monotonic data.
4. Extend the curve scheme in Section 8.6 to a parametric curve scheme such that it preserves the positive data.
5. Write a program to visualize the results of the scheme in Exercises 4–6.
6. Extend the curve scheme in Section 8.2 to a C^1 curve scheme.
7. Extend the curve scheme in Section 8.4 to a C^1 curve scheme.
8. Extend the curve scheme in Section 8.5 to a C^1 curve scheme.
9. Extend the curve scheme in Section 8.6 to a C^1 curve scheme.

References

1. Brodlie, K.W., and Butt, S. (1991), Preserving convexity using piecewise cubic interpolation, *Comput Graphics* 15(1), 15–23.
2. Butt, S., and Brodlie, K.W. (1993), Preserving positivity using piecewise cubic interpolation, *Comput Graphics* 17(1), 55–64.
3. Delbourgo, R., and Gregory, J.A. (1985), Shape-preserving piecewise rational interpolation, *SIAM J Stat Comput* 6, 967–976.
4. Fritsch, F.N., and Butland, J. (1984), A method for constructing local monotone piecewise cubic interpolants, *SIAM J Sci Stat Comput* 5, 300–304.
5. Fritsch, F.N., and Carlson, R.E. (1980), Monotone piecewise cubic interpolation, *SIAM J Numer Anal* 17(2), 238–246.

6. Gregory, J.A., and Sarfraz, M. (1990), A rational spline with tension, *Comput Aided Geom Des* 7, 1–13.

7. Gregory, J.R., and Delbourgo, R. (1983), Piecewise rational quadratic interpolation to monotonic data, *SIAM J Numer Anal* 3, 141–152.

8. McAllister, D.F., Passow, E., and Roulier, J.A. (1977), Algorithms for computing shape-preserving spline interpolations to data, *Math Comp* 31, 717–725.

9. McAllister, D.F., and Roulier, J.A. (1981), An algorithm for computing a shape-preserving osculatory quadratic spline, *ACM Trans Math Software* 7, 331–347.

10. Sakai, M., and Schmidt, J.W. (1988), Positive interpolation with rational splines, *Computing*, 140–147.

11. Sarfraz, M. (1992), Convexity-preserving piecewise rational interpolation for planar curves, *Bull Korean Math Soc* 29(2), 193–200.

12. Sarfraz, M., Al-Mulhem, M., and Ashraf, F. (1997), Preserving monotonic shape of the data using piecewise rational cubic functions, *Comput Graphics* 21(1), 5–14.

13. Sarfraz, M. (2003), A rational cubic spline for the visualization of monotonic data: an alternate approach, *Int J Comput Graphics*, Elsevier Science, 27(1), 107–121.

14. Sarfraz, M. (2002), Visualization of positive and convex data by a rational cubic spline, *Int J Information Sci*, Elsevier Science Inc., 146(1–4), 239–254.

15. Sarfraz, M., Butt, S., and Hussain, M.Z. (2001), Visualization of shaped data by a rational cubic spline interpolation, *Int J Comput Graphics*, Elsevier Science, 25(5), 833–845.

16. Sarfraz, M. (2000), A rational cubic spline for the visualization of monotonic data, *Int J Comput Graphics*, Elsevier Science, 24(4), 509–516.

17. Sarfraz, M., Hussain, M.Z., Chaudhry, F.S. (2005), Shape-preserving data visualization with cubic splines, *Proceedings of the International Joint Conference on Information Sciences-JCIS'2005-USA*, Etienne E. Kerre, Donald Hung, Dan Ventura, Manuel Grana Romay, Heng-Da Cheng, Hong Va Leong, Shu-Heng Chen, David K.Y. Chiu, Steve Blair, Paul P. Wang, Chris Tseng, Chang-Tien Lu, Jie Lu, M. Sarfraz (Eds.), pp. 1661–1664.

18. Sarfraz, M., Hussain, M.Z., and Chaudhry, F.S. (2005), Shape-preserving cubic spline for data visualization, *Int J Comput Graphics CAD/CAM,* International Scientific 1(6), 185-194.

9
Approximation with B-Splines Curves

Abstract. *B-spline curves have been used to approximate the functional data. Two curve approximation techniques are presented here. One scheme is based on a deterministic approach using quadratic B-splines. The other scheme uses a genetic algorithm in its formulation where the B-spline can have any order. Both schemes automatically compute data points to minimize errors.*

9.1 Introduction

Curve approximation [6,8–14] is all about finding accurate locations of data points from the given curve. It is an important area of computer graphics and can be utilized in computer vision and imaging applications too. B-splines curves [4] are popular models for curve design and can be defined by their degrees and control points. They have been used here to present curve approximating techniques. Both of the schemes presented in this chapter automatically compute data points to minimize errors. These techniques can be useful for efficient storage of geometric shapes in any applications of graphics, vision and imaging. The first technique presented is based on a deterministic approach; it uses a quadratic B-spline curve for approximating functions or functional data. The second scheme is based on a nondeterministic approach, namely, a genetic algorithm. It has the freedom to utilize any degree B-spline formulation.

In the first technique [12] presented here, quadratic B-spline data points are computed by exploiting the properties of its knots. This technique consists of three steps of approximation. Step 1 involves computation/plotting of opening angles. In Step 2, knots are inserted at appropriate locations, which bring approximation error within specified threshold limits. Step 3 is a further optimization of approximation results by changing knot positions. A general quadratic B-spline curve through these data points (control points and knots) would be an approximating curve. Demonstrated results will show that very precise approximation can be achieved with quite lesser data points. This curve approximation technique is simple, efficient and robust for any parametric curve(s). It does not require an extensive search for data points. Data points once computed are not discarded.

The second technique is also based on B-spline formulation [13,14]; it has more freedom and can use any degree B-spline formulation for curve representation. A genetic approach has been adopted to locate appropriate B-spline knots so that the approximation error is minimized.

The rest of the chapter is organized as follows. Section 9.2 gives a general description of quadratic B-splines. Section 9.3 highlights properties of knots together with the approximating technique (in three steps). Section 9.4 describes the technique based on a genetic algorithm (GA). Both schemes have been illustrated with examples. Section 9.5 summarizes the chapter.

9.2   B-Splines

The general expression for calculation of any coordinate position along a B-spline curve in a blending function formulation [5] can be given as:

$$P(u) = \sum_{k=0}^{n} p_k B_{k,d}(u), u_{\min} \leq u \leq u_{\max}, 2 \leq d \leq n+1 \qquad (9.1)$$

In Equation (9.1) above, p_k is an input set of $n+1$ control points. The B-spline blending function $B_{k,d}$ are polynomials of degree $d-1$. Blending functions for B-spline curves can be defined by the Cox-deBoor recursion formulas [3]:

$$\left. \begin{aligned} B_{k,d}(u) &= \frac{u - u_k}{u_{k+d-1} - u_k} B_{k,d-1}(u) + \frac{u_{k+d} - u}{u_{k+d} - u_{k+1}} B_{k+1,d-1}(u) \\ B_{k,1}(u) &= \begin{cases} 1, & \text{if } u_k \leq u < u_{k+1} \\ 0, & \text{otherwise} \end{cases} \end{aligned} \right\} \qquad (9.2)$$

Each blending function is defined over d subintervals of the total range of u. We can choose any values for the subinterval endpoints u_j satisfying the relation $u_j \leq u_{j+1}$.

9.3   Deterministic Approach

In this section, we assign $d = 3$, $u_{\min} = 0$ & $u_{\max} = 1$ for the quadratic B-spline (QBS) curves that would be used for approximation of given curves. The range of parameter u is divided into $n + d + 1$ knot values labeled as $\{u_0, u_1, \ldots, u_{n+d}\}$ and the resulting QBS curve is defined in the range from knot value u_{d-1} up to u_{n+1}. For the uniform QBS, the spacing between knots remains constant as in $\{0.0, 0.2, 0.4, 0.6, 0.8, 1.0\}$. Figure 9.1 shows QBS with five control points and uniform knot spacing. For the open uniform QBS, the knot spacing is uniform except at the ends where knot values are repeated d times as given below:

$$\{0, 0, 0, 0.25, 0.5, 0.75, 1, 1, 1\} \text{ for } d = 3 \text{ and } n = 5 \qquad (9.3)$$

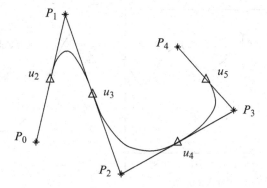

FIGURE 9.1. QBS with five control points ($n = 4$). The curve is defined between knot u_2 to u_5.

For a nonuniform QBS, we can choose unequal knot spacing and multiple knot values. Similarly, in open nonuniform QBS (used in this chapter), knot spacing is nonuniform, and at the ends knot values are repeated d times. We observe following properties of QBS knots:

- Knots are the interpolating points along the curve.
- Only one knot lies between two successive control points.
- The QBS curve touches its convex hull at each knot position.
- The opening angle along the QBS curve maximizes at its knot positions (Section 9.3).

9.3.1 Approximation Technique

The presented approximation technique is developed by exploiting the QBS knot properties. This technique is suitable for approximation of any spline/mathematical curve(s). The QBS approximation is a three-step process.

9.3.1.1 Initial Data Points (Step 1)

Curvature measure, based on opening angles of each point along the curve, is used for analysis/detection of initial knot positions. Opening angle, $\theta \in |0, \pi|$, for any curve point C_i can be computed as:

$$\theta = \arccos \frac{a^2 + b^2 + c^2}{2ab} \tag{9.4}$$

where a, b and c are the distances $|C_i - C_{i-w}|$, $|C_i - C_{i+w}|$ and $|C_{i-w} - C_{i+w}|$, respectively, for $w \le i \le n - w$, where w is the window size and n is the number of points in a given curve. The value of w depends on the smoothness of the given curve. We use $w = 1$ as the curve under approximation, which is very smooth. Figure 9.2(a) shows a plot of opening angle θ for a QBS of Figure 9.1. Maxima points of this plot, including two endpoints of given curve, are selected

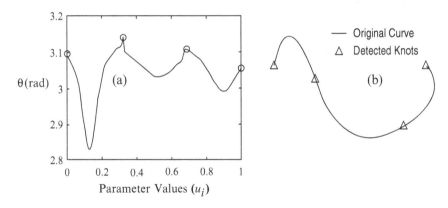

FIGURE 9.2. Initial data points: (a) Opening angle plot of QBS curve of Figure 9.1. Maxima points (circles) are the detected knots; (b) Detected knots are placed on the original curve.

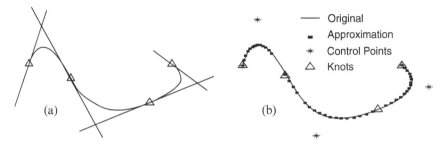

FIGURE 9.3. Control points evaluation: (a) Intersection points, of the tangents of the curve at its knots, representing expected location of control points, (b) Curve approximation of QBS curve of Figure 9.1 after Step 1.

as the initial knot positions (Figure 9.2(b)). One can observe that the positions of detected knots are very close to their actual locations (compare Figure 9.1 and Figure 9.2(b)). Using this method, detected positions of knots, for any QBS curve, are always precise and accurate.

Location of control points can be calculated very easily from the detected knots. Intersection points of tangents, for the curve at its knot positions, are the locations of control points (Figure 9.3(a)). Knots at curve endpoints are also selected as two control points because the approximation curve is intended to be open nonuniform QBS. The B-spline curve through these detected control points and knots is an approximation curve (Figure 9.3(b)). The computed curve is accurate enough, requiring no future working. Step 1 provides an accurate curve approximation if the given curve is quadratic but requires Step 2 and/or Step 3 approximation for higher polynomial curves. Therefore, if the approximation error (the area between two curves) exceeds the specified threshold limits, approximation results are transferred to the next step for further processing.

9.3.1.2   Knot Insertion (Step 2)

This step increases flexibility of approximating QBS by insertion of additional knots/control points at appropriate locations. We take the cubic B-spline curve (Figure 9.4(a)) as input for explanation of this step. Its opening angle plot is shown in Figure 9.4(b) and maxima points of this plot represent the initial knot positions. As the input curve is a cubic spline, detected knot positions may not be at their actual knot positions. However, minima points in Figure 9.4(b) represent the actual knot positions of the cubic B-spline which can lead to approximation techniques using cubic B-splines. Here we restrict ourselves to approximation with QBS, which should be applicable to the curves with any degree of polynomial/type of spline.

Approximating the curve through the detected knots is shown in Figure 9.5(a). The amount of error between two curves (Figure 9.5(a)) is undesirable. The acceptable error limit depends on the size/resolution of given curve. We use three-pixel error limits in our method. Therefore the default value of 3 can be assigned as the error limit when each curve point represents one pixel.

Additional knots are introduced to minimize error between two curves [2]. Approximation error minimizes at knot positions and maximizes in between.

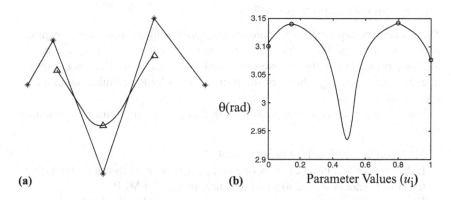

(a)   **(b)**   Parameter Values (u_i)

FIGURE 9.4. (a) Cubic B-spline with five control points; (b) the opening angle plot.

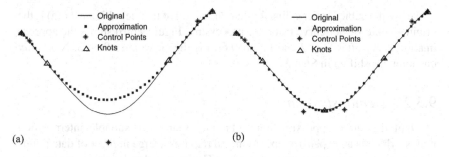

FIGURE 9.5. Curve approximation of Figure 9.4(a): (a) after Step 1; (b) after Step 2.

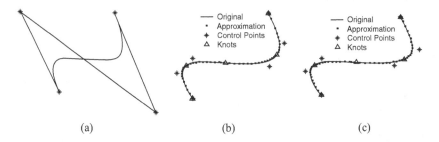

(a)   (b)   (c)

FIGURE 9.6. (a) Cubic Bezier curve. (b) Curve approximation after Step 2. (c) Curve approximation after Step 3.

The maximum errors between each pair of knots are called maximum error points (MEPs). New knots are inserted at the MEPs that exceed the threshold error limit. Approximating a curve after inserting these knot(s) is shown in Figure 9.5(b). Note that only one knot was added and approximation error decreased below the threshold value. Step 2 is expected to bring approximation error below threshold limits in a single iteration. The results of this step are fed to Step 3 for further refinement.

9.3.1.3 Error Minimization (Step 3)

This refinement step minimizes approximation error without introducing any more knots/control points. The shape of the approximating curve can change by changing knot positions [7]. In this step, detected knots are moved along the curve to exploit the design flexibility of the B-spline in order to optimize the ultimate approximation curve.

The following search technique is used to find the new (optimized) location of knots:

1. MEP between each pair of knots is located.
2. If the error at that point exceeds one-half of the specified threshold limit, then the closest knot is shifted to a half distance toward that MEP.
3. If the approximation error does not improve by shifting the knot, it is taken back to its original position.

We use the cubic Bezier spline for demonstration of this step. Figure 9.6(a) is the original cubic Bezier curve taken for processing. Figure 9.6(b) shows the approximation curve after Step 2 and Figure 9.6(c) is the curve after Step 3. Note only one knot has shifted in Step 3.

9.3.2 Demonstration

Most of the curve approximation techniques search for suitable interpolation points, which is an expensive operation and requires a large number of data points to present a good quality of approximation. The proposed technique, using general QBS curves, is based on approximation of data points and outperforms previous

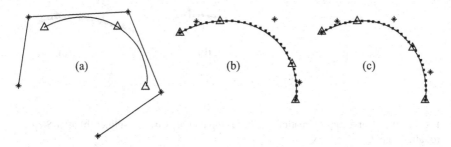

FIGURE 9.7. Curve approximation result: (a) cubic B-spline; (b) after Step 1; (c) after Step 3.

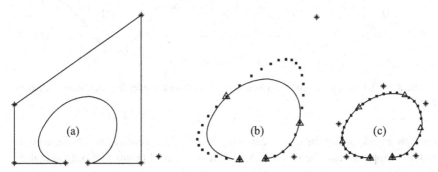

FIGURE 9.8. Curve approximation result: (a) input Bezier spline of degree 5; (b) after Step 1; (c) after Step 2.

methods in quality. Quality of any curve approximation technique can be gauged on various parameters such as computational efficiency, robustness of algorithm, approximation error, number of data points (control points or knots) and visual appearance.

The presented algorithm is computationally very efficient because it does not require any extensive search technique for detection of data points (Figure 9.7). Data points are located without any search in Steps 1 and 2, and Step 3 is a simple optimization of approximation results. Data points once detected are not discarded. The presented algorithm is very robust (even if no data points are found in Step 1); it performs well on any given curve. The detected data points are very well located and only few data points can demonstrate approximation of quite flexible and higher polynomial curves. Human judgment with visual appearance of computed curves is the most important factor in any curve approximation results. Various results are demonstrated in this section to analyze the quality of approximation with the proposed technique.

Figure 9.8(a) is a Bezier curve [1] constructed, with polynomial of degree 5, for approximation. Figure 9.8(b) and 8(c) are the approximation results after Step 1 and Step 2, respectively. The approximation result after Step 2 was accurate

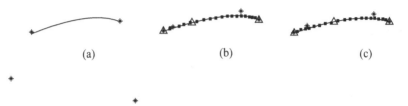

FIGURE 9.9. Curve approximation result: (a) input cubic cardinal spline; (b) after Step 1; (c) after Step 2.

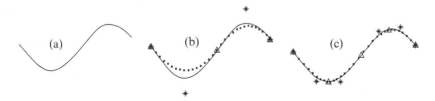

FIGURE 9.10. Curve approximation result: (a) input cosine curve; (b) after Step 1; (c) after Step 2.

enough, avoiding any further processing (Step 3). Seven control points were computed to approximate the given curve (with six control points and polynomial of degree 5).

Figure 9.9(a) is a Cardinal spline [5] specified with four control points. Its approximation after Step 1 and Step 3 is demonstrated in Figures 9.9(b) and 9.9(c), respectively. Step 2 approximation was not needed/performed. The curve is approximated with four control points, which is equal to the control points of the original curve.

Figure 9.10(a) is a plot of cosine function. Its approximation results after Step 1 and Step 2 are shown in Figures 9.10(b) and 9.10(c), respectively. Step 3 approximation was not required due to the good quality of result after Step 2.

In all the above results, note that the algorithm performs quite well on a variety of input curve models. Remember that the computed curve is a QBS, even though (in most of the cases) the number of computed control points (on which it is constructed) equalizes to the number of control points of the original (higher polynomial) curves. Also note that two steps of approximation are normally involved for computing approximating curves. Thus, the efficiency of this algorithm is in general much higher than it looks.

9.4   Nondeterministic Approach

Approximating data or curves with spline [3–7] is an important topic in the area of computer graphics. If we have to make a good model from complex data or a complex function, it is difficult to approximate it by a single polynomial. In this case, a spline is one of the most appropriate approximating functions. The key to using a B-spline formulation is the determination of good knots and obtaining good approximation. One needs to place the knots as precisely as possible for a good approximation. In such cases, one need to deal with knots as variables. Then the problem becomes a continuous nonlinear and multivariate optimization problem with many local optima. Therefore, it is difficult to obtain a global optimum [3].

In the current literature, *genetic algorithms (GAs)* have been widely rcognized as a useful vehicle for obtaining high-quality or even optimal solutions in this area. However, the knots of a spline do not need to be optimal: usually suboptimal is sufficient. So, GAs can be conveniently applied for the determination of good *knots* [1].

9.4.1   A Brief Overview of GAs

In the last decade, genetic algorithms (GAs) have emerged as practical robust optimization search methods. Introduced by Holland in the 1970s, GAs are search techniques based on the concept of evolution [8]. Given a well-defined search space in which each solution is represented by a bit string, called a chromosome, a GA is applied with its three genetic search operators, namely, selection, crossover and mutation, to transform a population of chromosomes with the objective of improving the quality of the chromosomes. The individual bits of a chromosome are called genes. Before the search starts, a set of chromosomes is randomly chosen from the search space to form the initial population. The three genetic search operations are then applied one after the other to obtain a new generation of chromosomes in which the expected quality over all the chromosomes is better than that of the previous generation. The process is repeated until the stopping criterion is met (e.g., a predefined number of generations are processed). In the end the best chromosome of the last generation is reported as a final solution. The outline for the GA algorithm is shown in Figure 9.11.

9.4.2   Implementation Summary

In this section, the summary of the work proposed in [1] has been presented. The details of the scheme can be seen in [1]. It can be summarized in the following steps:

1. Individuals are constructed by considering the candidates of the locations of knots as genes, as shown in Figure 9.12.
2. A control parameter called the *knot ratio*, R, has been used, where R is the ratio of the numbers of 1's and 0's in an individual (see Figure 9.13).
3. If the procedure of knot detection is applied, these knots are kept constant by applying the OR operation between the chromosome and the chromosome representing the detected knots, as shown in Figure 9.13. The OR operation is

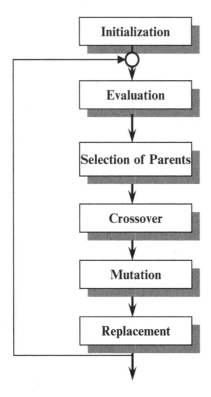

FIGURE 9.11. A GA outline.

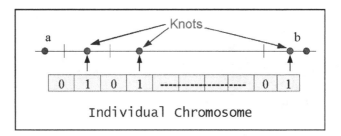

FIGURE 9.12. Genetic formulation.

applied after both the crossover and mutation have been applied so that we don't lose these knots during these operations. In this way the detected knots remain unchanged in the subsequent generations.

4. Akaike's information criterion (AIC) [2] has been used as the fitness function. It is given by:

$$AIC = N \log_e Q_1 + 2(2n + m) \tag{9.5}$$

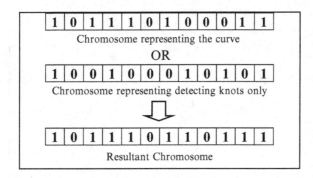

FIGURE 9.13. Preservation of significant knots.

where

$$Q_1 = \sum_{j=1}^{N} w_j \left\{ \{Sx_j(t) - x_j(t)\}^2 + \{Sy_j(t) - y_j(t)\}^2 \right\} \qquad (9.6)$$

where N is the number of data, n is the number of interior knots, and m is the order of the spline to be fitted on the given data. It should be noted that the smaller value of (9.5) gives better fitness. The $Sx(t)$ and $Sy(t)$ are the x and y components, respectively, of the approximated spline $S(t)$ over the data F, and w_j is the weight of data, taken to be 1 for all data points in our case. The subscript Q indicates the dimension of the data.

5. The fitness value of the solution is determined through AIC.
6. The control parameters constitute population size K, genelength L, crossover probability C, mutation probability M and knot ratio R.

9.4.3 Demonstration

In this section some results have been presented that demonstrate the curve scheme in different scenarios. Figure 9.14 displays an exponential function:

$$f(x) = \frac{1}{1 + e^{-x}}. \qquad (9.7)$$

The GA scheme was applied to find out the approximate spline curve for this function data in Figure 9.15. A gene size of 101 knots (see the points indicated as "x") was taken; a cubic B-spline curve was selected as the computational model; a knot ratio was taken as 0.3; population size was 30 (see bullets); and data was considered without noise. After five iterations, the approximated curve (loose curve) achieved can be seen in Figure 9.15; it requires more iterations to converge to the original function. Table 9.1 shows all the selected parameters.

The same parameter choice as in Table 9.1, but with noise generated in the data, was used to demonstrate the scheme in Figure 9.17. Figure 9.16 has been plotted by introducing some noise in the actual function, that is,

$$F_j = f(x_i) + \varepsilon_j, \, j = 1, 2, \ldots, N, \qquad (9.8)$$

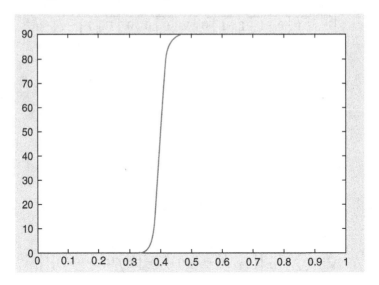

FIGURE 9.14. Input function.

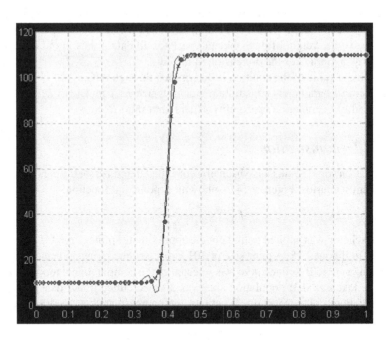

FIGURE 9.15. The result (loose curve) after five iterations of GA implemented.

TABLE 9.1. Description of parameter selection.

Function	Gene length	Population	Knot ratio	Number of generations	Order of spline	Noise
Exponential	101	30	0.3	05	4	No

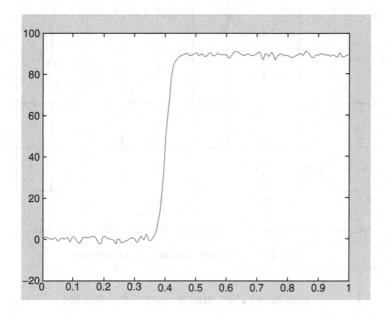

FIGURE 9.16. Exponential function data with noise addition.

where $f(x)$ is the underlying function in Equation (9.7), and ε_j is a measurement error.

Figure 9.17 is the cubic B-spline fitted to a uniformly distributed noisy data. Analysis of various other facts regarding the output in Figure 9.17 are given in Figures 9.18–9.20. For example, Figure 9.18 is the demonstration of the sum of the squares errors versus the number of generations. The details of other related parameters is also given in Figure 9.18. Figure 9.19 demonstrates the AIC versus the number of generations. Figure 9.20 is the display of the graph showing knot/generation versus number of generations.

Another implementation is made in Figure 9.21. This is to fit a cubic spline to a sine function. Analysis of various facts regarding the output in Figure 9.21 are given in Figures 9.22–9.24. For example, Figure 9.22 is the demonstration of the sum of the squares errors versus the number of generations. The details of other related parameters is also given in Figure 9.22. Figure 9.23 demonstrates the AIC versus the number of generations. Figure 9.24 is the display of the graph showing knot/generation versus number of generations.

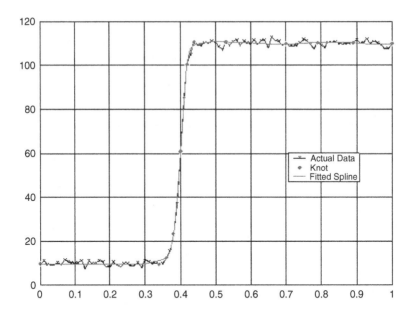

FIGURE 9.17. Cubic B-spline fitted to a uniformly distributed noisy data.

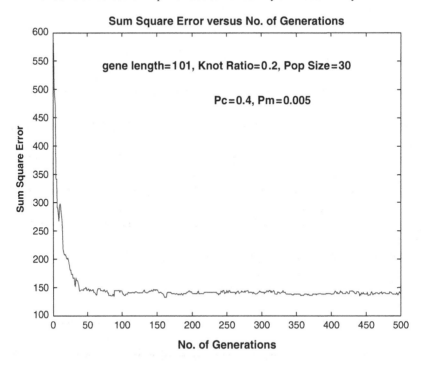

FIGURE 9.18. Sum of the squares errors versus the number of generations.

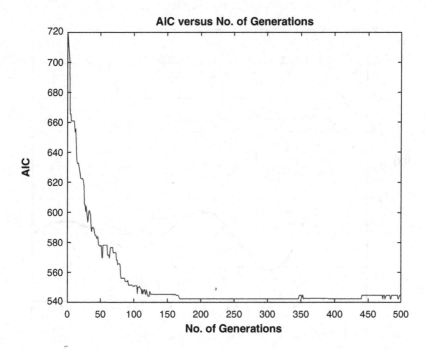

FIGURE 9.19. The AIC versus the number of generations.

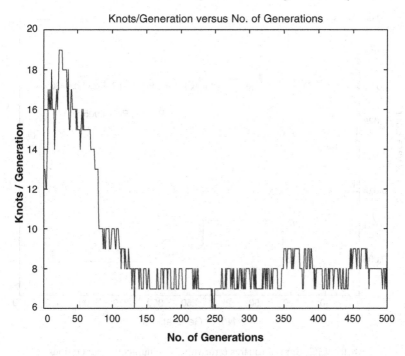

FIGURE 9.20. The graph showing knot/generation versus number of generations.

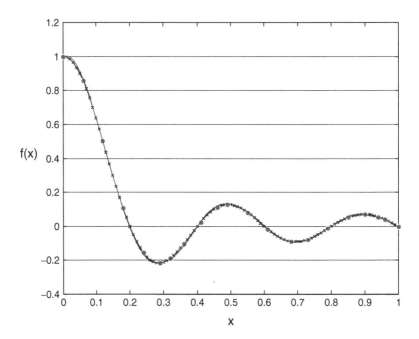

FIGURE 9.21. A sine function and fitted spline.

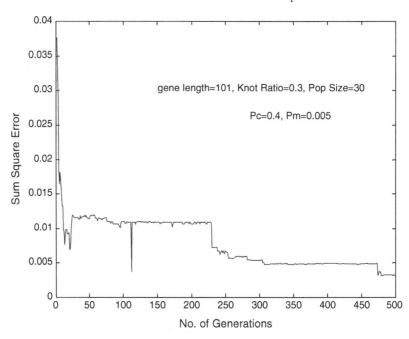

FIGURE 9.22. Sum of squares error versus the number of generations.

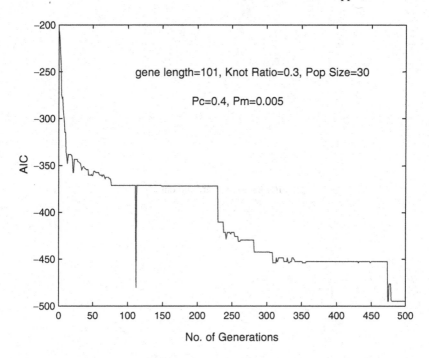

FIGURE 9.23. The AIC versus the number of generations.

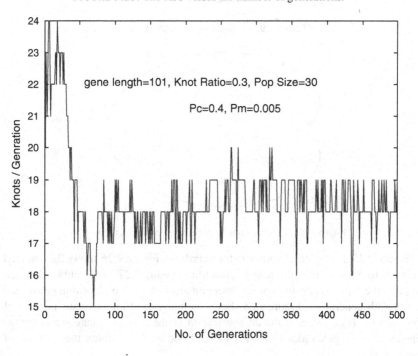

FIGURE 9.24. The graph showing knot/generation versus number of generations.

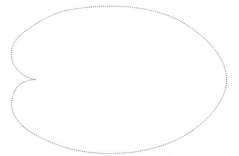

FIGURE 9.25. Cardioid data.

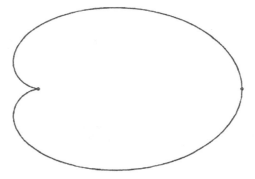

FIGURE 9.26. Showing detected points.

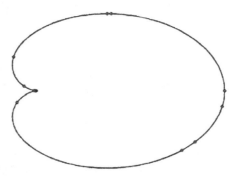

FIGURE 9.27. After convergence (with corner detection).

Figure 9.25 displays the input data for a cardioid. Figure 9.26 shows the detected knots before executing the genetic algorithm. Figure 9.27 is the cubic B-spline fitted to the input data using corner detection algorithm. The algorithm converged at the 98th generation. Figure 9.28 shows the number of knots versus number of generations, Figure 9.29 is the demonstration of the sum of square errors versus the number of generations and Figure 9.30 shows AIC versus the number of generations.

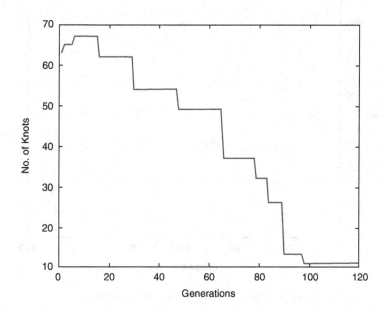

FIGURE 9.28. Knots versus number of generations.

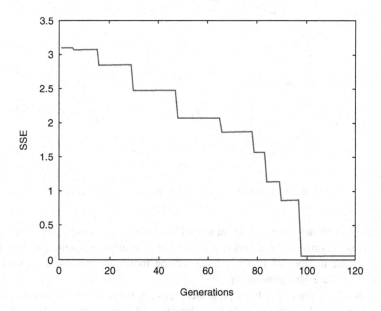

FIGURE 9.29. Sum of squares error versus number of generations.

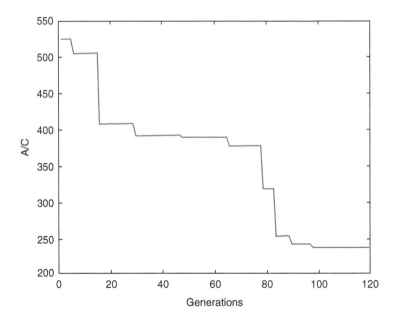

FIGURE 9.30. AIC versus number of generations.

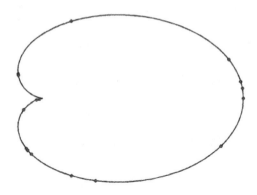

FIGURE 9.31. After convergence (without detected knots).

Figure 9.31 shows the result obtained without using the corner detection technique. This version of the algorithm converged to almost the same solution but with a greater number of knots and consuming more generations. This version converged at the 104th generation.

A comparative study has been presented between the results obtained by using detected knots and results without knot detection. A very interesting observation that can be made on the basis of these results is that the algorithm showed better

TABLE 9.2. Performance with and without detected knots.

Shape: Cardioid	With detected knots	Without detected knots
Generation converged on	98	104
No. of knots obtained	11	16

performance when aided by the detected knots. That is, the former version converged earlier than the other. However, both in the end reached almost the same solution in terms of sum square error. Sometimes the solution also shows a difference in the number of knots obtained. Table 9.2 shows a comparison between the results obtained with and without the detected knot technique.

9.5 Summary

Two curve approximation techniques have been presented. One is deterministic and the other is nondeterministic. The deterministic technique is the curve approximation algorithm with QBS. The algorithm is a three-step process that is very simple and does not involve heavy computations. The algorithm is based on detection of data points that are approximated (not interpolated) to get the ultimate approximation curve. The nondeterministic technique is based on a genetic algorithm. It is similar to the first technique except that its mechanism is to locate the most optimal knots. Both algorithms are simple, efficient and robust for any given curve(s). These schemes can lead to various applications in CAD and CAGD.

9.6 Exercises

1. Write a program to implement the B-spline curve in Equation (1).
2. Write a program to implement the curve approximation technique in Section 9.3.
3. Extend the curve approximation technique of Section 9.3 for a cubic B-spline.
4. Write a program to implement the curve approximation technique in Section 9.4.
5. Make a comparative study of the two schemes in Sections 3 and 4 about the time cost when a quadratic B-spline is used in both cases.
6. Make a comparative study of the two schemes in Sections 3 and 4 about the time cost when a cubic B-spline is used in both cases.
7. B-spline curve in Equation (1).

References

1. Bezier, P. (1974), Mathematical and practical possibilities of UNISURF. In: Barnhill. R.E., and Riesenfeld R.F., eds. *Computer Aided Geometric Design*, Academic Press, New York.
2. Boehm, W. (1980), Inserting new knots into B-spline curves. *Comput Aided Des* 12, 199–201.
3. DeBoor, C. (1977), Package for calculating with B-splines. Society for Industrial and Applied Mathematics. *J Numer Anal* 14(3), 441–472.
4. Farin, G. (1998), *Curves and Surfaces for CAGD: A Practical Guide*. Academic Press.
5. Hearn, D., and Baker. M.P. (1997). *Computer Graphics*. Prentice-Hall, Englewood Cliffs, NJ.
6. Hölzle, G.E. (1983), Knot placement for piecewise polynomial approximation of curves. *Comput Aided Des* 15(5):295–296.
7. Juhász, I., and Hoffmann. M. (2001), The effect of knot modifications on the shape of B-spline curves. *J Geom Graphics* 5(2), 111–119.
8. Pratt, M., Goult, R., and He. L. (1993), On rational parametric curve approximation. *Comput Aided Geom Des* 10(3/4):363–377.
9. Razdan, A. (1999), A knot placement for B-spline curve approximation. PRISM Publications, http://prism.asu.edu/research/data/publications/paper99_kpbsca.pdf
10. Sarfraz, M., Asim, M.R., Masood. A. (2004), Capturing outlines using cubic Bezier curves. *The Proceedings of 1st IEEE International Conference on Information and Communication Technologies: From Theory to Applications*.
11. Speer, T., Kuppe, M., and Hoschek. J. (1998), Global reparametrization for curve approximation. *Comput Aided Geom Des* 15, 869–877.
12. Masood, A., Sarfraz, M., and Haq, S.A. (2005), Curve approximation with quadratic B-splines, *The Proceedings of IEEE International Conference on Information Visualisation (IV'2005)-UK*, IEEE Computer Society Press, pp. 991–996.
13. Sarfraz, M, and Raza, A, (2002), Visualization of data using genetic algorithm, *Soft Computing and Industry: Recent Applications*, eds.: R. Roy, M. Koppen, S. Ovaska, T. Furuhashi, and F. Hoffmann, Springer-Verlag, New York, pp. 535–544.
14. Sarfraz, M, and Raza, A., (2002), Visualization of data with spline fitting: a tool with a genetic approach, *The Proc. International Conference on Imaging Science, Systems, and Technology (CISST'2002), Las Vegas, Nevada*, CSREA Press, pp. 99–105.

10
Spirals

Abstract. *Spirals are desirable for applications such as in highway route designing, robot path planning, data-fitting problems, shape design, and curve/surface fairing in geometric modeling. This chapter presents an efficient geometric algorithm for visualization of two-point geometric Hermite conic and arc/conic spiral segments. A comparative study is made with those of Tschirnhausen cubic spirals.*

10.1 Introduction

Manipulating and designing of curves and surfaces [1–20] is an important area of computer graphics and geometric modeling. The rational quadratic Bézier curves, which are usually called the *conic* section curves, have been widely used for computer graphics applications in various industries due to their well-known properties and convenience for users [4, 5]. Traditionally, conic sections, when represented by NURBS [1], are in the form of a rational quadratic Bézier curve.

The curvature is one of the most important geometric concepts of curves and surfaces. Conics have no inflection points; however, they do have curvature extrema. Therefore, only well-chosen conic segments will have monotone curvature. Spirals are visually pleasing curves of monotone curvature; and they have the advantage of not containing curvature maxima, curvature minima, inflection points and singularities. Spirals are desirable for applications such as in highway route designing [2], robot path planning [6, 17], data-fitting problems [10], shape design [12], and curve/surface fairing in geometric modeling [11].

A method to create a two-point geometric Hermite planar curve by joining spiral segments is described in [3, 7, 8]. The spiral segments are either spirals taken from the Tschirnhausen cubic curve (referred to as the T-cubic) or spirals created by joining circular arcs to segments of the T-cubic (referred to as the arc/T-cubic) in a G^3 fashion. However, it has not been possible so far to visualize the arc/T-cubic spiral on the Web due to its lot of complications in the scheme and some limitations of Java. We solve this problem by using a conic segment instead of a T-cubic, and achieve the same level of smoothness but with a more simplified and flexible algorithm suitable for demonstration as a graphics tool.

In this chapter, the spiral segments have been created in two ways. The first is by taking a spiral segment from a conic, which gives a curve referred to as a conic spiral. The second is by joining a circular arc to a conic spiral in a G^3 manner, which gives a curve referred to as an arc/conic spiral. The method is local. Changing one point of a local interpolant does not affect the whole curve, just the part of the curve near that point. The rapid growth of information technology and the World Wide Web motivates us to make the system appear over the Web. In this paper, we also present a flow chart of an efficient algorithm to implement two-point Hermite conic and arc/conic spiral segments as a graphics tool for the designers. It is implemented through a Java applet and a user interface is provided for demonstration on the Web. Online interactive graphics tool is easy to use and comfortable for computer-aided designers or manufacturers. Both a Java implementation and the source code are available online at the address listed at the end of this paper.

10.2   The Rational Quadratic Bézier Curve

A rational quadratic Bézier curve, i.e., a conic segment in normalized local coordinate system, is shown in Figure 10.1. Its standard form for $t \in [0, 1]$ is

$$z(t) = \frac{(1-t)^2 b_0 + 2wt(1-t) b_1 + t^2 b_2}{(1-t)^2 + 2wt(1-t) + t^2}, \tag{10.1}$$

where b_0, b_1, $b_2 \in R^2$ are noncollinear control points, $w \in R$ is the weight associated with b_1, $(1-t)^2 = B_{2,0}(t)$, $2t(1-t) = B_{2,1}(t)$, $t^2 = B_{2,2}(t)$ are Bernstein basis functions. Without loss of generality, assume the points of the geometric Hermite data are $b_0(= (-1, 0))$, and $b_2(= (1, 0))$. Assume the total rotation of the tangent vector is less than π, so that the initial and final tangent

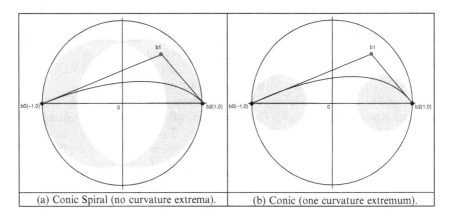

| (a) Conic Spiral (no curvature extrema). | (b) Conic (one curvature extremum). |

FIGURE 10.1. A rational quadratic Bézier curve.

vectors at b_0, and b_2, making angles θ_0 and θ_1, respectively, can be extended to intersect at a point $b_1 (= (b, c))$ with $c \neq 0$.

The type of conic is characterized by the value of the middle weight w: $z(t)$ is an ellipse when $w < 1$, a parabola when $w = 1$ and a hyperbola when $w > 1$. If the control polygon $b_0 b_1 b_2$ forms an isosceles triangle (i.e., $\theta_0 = \theta_1$), set the weight $w = \cos \theta_0$, then the rational quadratic Bézier curve is a circular arc. Also, when w is negative, $z(t)$ is the complementary segment of the original conic segment.

10.3   The Conic Spiral

With reference to [1, 4], the signed curvature $\kappa(t)$ of rational quadratic Bézier curve (10.1) is given by:

$$\kappa(t) = \frac{z'(t) \times z''(t)}{\|z'(t)\|^3}, \tag{10.2}$$

where $\times$ stands for the two-dimensional cross product $(x_0, y_0) \times (x_1, y_1) = x_0 y_1 - x_1 y_0$ and $\|\bullet\|$ means the Euclidean norm. Suppose K is the number of curvature extrema; then if the control point b_1 is on

 (i) the yellow region then $K = 0$, see Figure 10.1(a).
 (ii) the white region then $K = 1$, see Figure 10.1(b).
(iii) the gray region then $K = 2$, see Figure 10.2(a).

(The corresponding curvature plots of Figures 10.1(a), 10.1(b), 10.2(a) and 10.2(b) are shown in Figures 10.3(a), 10.3(b), 10.3(c), and 10.3(d), respectively.) If the control point b_1 is on the boundaries, then K is the smaller one of K for the regions beside the boundaries. The number of curvature extrema within the segment (10.1) depends on w, b and c. It can be seen in Figure 10.4 as a function on R^3. If w, b and c are varied continuously, then the number of curvature extrema changes only if the curve segment has a curvature extremum at the boundary. This can be checked easily by evaluating the derivatives of curvature κ' at $t = 0$ and $t = 1$, which gives

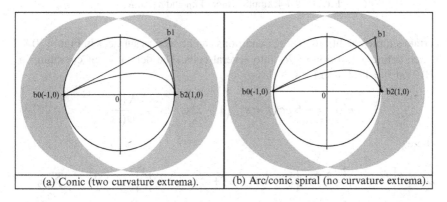

| (a) Conic (two curvature extrema). | (b) Arc/conic spiral (no curvature extrema). |

FIGURE 10.2. A rational quadratic Bézier curve.

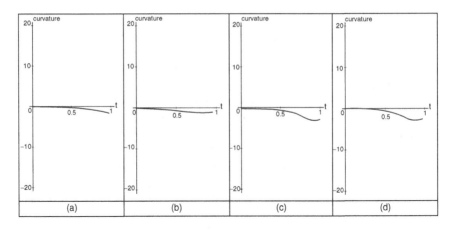

FIGURE 10.3. Curvature plots of the curves in Figures 10.1(a), 10.1(b), 10.2(a), and 10.2(b), respectively.

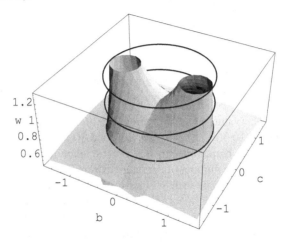

FIGURE 10.4. Implicit plot of a_0 and a_4 on R^3.

certain simple conditions. These conditions can be seen as surfaces in Figure 10.4, which define a partition of R^3 into several cells. The derivative of curvature in (10.2) at $t = 1/(1+s)$ for $s > 0$ is

$$\kappa'(t) = -6wc(1+s)^2 \left(1 + 2sw + s^2\right)^2 \frac{N(s)}{D(s)}, \qquad (10.3)$$

where

$$D(s) = \left[\left(1 - s^2\right)^2 w^2 c^2 + \left\{ 2s + w(1-b) + s^2 w(1+b) \right\}^2 \right]^{\frac{5}{2}} \text{ and } N(s) = \sum_{i=0}^{4} a_i s^i, \qquad (10.4)$$

TABLE 10.1. The number K of curvature extrema for rational quadratic Bézier curve (10.1) determined by Descartes' rule of signs.

	Case 1 $a_4 \geq 0, a_0 \leq 0$		Case 2 $a_4 \geq 0, a_0 \geq 0$					
	$w^2c^2 \geq \max[q(b), q(-b)]$ $w > 0$		$q(b) \leq w^2c^2 \leq q(-b)$ $w^2 > 1/2$ $\quad$ $w^2 = 1/2$			$q(b) < w^2c^2 < q(-b)$ $0 < w^2 < 1/2$ $b \leq 0$		
	$b \geq 0$	$b < 0$	$b \geq 0$	$b \geq 0$	$b < 0$	$a_4 > 0$ $a_0 > 0$	$a_4 > 0$ $a_0 = 0$	$a_4 = 0$ $a_0 > 0$
a_4	+	+	+	0	0	+	+	0
a_3	+	?	+	+	−	?	?	−
a_2	+	−	+	+	−	−	−	−
a_1	?	−	+	+	−	?	−	?
a_0	−	−	+	0	0	+	0	+
K	1	1	0	0	0	2	1	1

	Case 3 $a_4 \leq 0, a_0 \geq 0$		Case 4 $a_4 \leq 0, a_0 \leq 0$					
	$w^2c^2 \leq \min[q(b), q(-b)]$ $0 < w \leq 1$		$q(-b) \leq w^2c^2 \leq q(b)$ $w^2 > 1/2$ $\quad$ $w^2 = 1/2$			$q(-b) < w^2c^2 < q(b)$ $0 < w^2 < 1/2$ $b \geq 0$		
	$b \geq 0$	$b < 0$	$b \leq 0$	$b \geq 0$	$b < 0$	$a_4 < 0$ $a_0 < 0$	$a_4 < 0$ $a_0 = 0$	$a_4 = 0$ $a_0 < 0$
a_4	−	−	−	0	0	−	−	0
a_3	?	−	−	+	−	?	?	+
a_2	+	−	−	+	−	+	+	+
a_1	+	?	−	+	−	?	+	?
a_0	+	+	−	0	0	−	0	−
K	1	1	0	0	0	2	1	1

for

$$a_4 = -wp(b), a_3 = -2\{p(b) - b\}, a_2 = 6wb,$$
$$a_1 = 2\{p(-b) + b\}, a_0 = wp(-b),$$

where

$$p(t)\,(= p_c(t)) = 1 + t - w^2 \left\{c^2 + (1+t)^2\right\}.$$

Depending on the signs of a_4 and a_0, we consider the four cases highlighted in Table 10.1, where "+" and "−" include "0." "?" means either "+" or "−", and $q(t) = p_0(t)$. In fact, the cross-section of two surfaces $a_0 = 0$ and $a_4 = 0$ with planes $w = $ constant are the circles.

Within each cell the number of curvature extrema is constant. Therefore, it suffices to check one representative for each cell in order to determine the corresponding number of vertices.

Remark 10.1. *For any point within unit circle $b^2 + c^2 = 1$, there exists a weight w such that the number of curvature extrema equals 0. Therefore, the sufficient conditions for conic spiral matching geometric Hermite data are $\theta_0, \theta_1 \leq \pi/2$.*

The segment (10.1) for $w^2 \geq 1/2$ and $b^2 + c^2 \leq 1$ has no curvature extrema (i.e., conic spiral) if

$$\min\left[\sqrt{\frac{1+b}{(1+b)^2 + c^2}}, \sqrt{\frac{1-b}{(1-b)^2 + c^2}}\right] \leq w$$

$$\leq \max\left[\sqrt{\frac{1+b}{(1+b)^2 + c^2}}, \sqrt{\frac{1-b}{(1-b)^2 + c^2}}\right]. \tag{10.5}$$

10.4   Comparison of Conic and T-cubic Spirals

This section gives the region for the curvature at the end points of the conic segment to compare our scheme with T-cubic spirals in [3,7,8]. To simplify the comparison, we treat the case when the curve is a spiral of positive curvature. The curvature is monotone increasing and positive if (b, c) is in the fourth quadrant of bc-plane. One should note that

$$\kappa(0) = \frac{c}{w^2 \left\{c^2 + (1+b)^2\right\}^{3/2}}, \quad \kappa(1) = \frac{c}{w^2 \left\{c^2 + (-1+b)^2\right\}^{3/2}}, \tag{10.6}$$

to obtain the spiral region for $(\kappa(0), \kappa(1))$ in Figure 10.5(a). Similarly, we consider the spiral condition of positive curvature on $(\kappa(0), \kappa(1))$ for T-cubic spline of six parameters. Let

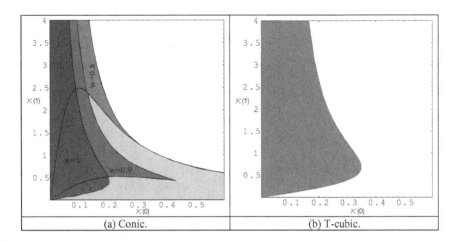

FIGURE 10.5. The spiral conditions of positive curvature on $(\kappa(0), \kappa(1))$: (a) Conic, (b) T-cubic.

$$U(t) = \alpha(t) + \beta(1 - t), \, V(t) = \gamma(t) + \delta(1 - t),$$

and T-cubic spline $z(t) = ((x(t), y(t)))$ is satisfying $z(0) = b_0$ and $z(1) = b_2$ where

$$x'(t) = U(t)^2 + V(t)^2, \, y'(t) = 2U(t)V(t). \tag{10.7}$$

Note the positive curvatures and use a change of variables:

$$(\gamma, \delta) = \frac{1}{\sqrt{2}}(Y + X, Y - X),$$

the curvature is monotone increasing if $\kappa(t) \geq 0$ and $\kappa'(t) \geq 0$, i.e., $\alpha(\beta - \alpha) \geq \gamma(\gamma - \delta)$ which is equivalent to

$$\left(X^2 + 3Y^2\right)^2 + 36Y^2 \leq 12XY, \tag{10.8}$$

therefore, we have the following curvatures at end points:

$$(\kappa(0), \kappa(1)) = \frac{3\sqrt{3}}{2}\left(X^2 + 3Y^2\right)^{\frac{5}{2}} \times \sqrt{X^2 + 3\left(4 + Y^2\right)}\left(\frac{1}{a_0^2}, \frac{1}{a_1^2}\right), \tag{10.9}$$

where

$$(a_0, a_1) = X^4 + 9Y^2\left(3 + Y^2\right) + X^2\left(3 + 6Y^2\right) + 18XY\,(1, -1).$$

Since the region (10.8) and the above curvatures (10.9) are symmetric with respect to the origin, we only have to consider the region in the first quadrant of bc-plane and combine (10.8) and (10.9) to obtain Figure 10.5(b). Figure 10.5 shows the spiral conditions of positive curvatures on $(\kappa(0), \kappa(1))$ with gray color. The spiral region for conic case in Figure 10.5(a) is shown with different shades of gray color for $w^2 = 1, 0.81, 0.5$. The region with all the gray shades is represented by $0.5 \leq w^2 \leq 1$ which is greater than T-cubic case in Figure 10.5(b). Finally, we have a simple example in Figure 10.6 for $\kappa(0) = 0.4$ and $\kappa(1) = 0.5$ which can not be covered by T-cubic spiral in [3, 7, 8].

10.5   The Arc/Conic Spiral

The arc/conic spiral that matches given geometric Hermite data is described below. If the point of intersection b_1 of the tangent lines is outside the unit disk: $b_2 + c_2 \leq 1$, i.e., $\pi/2 < \theta_0 + \theta_1$, then the arc/conic is formed by joining a circular arc to the point of extreme curvature of a conic spiral in such a way that the unit tangents match at the join.

The curvature of the circle is chosen to match the curvature of the conic spiral at the join point, making the circle a circle of curvature and making the composite

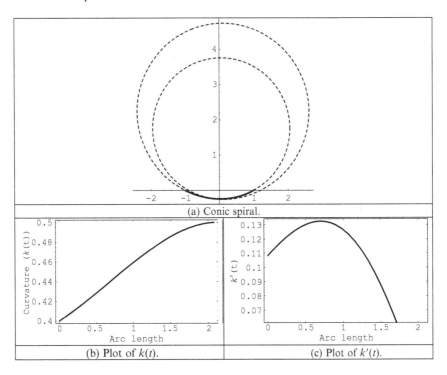

(a) Conic spiral.

(b) Plot of $k(t)$.

(c) Plot of $k'(t)$.

FIGURE 10.6. The conic spiral with $\kappa(0) = 0.4$, $\kappa(1) = 0.5$, and $w = 0.9$.

curve a spiral. This join is G^3 since the derivative of the curvature of the circular
arc and the derivative of the curvature of the conic spiral at the join point are both
zero.

With reference to Remark 10.1, the sufficient spiral conditions for the conic part
of arc/conic are $\theta_1 + \theta_0 - \pi/2 \le \theta \le \theta_1 - \theta_0 + 2\phi$ and $0 < \phi < \theta_0$ for some suitable
choice of w. To simplify the analysis for Web application, we assume $w^2 = 0.5$
and $\theta = \theta_1 + \theta_0 - \pi/2$. For $0 < \theta_0 < \theta_1 < \pi$ and referring to Figure 10.7 and flow
chart in Figure 10.8, let the conic part of the arc/conic start at the point $b_0(-1, 0)$
with tangent vector at angle θ_0 with parameter $t = 0$, and end at the joining point:

$$Q \left(= \left(q_x, q_y\right)\right) = (1 + r \left(\sin\left(\theta_1 - \theta\right) - \sin\theta_1\right), r \left(\cos\theta_1 - \cos\left(\theta_1 - \theta\right)\right))$$
(10.10)

with tangent vector at angle $\pi/2 - \theta_0$ with parameter value $t = 1$. Both tangent
vectors intersect at:

$$b_1^1 = (\cos\left(2\theta_0\right) + r \cos\theta_0 \left(1 - \sin\left(\theta_0 + \theta_1\right)\right),$$
$$- \sin\theta_0 \left(2 \cos\theta_0 + r \left(1 - \sin\left(\theta_0 + \theta_1\right)\right)\right)),$$
(10.11)

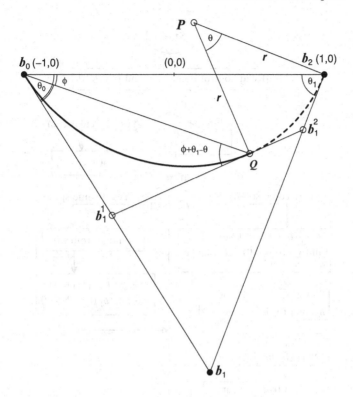

FIGURE 10.7. Arc/conic spiral.

Let the arc part of the arc/conic with radius

$$r = \frac{1}{\sin(\theta_0 + \theta_1)(\sin(\theta_0 + \theta_1) - 1)}\Big\{\sin(2\theta_0 + \theta_1) \\ + \sqrt{4 - 3\cos^2\theta_0 - 4\cos\theta_1\sin\theta_0} - \cos\theta_0 - \sin\theta_1\Big\}, \quad (10.12)$$

starting from the point Q with tangent vector at angle $\pi/2 - \theta_0$, sweep through an angle θ and end at the point $b_2(1, 0)$ with tangent vector at angle $\pi + \theta_1$. Both tangent vectors intersect at

$$b_1^2 = \frac{(m_0 q_x - m_1 - q_y, m_0 m_1 (q_x - 1) - m_1 q_y)}{m_0 - m_1} \quad (10.13)$$

where

$$m_0 = \tan\left(\frac{\pi}{2} - \theta_0\right), m_1 = \tan(\pi + \theta_1).$$

Then quadratic Bézier curve (10.1) is the desired arc for $b_1 = b_1^2$, $w = \cos\left(\frac{\theta}{2}\right)$. A simple example of an arc/conic spiral segment is shown in Figure 10.2(b) with corresponding curvature plot in Figure 10.3(d).

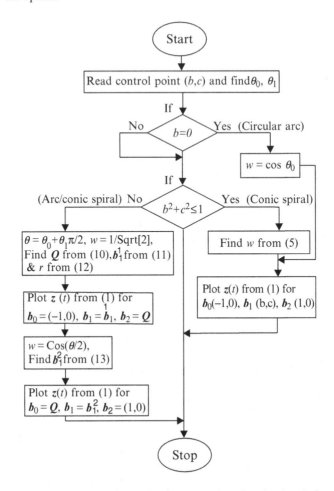

FIGURE 10.8. Flow chart to implement conic and arc/conic spirals.

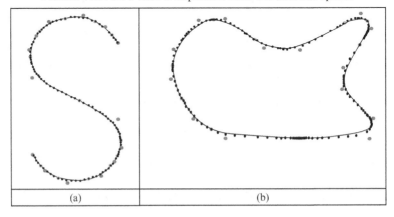

FIGURE 10.9. A curve made of conic spirals fitting given points.

10.6   Examples

Figure 10.9 is a data-fitting example where the data are a set of points taken from a smooth curve. The given points are shown as dots, each given point that is a critical point is indicated by a circle around the given point and control points are shown as disk. Conic and arc/conic spiral splines are shown as solid line matching the given points well in these simple examples. Figure 10.10(a) is an outline of a cup made of Hermite conic and arc/conic spiral segments. The shaded rendition of the smooth curve in Figure 10.10(a) is shown in Figure 10.10(b). Figure 10.11(a) and Figure 10.11(b) demonstrate the use of conic and arc/conic spirals for highway design and obstacle avoidance when designing a robot path, respectively.

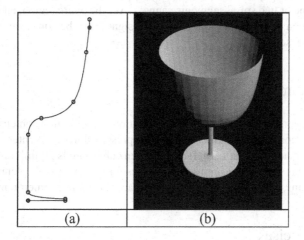

FIGURE 10.10. Hermite conic spiral interpolation: (a) Conic and arc/conic spiral spline, (b) Shaded rendition.

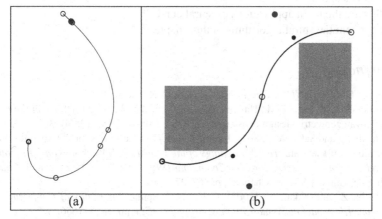

FIGURE 10.11. Route planning with conic and arc/conic spiral spline: (a) Highway design with third and last segments as a straight line. (b) Obstacles avoiding robot path.

10.7   Limitations

Although both arc/conic and T/cubic spirals have G^3 continuity internally, the joining of neighboring pairs of spirals gives a curve that has only tangent continuity. Meek and Walton [9] presented a method for C-shaped interpolating curve made of one or two conic spiral segments. This curve is curvature continuous with monotone curvature, but this fairness is achieved at the cost of nonflexibility and inconvenience of use in practical applications. For example, in their method the angle between tangents at end points must be less than $\pi/2$, where as in our arc/conic case it is less than π. Their method is also restricted for the case when the sign of curvatures at end points are same and nonzero, so user has to compromise on tangent continuity to interpolate an S-shaped curve. Further, their C-shaped curve with one or two spiral segments cannot cover the entire region, and therefore the examination of reachable regions for a designer may be confusing to develop the two curves separately.

10.8   Summary

An efficient geometric algorithm, for visualization of two-point geometric Hermite conic and arc/conic spiral segments, has been presented in this chapter. A comparative study is made with those of Tschirnhausen cubic spirals. Spirals are desirable for applications such as in highway route designing, robot path planning, data-fitting problems, shape design, and curve/surface fairing in geometric modeling.

10.9   Exercises

1. What is a spiral?
2. What are the main applications of spiral curves?
3. Implement the spiral algorithms in this chapter.

References

1. Farin, G. (1995), *NURB Curves and Surfaces*. A.K Peters, 1995.
2. Gibreel, G.M., Easa, S.M., Hassan, Y., and El-Dimeery, I.A. (1999), State of the art of highway geometric design consistency. *ASCE J Transport Eng* 125(4), 305–313.
3. Habib, Z., and Sakai, M. (2002), T-cubic and arc/T-cubic spirals for Web-based visualization of planar data. *The Proceedings of the Fourth IEEE Workshop on Information and Computer Science: Internet Computing* (WICS'2002), KFUPM, Saudi Arabia, IEEE Computer Society Chapter, pp. 267–278.
4. Habib, Z., and Sakai, M. (2005), Conic spiral spline, *International Conference on Geometric Modeling, Visualization & Graphics, JCIS,* pp. 1653–1656.
5. Habib, Z., Sarfraz, M., and Sakai, M. (2005), Rational cubic spline interpolation with shape control. *Comput Graphics*, Elsevier Science, 29(4), 594–605.

6. Liang, T., Liu, J., Hung, G., and Chang, Y. (2005), Practical and flexible path planning for carlike mobile robot using maximal-curvature cubic spiral. *Robot Autonomous Sys* 52, 312–335.

7. Meek, D.S. (2002), Coaxing a planar curve to comply. *J Computational Appl Math* 140, 599–618.

8. Meek, D.S., and Walton, D.J. (1997), Hermite interpolation with Tschirnhausen cubic spirals. *Comput Aided Geom Des* 14, 619–633.

9. Meek, D.S., and Walton, D.J. (2002), Planar G^2 Hermite interpolation with some fair, C-shaped curves. *J Computational Appl Math* 139, 141–161.

10. Sarfraz, M. (2003), Optimal curve fitting to digital data. *Int J WSCG* 11(1), 128–135.

11. Sarfraz, M., Ed. (2004), *Geometric Modeling: Techniques, Applications, Systems and Tools*, Kluwer, Netherlands.

12. Sarfraz, M., & Razzak, M. (2003), A Web-based system to capture outlines of Arabic fonts. *Int J Information Sci*, Elsevier Science, 150(3–4), 177–193.

13. Sarfraz, M., Raza, S.A., and Baig, M.H. (2005), computing optimized curves with NURBS using evolutionary intelligence, Lecture Notes in Computer Science, Vol. 3480: *Computational Science and Its Applications*, eds.: Gervasi, O., Gavrilova, M.L., Kumar, V., Laganà, A., Lee, H.P., Mun, Y., Taniar, D., Springer-Verlag, New York, pp. 806–815.

14. Sarfraz, M. (2004), A rational spline with point tension: an alternative to NURBS of Degree Three, In: *Geometric Modeling: Techniques, Applications, Systems and Tools*, Ed.: M. Sarfraz, Kluwer, pp. 131–148.

15. Sarfraz, M. (2004), Representing shapes by fitting data using an evolutionary approach, *Int J Comput Aided Des Applications*, 1(1–4), 179–186.

16. Sarfraz, M. (2003), Weighted Nu splines: an alternative to NURBS, In: *Advances in Geometric Modeling*, Ed.: M. Sarfraz, John Wiley, New York, pp. 81–95.

17. Yongguo, M., Yung-Hsiang, L., Charlie, H., and George, L. (2004), Energy-efficient motion planning for mobile robots. *The Proceedings IEEE International Conference on Robotics and Automation,* IEEE Computer Society Press, pp. 4344–4349.

18. Sarfraz, M. and Khan, M. A. (2004), An automatic algorithm for approximating boundary of bitmap characters, In: *Future Generation Computer Systems*, Elsevier Science, 20, 1327–1336.

19. Sarfraz, M. (2004), Some algorithms for curve design and automatic outline capturing of images, *Int J Image Graphics*, World Scientific, 4(2), 301–324.

20. Sarfraz, M. (2004), Weighted Nu splines with local support basis functions, International *J Comput Graphics*, Elsevier Science, 28(4), 539–549.

21. Habib, Z., and Sakai, M. (2005), Web-based visualization of conic and arc/conic spirals, *Int J Comput Graphics CAD / CAM*, 1(1), 16–26.

11
Corner Detection for Curve Segmentation

Abstract. *Corners in digital images give important clues for shape representation and analysis. Corner points represent important features of an object that may be useful at subsequent levels of processing. Corners are robust features in the sense that they provide important information regarding objects under translation, rotation and scale change. If the corner points are identified properly, a shape can be represented in an efficient and compact way with sufficient accuracy in many shape analysis problems. Shape representation and image interpretation depends, in most cases, on how correctly and efficiently the corner points are located. Specifically, in the area of vectorizing planar images, contour segmentation is very often managed by locating the exact corner points. This leads to the piecewise solution of the problem.*

11.1   Introduction

Corners in digital images give important clues for shape representation and analysis. Since dominant information regarding shape is usually available at the corners, they provide important features for object recognition, shape representation and image interpretation. Corners are robust features in the sense that they provide important information regarding objects under translation, rotation and scale change. If the corner points are identified properly, a shape can be represented in an efficient and compact way with sufficient accuracy in many shape analysis problem.

Corner points represent important features of an object that may be useful at a subsequent level of computer vision. Guru et al. [12] state that information about a shape is concentrated at the corners and that corners practically prove to be descriptive primitives in shape representation and image interpretation. Asada and Brady [2] insist that these points play a dominant role in shape perception by humans. Attneave [3] proposed that information along a visual contour is concentrated in the regions of high magnitude of curvature. Corner points are used in various computer vision, computer graphics, and pattern recognition applications. It can be used as a step in document image analysis, such as chart and diagram processing [15], and is also important from the view point of understanding human perception of objects [3]. Corner points play a crucial role in decomposing or describing a curve [1]. They are also used in scale space theory [8, 18], image representation [5], stereo vision [9, 33], motion tracking [10, 34], image matching [29, 32], building 2D mosaics [35] and preprocessing phase of outline capturing systems [26, 27].

Corner detection schemes can be broadly divided into two categories based on their applications:

- binary (suitable for binary images) and
- gray level (suitable for gray level images)

Corner detection approaches for binary images usually involve segmenting the image into regions and extracting boundaries from those regions that contain them. The techniques for gray-level images can be categorized into two classes: (a) template based and (b) gradient based. The template-based technique utilizes correlation between a subimage and a template of a given angle. A corner point is selected by finding the maximum of the correlation output. Gradient-based techniques require computing the curvature of an edge that passes through a neighborhood in a gray-level image.

Many corner detection algorithms have been proposed which can be broadly divided into two parts. One is to detect corner points from grayscale images [13, 16, 19, 30] and another relates to boundary-based corner detection [4, 6, 11, 13, 17, 20, 24, 28, 38]. This chapter mainly deals with techniques adopted for later approach.

11.2   Basic Formulation

Visually, corners are the endpoints of straight-line segments of polygonal shapes. But it is difficult and complicated to determine corners in case of nonparametric curves as well as outlines of natural objects especially when the noise is carried. In general, corners represent significant features of an object that human beings would perceive as the meaningful points. Detection of these points is not an easy job since accuracy of detected corners is gauged purely by human judgment and no standard definition/criteria exists. In order to compute the corners, it is important to give them some mathematical representation. In the literature, different authors have described them in different ways. Abe and Kandonaga [1] described corners as local maxima points. They proposed a method for decomposing curves into straight segments and curved arcs, based on the slope at each point. Guru et al. [12] smoothed the boundary curve and found a difference at each curve point called a "cornerity index." The larger values of the cornerity index were taken to be corners.

Rosenfeld and Johnston [23] took curvature maxima points using k-cosine as corners. Rosenfeld and Weszka [24] proposed a modification of [23] in which averaged k-cosines were used. Freeman and Davis [11] found corners at a maximum curvature change in which a straight-line segment moved along the curve. The angular difference between successive segments was used to measure the local curvature. Beus and Tiu's [4] algorithm was similar to [11] except that they proposed an arm cutoff parameter τ to limit length of straight line. Davies [7] has described a method for detecting corners using the Hough transform. Chetverikov and Szabo [6] located corners at significant change in curve slope. In their algorithm, corners are the locations where a triangle of specified size and opening angle can be inscribed in a curve. Pritchard et al. [20] used similar triangles, as in Chetverikov and Szabo [6], to identify the corners in which they compared area of triangle with the actual area under the curve.

In general, the accuracy of any corner detection algorithm changes with noise, size and resolution of input shape and nature of corner (sharpness). It may perform well for a particular shape and display poor results for others. This does not happen in cases of human judgment because they are gifted with an adaptive nature and automatically adapt themselves to the changing environment. Study of this human behavior may lead to development of adaptive algorithms. Various parameters are generally introduced to compensate for such variations. But it would be preferable if one could go for an algorithm that covered a wide range of shape variations without changing its parameters.

Accuracy of any corner detector can be judged only if the actual corner positions are already known. A panel of ten human observers was used to judge the actual location of corners for eight test shapes. Corners marked by a majority were taken as actual corner positions which were then used in measuring the accuracy of different corner detectors. Figure 11.2 shows them as marked with actual corner points on the shapes in Figure 11.1. Figure 11.1 shows the test shapes that introduced some noise into the original noise-free pictures. In addition, limited random noise was added to the scanned images to better test the robustness of the algorithms. These shapes (let us call them as im1, im2, ..., im8 throughout this chapter) are available in various references [6,37,38]. These shapes as well as few

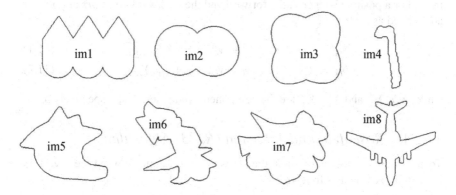

FIGURE 11.1. Shapes used in the tests.

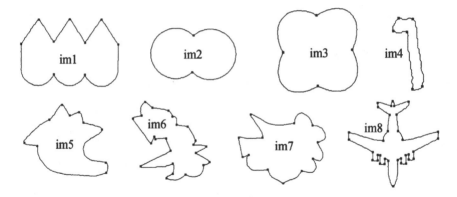

FIGURE 11.2. Test shapes marked with actual corner points.

more shapes will be used to test corner detector algorithms in this chapter. Seven corner detection algorithms have been implemented and tested. Four of them are summarized in Section 11.3, while the rest are reported in Sections 11.4–11.6.

11.3   Summary of Commonly Referred Corner Detectors

This section is devoted to the summary of four corner detection algorithms used by different authors. The summary is based on the survey in [6]. Each algorithm inputs a chain-coded curve that is converted into a connected sequence of grid points $P_i = (x_i, y_i)$, $i = 1, 2, \ldots, N$. A measure of corner strength (cornerity) is assigned to each point; then corner points are selected based on this measure. For each approach, main steps are summarized together with the list of parameters used in the algorithm and their default ("best") values.

When processing a point P_i, the algorithms consider a number of subsequent and previous points in the sequence as candidates for the arms of a potential corner in P_i. For a positive integer k, the forward and the backward k-vectors at point P_i are defined as

$$a_{ik} = (x_i - x_{i+k}, y_i - y_{i+k}) = \left(X_{ik}^+, Y_{ik}^+\right), \tag{11.1}$$
$$b_{ik} = (x_i - x_{i-k}, y_i - y_{i-k}) = \left(X_{ik}^-, Y_{ik}^-\right), \tag{11.2}$$

where X_{ik}^+, Y_{ik}^+ and X_{ik}^-, Y_{ik}^- are the components of a_{ik} and b_{ik}, respectively.

11.3.1   *Rosenfeld and Johnston (RJ73) Algorithm*

To determine the corner strength, the k-cosine of the angle between the k-vectors is used. It is defined as follows:

$$c_{ik} = \frac{(a_{ik} \cdot b_{ik})}{|a_{ik}| \, |b_{ik}|}. \tag{11.3}$$

where a_{ik} and b_{ik} are explained in Equations (11.1) and (11.2), respectively. The selection procedure for the corner points is as follows. Starting from $m = kN$, k is decremented until c_{ik} stops to increase. That is:

$$c_{im} < c_{i,m-1} < \dots < c_{in} \not< ci, n-1.$$

Then $k = n$ is selected as the best value for the ith point. A corner is indicated in i if $c_{in} > c_{jp}$ for all j such that $|i - j| \leq n/2$, where p is the best value of k for the jth point. The single parameter κ specifies the maximum considered value of k as a fraction of the total number of curve points N. This limits the length of an arm at κN. The default value is taken as $\kappa = 0.05$.

For more details of the algorithm, the reader is referred to [23]. Demonstration of the algorithm, for the shapes im1, im2, …, im8, is made in Figure 11.24. The choice of the selected parameters, for these figures, can be seen in Table 11.2. The "D" in Table 11.2 is meant for the default values; the deviations from the "D" are shown otherwise. The proposed algorithm yields reasonable results at the shown values for all the eight shapes. Points not well located are indicated with arrows.

11.3.2 Rosenfeld and Weszka (RW75) Algorithm

To determine the corner strength, the averaged k-cosine of the angle between the k-vectors is used, which is defined as follows:

$$\bar{c}_{ik} = \begin{cases} \frac{2}{k+2} \sum\limits_{t=k/2}^{k} c_{it}, & \text{if } k \text{ is even,} \\[2ex] \frac{2}{k+3} \sum\limits_{t=(k-1)/2}^{k} c_{it}, & \text{if } k \text{ is odd,} \end{cases}$$

where c_{it} are given by Equation (11.3). The selection procedure for the corner points is the same as in RJ73, but it is performed for $\bar{c}_{ik}$. Similarly, the choice of parameter is also same as in RJ73, with the same default value $\kappa = 0.05$.

For more details of the algorithm, the reader is referred to [24]. Demonstration of the algorithm, for the shapes im1, im2, …, im8, is made in Figure 11.25. The choice of the selected parameters, for these figures, can be seen in Table 11.2. The "D" in Table 11.2 is meant for the default values; the deviations from the "D" are shown otherwise. The proposed algorithm yields reasonable results at the shown values for all the eight shapes. Points not well located are indicated with arrows.

11.3.3 Freeman and Davis (FD77) Algorithm

To determine the corner strength at the ith point, the angle between the x-axis and the backward k-vector defined in Equation (11.2) is given as:

$$\theta_{ik} = \theta_{ik} = \begin{cases} \tan^{-1}\left(Y_{ik}^{-}/X_{ik}^{-}\right), & \text{if } |X_{ik}^{-}| \geq |Y_{ik}^{-}|, \\[1ex] \cot^{-1}\left(X_{ik}^{-}/Y_{ik}^{-}\right), & \text{otherwise.} \end{cases}$$

The incremental curvature is then defined as

$$\delta_{ik} = \theta_{i+1,k} - \theta_{i-1,k}. \tag{11.4}$$

Finally, the k-strength in i is computed as

$$S_{ik} = \ln t_1 . \ln t_2 \sum_{j=i}^{i+k} \delta_{jk}, \tag{11.5}$$

where

$$t_1 = \max \left\{ t : \delta_{i-v,k} \in (-\Delta, \Delta), \forall\, 1 \leq v \leq t \right\},$$

and

$$t_2 = \max \left\{ t : \delta_{i+k+v,k} \in (-\Delta, \Delta), \forall\, 1 \leq v \leq t \right\},$$

account for the effect of the forward and backward arms as the maximum spacings (i.e., numbers of steps from i) that still keep the incremental curvature δ_{ik}, within the limit $\pm\Delta$. The Δ is set as follows:

$$\Delta = \arctan \left(\frac{1}{k-1} \right). \tag{11.6}$$

The selection procedure for the corner points is as follows. The ith point is selected as a corner if S_{ik} exceeds a given threshold S and individual corners are separated by a spacing of at least $k+1$ steps. Two parameters are involved in the procedure. These parameters are the spacing k and the corner strength threshold S. The default values for the parameters are set as $k = 5$ and $S = 1500$.

For more details of the algorithm, the reader is referred to [11]. Demonstration of the algorithm, for the shapes im1, im2, ..., im8, is made in Figure 11.26. The choice of the selected parameters, for these figures, can be seen in Table 11.2. The "D" in Table 11.2 is meant for the default values; the deviations from the "D" are shown otherwise. The proposed algorithm yields reasonable results at the shown values for all the eight shapes.

11.3.4   Beus and Tiu (BT87) Algorithm

The corner strength for this algorithm is determined in the same manner as in FD77. However, the following modifications are made. The arm cutoff parameter τ is introduced to specify the upper limit for t_1 and t_2 as a fraction of N. These are explained as follows:

$$t_1 = \max \left\{ t : \delta_{i-v,k} \in (-\Delta, \Delta), \forall\, 1 \leq v \leq t, \quad \text{and} \quad t \leq \tau N \right\},$$

and

$$t_2 = \max \left\{ t : \delta_{i+k+v,k} \in (-\Delta, \Delta), \forall\, 1 \leq v \leq t, \quad \text{and} \quad t \leq \tau N \right\},$$

where δ_{ik} and Δ are given by Equations (11.4) and (11.6), respectively. The corner strength is obtained by averaging Equation (11.5) between two values k_1 and k_2 as follows:

$$S_i = \frac{1}{k_2 - k_1 + 1} \sum_{k=k_1}^{k_2} S_{ik}.$$

The selection procedure follows exactly in the same manner as in FD77. There is an involvement of two parameters for the procedure. These parameters are the averaging limits k_1 and k_2, the arm cutoff parameter τ and the corner strength threshold S. The default values for the parameters are set as $k_1 = 4, k_2 = 7$, $\tau = 0.05$, and $S = 1500$.

For more details about the algorithm, the reader is referred to [4]. Demonstration of the algorithm, for the shapes im1, im2, ..., im8, is made in Figure 11.27. The choice of the selected parameters, for these figures, can be seen in Table 11.2. The "D" in Table 11.2 is meant for the default values; the deviations from the "D" are shown otherwise. The proposed algorithm yields reasonable results at the shown values for all the eight shapes. Points not well located are indicated with arrows.

11.4 Chetverikov and Szabo (CS99) Algorithm

In this algorithm [6] a corner point is defined as a point where a triangle of specified angle can be inscribed within a specified distance from its neighbor points. The number of neighbor points to be checked are also predefined. It is a two-pass algorithm. In the first pass, the algorithm scans the sequence of points and selects candidate corner points. The second pass is postprocessing to remove superfluous candidates.

11.4.1 First Pass

In each curve point P, the detector tries to inscribe in the curve a variable triangle (P^-, P, P^+) constrained by a set of simple rules. For each point P_i, it is checked if a triangle of specified size and angle is inscribed or not. The following three conditions are used:

$$d_{min}^2 \leq |P - P_k^+|^2 \leq d_{max}^2, \tag{11.7}$$

$$d_{min}^2 \leq |P - P_k^-|^2 \leq d_{max}^2, \tag{11.8}$$

$$\alpha \leq \alpha_{max}, \tag{11.9}$$

where

P is the point under consideration for corner point,

P_k^+ is the kth clockwise neighbor of P,

P_k^- is the kth anticlockwise neighbor of P.

Taking

$a = |P - P_k^+|$, the distance between P and P_k^+,

$b = |P - P_k^-|$, the distance between P and P_k^-,

$c = |P_k^+ - P_k^-|$, the distance between P_k^+ and P_k^-.

The angle α can be computed by using cosine law as follows:

$$a^2 + b^2 - c^2 - 2ab \cos \alpha = 0,$$

which yields:

$$\alpha = \cos^{-1} \left(\frac{a^2 + b^2 - c^2}{2ab} \right)$$

All the three conditions described in Equations (11.7), (11.8) and (11.9) are necessary for the first pass. Now each point P may have zero, one or more than one alpha values. Among all alpha values, minimum value is taken as the alpha value of that point P.

11.4.2 *Second Pass*

The second pass removes some super points. A candidate corner point P from the first pass is discarded if it has a sharper valid neighbor $P_v : \alpha(P) > \alpha(P_v)$. A candidate point P_v is a valid neighbor of P if $|P - P_v|^2 \leq d_{max}^2$. As an alternative definitions, one can use $|P - P_v|^2 \leq d_{min}^2$ or the points adjacent to P in the same manner.

The values d_{min}, d_{max} and α_{max} are the parameters of the algorithm. Small values of d_{min} respond to fine corners. The upper limit d_{max} is necessary to avoid false sharp triangles formed by distant points in highly varying curves. The α_{max} is the angle limit that determines the minimum sharpness accepted as high curvature.

11.4.3 *Demonstration*

Practical demonstration of the corner detection algorithm CS99 is shown in Figures 11.3–11.6. The outer boundaries of different images are selected to show the results with the default values as well as with different values of d_{min} and α_{max}. The effects of changing the parameters d_{min} and α_{max} are compared in Table 11.1. Although the algorithm works fine and detects corners correctly in most of the images, in some cases it may not find all of the corners at their most appropriate positions such as in Figures 11.3 and 11.5. But the method, in general, takes care of the points which can be considered as corner points for various applications. However, appropriate parameter selection is a manual factor that a user needs to select carefully.

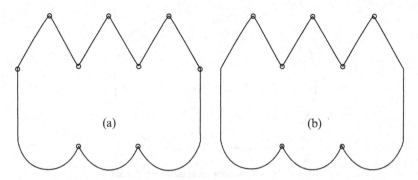

FIGURE 11.3. Corner detection with CS99: (a) corner points at default parameters; (b) corner points at $d_{min} = 7$ and $\alpha_{max} = 160$.

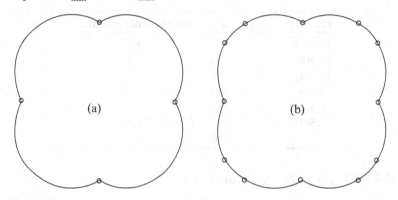

FIGURE 11.4. Corner detection with CS99: (a) corner Points at default parameters; (b) corner points at $d_{min} = 8$ and $\alpha_{max} = 160$,

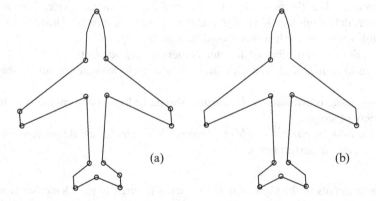

FIGURE 11.5. Corner detection with CS99: (a) corner points at default parameters; (b) corner points at $d_{min} = 7$ and $\alpha_{max} = 140$.

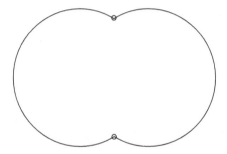

FIGURE 11.6. Corner points at default parameters.

TABLE 11.1. Effects of changing parameter d_{min} and α_{max} on number of detected corner points.

Figure #	d_{min}	α_{max}	No of corner points
11.3(a)	7	150	9
11.3(b)	7	160	7
11.4(a)	7	150	4
11.4(b)	8	160	12
11.5(a)	7	150	15
11.5(b)	7	140	11
11.6	7	150	2

11.4.4 *Performance Evaluation*

Criteria for performance evaluation of corner detectors were given by Chetverikov and Szabo [6], as follows:

- *Selectivity*: It is the most important factor for any corner detector. The rate of correct detections should be high and the wrong ones should be low.
- *Single response*: Each corner should be detected only once.
- *Precision*: The positions of detected corners should be precise.
- *Robustness to noise*: The algorithm should perform well for noisy shapes as well.
- *Easy setting of parameters*: Parameters should be logical and easy to tune for a variety of shapes.
- *Robustness for parameters*: Minor changes in parameter should not cause drastic changes in performance.
- *Speed*

For more details of the algorithm, the reader is referred to [6]. Demonstration of the algorithm, for the shapes im1, im2, ..., im8, is made in Figure 11.27. The choice of selected parameters for these figures can be seen in Table 11.2. The "D" in Table 11.2 is meant for the default values; the deviations from the "D" are shown otherwise. The proposed algorithm yields reasonable results at the shown values for all the eight shapes. Points not well located are indicated with arrows.

TABLE 11.2. Parameter values for eight tested shapes.

Algorithm	im1	im2	im3	im4	im5	Im6	im7	im8
SAM06	D	D	D	D	D	D	D	D
CS99	D	D	D	D	D	D	D	D
BT87	D	D	D	500	1000	1300	D	1000
FD77	D	7,2500	5,2500	5,500	D	7,1000	D	D
RW75	D	0.15	D	D	D	D	D	D
RJ73	D	0.15	D	D	D	D	D	D

It has been observed that, for RJ73 and RW75, somewhat better results can be obtained when the parameters are slightly modified. However, for stable performance, FD77 and BT87 need more frequent modifications of their parameters. In case of BT87, only S needed to be varied. CS99, of course, outperforms RJ73, RW75, FD77 and BT87.

11.5 Sarfraz, Asim and Masood (SAM06) Algorithm

In this algorithm, detection of corner points is based on calculation of distances from the straight line joining two contour points on two sides of that corner. The algorithm is robust, simple to implement, efficient and performs well on noisy shapes as well. The algorithm is divided into two passes. Candidate corner points are detected in the first pass and superfluous candidate corner points are discarded in the second pass. The two passes are explained below in detail.

11.5.1 *First Pass*

Any contour point P_j is a candidate corner point if it satisfies two conditions. First, P_j (located between two contour points P_i and P_k) is at maximum perpendicular distance from the straight line joining these two contour points. Second, the maximum perpendicular distance is greater than the given threshold value D.

For the contour point P_i where $1 \leq i \leq n$ and n is the number of contour points in a closed loop, the contour point P_k is given as:

$$P_k = \begin{cases} P_{i+L}, & \text{if } (i+L) \leq n, \\ P_{i+L-n}, & \text{otherwise}, \end{cases} \qquad (11.10)$$

where L is a length parameter whose default value is 14. The perpendicular distance of all contour points between P_i and P_k are calculated from the straight line joining these contour points. Point P_j is the point with maximum perpendicular distance as shown in Figure 11.7. P_j is selected as a candidate corner point if its perpendicular distance (d_j) from the straight line is greater than the parameter D and the distance d_j is assigned to P_j. The perpendicular distance d_j of point

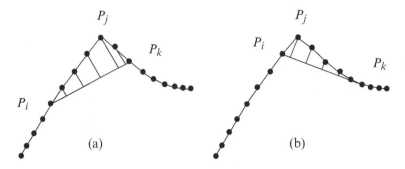

FIGURE 11.7. The contour point at maximum perpendicular distance from the straight line $P_i P_k$ is marked as P_j. Same P_j respond to the two different straight lines in (a) and (b).

$P_j(x, y)$ from the straight line joining the point $P_i(x, y)$ and $P_k(x, y)$ can be calculated as:

$$
d_j = \begin{cases} \left| P_{j,x} - P_{i,x} \right|, & \text{if } m_x = 0, \\[2mm] \dfrac{\left| P_{j,y} - m P_{j,x} + m P_{i,x} - P_{i,y} \right|}{\sqrt{m^2 + 1}}, & \text{otherwise,} \end{cases}
\tag{11.11}
$$

where

$$
m = \frac{m_y}{m_x} = \frac{P_{k,y} - P_{i,y}}{P_{k,x} - P_{i,x}}.
\tag{11.12}
$$

The next candidate corner point is detected for a new straight line by incrementing both i and k. The process continues for $i = 1$ to n. For one straight line, there can be only one candidate corner point or no candidate corner point at all. More than one straight line may respond to the same point P_j as shown in Figure 11.7(a) and 11.7(b). In this case, the higher value of d_j is assigned to P_j.

11.5.2   Second Pass

Sometimes the corners to be detected are not the sharp angle points and we may detect superfluous candidate corner points in first pass, as shown in Figure 11.8. These superfluous points are discarded in second pass. The candidate corner point is superfluous if any other candidate with higher value of d_j is in the range R. The default value of parameter R is equal to parameter L. Therefore for any candidate point to be selected as a corner point, it must have its highest value of d_j among the R number of points on both of its sides. Three different points are detected as candidate corner points in Figure 11.8(a), 11.8(b) and 11.8(c). P_j of Figure 11.8(a) and 11.8(c) are discarded as P_j of Figure 11.8(b) has higher d_j, which is in the range R.

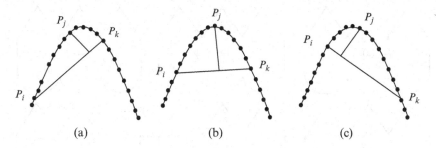

FIGURE 11.8. Superfluous candidate corner points are P_j in (a) and (c).

11.5.3 Parameters

The algorithm needs three external parameters—L, D and R, as given above. The length of the straight line $P_i P_k$ is fixed as per length parameter L throughout the corner detection process. Thus, the straight line will always join the two contour points, L points apart. The default value of L is 14. This parameter takes care of object scaling and resolution. The default value assigned to L suits the size of all test shapes demonstrated in Section 11.4.

Corners are the high curvature points which are recognized by their local sharpness and opening angle. We use the distance parameter D as a substitute for the sharpness and opening angle, to check their validity as a corner point. Any point whose distance from the straight line $P_i P_k$ goes beyond parameter D can be selected as a valid corner point. The default value of D is 2.6. This is an important parameter to control false selection of corners due to noise and other irregularities in a curve. Higher values of D may miss some valid corners and lower values may hit the wrong corners as well. For noisy shapes, accurate corners can be detected by adjusting this parameter (see Figure 11.17(a)).

Sometimes local sharpness of a corner is not high enough, but a global view of shape identifies it as a valid corner (Figure 11.8). Such corners are also detected successfully with this method at the cost of some additional invalid (superfluous) corners. These invalid corners are removed in the second pass by fixing the domination range R. Only the most dominant corner (with highest d_j) in the range R is selected as a valid corner and all others are discarded. The default value of R is equal to L but it must be given lower value to enable detection of closely located corner.

11.5.4 Demonstration

The criteria for performance evaluation in this algorithm is the same as given by Chetverikov and Szabo [4], which is explained in Section 11.4.4. Test results of this algorithm are compared with five corner detectors presented in Chetverikov and Szabo [6] and explained in Sections 11.3–11.4. These are based on scanned images presented in [7], with the inclusion of some noise into the original noise-free pictures. It also uses the same noisy test shapes, which were downloaded from

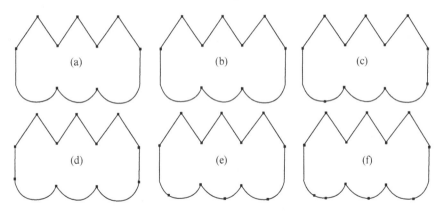

FIGURE 11.9. Detected corner points for im1 as per parameters given in Table 11.2: (a) SAM06, (b) CS99, (c) BT87, (d) FD77, (e) RW75, (f) RJ73.

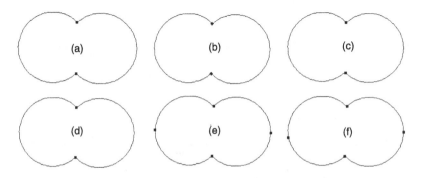

FIGURE 11.10. Detected corner points for im2 as per parameters given in Table 11.2: (a) SAM06, (b) CS99, (c) BT87, (d) FD77, (e) RW75, (f) RJ73.

the website [17]. Very minor variations in demonstrated test shapes from [6] are possible; however, efforts have been made to keep them close to [6].

Comparative results are demonstrated for eight different shapes (im1 to im8; see Figure 11.1). Results of the six algorithms in Sections 11.3–11.4 are presented together for each shape to have an effective comparison (see Figures 11.9– 11.16). Parameters assigned for each test shape in a particular algorithm are also kept closer to ones demonstrated in [6]. Parameters assigned in each test are summarized in Table 11.1. In that table, parameter value "*D*" stands for a default value. For BT87, the corner strength parameter S was modified for im4, im5, im6 and im8. For FD77, the spacing parameter k and corner strength parameter S were modified for im2, im3, im4 and im6. For RW75 and RJ73, parameter k was modified for im2. For details of these parameters, the reader is referred to [4,6,7,28,38].

For the results of im1 in Figure 11.9, SAM06 and CS99 produced similar results and detected precise corners without selecting any wrong ones. One may accept corners of FD77 as well. All other algorithms tend to hit the wrong corners.

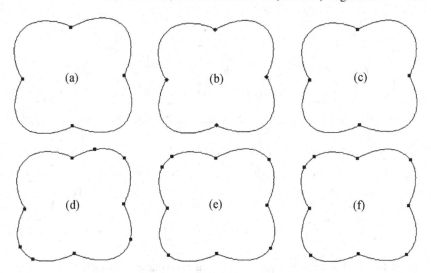

FIGURE 11.11. Detected corner points for im3 as per parameters given in Table 11.2: (a) SAM06, (b) CS99, (c) BT87, (d) FD77, (e) RW75, (f) RJ73.

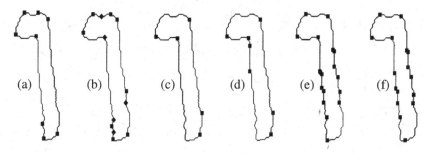

FIGURE 11.12. Detected corner points for im4 as per parameters given in Table 11.2: (a) SAM06, (b) CS99, (c) BT87, (d) FD77, (e) RW75, (f) RJ73.

For im2 in Figure 11.10, results of all algorithms were the same except RW75 & RJ73. For im3 in Figure 11.11, SAM06, CS99 and BT87 precisely detected corners, and all other algorithms detected few additional wrong corners.

For im4 in Figure 11.12, very different results were obtained by each algorithm due to heavy noise along the object boundary. SAM06 detected corners with one or two additional wrong corners, but all of them were well separated. All other algorithms either detected many wrong corners or missed the actual corners. Results of RW75 and RJ73 were badly affected by the irregularities along the curve. Because the image contained heavy noise along its curve boundary, SAM06 did produce precise results with slight modification of parameter D as shown in Figure 11.16(a), which has not been possible due to any other algorithm. For im5 in Figure 11.13, SAM06 again outperformed all other algorithms in corner selectivity. CS99 achieved similar corners by adjusting parameters.

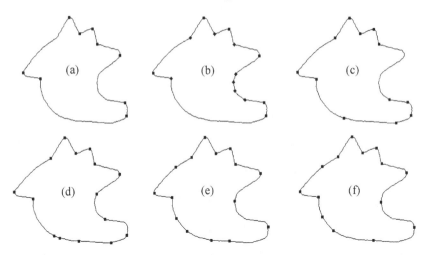

FIGURE 11.13. Detected corner points for im5 as per parameters given in Table 11.2: (a) SAM06, (b) CS99, (c) BT87, (d) FD77, (e) RW75, (f) RJ73.

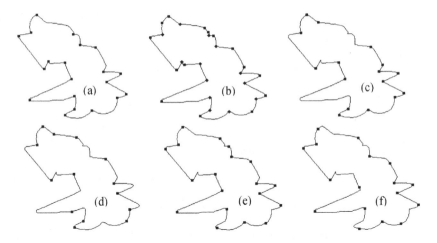

FIGURE 11.14. Detected corner points for im6 as per parameters given in Table 11.2: (a) SAM06, (b) CS99, (c) BT87, (d) FD77, (e) RW75, (f) RJ73.

For im6 in Figure 11.14, results of SAM06 did not find any wrong corner. However, it missed approximately four corners according to the human vision decision as shown in Figure 11.2. By slightly reducing the dominant range parameter R, SAM06 has added one missed corner to the list (see Figure 11.17(b)). Detected corners by SAM06 were precise and without detecting any wrong ones. For im7 in Figure 11.15, detected corners by SAM06 were precise, well located and without wrong ones. Results of RJ73 were close to the results by SAM06 but few detected corners (indicated with arrows) were not at their perfect locations.

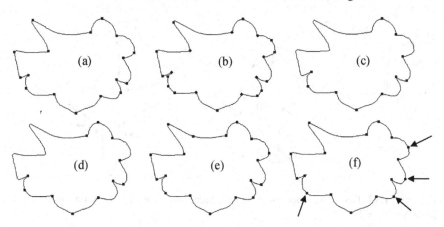

FIGURE 11.15. Detected corner points for im7 as per parameters given in Table 11.2: (a) SAM06, (b) CS99, (c) BT87, (d) FD77, (e) RW75, (f) RJ73.

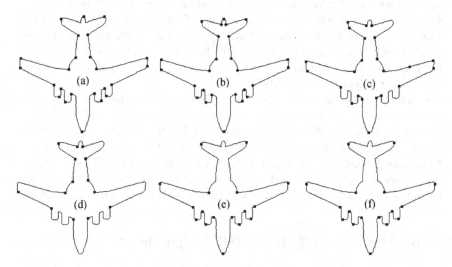

FIGURE 11.16. Detected corner points for im8 as per parameters given in Table 11.2: (a) SAM06, (b) CS99, (c) BT87, (d) FD77, (e) RW75, (f) RJ73.

For im8 in Figure 11.16, results of SAM06 were good but not of the quality demonstrated for other shapes. This was because the corners of this shape were closely located. Therefore, the dominant range parameter R could be modified for better results. Results of this shape after adjusting parameter R is demonstrated in Figure 11.17(c). CS99 produced the same results by adjusting its parameters [4].

It can be observed in all above demonstrated results of SAM06 that the rate of selecting wrong corners is almost zero; this is only in im4 and only with default parameters. Figure 11.17 shows results of im4, im6 and im8 with a slight variation in the parameters of SAM06. A change in parameter was required due to variations

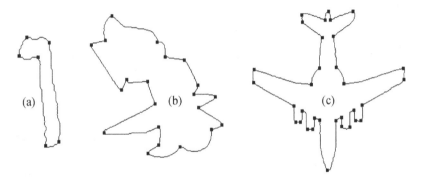

FIGURE 11.17. Detected corner points with SAM06: (a) im4 at $D = 3$; (b) im6 at $R = 13$; (c) im8 at $R = 7$.

in the nature of shapes as discussed above. It is not possible to develop a corner detector, with fixed parameter values, that performs equally well on shapes of varying scale, resolution, noise level and nature of corners (sharpness). Therefore, variation of parameters for different test shapes is perfectly fine but the algorithm should then be able to detect proper corners. SAM06 gets very close to that level; however, automatic calculation of parameters will be a good contribution, which can make this algorithm self- sufficient.

It is not easy to compare computational efficiency of different algorithms due to implementation variations. However, a rough estimate of their efficiency can be made by looking at the calculations involved. The SAM06 algorithm traverses around the closed loop only once in the first pass and detects candidate corners by calculating simple distances (no angles or curvature evaluation involved). Candidate corners are then traversed once in the second pass to discard superfluous candidates. This definitely indicates the computational efficiency of the algorithm.

11.6   Masood and Sarfraz (MS06) Algorithm

This algorithm is different from traditional approaches as it does not involve calculation of the cosine angle and curvature and incorporates both local and global views of a given shape. A set of three rectangles represents the three views of a given shape. These rectangles are moved along the shape boundary and contour points in each rectangle as each step is counted. This information (i.e., the count of points in each rectangle) is used to make a final decision about the corner. This algorithm covers a wide range of shape variations without changing its parameters.

This algorithm works on sequence of n integer coordinate points describing a closed curve C,

$$C = \{C_i = (x_i, y_i), i = 1, \ldots, n\}$$

where C_{i+1} is a neighbor of C_i (modulo n). This technique of corner detection is based on three sliding rectangles (Figure 11.18) along the given curve. Information

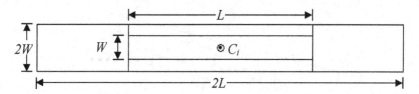

FIGURE 11.18. Three sliding rectangles (R_1, R_2 and R_3) used to detect corners.

about location of the surrounding contour points is gathered in its way. Three sliding rectangles with common centroid at C_i are given as:

$$\left.\begin{array}{l} R_1 = 2L \times 2W, \\ R_2 = L \times 2W, \\ R_3 = L \times W. \end{array}\right\}$$

Rectangles must lie along the slope S of curve with center at contour point C_i. The slope of contour at C_i is a straight line between two points (P_1 and P_2), obtained by taking the mean of $k + 1$ points (including C_i) on both sides of C_i. It is given as follows:

$$\left.\begin{array}{l} P_1 = \frac{1}{k+1} \sum\limits_{i}^{i-k} C_i, \ k = 4, \\[2mm] P_2 = \frac{1}{k+1} \sum\limits_{i+k}^{i} C_i, \ k = 4. \end{array}\right\} \quad (11.13)$$

The contour point C_i automatically adjusts at the center when length and width of R_1 is adjusted at the L and W distance from C_i. The length is taken along the slope S and the width is taken perpendicular to the slope S. The point at unit distance from C_i along the slope S may be calculated as $C_i \pm \frac{P_2-P_1}{|P_1 P_2|}$, where $|P_1 P_2|$ is the length of straight line between point P_1 and P_2. Rectangles R_2 and R_3, sharing a common center C_i, are also drawn with this method. Thus, $R_3 \subset R_2 \subset R_1$.

The set of rectangles is moved along the given curve/contour and a number of neighboring points in each rectangle are counted, which can range from C_{i-L} to C_{i+L}. Let $nR_{1,i}$, $nR_{2,i}$ and $nR_{3,i}$ represent the number of points in rectangles R_1, R_2 and R_3, respectively, having the ith contour point at the centroid. For example, in Figure 11.19, $nR_{1,i} = 21$, $nR_{2,i} = 15$ and $nR_{3,i} = 13$. The value of nR_1, nR_2 and nR_3, for each contour point is ultimately used while making final decision about the corners.

Corners may be found easily from computer-generated curves and shapes by simple analysis of their curvature. Finding corners from outlines of natural shapes and scanned images imposes a challenging task. This is due to noise and low resolution of images, which introduces irregularities along the object boundary. Such irregularities of a curve do not impose much of a problem in human judgment of corners because people have the inherent quality of automatically adjusting their scale/view (local, global or in-between), which is the most appropriate to keep in view noise and size of image. In a smaller view, only a small part of a curve is observed, whereas in a broader view a bigger part is considered. A broader view

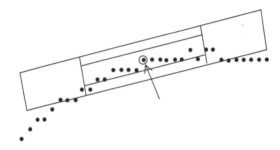

FIGURE 11.19. A snapshot of sliding rectangles at the ith contour point indicated with an arrow.

gives the general area of a curve that may have a corner and hence the effect of noise (irregularities) is lesser in that view. Similarly, in a smaller view, the effect of noise is higher, but the absolute position of corners may be located in that area. Relying solely on one view (by fixing a region of support) is one major drawback of most corner detectors.

The MS06 algorithm combines three levels of view, following the natural corner detection methodology. A set of three rectangles (described above) takes three different views of contour points. A record of their count ($nR_{1,i}$, $nR_{2,i}$ and $nR_{3,i}$), for each curve point, finds enough information to locate the proper corners. Rectangle R_1 takes a broader picture of a curve and passes only those contour points for which no part of curve lies in the area (R_1–R_2). Such curve points can be described as set G as follows:

$$G = \{C_i : nR_{1,i} - nR_{2,i} = 0\}, \tag{11.14}$$

Or

$$G = \{C_i : nR_{1,i} = nR_{2,i}\}.$$

Set G represents a wider view of an image and does not respond to fake corners (at curve irregularities) as discussed above. For example, in Figure 11.20 some snapshots along irregular/noisy curves are shown. Centroids in Figure 11.20(a) and 11.20(b) appear to be corners if a smaller part of a curve is viewed, but these are not the valid corners that can be observed in their broader view. Such points are rejected in a MS06 algorithm as it does not fulfill condition of Equation (11.14). In other words, some parts of a curve lie in the area ($R_1 - R_2$) which is indicated by arrows. The curves in Figure 11.20(c) and 11.20(d) would only be taken in set G.

Set G does not consist of simple corners; rather it gives a general area of curve around the corner. Figure 11.21 shows some images marked with set G. Connected points in set G form one group and a number of groups may exist in set G. The maximum of one corner point can exist in each group. In each group, all points with $nR_{3,i}$ value below the threshold "η" are determined, and the point with minimum $nR_{3,i}$ among them is selected as a corner. Curve point in Figure 11.20(c) was part of set G but does not fall below threshold η; thus it cannot be considered as a corner. Sometimes, none of the points in a group with $nR_{3,i}$ below η exist,

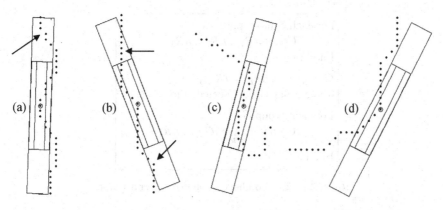

FIGURE 11.20. Some snapshots of a rectangle sliding over noisy/irregular curves. Set G of the curve does not support (a) and (b). Part (c) is also rejected as its $nR_{3,i}$ value is above threshold "η."

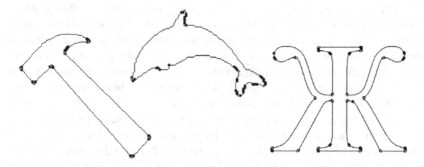

FIGURE 11.21. Some shapes marked (bold) with contour points in set G. Corners are marked in gray.

which means a corner does not exist in that group. The corners for Figure 11.21, found with this method, are marked by gray circles.

Pseudo code of MS06 algorithm is given in Figure 11.22. In this algorithm, the default value of L is set as 16. The values of $L/8$ and $3L/4$ are assigned to W and η, respectively. All others parameters (lengths and widths of all rectangles) are relative to L (Figure 11.18). The value of parameter L depends on the noise, resolution and size of the image. Assigned sizes of rectangles are suitable to a certain range of size and resolution, which covers all demonstrated shapes in this chapter. These sizes were found after extensive testing on many shapes of similar size and resolution. The relationship between relative size of rectangles is set (again with extensive testing) for the convenience of using these parameters. The user needs to tune only one parameter instead of three. One can improve the accuracy of corner detection by assigning independent sizes to these rectangles, but that would be at the cost of complex tuning of parameters.

For each contour point C_i
    Count $nR_{1,i}, nR_{2,i}, nR_{3,i}$
End For

$G = \{C_i : nR_{1,i} = nR_{2,i}\}$
Make groups of connected points in G

For each group G_k
    Corner $= \min_{nR_{1,j}}\{G_{k,j} : nR_{1,j} < \eta\}$
End For

FIGURE 11.22. Algorithm of proposed corner detector.

11.6.1 *Performance Criteria*

A variety of corner detectors have been proposed for digital curves. Their comparative study has also been presented by some authors. Abe and Kandonaga [1] compared seven corner detectors. In their testing, they used flow chart symbols and sample figures (used for dominant point detection). Their evaluation criteria consisted of (a) degree of coincidence with the corner points detected by human subjects, (b) processing time, and (c) invariance of results against rotation, size change and reflection of input image. Guru et al. [12] presented a comparison of three corner detectors on the basis of similar criteria. In both comparisons, the role of noise/irregularity along the curve was ignored, which can adversely affect the results of any corner detection algorithm. Liu and Srinath [17] proposed evaluation criteria that included noise sensitivity. Performance evaluation criteria by Chetverikov and Szabo [6] was (a) selectivity: rate of correct detection; (b) single response: each corner should be detected only once; (c) precision: precise position of detected corners; (d) robustness to noise; and (e) easy setting of parameters.

Unfortunately no standard test shapes and evaluation criteria (especially for digital curves) have been decided for comparison of corner detection results. Corner detection algorithms are normally very sensitive to size/resolution of tested shapes, noise/irregularities along the boundary curve, sharpness of expected corner points and parameter values used.

Corners are sometimes confused with dominant points. Teh and Chin [31] proposed a dominant point detection algorithm and compared with other algorithms (including corner detectors) on the basis of maximum error, integral square error and figure of merit. Such criteria are suitable for polygonal approximation and poor for corner detectors. Rattarangsi and Chin [21] have also made similar comparisons. Care must be taken while comparing corner detection algorithms. Masood and Sarfraz [38] proposed a criteria for evaluation/comparison of corner detection algorithms. It is given as follows:

- *Accuracy*: This is the most important criterion without which all other merits of any corner detector have no value. Accuracy of detected corners will be measured by calculating: (a) percentage of correctly determined corners, (b) percentage of wrongly detected corners, and (c) percentage of missed corners.

- *Localization error*:
- *Noise sensitivity:* Noise can adversely affect the accuracy of detected corner points.
- *Transformation invariance*:
- *Single response*: Sometimes one corner point is selected more than once and sometimes two or three closely located points represent the same corner position. A corner should produce a single response.
- *Parameter setting:* In corner detection, parameters are very important to compensate for noise and size variations. One setting of parameters should be robust to minor shape variations.
- *Computation time.*

11.6.2 Demonstration

Testing of six corner detectors BT87, FD77, RW75, RJ73, CS99, and SAM06 has been shown in Sections 11.3– 11.5. Figures 11.24– 11.29 show the results for these tests against the test shapes im1, im2, ..., im8. Detected corners by MS06 algorithm are shown in Figure 11.30. Best results for each algorithm were obtained by assigning optimum parameter values, and all results of the MS06 algorithm were taken on default parameters. A list of parameters assigned for each algorithm is summarized in Table 11.3. The letter "*D*" is used for the default setting. For details of these parameters, readers are referred to respective algorithms in this

TABLE 11.3. Parameter values assigned for results in Figures 11.24–11.29.

			Parameter Values				
Shapes	RJ73	RW75	FD77	BT87	CS99	SAM06	MS06
im1	D	D	D	D	D	D	D
im2	Kappa $(\kappa) = 0.15$	Kappa $(\kappa) = 0.15$	Spacing $(k) = 7$, corner strength $(S) = 2500$	D	D	D	D
im3	D	D	$S = 6$, $K = 2500$	D	D	D	D
im4	D	D	Spacing $(k) = 5$, corner strength $(S) = 500$	Corner strength $(S) = 500$	$d_{min} = 8$, $\alpha_{max} = 140$	D	D
im5	Kappa $(\kappa) = 0.06$	Kappa $(\kappa) = 0.07$	D	Corner Strength $(S) = 1000$	$d_{min} = 8$, $\alpha_{max} = 140$	D	D
im6	D	D	Spacing $(k) = 7$, corner strength $(S) = 1000$	Corner strength $(S) = 1300$	D	D	D
im7	D	D	D	D	D	D	D
im8	D	D	D	Corner strength $(S) = 1000$	D	D	D

chapter. Table 11.4 summarizes the number of correctly and incorrectly detected corner points for each algorithm (see Figures 11.24–11.30). Some corner points were not well located, which are indicated with arrows in each of Figures 11.24–11.30 whereever applicable. Figure 11.23 shows overall accuracy comparison of all algorithms.

TABLE 11.4. Number of correctly and incorrectly detected corner points (Figures 11.24–11.29).

	Correct							Incorrect						
	RJ	**RW**	**FD**	**BT**	**CS**	**SAM**	**MS**	**RJ**	**RW**	**FD**	**BT**	**CS**	**SAM**	**MS**
im1	9	9	9	8	9	9	9	3	3	2	2	0	0	0
im2	2	2	2	2	2	2	2	2	2	0	0	0	0	0
im3	4	4	3	4	4	4	4	5	5	5	0	0	0	0
im4	5	5	4	4	6	6	6	11	12	3	1	4	2	0
im5	7	8	9	10	9	9	9	3	3	6	3	0	0	0
im6	13	17	12	16	24	20	24	4	2	2	0	4	0	1
im7	12	12	8	7	12	12	12	5	6	3	3	9	4	5
im8	16	15	14	22	25	26	27	2	2	0	1	1	0	0

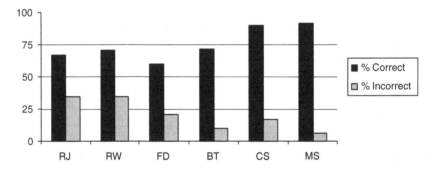

FIGURE 11.23. Overall accuracy comparison for eight test shapes of in Figure 11.1.

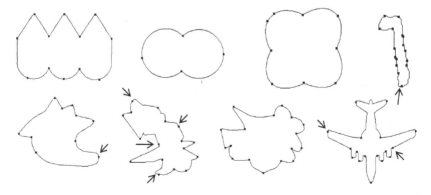

FIGURE 11.24. Corner detection by the RJ73 algorithm [23]. Points not well located are indicated with arrows.

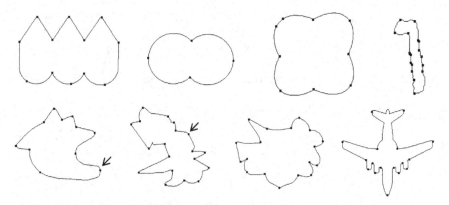

FIGURE 11.25. Corner detection by the RW75 algorithm [24]. Points not well located are indicated with arrows.

FIGURE 11.26. Corner detection by the FD77 algorithm [11].

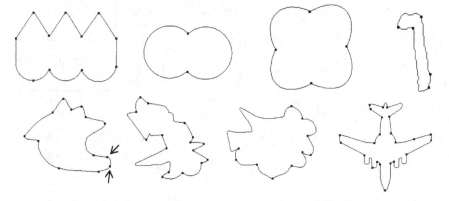

FIGURE 11.27. Corner detection by the BT87 algorithm [4]. Points not well located are indicated with arrows.

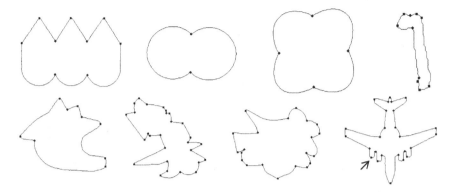

FIGURE 11.28. Results of corner detection by the CS99 algorithm [6]. Points not well located are indicated with arrows.

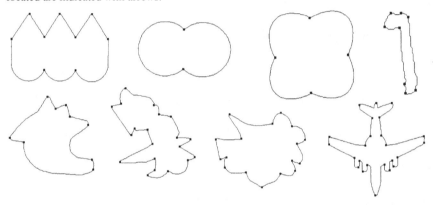

FIGURE 11.29. Results of corner detection by the SAM06 algorithm [28].

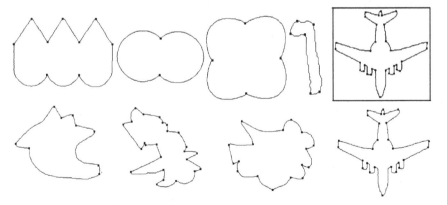

FIGURE 11.30. Corner detection by the MS06 algorithm. The rectangular box shows im8 with parameter value $L = 11$.

11.7   Overall Analysis

Overall accuracy of correctly detected corners in the FD77 algorithm was the lowest (60%) for presented test shapes. One can observe (in im3, im4, im6, im7, im8 of Figure 11.26) that the FD77 algorithm misses some important corner points. For the RJ73 algorithm, although the accuracy of correctly detected corners (67%) was higher than the FD77 algorithm, it falls behind the FD algorithm in the case of localization error (indicated by arrows in the respective figures) and the percentage of incorrectly detected corners (see Figure 11.23). Overall, correctly detected corners by the RW75 algorithm (71%) was better than both algorithms, but the percentage of wrong (incorrect) corners (34%) was equal to the RJ73 algorithm.

The reason for a higher percentage of incorrect detection in the RJ73 and RW75 algorithms was high noise sensitivity (see im4 in Figures 11.24 and 11.25). The percentage of correct corner detection by the BT87 algorithm is higher (72%) than the RJ73, RW75, and FD77 algorithms, but it also tends to miss some important corners (in im4, im6, im7 of Figure 11.27). Performance of the BT87 algorithm is better than the RJ73, RW75, and FD77 algorithms with respect to localization error and incorrect detection (10%). Considerable improvement of overall accuracy can be seen in the CS99 algorithm with 92% of correct detection, 17% of incorrect detection and improvement in localization error. Some incorrect detection was observed (in im4 and im7 of Figure 11.28) due to heavy noise, which affected the overall performance of their algorithm.

The percentage of correctly detected corners by the SAM06 algorithm is around 90%, which is better than the BT87, RJ73, RW75, and FD77 algorithms. By slightly reducing the dominant range parameter R, SAM06 has the ability to add more missed corners, as was seen in Figure 11.17. Detected corners by SAM06 are precise, and no wrong corners are detected. It has the upper hand in the sense that it does not find wrong corners. Moreover, it has the lowest percentage of incorrect detection (6%), which is another big advantage of this algorithm over the five algorithms BT87, RJ73, RW75, FD77, and CS99. One can hardly find a error at any detected corner points.

The percentage of correctly detected corners by the MS06 algorithm (93%) is slightly better than the CS99 algorithm. There was hardly any corner missed by this algorithm except in im8 of Figure 11.30. This was due to low resolution of that shape. Modifying the parameter value for im8 (at $L = 11$) raised accuracy of correct detection to 98%. Result of im8 with new a parameter value is shown in the rectangular box in Figure 11.30. The lowest percentage (equal to that of SAM06) of incorrect detection (6%) is another big advantage of this algorithm. One can hardly find localization error at any detected corner points. No other algorithm can accurately find all the corners of im4 due to heavy noise except the MS06 algorithm and that is without any incorrect corner(s). Results of he MS06 algorithm were taken on default parameter value (i.e., $L = 16$) and performance is expected to improve with fine tuning (e.g., im8 in Figure 11.30). A corner point is represented by a single point with minimum localization error.

11.8   Piecing Boundaries

Segmentation of object boundaries was one of the main objectives behind the work on corner detection. The boundary/outline is divided into different pieces or segments of curves from detected corners, and each segment can be processed for capturing separately or in a parallel way. Figure 11.31 shows outline segmentation from detected corners. Figure 11.31(a) is the outline of the original object marked with detected corner points. These corner points were found using the SAR06 method. Figure 11.31(b) is the object after segmentation. The object was broken into eight segments in total.

Converting the outline segments into vector form, which is the objective of the next chapter, is one of the useful applications of the corner detection algorithms. After segmenting successfully, vectorizing the outline can be managed in a computationally economical way by using a suitable technique from the next chapter. The interested reader is referred to [26,27] for some efficient vectorization techniques.

The image in Figure 11.32(a) has been tested for the vectorized outline capture using the Bézier cubic approximating technique in [26]. Test results of the self-generated shape at threshold 3 is shown in Figure 11.32. Figure 11.32(a) is the original bitmap image; Figure 11.32(b) is the extracted outline; and Figure 11.32(c) shows the detected corner points through the MS algorithm. Figure 11.32(d) shows the end points of the curve segments (over the computed outline) after segment subdivision. Figure 11.32(e) shows the cubic Bézier control

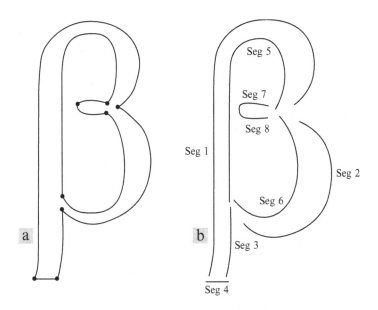

FIGURE 11.31. Outline segmentation from corners: (a) Detected corners; (b) segmented boundary with allotted segment numbers.

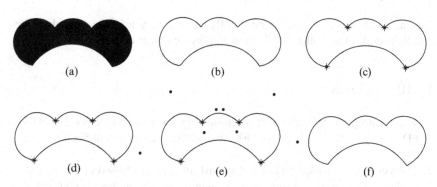

FIGURE 11.32. Capturing an outline object: (a) bitmap image; (b) extracted boundary; (c) detected high curvature points; (d) segment end points after segment sub-division; (e) detected piecewise cubic Bézier control points; (f) computed boundary.

points detected in each segment. Cubic Bézier control points (segment end points or corner points) are shown by ($*$), and computed control points are shown by ($\bullet$). The computed (vectorized) outline is shown in Figure 11.32(f) for easy comparison with the original outline in Figure 11.32(b). Note that very few segments are making a very elegant approximation.

11.9   Summary

Corners are not simply the local maxima, high curvature or dominant points. Points of abrupt change from where the shape can be segmented, and which human beings perceive as meaningful points, are the true corners. Seven corner detection approaches, namely, BT87, RJ73, RW75, FD77, CS99, SAM06, and MS06, have been discussed, experimented with, and analyzed. The SAR06 and MS06 algorithms have been found to be the most accurate and efficient as they do not involve curvature analysis and determination of trigonometric functions such as a cosine angle. A comparative study, based on proposed parameters, shows that the SAR06 and MS06 algorithms have various advantages over previous techniques. Some of the advantages are that (1) they are the most consistent with human judgment of corners; (2) the ratio of false detection is extremely low; (3) they are computationally efficient; (4) they are invariant to transformation changes; (5) they are highly insensitive to noise/irregularities along the curve; (6) they are robust to minor changes in size and resolution; and (7) they are very suitable for natural shapes/objects. Independent tuning of the parameters can further fine tune the results if needed in some extreme case.

Object segmentation is used as a preprocessing step in a capturing process. Objects are segmented from the detected corner points. SAM06 and MS06 seem to be most optimal methods presented in this chapter, which meet the needs of capturing process. Results of both of the algorithms were compared with five commonly referred algorithms and the two methods outperformed in all comparisons.

Specifically, MS06 was found to be slightly superior to Sam6. The algorithms are equally useful for any other application employing corner detection.

11.10   Exercises

1. Write a program to implement the following seven corner detectors—BT87, FD77, RW75, RJ73, CS99, SAM06, and MS06— described in Sections 11.3–11.6.
2. Test your programs for the test shapes im1, im2, ..., im8 used in this chapter.
3. Collect six different test images other than those used in this chapter and test your programs for these test shapes.
4. Using your program in Exercise 11.10.2, verify the results in Table 11.4 using the parameter settings in Table 11.3.
5. Using your program in Exercise 11.10.2, develop similar results as those in Table 11.4 using the parameter settings in Table 11.3.
6. Using your program in Exercise 11.10.2, develop similar results as those in Table 11.4 using the parameter settings other than in Table 11.3.
7. Develop a comparative study between your results obtained in Exercises 11.10.5 and 11.10.6.

References

1. Abe, K., Morii, R., Nishida, K., and Kadonaga T. (1993), Comparison of methods for detecting corner points from digital curves—a preliminary report, *Int Conf Document Anal Recog* 954–857.
2. Asada, H., and Brady, M. (1986). The curvature primal sketch, *IEEE Trans Pattern Anal Mach Intell* PAMI-8, 2–4.
3. Attneave, F. (1954), Some informational aspects of visual perception, *Psychol Rev* 61:183–193.
4. Beus, H.L., and Tiu, S.S.H. (1987), An improved corner detection algorithm based on chain coded plane curves, *Pattern Rec* 20:291–296.
5. Cabrelli, C.A., and Molter, U.M. (1990), Automatic representation of binary images, *IEEE Trans Pattern Anal Mach Intell* PAMI-12, 1190–1196.
6. Chetverikov, D., and Szabo, Z. (1999), A simple and efficient algorithm for detection of high curvature points in planner curves, *Proc. of 23rd Workshop of Australian Pattern Recognition Group*, Steyr, pp.175–184.
7. Davies, E.R. (1988), Application of generalized Hough transform to corner detection, *IEE-P(E:135)*, No. 1, pp. 49–54.
8. Deriche, R., and Giraudon, G. (1990), Accurate corner detection: an analytical study, *Third International Conference on Computer Vision*, pp. 66–70.
9. Deriche, R., and Faugeras, O.D. (1990), 2D curve matching using high curvature points: application to stereo vision, *10th IAPR*, pp. 18–23.
10. Dreschler, L., and Nagel, H.H. (1982), On the selection of critical points and local curvature extrema of region boundaries for interframe matching, *Proc. Of ICPR,* pp. 542–544.

11. Freeman, H., and Davis, L.S. (1977), A corner finding algorithm for chain-coded curves, *IEEE Trans Comput* 26:297–303.
12. Guru, D.S., Dinesh, R., and Nagabhushan P. (2004), Boundary-based corner detection and localization using new "cornerity" index: a robust approach, *Proceedings of 1st Canadian Conference on Computer and Robot Vision*, pp. 417–423.
13. Harris, C., and Stephens, M. (1988), A combined corner and edge detector, *Proc Alvey Vis Con, pp.* 147–151.
14. Kadonaga, T., and Abe, K. (1996), Comparison of methods for detecting corner points from digital curves, *GRMA95*, pp 23–34.
15. Kasturi, R., Siva, S., and O'Gorman, L. (1990), Techniques for line drawing interpretation: an overview, *Proc. IAPR Workshop on Machine Vision Applications*, pp. 151–160.
16. Kitchen, L., and Rosenfeld, A. (1982), Gray-level corner detection, *Pattern Recog Lett* 1: 95–102.
17. Liu, H.C., and Srinath, L.S. (1990), Corner detection from chain- code, *Pattern Recog* 23:51–68.
18. Mokhtarian, F., and Mackworth, A.K. (1992), A theory of multiscale, curvature-based shape representation for planar curves, *IEEE Trans Pattern Anal Machine Intell* 14:789– 805.
19. Noble, J.A. (1988), Finding corners, *Image Vision Comput* 6:121–128, 1988.
20. Pritchard, A.J., Sangwine, S.J., and Horne, R.E.N. (1993), Corner and curve detection along a boundary using line segment triangles, *Electronics Division Colloquium on Hough Transforms*, Digest No. 1993/106, pp. 1–4.
21. Rattarangsi, A., and Chin, R.T. (1992), Scale-based detection of corners of planar curves, *Trans Pattern Anal Machine Intell* 14:430–449.
22. Ray, B.K., and Pandyan, R. (2003), ACORD: an adaptive corner detector for planar curves, *Pattern Recog* 36:703–708.
23. Rosenfeld, A., and Johnston, E. (1973), Angle detection on digital curves, *IEEE Trans Comput* 22:875–878.
24. Rosenfeld, A., and Weszka, J.S. (1975), An improved method of angle detection on digital curves, *IEEE Trans Comput* 24:940–941.
25. Rutkowski, W.S., and Rosenfeld, A. (1978), A comparison of corner-detection techniques for chain-coded curves, *TR- 623*, Computer Science Center, University of Maryland.
26. Sarfraz, M., Asim, M.R., and Masood, A. (2004), Capturing outlines using cubic bézier curves, *Proc. of IEEE 1st International Conference on Information & Communication Technologies: from Theory to Applications*, pp. 539–540.
27. Sarfraz, M., Masood, A., and Asim, M.R. (2004), A web-based system for capturing outlines of 2D objects, *Proceedings of International Conference on Information & Computer Science*, Dhahran, Saudi Arabia.
28. Sarfraz, M., Asim, M.R., and Masood, A. (2006), A new approach to corner detection:*Computer Vision and Graphics*, eds.: K. Wojciechowski, B. Smolka, H. Palus, R.S. Kozera, W. Skarbek, and L. Noakes, Springer-Verlag, New York, pp. 528–533.
29. Smith, P., Sinclair, D., Cipolla R., and Wood, K. (1998), Effective corner matching. In: P.H. Lewis and M.S. Nixon, eds., *Proceedings of 9th British Machine Vision Conference*, volume II, pp. 545–556.
30. Smith, S., and Brady, J. (1995). SUSAN: a new approach to low- level image processing, *Int J Comput Vis* 23, 45–78.

31. Teh C., and Chin, R. (1990), On the detection of dominant points on digital curves, *IEEE Trans PAMI* 8:859–873.

32. Vincent, E., and Laganiere, R. (2005), Detecting and matching feature points, *J Visual Commun Image Representation* 16(1), 38–54.

33. Vincent, E., and Laganire, R. (2001), Matching feature points in stereo pairs: a comparative study of some matching strategies, *Mach Graph Vis.* 10:237–259.

34. Wang, H., and Brady, M. (1995), Real-time corner detection algorithm for motion estimation, *Image Vision Comput*, 13(9), 695–703.

35. Zoghlami, I., Faugeras, O., and Deriche, R. (1997), Using geometric corners to build a 2D mosaic from a set of images, *Proc Comput Vis Pattern Recogn* 420–425.

36. http://visual.ipan.sztaki.hu

37. http://visual.ipan.sztaki.hu/publ/oagm99_corn.ps.gz

38. Masood, A., and Sarfraz, M. (2006), A novel corner detector approach using sliding rectangles, *The Proceedings of the 4th ACS/IEEE International Conference on Computer Systems and Applications (AICCSA-06)*, Sharja, UAE, pp. 621–626, IEEE Computer Society Press.

12
Linear Capture of Digital Curves

Abstract. *This chapter is devoted to the detailed study of linear or polygonal approximation needed in various applications, including shape recognition, point-based motion estimation, coding methods, and so on., in the areas of computer graphics, imaging and vision. Some important aspects related to capturing with linear approximation have been addressed. A detailed survey of many methods, in the current literature has been made. Some commonly referred algorithms have been explained and their results are demonstrated and compared.*

12.1 Introduction

The most appealing representation of information to humans is in a visual form. Effective computer representation of these visual shapes is an important task. Boundary representation of shapes and their approximation economizes memory storage and processing time for subsequent procedures.

The goal of a linear approximation is to capture the essence of boundary shapes with the fewest possible segments. The term *dominant point* (DP) is assigned to the end points of these segments. Linear approximation for closed curves is referred to as polygonal approximation because approximating line segments joined together form a polygon. This is one of the popular approaches, which can provide good representations of 2D shapes at different resolutions. One obvious advantage of using this approach is high data reduction and its immediate impact on the efficiency of the subsequent feature extraction and/or shape-matching algorithms. It has been applied in shape recognition, point-based motion estimation, and coding methods. This representation gained popularity due to its simplicity, locality, generality and compactness [22].

The development of this approach has its roots back to the research carried out in psychology toward the study of shape perception and shape understanding. In one of his experiments, Attneave [1] created the picture of a cat by identifying high curvature points in an ordinary snapshot, and linking them by line segments. A human observer easily recognized the resulting sketch. The conclusion was that those high curvature points are rich in information content, and they are able and sufficient to characterize a contour. These points are considered as representative features for the object contours. This idea has been the starting point for most of the subsequent efforts in this direction. Following Attneave's [1] observation, there are many approaches developed for detection of dominant points.

Algorithms on polygonal/linear approximation can be classified into three main groups, namely, sequential approach, split-and-merge approach and heuristic-search approach. For sequential approaches, Sklansky and Gonzales [23] proposed a scan-along procedure that starts from a point and tries to find the longest line segments sequentially. Ray and Ray [11] proposed a method that determines the longest possible line segments with the minimum possible error. Teh and Chin [18] determined the region of support for each point based on its local properties and computed its relative significance (curvature) and finally detected dominant points by a process of nonmaxima suppression. Kurozumi and Davis [7] proposed a minimax method that derives the approximating segments by minimizing the maximum distance between a given set of points and the corresponding segments. Most of the sequential approaches are simple and fast, but the quality of their approximating results depends on the location of the point where they start the scan-along process.

For split-and-merge approaches, Ramer [10] presented a recursive method starting with initial boundary segmentation. At each iteration, the segment was split at the point that has the farthest distance from the corresponding segment unless the approximation error is no more than the prespecified error tolerance. Sarfraz et al. [14] proposed a recursive algorithm in which the longest line segments within the specified threshold were determined. Common points were marked as dominant points and curve segment was split into subsegments from each dominant point and processed recursively. Held et al, [24] proposed a split-and-merge technique in which difference of slope was used to split segments and these were merged on the criteria of perceptual significance. The approximation results of the split-and-merge approaches may be far from the optimal one if a poor initial segmentation is used.

For the heuristic-search approach, an exhaustive search for the vertices of the optimal polygon from the given set of data points will result in an exponential complexity. Dunham [25] and Sato [26] used dynamic programming to find the optimal approximating polygon. However, when the starting point is not specified, these methods require a worst-case complexity of $O(n^4)$ where n is the number of data points. Some authors [27–30] have used a genetic algorithm for polygonal approximation of digital curves. Tabu search [31] have been proposed to solve the polygonal approximation problem and to obtain better results than most of those due to the local optimal methods. Yin [32] has proposed polygonal approximation technique using ant colony search algorithm. Heuristic-search algorithms are computationally expensive and are not guaranteed to be optimal.

This chapter, in addition to the summary of various algorithms in the literature, is dedicated for the recursive algorithm devised by Sarfraz et al. [14] for piecewise polygonal approximation of digital curves. For simplicity, the algorithm will be called SAMAPA (Sarfraz-Asim-Masood Algorithm for Polygonal Approximation).

Algorithms developed for polygonal approximation and dominant point detection can be classified into two categories. The first is to extract dominant points by curvature evaluation [9, 11, 15, 18–20] and second is by fitting the longest straight-line segments [5, 7, 10, 16, 17, 21]. Extraction of dominant points depends on the accuracy of curvature evaluation and correct determination of the region of support at each contour point. It is computationally more expensive and the results are far from optimal. Polygonal approximation of curves by fitting straight lines is more logical and is an efficient approach. The SAMAPA technique explained in this chapter belongs to the second category.

The break points, in this chapter, will be extracted as a preprocessing step toward polygonal approximation. These break points are the candidates to be selected as the end points of approximating straight lines. While approximating the curve with straight lines, it is important to select the best end points of lines such that the number of line segments and approximation error are minimized. The polygonal approximation will be carried out in clockwise as well as anticlockwise directions around the given curve to look for an optimal solution between the two.

The organization of the chapter is as follows. Some important aspects related to capturing with linear approximation have been addressed in the following section. The preprocessing stage is discussed in Section 12.2. The polygonal approximation algorithm is discussed in Section 12.3. Experimental results are evaluated in Section 12.4. Finally, Section 12.5 concludes the chapter.

12.2   Some Important Issues

Research on polygonal approximation is based on the number of issues that have a direct impact on the quality and performance of these algorithms. These are selection of input parameters, finding region of support, error calculation, shapes to be used for testing, min-# and min-ε problems. A standard algorithm is expected to address these issues and propose a solution. These issues are described below in detail.

12.2.1   *Input Parameters*

Most of the algorithms are based on one or more input parameters. These parameters are selected based on the level of detail represented by the digital curve. In general, it is difficult to find a set of parameters suitable for a curve that consists of multiple size features. This is a fundamental problem of scale because the features describing the shape of a curve vary enormously in size and extent, and there is seldom a well-defined basis for choosing an appropriate scale (or smoothing) parameter that correspond to a particular feature size [33]. Some of the researchers have proposed algorithms that require no input parameters [18, 34–36].

12.2.2 *Region of Support*

The determination of the region of support constitutes the major problem in various dominant point detection algorithms. Although the exact term is attributed to Teh and Chin [18], a similar concept has been presented by Langridge [38], who pointed out that each boundary point of a closed curve should have its own view of the curve. A dominant point should have a view that constitutes a meaningful region of support of the curve and should block the view from neighboring nondominant points. Rosenberg [39] noted that certain points of a convex blob perceptually dominate other points of the blob. He further presented methods for the determination of regions of support with specific reference to convex blobs.

Teh and Chin [18] argued that the detection of dominant points relies primarily on the precise determination of the region of support. To support their argument, they applied three different significance measures (k-curvature, 1-curvature and k-cosine) to different test shapes, and showed that once the region of support is determined properly, the choice of a particular significance measure does not produce much difference. Marji and Siy [9] suggested that the choice of the significance measure is also an important factor that has to be chosen properly, even in the presence of an accurate region-of-support measure. They proposed an algorithm for determination of correct region of support, which is sum of the lengths of the left and right support arms. This issue is addressed in many other places also [9, 20, 40, 42].

12.2.3 *Error Measurement*

Error measurement represents the deviation of an approximating polygon from the original shape. Various types of errors are used for this purpose, depending on the type of distortion under consideration. Let $C = \{p_i = (x_i, y_i), i = 1, \ldots, n\}\}$ be the set of points describing a closed curve, where p_{i+1} is the neighbor of p_i (modulo n). Let $\overline{p_j p_k}$ be a straight line of the approximating polygon. The basic error for that straight line is calculated as a perpendicular distance of all points between p_j and p_k from that straight line. Variations of this error measurement in the polygonal approximation are described as follows:

- *Integral square error (ISE)*: It is used to assess the overall distortion caused by the approximating polygon. It is defined as:

$$ISE = \sum_{i=1}^{n} e_i, \tag{12.1}$$

  where e_i is the squared distance of ith curve point from the approximating polygon.
- *Maximum error (MaxError)*: Maximum error is the maximum deviation of the approximating polygon from the original curve. It is described as follows:
-

$$MaxError = \max_{i=1}^{n}\{e_i\}, \tag{12.2}$$

  where e_i is error in ith point (squared distance).

- *Normalized error (NE)*: Lowe [43] suggest that long approximating lines should be permitted greater deviations by dividing them by the length (L) of the approximating line. It is defined as:

$$NE = \frac{ISE}{L}. \tag{12.3}$$

- *Other errors*: Few other error measurements are the area between two curves, the Hausdorff distance and the Euclidean distance.

12.2.4   *Min-# and Min-ε Problems*

Min-# problem states that for a given boundary, polygonal approximation has a given number of segments so that the approximation error is minimized. Similarly, min-ε states that polygonal approximation has a minimum number of segments so that the approximation error does not exceed a given maximum tolerance ε. This restriction is applied for optimal algorithms. For the case of open curve, the min-# and min-ε problems can be solved by dynamic programming [5,44–46] with the time complexities of $O(N^2)$ to $O(N^3)$, depending on the number of output segments. In the case of closed curves, we have to find the optimal location of the starting point also. A straightforward approach is to try all vertices as a starting point, and to choose the one with minimal error. However, this would multiply the complexity by N, leading to time complexities of $O(N^3)$ to $O(N^4)$.

12.2.5   *Test Shapes*

Some shapes are commonly used for demonstration of polygonal approximation results. These shapes are shown in Figure 12.1. The chromosome-shaped curve in

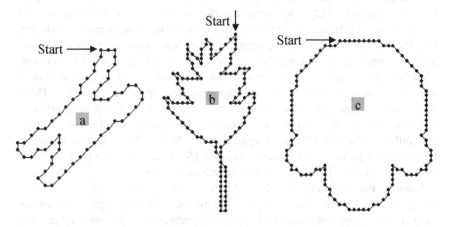

FIGURE 12.1. Standard shapes used in polygonal approximation: (a) chromosome, (b) leaf, and (c) semicircle.

Chain Code for the shape of Chromosome
55454 32011 01111 12112 12006 65655 60010 10765 55455 ˇ55555 55431 12122

Chain Code for the shape of Leaf
33332 30700 00003 32307 00003 32322 26776 22212 76661 11116 66566 55000
10056 65655 00110 66565 65555 56667 66666 66664 22222 22222 232243433

Chain Code for the shape of semicircle
00007 00777 77766 76666 66665 76766 56454 43436 66656 55454 44434 33232
22254 54434 23221 21322 22222 21221 11111 00100 00

FIGURE 12.2. Chain codes for the shapes of a chromosome, leaf, and semicircle.

Figure 12.1(a) consists of 60 boundary points. Similarly, the leaf in Figure 12.1(b) and the semicircle in Figure 12.1(c) consist of 120 and 102 points, respectively. These shapes will be used for demonstration/comparison of results in this chapter. Shapes in Figures 12.1(a) and 12.1(b) were initially presented by Rosenfeld and Johnston [41] and the shape in Figure 12.1(c) was presented by Teh and Chin [18]. The Freeman's chain code [6] of each curve, which constitutes the input to all the algorithms, was coded in clockwise direction starting from the point marked with arrow in Figure 12.1. The chain codes of all the shapes are shown in Figure 12.2.

12.3   Approximation Techniques

The subject of polygonal/linear approximation has been explored thoroughly by the researchers. Polygonal approximation approaches for handling various problems can be found in literature such as dynamic programming approach [47, 48], Newton's method [49], iterative point elimination approach [50], minimax approach [51], split-and-merge approaches [52, 53], dominant points or angle detection approach [54], k–means based-approach [55], genetic algorithm (GA)-based approaches [27–30], and segment fitting approaches [56, 57]. These techniques are generally based on curvature measure [11, 20, 41, 42, 58], curvature morphology [59, 60], local neighborhood of curve points in the plane [34, 61], arc-cord distance [62–64], local symmetry of shapes [65], adaptive Gaussian smoothing [66], direct chain code analysis [2, 15], neural networks [68], wavelets [69, 70], fuzzy logic [71], and different search techniques [27–32].

Some of the algorithms [2, 11, 18, 35, 40, 42, 66, 73] have gained more popularity due to various aspects such as simplicity, efficiency, high compression ratio and low approximation error. These algorithms are commonly referred to by the authors and are used for comparison with their results. Results of the proposed algorithm will also be compared with these algorithms in the next chapter.

A brief summary of more recent and innovative algorithms [18, 40] among them is given below. Readers are referred to the respective algorithms for details.

12.3.1 Teh and Chin Algorithm

Let the sequence of n integer-coordinate points describe a closed curve C as follows:

$$C = \{p_i = (x_i, y_i), i = 1, \ldots, n\}. \tag{12.4}$$

The algorithm consists of three steps. These are given as follows:

Step 1: *Determining the region of support:*

1. Define the length of the chord joining the points p_{i-k} and p_{i+k} as:

$$l_{ik} = |\overline{p_{i-k}p_{i+k}}|. \tag{12.5}$$

Let d_{ik} be the perpendicular distance of the points p_i to the chord $\overline{p_{i-k}p_{i+k}}$

2. Start with $k = 1$. Compute l_{ik} and $d$ik until

(a)

$$l_{ik} \geq l_{i,k+1} \tag{12.6}$$

or

(b)

$$\frac{d_{ik}}{l_{ik}} \geq \frac{d_{i,k+1}}{l_{i,k+1}}, \text{ for } d_{ik} > 0 \tag{12.7}$$

$$\frac{d_{ik}}{l_{ik}} \leq \frac{d_{i,k+1}}{l_{i,k+1}}, \text{ for } d_{ik} < 0 \tag{12.8}$$

Then the region of support of p_i is the set of points that satisfies either condition (a) or (b); it is given as:

$$D(p_i) = (p_{i-k}, \ldots, p_{i-1}, p_i, p_{i+1}, \ldots, p_{i+k}). \tag{12.9}$$

Step 2: *Selecting measure of significance.*
Three different measures of curvature are used, which are given as follows:

(a) k cosine measure:

$$\cos_{ik} = \frac{a_{ik} \cdot b_{ik}}{|a_{ik}||b_{ik}|}, \tag{12.10}$$

where $a_{ik} = (x_{i-k} - x_i, y_{i-k} - y_i), b_{ik} = (x_{i+k} - x_i, y_{i+k} - y_i)$.

(b) k curvature measure:

$$CUR_{ik} = \frac{1}{k} \sum_{j=-k}^{-1} f_{i-j} - \frac{1}{k} \sum_{j=0}^{k-1} f_{i-j}, \tag{12.11}$$

where f is assigned Freeman's chain code.

(c) 1 curvature measure:

$$CUR_{ik} = f_{i+1} - f_i. \tag{12.12}$$

Step 3: *Performing nonmaximal suppression.*

This step consists of three passes. which are as follow:

1st Pass: Perform nonmaxima suppression as follows: retain only those points p_i where

$$|S(p_i)| \ge |S(p_j)|, \tag{12.13}$$

for all j such that

$$|i - j| \le \frac{k_i}{2} \tag{12.14}$$

2nd Pass: Further suppress those points having zero 1 curvature (CURi1 $= 0$).

3rd Pass: For those points that have survived after the 2nd pass
if ($[k_i$ of $D(p_i)] = 1$) and (p_{i-1} or p_{i+1} still survived)
then further suppress p_i if ($|S(p_i)| \le |S(p_{i-1})|$) or ($|S(p_i)| \le |S(p_{i+1})|$)
if 1 curvature is selected as a measure of significance
then goto step 4th pass
else those points survived are the dominant points.

4th Pass: For those groups of more than two points that still survived, suppress all the points except the two end points of each of the groups. For those groups of exactly two points that still survived,

if	($|S(p_i)| > |S(p_{i+1})|$)
then	suppress p_{i+1}
elseif	($|S(p_i)| < |S(p_{i+1})|$)
then	suppress p_i
elseif	($k_i > k_{i+1}$)
then	suppress p_{i+1}
else	suppress p_i

12.3.2   *Marji and Siy Algorithm*

Let the sequence of n integer-coordinate points be described as a closed curve C similar to that in Section 12.3.1. The main algorithm is followed by the algorithm for the region of support. Let p_j be the point for which the region of support is to be determined.

Right region of support:

a. Initially

$$k = j + 2, F_{\text{old}} = 0, \tag{12.15}$$

where F represents the objective function.

b. Calculate L_{jk}, the length of the line segment that joins point p_j and p_k.

c. Calculate E_{jk}, the sum of the squared perpendicular distance from all the points between p_j and p_k to the line segment that joins point p_j and p_k.

d. Calculate $F_{\text{new}} = L_{jk} - E_{jk}$.

e. If $F_{new} < F_{old}$ then return p_{k-1} as the end support point.

f. Else, set $F_{old} = F_{new}$, increment k and goto step b.

Left region of support:

Follow the same steps described for the right region of support in the opposite direction.

Main algorithm:

a. The end points of the right and left support arms are called nodes and their strength is measured by the frequency of their selection.

b. Initially all points are marked as nondominant and uncovered.

c. If the considered node lies in an uncovered territory, that point is set as dominant and all the points within its region of support are marked as covered.

d. If a support end point is crossed while covering a certain node in any direction, the overlap segment is further investigated for valid split points. The strongest nodes in the overlap segment are marked as candidate split points. At the end of each iteration, candidate split points are marked as dominant point if their perpendicular distance to the line that joins the immediate (left and right) dominant points exceeds 0.95.

e. If the point next to the support end point is also marked, the stronger node is marked as dominant. If both nodes have the same strength, both are marked as dominant.

f. If the considered node resides in the covered area, its perpendicular distance to the line that joins its immediate left and right dominant points is checked. If the distance exceeds 0.95, then this point is marked as dominant and its domain is covered.

12.3.3   *Wu Algorithm*

This algorithm is implemented in three steps.

Step 1: Contour is tracked to find the chain codes of the curve and break points are extracted. Chain coding is given in Appendix A in detail. Point p_i is a break point if its chain code $c_i \neq c_{i-1}$.

Step 2: The best length of support for each break point is found and its approximated curvature is computed. The k-cosine (Equation (12.10)) is used to determine the length of support region. The length of support region lies between lower bound (K_{min}) and the upper bound (K_{max}). Let k_i be the best length of support region at the ith point. It can be simply defined as the following:

$$k_i = k, \text{ if } \cos_{ik} = \max\{\cos_{ij} \mid j = K_{min}, \ldots, K_{max}\}, \text{ for } i = 1, 2, \ldots, n.$$
$$(12.16)$$

The region of support of the ith point is the set of points given by

$$D_i = \{p_{i-k}, \ldots, p_{i+k}\}, \qquad (12.17)$$

The approximated curvature at the ith point, c_{vi}, can be defined by averaging the k-cosines:

$$c_{vi}cv_i = \frac{1}{k_i}\sum_{j=1}^{k_i}\cos_{ij}.$$ (12.18)

Step 3: The redundant dominant points are from the list of candidate dominant points if one of the following conditions is satisfied:

a.
$$cv_i < \varepsilon,$$ (12.19)

b.
$$cv_i < cv_j \quad \text{for} \quad j \in \{i - k_i, \ldots, i + k_i\},$$ (12.20)

c.
$$cv_i = cv_{i-1} \quad \text{and} \quad k_i < k_{i-1},$$ (12.21)

d.
$$cv_i = cv_{i+1} \quad \text{and} \quad k_i \le k_{i+1},$$ (12.22)

The break points with maximum curvature among their region of support are marked as the dominant points.

12.3.4 Some Other Algorithms

Some other algorithms, in addition to above three algorithms [18, 36, 40], would also be briefly discussed and compared from an analysis view. These are mostly the improvements of the Teh and Chin algorithm [18]. One of the improved versions of the Teh and Chin [18] algorithm was proposed by Ansari and Huang [2]. In this method, for each boundary point, a support region is assigned to the point based on its local properties. Each point is then smoothed by a Gaussian filter with a width proportional to its determined support region. A significance measure for each point is then computed. Dominant points are finally obtained through non-maximum suppression. The method does not require any input parameter, and the dominant points obtained by this method remain relatively the same even when the object curve is scaled or rotated. The algorithm was compared with Teh-Chin algorithm in [66] in terms of the computational complexity, the approximation errors and the number of detected dominant points of an object curve.

Another improved version of the Teh and Chin [18] algorithm proposed by Ray and Ray [11] determines the support region by the k-cosine itself and the significant points are detected with the help of the smoothed k-cosine. The procedure is parallel and requires no input parameter. It detects not only the curvature maximum points, but also the curvature minimum points. A polygonal approximation is suggested by joining the successive significant points. Ray and Ray proposed another algorithm [60] that introduced the concept of an asymmetric region of support and k-l-cosine which is the angle between the k-vector and the 1-vector of the point of interest. The dominant points are the local maxima of $k - l$-cosine. The procedure needs no input parameter and remains reliable even when features of multiple sizes are present.

Sarkar [15] proposed a simple but efficient method for detection of significant points of chain-coded curves. The algorithm is based on manipulation with chain codes only. The polygonal approximation is achieved by joining successive significant vertices. Cornin [4] pointed out that, as far the Teh and Chin algorithm [18], the Ray and Ray [11] algorithm is not robust in presence of noise. In addition, the procedure for choosing three consecutive increasing angles in the Ray and Ray algorithm is subjective. In his method, the concavity code was constructed from the chain code to classify the degree of concavity or convexity of boundary coordinates. Dominant points are then extracted by throwing away points one at a time that contribute the least curvature to the boundary shape, using an appealing technique called error budgeting.

12.4 Piecewise Polygonal Approximation

This section is dedicated to the recursive algorithm, devised by Sarfraz et al. [14], for piecewise polygonal approximation of digital curves. For simplicity, the algorithm will be called SAMAPA (Sarfraz-Asim-Masood Algorithm for Polygonal Approximation). The SAMAPA technique belongs to the category of polygonal approximation of curves by fitting straight lines. It is more logical and is an efficient approach.

The break points, in SAMAPA, are extracted as a preprocessing step toward polygonal approximation. These break points are the candidates to be selected as the end points of approximating straight lines. While approximating the curve with straight lines, it is important to select the best end points of lines such that the number of line segments and approximation errors are minimized. The polygonal approximation is carried out in clockwise as well as anticlockwise directions around the given curve to look for an optimal solution between the two.

12.4.1 *Preprocessing Stage*

Break points (BP) and initial dominant points (IDP) are extracted in this preprocessing stage. The extracted BPs are the only candidate points to be taken as the end points of approximating straight lines and IDPs are the start points for this algorithm. This preprocessing will considerably reduce the subsequent computation of polygonal approximation.

BP are the nonlinear points along the curve. To find BP, we assign Freeman's chain code [6], C_k varying from 1 to 7, to each contour point P_i, according to the direction of the next point P_{i+1}. From the chain-coded contour points if $abs(C_k - C_{k+1}) = 0$, then it is a linear point; otherwise it is break point.

The point(s) with angle of 135° are marked as IDP. It can be calculated from chain-coded contour points. If $abs(C_k - C_{k+1}) = $ (3 or 5) then the angle is 135°.

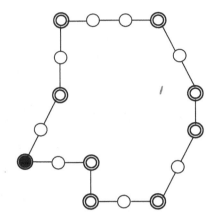

FIGURE 12.3. Single line, double line and shaded circles are the linear points, BP and IDP, respectively.

If no point is found with the 135° angle, then the point(s) with angle of 90° are selected as IDP. If abs($C_k - C_{k+1}$) = (2or6) then the angle is 90°. In the worst case, if the points with 90° angle are not available then the first BP is selected as IDP. Figure 12.3 shows the extracted linear points, BP and IDP.

12.4.2   *SAMAPA Algorithm*

The curve is split into segment(s) at each IDP and an independent polygonal approximation is performed for each segment. The SAMAPA algorithm is divided into two steps explained as follows:

Step I: The first step is to perform segment approximation to find the farthest end points of approximating straight lines such that the maximum perpendicular squared distance from all the points between two end points to the line joining end points is less than the given threshold value (ε). Segment approximation is performed in a clockwise direction (from first point to the last point of segment) and in an anticlockwise direction (from last point to the first point of segment). Pseudo-code for segment approximation in the clockwise direction is given as follows (algorithm for anticlockwise direction will also be on similar lines):

Pseudo-Code for a Function SegAppxC( )

COMMENTS START

EP	End points, i.e., EP-1 and EP-2
DP_{max}	Maximum perpendicular squared distance among all the points between end points to respective line joining end points.
DP_C	List of dominant points in clockwise direction.
ε	Threshold, default value is 0.7
$DP_{C\text{-new}}$	New list of detected dominant points in clockwise direction.
MaxError()	Function maximum error – Finds the maximum perpendicular squared distance between two segments

COMMENTS END

Function DP$_C$ = SegAppxC(Segment)
DP$_C$ = [ ]
Do
EP-1 = first point of segment
EP-2 = next BP in sequence
DP$_{C-new}$ = [ ]
Do
Do
Calculate D$_{max}$
If D$_{max}$ < ε
  P = EP-2
    End If
EP2 = next BP
    While ((D$_{max}$ < 2*ε) OR (End of Segment))
EP-1 = P
Add P in the list DP$_{C-new}$
While (End of Segment)
If isempty (DP$_C$)
DP$_C$ = DP$_{C-new}$
End If
ε = MaxError ( )
While Length (DP$_{new}$) == Length(DP$_C$)

Step II: The second step is to find an optimum solution between the two segment approximations. The pseudo-code for the complete SAMAPA algorithm, as a recursive function "SAMAPA()", is given as follows:

Pseudo-Code for the Function SAMAPA( )

Function DP = SAMAPA(Segment)
DP = [ ]
DP$_C$ = SegAppxC(Segment)
DP$_A$ = SegAppxA(Segment)
  If $DP_C \cup DP_A = \phi$
  DP = segment end points
  Return DP
End If
  If $DP_C \cap DP_A \neq \phi$
  Divide segment into subsegments at $(DP_C \cap DP_A)$
  For (each subsegment)
  DP = DP + SAMAPA(subsegment)
  End For
  Return DP

ElseIf
    Length (DP$_C$) $\neq$ Length (DP$_A$)
If Length (DP$_C$)   < Length (DP$_A$)
DP = DP$_C$
    Else
DP = DP$_A$
    End IF
Else
    DP2 = Sort ($DP_C \cup DP_A$)
    Make pair(s) of DP2 (two consecutive points make one
pair)
    Select one point from each pair(s) so that it minimizes
integral square error.
End IF

In this function, end points of the approximating straight lines are determined
first, from the two-segment approximations (clockwise and anticlockwise). Segments are divided into sub-segments at the common end points and processed
again recursively. Results of this approximation can be seen in Figures 12.4(h),
12.5(h) and 12.6(h) for three shapes, namely, chromosome, leaf, and semicircle,
respectively.

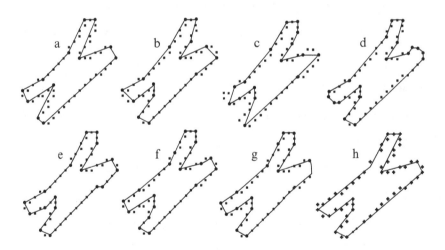

FIGURE 12.4. Results of under comparison algorithms for the shape of a chromosome:
(a) Marji and Siy [9] algorithm, (b) Teh and Chin [18] algorithm, (c) Ansari and Huang
[2] algorithm, (d) Sarkar [15] algorithm, (e) Cronin [4] algorithm, (f) Ray and Ray [11]
algorithm, (g) Wu [20] algorithm, (h) SAMAPA [14] algorithm.

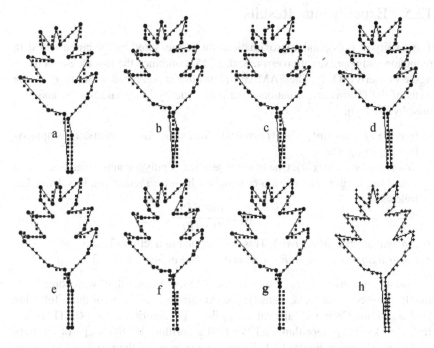

FIGURE 12.5. Results of under comparison algorithms for the shape of a leaf: (a) Marji and Siy [9] algorithm, (b) Teh and Chin [18] algorithm, (c) Ansari and Huang [2] algorithm, (d) Sarkar [15] algorithm, (e) Cronin [4] algorithm, (f) Ray and Ray [11] algorithm, (g) Wu [20] algorithm, (h) SAMAPA [14] algorithm.

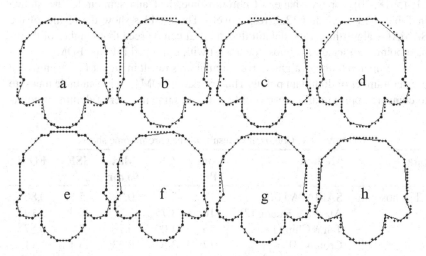

FIGURE 12.6. Results of under comparison algorithms for the shape of a semicircle: (a) Marji and Siy [9] algorithm, (b) Teh and Chin [18] algorithm, (c) Ansari and Huang [2] algorithm, (d) Sarkar [15] algorithm, (e) Cronin [4] algorithm, (f) Ray and Ray [11] algorithm, (g) Wu [20] algorithm, (h) SAMAPA [14] algorithm.

12.5   Experimental Results

The quality of polygonal approximation can be measured by the amount of data reduction and approximation error. Sarkar [15] combined the two measures using figure of merit (FOM). The SAMAPA algorithm is compared with others on the basis of the following evaluation criteria as done by Marji and Siy [9] and also used by Wu [20]:

- *Number of dominant points* (*Dom Pts*): The extracted end points of the approximating straight lines.
- *Compression ratio* (*CR*): One of the objectives of polygon approximation is data reduction. Larger compression ratio means high data reduction. It is defined as follows:

$$CR = \frac{TotalPts}{DomPts}.$$

- *Maximum error* (*MaxError*): This is described in Section 12.2.3.
- *Integral Square Error* (*ISE*): This is described in Section 12.2.3.

Visual comparison of the results of the SAMAPA algorithm, with some commonly referred algorithms, namely, the Ansari-Huang [2] algorithm, Teh-Chin [18] algorithm, Cronin [4] algorithm Marji-Siy [9] algorithm, Ray-Ray [11] algorithm, Sarkar [15] algorithm, and Wu [20] algorithm, for the shape of chromosomes are shown in Figure 12.4. Visual comparisons of the results of two other popular shapes, leaf and semicircle, are shown in Figures 12.5 and 12.6 respectively.

The quantitative comparisons of SAMAPA algorithm with those in [2, 4, 9, 11, 15, 18, 20], for the shapes of chromosome, leaf and semicircle, are shown in Tables 12.1, 12.2 and 12.3, respectively. These tables show the results of the SAMAPA algorithm at the default threshold. It can be seen that number of dominant points extracted are almost the lowest with improved ISE and FOM.

As compared to the straighter arcs, circular arcs result in higher ISE even with a greater number of dominant points. Thus, Sarkar's FOM [15] is a suitable measure to compare approximation results only with the same number of dominant points

TABLE 12.1. Comparative results of the chromosome shape.

Shape	Method	Dom Pts	CR	Max Error	ISE	FOM
Chromosome	SAMAPA [14]	12	5	0.79	5.82	0.86
	Ansari & Huang [2]	16	3.75	2	20.3	0.19
	Teh &Chin [18]	15	4.00	0.74	7.2	0.57
	Cronin [4]	17	3.53	0.63	3.18	1.11
	Marji & Siy [9]	11	5.45	0.90	9.96	0.55
	Ray & Ray [11]	18	3.33	0.71	5.57	0.60
	Sarkar [15]	19	3.16	0.55	3.86	0.82
	Wu [20]	17	3.53	0.64	5.01	0.70

TABLE 12.2. Comparative results of the leaf shape.

Shape	Method	Dom Pts	CR	Max Error	ISE	FOM
Leaf	SAMAPA [14]	21	5.71	0.78	13.6	0.42
	Ansari and Huang [2]	30	4.00	2.13	25.6	0.16
	Teh and Chin [18]	29	4.14	0.99	14.96	0.28
	Cronin [4]	28	4.29	0.74	7.30	0.59
	Marji and Siy [9]	21	5.71	0.78	14.1	0.40
	Ray and Ray [11]	32	3.75	1	14.7	0.26
	Sarkar [15]	23	5.22	0.784	13.1	0.40
	Wu [20]	23	5.22	1	20.34	0.23

TABLE 12.3. Comparative results of the semicircle shape.

Shape	Method	Dom Pts	CR	Max Error	ISE	FOM
Semicircle	SAMAPA [14]	19	5.37	0.74	12.9	0.42
	Ansari and Huang [2]	28	3.64	1.26	17.8	0.20
	Teh and Chin [18]	22	4.64	1	20.6	0.23
	Cronin [4]	30	3.40	0.485	2.91	1.17
	Marji and Siy [9]	18	5.67	1	24.2	0.23
	Ray and Ray [11]	29	3.52	0.833	11.8	0.30
	Sarkar [15]	19	5.37	1.474	17.4	0.31
	Wu [20]	27	3.78	0.83	9.01	0.42

TABLE 12.4. Quantitative results of the SAMAPA method for chromosome shape at different thresholds.

Shape	SAMAPA Method	Dom Pts	CR	Max Error	ISE	FOM
Chromosome	$\varepsilon = 1$	11	5.45	0.89	7.78	0.70
	$\varepsilon = 0.9$	11	5.45	0.89	7.78	0.70
	$\varepsilon = 0.8$	12	5	0.79	5.82	0.86
	$\varepsilon = 0.7$ (default)	12	5	0.79	5.82	0.86
	$\varepsilon = 0.6$	13	4.62	0.75	4.81	0.96
	$\varepsilon = 0.5$	14	4.29	0.69	4.82	0.89
	$\varepsilon = 0.4$	15	4	0.63	4.14	0.97
	$\varepsilon = 0.3$	16	3.75	0.51	3.84	0.98
	$\varepsilon = 0.25$	19	3.16	0.45	2.68	1.18

in the same shape. However, if an algorithm produces better ISE with lesser number of dominant points for the same shape, the algorithm proves itself better. For a meaningful evaluation of results, approximation results of SAMAPA algorithm at different thresholds are shown in Tables 12.4, 12.5 and 12.6 for the shapes of chromosome, leaf, and semicircle, respectively.

For the shape of the chromosome, the results of the SAMAPA algorithm prove better as compared to Ansari-Huang [2], Teh-Chin [18], Marji-Siy [9] and Sarkar

TABLE 12.5. Quantitative results of the SAMAPA method, for leaf shape, at different thresholds.

Shape	SAM [14] Method	Dom Pts	CR	Max Error	ISE	FOM
Leaf	$\varepsilon = 1$	19	6.32	0.99	16.63	0.38
	$\varepsilon = 0.9$	20	6	0.89	15.73	0.38
	$\varepsilon = 0.8$	21	5.71	0.78	13.57	0.42
	$\varepsilon = 0.7$ (default)	21	5.71	0.78	13.57	0.42
	$\varepsilon = 0.6$	22	5.45	0.74	11.47	0.48
	$\varepsilon = 0.5$	25	4.8	0.69	9.67	0.50
	$\varepsilon = 0.43$	29	4.14	0.63	6.63	0.62
	$\varepsilon = 0.4$	30	4	0.59	6.13	0.65
	$\varepsilon = 0.31$	32	3.75	0.55	5.14	0.73

TABLE 12.6. Quantitative results of the SAMAPA method, for a semicircle shape, at different thresholds.

Shape	SAM [14] Method	Dom Pts	CR	Max Error	ISE	FOM
Semicircle	$\varepsilon = 1$	17	6	0.85	15.01	0.40
	$\varepsilon = 0.9$	17	6	0.85	15.01	0.40
	$\varepsilon = 0.8$	17	6	0.85	15.01	0.40
	$\varepsilon = 0.7$ (default)	19	5.37	0.74	12.93	0.42
	$\varepsilon = 0.6$	19	5.37	0.74	12.93	0.42
	$\varepsilon = 0.55$	21	4.86	0.72	9.82	0.49
	$\varepsilon = 0.5$	24	4.25	0.66	6.18	0.69
	$\varepsilon = 0.43$	26	3.92	0.63	4.91	0.80
	$\varepsilon = 0.4$	29	3.52	0.63	3.41	1.03

[15] at the threshold of 0.3, 0.4, 0.9 and 0.25, respectively. It can be seen that the SAMAPA algorithm at threshold of 0.3 gives ISE = 3.84 with 16 dominant points, which is better that Wu [20] with 18 dominant points and Ray-Ray [11] with 17 dominant points. Thus, the results are better than Wu and Ray-Ray also. It is difficult to compare with Cronin [4] but looking at the results at threshold of 0.3 and 0.25 gives some idea of the results of SAMAPA algorithm as compared to Cronin.

For the shape of a leaf, the results of the SAMAPA algorithm prove better as compared to the Ansari-Huang [2], Teh-Chin [18], Marji-Siy [9] and Ray-Ray [11] at the threshold of 0.4, 0.43, 0.7 and 0.55, respectively. At a threshold of 0.6 the ISE = 11.47 with 22 dominant points; the ISE is better than Sarkar [15] and Wu [20] even with 23 dominant points. Thus, the results are better than Sarkar [15] and Wu [2] too. Again the results with 28 dominant points were not available with the SAMAPA algorithm at any threshold to compare with Cronin [4].

For the shape of a semicircle, the results of the SAMAPA algorithm prove better as compared to Ray-Ray [11] and Sarkar [15] at the threshold of 0.4 and 0.6

respectively. The results also prove better with even lesser number of dominant points than Ansari-Huang [2], Teh-Chin [18], Marji-Siy [9] and Wu [20] at threshold of 0.3, 0.55, 0.8, and 0.43. The results of the SAMAPA algorithm at threshold of 0.3 and Cronin [4] are the same. The algorithm by Cronin [4] looks to perform better in all three shapes but it can be seen that the number of dominant points detected by Cronin are always larger.

Another additional advantage of the SAMAPA algorithm is its computational efficiency. Break points are selected in the start and only these points, as candidate end points of approximating straight lines, are considered during the further processing of polygonal approximation algorithm. As the given curve is divided into pieces and processing of each piece of curve is independent from other pieces; therefore parallel processing can be applied.

12.6 Optimal Algorithms

Polygonal approximation is a common and efficient representation of digital curves. A problem with natural interest is the detection of optimal polygonal approximation. Optimal approaches tend to find the optimal polygonal approximation based on specified criteria and error-bound constraints. One desired criterion for optimality is approximation with minimal number of vertices, distant from the original curve by no more than a prespecified value. The optimal polygonal approximation is formulated as an optimization problem, which seeks to minimize the error measure of fitness by locating a given number of vertices. This problem can be solved by using a dynamic programming [4, 8, 73, 74], A*, search [75], or by algorithms developed for the shortest-path problem in digraph [76–78].

12.6.1 *Dynamic Programming*

The problem of polygonal approximation of digital curves is stated as follows: given a digital curve of N points, find M vertices amount them so that the polygon constructed by directly connecting these vertices best fits the given digital curve. The set of N given points is denoted by

$$S = \{s_1, s_2, \ldots, s_N\} = \{(x_1^s, y_1^s), (x_2^s, y_2^s), \ldots, (x_N^s, y_N^s)\}, \qquad (12.23)$$

The set of M vertices to be found among S is denoted by

$$V = \{v_1, v_2, \ldots, v_M\} = \{(x_1^v, y_1^v), (x_2^v, y_2^v), \ldots, (x_M^v, y_M^v)\}, \qquad (12.24)$$

The fitting error of the kth edge is denoted by $e(v_k, v_{k+1})$, which is the sum of error norms from each point between v_k and v_{k+1} to the corresponding edge $\overline{v_k v_{k+1}}$. The norm used is the integral square error. The polygonal approximation problem is formulated as follows: given a point set S of size N, find a subset V of size M from S, where $v_1 = s_1$ and $v_M = s_N$, such that the total error measure is minimized. That is, we seek to find the minimum error measure as follows:

$$E(N, M) = \min_{V \subset S} \sum_{K=1}^{M-1} e(v_k, v_{k+1}). \tag{12.25}$$

The dynamic programming technique can be applied to find the globally optimal solution of the above problem. Dynamic programming is an optimization method that makes an optimal decision based on all possible previous states with a proper recurrence relation. The following recursive function can be applied to solve the given problem:

$$E(n, m) = \min_{m-1 \leq j \leq n-1} [E(j, m-1) + e(s_j, s_n)], \tag{12.26}$$

where $E(n, m)$ denotes the minimum error of fitting first n points by using m vertices, $E(j, m-1)$ denotes the minimization error of fitting first j points by using $m-1$ vertices, and $e(s_j, s_n)$ denotes the error of fitting the curve segment between s_j and s_n by a single edge. The value of j ranges from $m-1$ to $n-1$, which is the possible range of distributing first $m-1$ vertices. The principle of dynamic programming is to derive $E(., m)$ from $E(., m-1)$ recursively. $E(n, m)$ is found by adjusting j, such that the sum of $E(j, m-1)$ and $s(s_j, s_n)$ reaches the minimum value. This process is initialized with $E(1, 1) = 0$ and $E(n, 1) = +\infty$ for $n = 2, \ldots, N$; and is terminated at $E(N, M)$. The number of vertices m must be smaller than or equal to the number of points n. As a result, the dynamic programming fills up the lower triangle of the array $E(., .)$ with size $N \times M$. The value of $E(N, M)$ is the global minimum error of fitting the given digital curve of length N by using a polygon of M vertices.

12.6.2 *Perez and Vidal Algorithm*

The work of Perez and Vidal is based on dynamic programming [8]. It is a well-known approach to define an algorithm that finds optimal results according to a specific criterion. Perez and Vidal algorithm is described as follows:

```
g[1, 0] = 0;
FOR n = 2 TO NP DO g[n, 0] = MaxReal;
(*arbitrary high value for initialization *)
FOR m = 1 TO NS DO
    FOR n = 2 TO NP DO
        BEGIN
            (*Search for the minimum error to reach point n with m segments:*)
            g[n, m] = Min{ g[i, m − 1] + error(i, n)/i ∈ [m, n − 1] }
            Father[n, m] = mini
        END;
TotalError = g(n, m];
```

For a clear understanding of the method, some important variables are presented as follows:

- *g*: array[1...*NP*, 0...*NS*] of real; *g* is used to memorize the minimum global error to reach any point of the contour, using any number of segments. For instance, *g*[30, 4] is the minimum global error to reach the 30th point using four line segments.
- *Points*: array[1...*NP*] of *RPoint*; *RPoint* is a structure with *x* and *y* coordinates.
- *Father*: array[1...*NP*, 1...*NS*] of integer; This array is used to memorize the starting point of the last segment. For instance, *Father*[30,4] is the number of the starting point of the 4th segment, the 30th being the ending point.

The Perez and Vidal algorithm employs dynamic programming, which has two major problems. First, in applying dynamic programming, the number of vertices to locate should be assigned a priori. This parameter value is hard to predict since the suitable number of vertices varies from case to case and depends largely on the geometric size and features of the given digital curve. Second, the dynamic programming is time consuming, especially while dealing with closed curves. All possible initial points should be examined to achieve the global minimum fitting error.

12.6.3   *Some Remarks on Optimal Algorithms*

A global optimum is the major advantage of the dynamic programming approach. However, this approach suffers from two severe problems. First, the proper number of vertices is hard to decide a priori. Secondly, the computational complexity is much higher than other existing methods. The time complexity of applying dynamic programming to polygonal approximation is in the order of $O(MN^3)$. The main task is to fill up the array $E(.,.)$ of size $N \times M$.

Each entry of array involves the $O(N^2)$ computation of Equation (12.26). For fitting close curves, an additional outer loop of size N is required to obtain a proper initial point that minimizes the global fitting error. The overall time complexity of constructing optimal polygonal approximation of closed digital curves by order of $O(MN^4)$. Thus, in its present form, applying this algorithm on large digital curves extracted from real images is impractical.

The problem of finding the minimum error of the best line segment approximating a curve is addressed in optimal algorithm by Perez and Vidal [45]. Unfortunately, a mathematical analysis of the error function shows that this minimum is hard to find. However, it is possible to determine a lower-bound on the error. The values of the least-square errors of both regression lines are required. The computation of the lower-bound is given by Salotti [75] and he uses the lower-bound, in his A* algorithm, to speed up the search and reduce the complexity. Various other improvements can be found in [4,76–79]. To sum up, the proposed approaches for closed curves are suboptimal, whereas the optimal choice of the starting point is time-consuming. Thus, the problem still remains unsolved.

12.7   Summary

Capturing with linear/polygonal approximation was covered in this discussion. In addition to providing a general overview of the topic, some algorithms were described that are subsequently used for comparison with the SAMAPA algorithm in this chapter. Piecewise polygonal approximation is a split-and-merge type of technique implemented by a recursive algorithm. Comparative study in Section 12.5 demonstrates that results of the SAMAPA technique are much better than for its predecessors.

12.8   Exercises

1. Write a program to implement the Freeman's chain code method and verify the code for the test shapes of chromosome, leaf, and semicircle in Figure 12.2.
2. Collect three different test images than those used in this chapter and compute their chain code using the program of Exercise 12.8.1.
3. Write programs to implement the Teh and Chin, Marji and Siy, Wu, and SAMAPA algorithms described in Sections 12.3–12.4.
4. Test your programs of Exercise 12.8.3 for the test shapes of chromosome, leaf, and semicircle used in this chapter.
5. Test your programs of Exercise 12.8.3 for the test shapes of Exercise 12.8.2.
6. Using your program in Exercise 11.10.2, verify the results in Tables 12.1–12.6.

References

1. Attneave, F. (1954), Some information aspects of visual perception. *Psychol Rev* 61:183–193.
2. Ansari, N., and Huang. K.W. (1991), Nonparametric dominant points detection. *Pattern Recognition* 24:849–862, 1991.
3. Arcelli, C., and Ramella. G. (1993), Finding contour-based abstractions of planner patterns. *Pattern Recognition* 26(10):1563–1577.
4. Cronin, T.M. (1999), A boundary concavity code to support dominant points detection, *Pattern Recognition Lett* 20, 617–634.
5. Dunham. J.G. (1986), Optimum uniform piecewise linear approximation of planner curves. *IEEE Trans Anal Mach Intell* 8:67–75.
6. Freeman. H. (1061), On the encoding of arbitrary geometric configurations. *IRE Trans Elec Comp* 10:260–268.
7. Kurozumi, Y., and Davis. W.A. (1982), Polygonal approximation by minimax method. *Comput Graphics Image Process* 19:248–264.
8. Lowe, D.G. (1987), Three-dimensional object recognition from single two-dimensional images. *AI* 31:355–395.
9. Marji, M., and Siy, P. (2003), A new algorithm for dominant points detection and polygonization of digital curves, *Pattern Recognition* 36, 2239–2251.
10. Ramer. U. (1972), An iterative procedure for the polygonal approximation of plane curves. *Comput Graphics Image Process* 1:244–256.

11. Ray, B.K., and Ray, K.S. (1992), Detection of significant points and polygonal approximation of digitized curves, *Pattern Recognition Lett* 13, 443–452.

12. Rosin. P.L. (1998), Assessing the behavior of polygonal approximation algorithms. *Ninth British Machine Vision Conference, Southampton, UK.*

13. Rosin. P.L. (1997), Techniques for assessing polygonal approximations of curves. *IEEE Trans PAMI* 19(6):659:666.

14. Sarfraz, M., Asim, M.R., and Masood, A. (2004), Piecewise polygonal approximation of digital curves, *The Proceedings of IEEE International Conference on Information Visualisation (IV'2004)-UK*, IEEE Computer Society Press, pp. 991–996.

15. Sarkar, D. (1993), A simple algorithm for detection of significant vertices for polygonal approximation of chain-coded curves, *Pattern Recognition Lett* 14, 959–964.

16. Sato, Y. (1992), Piecewise linear approximation of plane curves by perimeter optimization. *Pattern Recognition* 25:1535–1543.

17. Slansky, J., and Gonazlez. V. (1980), Fast polygonal approximation of digitized curves. *Pattern Recognition* 12:327–331.

18. The, C., and Chin, R. (1989), On the detection of dominant points on digital curves, *IEEE Trans PAMI* 8, 859–873.

19. Wang, M.J., Wu, W.Y., Huang, L.K., and Wang. D.M. (1995), Corner detection using bending value. *Pattern Recognition Lett* 16:575–583.

20. Wu, W.Y. (2003), An adaptive method for detecting dominant points, *Pattern Recognition* 36, 2231–2237.

21. Yin. P.Y. (2003), Ant colony search algorithms for optimal polygonal approximation of plane curves. *Pattern Recognition* 36:1783–1797.

22. Melkman, A., and Rourke, J.O. (1988), On polygonal chain approximation. *Proceedings of Computational Morphology*, North-Holland, Amsterdam, pp. 87–95.

23. Sklansky, J., and Gonzalez, V. (1980), Fast polygonal approximation of digitized curves, *Pattern Recognition* 12, 327–331.

24. Held, A., Abe, K., and Arcelli, C. (1994), Towards a hierarchical contour description via dominant point detection, *IEEE Trans Sys Man Cybernetics* 24, 942–949.

25. Dunham, J.G. (1986), Optimum uniform piecewise linear approximation of planar curves, *IEEE Trans PAMI* 8, 67–75.

26. Sato, Y. (1992), Piecewise linear approximation of plane curves by perimeter optimization, *Pattern Recognition* 25, 1535–1543.

27. Goldberg, D.E. (1989), *Genetic Algorithms in Search Optimization and Machine Learning*, Addison-Wesley, Reading, MA,.

28. Huang, S.C., and Sun, Y.N. (1999), Polygonal approximation using genetic algorithms, *Pattern Recognition* 32, 1409–1420.

29. Pal, N.R., Nandi, S., and Kundu, M.K. (1998), Self-crossover: a new genetic operator and its application to feature selection. *Int J Systems Sci* 2, 207–212.

30. Yin, P.Y. (1999), Genetic algorithms for polygonal approximation of digital curves, *Int J Pattern Recognition Artif Intell* 13, 1–22.

31. Yin, P.Y. (2000), A tabu search approach to the polygonal approximation of digital curves, *Int J Pattern Recognition Artif Intell* 14, 243–255.

32. Yin, P.Y. (2003), Ant colony search algorithms for optimal polygonal approximation of plane curves, *Pattern Recognition*, 36, 1783–1797.

33. Davis, L.S. (1977), Understanding shape angles and sides, *IEEE Trans Comput* 26, 236–242.

34. Sankar, P.V., and Sharma, C.V. (1978), A parallel procedure for the detection of dominant points on digital curve, *Comput Graphics Image Process* 7, 403–412.

35. Latecki, L.J., and Lakämper, R. (1999), Convexity rule for shape decomposition based on discrete contour evolution, *Comput Vision Image Understanding* 73, 441–454.

36. Latecki, L.J., Ghadially, R.R., Lakämper, R., and Eckhardt, U. (2000), Continuity of the discrete curve evolution, *J Electronic Imaging* 9, 317–326.

37. Sankar, P.V., and Sharma, C.V. (1978), A parallel procedure for the detection of dominant points on digital curve, *Comput Graphics Image Process* 7, 403–412.

38. Latecki, L.J., and Lakämper, R. (1999), Convexity rule for shape decomposition based on discrete contour evolution, *Comput Vision Image Understanding* 73, 441–454.

39. Latecki, L.J., Ghadially, R.R., Lakämper, R., and Eckhardt, U. (2000), Continuity of the discrete curve evolution, *J Electronic Imaging* 9, 317–326.

40. Rosenfeld, A., and Weszka, J.S. (1975), An improved method of angle detection on digital curves, *IEEE Trans Comput* 24, 940–941.

41. Rosenfeld, A. Johnston, E. (1973), Angle detection on digital curves, *IEEE Trans Comput* 22, 875–878.

42. Freeman, H., and Davis, L.S. (1977), A corner-finding algorithm for chain-coded curves, *IEEE Trans Comput* 26, 297–303.

43. Neumann, R., and Teisseron, G. (2002), Extraction of dominant points by estimation of the contour fluctuations, *Pattern Recognition* 35, 1447–1462.

44. Lowe, D.G. (1987), Three-dimensional object recognition from single two-dimensional images, *Artific Intell* 31, 355–395.

45. Perez, J.C., and Vidal, E. (1994), Optimum polygonal approximation of digitized curves, *Pattern Recognition Lett* 15, 743–750.

46. Chan, W.S., and Chin, F. (1996), On approximation of polygonal curves with minimum number of line segments or minimum error, *Int J Comput Geom Appl* 6, 59–77.

47. Saghri, J., and Freeman, H. (1981), Analysis of the precision of generalized chain codes for the representation of planar curves, *IEEE Trans PAMI* 3, 533–539.

48. Koplowitz, J. (1981), On the performance of chain codes for quantization of the line drawings. *IEEE Trans PAMI* 3, 180–185.

49. Li, L. Chen, W. (1999), Corner detection and interpretation on planar curves using fuzzy reasoning, *IEEE Trans PAMI*, 21, 1204–1210.

50. Kaneko, T., and Okudaira, M. (1985), Encoding of arbitrary curves based on the chain code representation, *IEEE Trans Comm* 33, 697–707.

51. Kurozumi, Y., and Davis, W.A. (1982), Polygonal approximation by the minimax method, *Comput Graphics Image Process* 19, 248–264.

52. Pikaz, A., and Dinstein, I. (1995), An algorithm for polygonal approximation of digital curves based on iterative points elimination, *Pattern Recognition Lett* 16, 557–563.

53. Leu, J.G., and Chen, L. (1988), Polygonal approximation of 2-D shapes through boundary merging, *Pattern Recognition*, 28, 571–579.

54. Ray, B.K., and Ray, K.S. (1995), A new split-and-merge technique for polygonal approximation of chain coded curves, *Pattern Recognition Lett* 16, 161–169.

55. Inesta, J.M., Buendia, M., and Sarti, M.A. (1988), Reliable polygonal approximations of imaged real objects through dominant point detection, *Pattern Recognition* 31, 685–697.

56. Yin, P.Y. (1998), Algorithms for straight-line fitting using K-means, *Pattern Recognition Lett* 19, 31–41.

57. Yukio, S. (1992), Piecewise linear approximation of plane curves by perimeter optimization, *Pattern Recognition*, 25, 1535–1543.

58. Imai, H., and Iri, M. (1986), Computational-geometric methods for polygonal approximations of a curve, *Comp Vis Image Proc* 36, 31–41.

59. Leymarie, F., and Levine, M.D. (1988), *Curvature Morphology*, Center of Intelligent Machines, TR-CIM-88-26, McGill University, Montreal.

60. Ray, B.K., and Ray, K.S. (1992), An algorithm for detecting dominant points and polygonal approximation of digitized curves, *Pattern Recognition Lett* 13, 849–856.

61. Zhang, X., and Zhao, D. (1997), A parallel algorithm for detecting dominant points on multiple digital curves, *Pattern Recognition*, 30, 239–244.

62. Cheng, K.H., and Hsu W.H., (1988), Parallel algorithms for corner following on digital curves, *Pattern Recognition Lett* 8, 47–53.

63. Phillips, T.Y., and Rosenfeld, A. (1987), A method for curve partitioning using arc-chord distance, *Pattern Recognition Lett* 5, 285–288.

64. Fischler, M.A., and Wolf, H.C. (1994), Locating perceptually salient points on planar curves, *IEEE Trans. PAMI* 16, 113–129.

65. Han, J.H., and Poston, T. (2001), Chord-to-point distance accumulation and planar curvature: a new approach to discrete curvature, *Pattern Recognition Lett* 22, 1133–1144.

66. Ogawa, H. (1989), Corner detection on digital curves based on local symmetry of the shape, *Pattern Recognition*, 22, 351–357.

67. Ansari, N., and Huang, K.W. (1991), Nonparametric dominant point detection, *Pattern Recognition*, 24, 849–862.

68. Koplowitz, J., and Plante, S. (1995), Corner detection for chain coded curves, *Pattern Recognition* 28, 843–852.

69. Tsai, D.M. (1997), Boundary-based corner detection using neural networks, *Pattern Recognition* 30, 85–97.

70. Lee, J.S., Sun, Y.N., Chen, C.H., and Tsai, C.T. (1993), Wavelet-based corner detection, *Pattern Recognition*, 26, 853–865.

71. Quddus, A., and Fahmy, M.M. (1999), Fast wavelet-based corner detection technique, *Electron Lett* 35, 287–288.

72. Pikaz, A., and Dinstein, I. (1995), Optimal polygonal approximation of digital curves, *Pattern Recognition* 28, 373–279.

73. Horng, J.H., and Li, J.T. (2002), An automatic and efficient dynamic programming algorithm for polygonal approximation of digital curves, *Pattern Recognition Lett* 23, 171–182.

74. Kolesnikov, A., and Fränti, P. (2003), Reduced search dynamic programming for approximation of polygonal curves, *Pattern Recognition Lett* 24, pp. 2243–2254.

75. Salotti, M. (2000), Improvement of Perez and Vidal algorithm for the decomposition of digitized curves into line segments, *15th International Conference on Pattern Recognition*, Vol. 2, pp. 878–882.

76. Zhu, Y., and Seneviratne, L.D (1997), Optimal polygonal approximation of digitized curves. *IEE Proc. of Vision, Image and Signal Processing*, Vol. 144, pp. 8–14.

77. Chan, W.S., and Chin, F. (1996), On approximation of polygonal curves with minimum number of line segments or minimum error, *Int J Comput Geom Appl* 6, 59–77.

78. Kolesnikov, A., and Franti, P. (2005), Min-# polygonal approximation of closed curves, *IEEE International Conference on Image Processing*, Vol. 2, pp. 522–525.

79. Horng, J.H. (2002), Improving fitting quality of polygonal approximation by using the dynamic programming technique, *Pattern Recognition Lett* 23, 1657–1673.

13
Digital Outline Capture with Cubic Curves

Abstract. *In this chapter, an automatic and efficient algorithm for outline capture of character images, stored as bitmaps, is presented. This method is well suited for characters of non-Roman languages such as Arabic, Japanese, Urdu, Persian, and so on. Contemporary word processing systems store shapes of characters in terms of their outlines, and outlines are expressed as cubic Bézier curves. The process of capturing outlines includes various steps including detection of the boundary, finding corner points and break points, and fitting the curve. The chapter discusses automating the above process to provide optimal results. As an alternate smoother scheme, the Hermite cubic spline curve scheme has also been introduced.*

13.1   Introduction

Fonts are an essential part of any computer system. Two fundamental approaches to storing fonts on a computer are bitmap and outline [1, 2]. In bitmap fonts, each character is stored as an array of pixels (a bitmap). Outline fonts describe the character outlines [18–29] with a combination of control points and curves. Outline representation has many advantages over the bitmap approach such as scaling, shearing, translation, rotation, and clipping. Therefore, most contemporary desktop publishing systems are based on outline fonts.

Characters of non-Roman languages are complex and their cursive nature requires much more attention. In traditional font design, a character is drawn initially on paper by hand and then it is scanned to obtain a gray-level image. From this gray-level image, the boundary, or contour, of the character is obtained. Then *corner points* of the character are determined from the contour. These *corner points* can be obtained by some interactive method or by some automated corner detection algorithm [3,4]. Curve fitting is done by segmenting the boundary at the corner points and fitting the parametric curve to these points.

This chapter includes an automatic algorithm [18] to obtain the outline of bitmap characters. The algorithm presented improves the work done in [5, 6]. The methodology adopted in this chapter gives a higher level of accuracy and speed compared with traditional approaches. Corner points are sometimes not sufficient to fit the curve, and a few additional points are needed to achieve a best fit. This chapter, in addition to corner points, identifies these additional points called break points. So the set of *significant points* consists of corner points and break points. Segmentation is done at significant points, and the cubic Bézier is used for curve fitting. The least square method is used to achieve the best fit. In the case when the fitted curve is not the desired shape, reparameterization improves the fit, and then break points are used ultimately to achieve the desired level of accuracy.

The algorithm of automatic approximation of the boundary of digital character images consists of the following steps.

1. Finding the boundary of the bitmap image
2. Detecting the corner points
3. Filtering noise
4. Curve fitting with a cubic Bézier
5. Reparameterization
6. Breaking segments

Steps 4-6 are iterative steps. Initially, the curve is fitted to only corner points, but if the fit is not up to the desired tolerance limit, then reparameterization is done. If needed, break points are determined and the curve is fitted to significant points (i.e., corner points and break points).

Since the Bézier curve scheme described above is not actually a smooth scheme at the joints of the segments, some alternate smoother scheme may be needed, which may be more useful for some applications such as smoother or blobby objects. A C^1 smooth scheme [??] has been described that uses a Hermite-like spline as a modeler. The scheme can be implemented in the same way as the Bézier curve scheme described above. It computes the tangent vectors and finds the intermediate points in the segments, keeping account of the error minimization. Although least square error has not been used for optimizing tangents, one can attempt this in a similar manner to what was done in the Bézier curve scheme.

The organization of the chapter is as follows. Section 13.2 discusses finding the boundary of bitmap images. Discussion of the corner detection process can be found in Section 13.3. Section 13.4 addresses the issue of noise filtering. The core of the algorithm, that is, the curve-fitting process, is elaborated in Section 13.5. The reparameterization step is described in Section 13.6. The issue of when and how to break the segments is discussed in Section 13.7. An alternate approach using the Hermite cubic is described in Section 13.8. The issue of transformation is discussed in Section 13.9. The chapter is summarized in Section 13.10.

13.2   Finding the Boundary of a Bitmap Image

A bitmap image of a character can be obtained by creating a bitmap character in some program such as Paint or Adobe Photoshop. Alternatively an image drawn on paper can be scanned and stored as a bitmap. Both methods are recommended. The quality of the bitmap image obtained directly from an electronic device

FIGURE 13.1. Bitmap image.

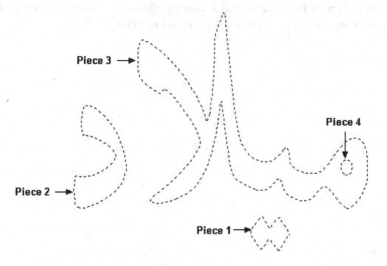

FIGURE 13.2. Detected boundary of the image of Figure 13.1.

depends on the resolution of device, type of image (e.g., BMP, JPEG, TIFF, etc.), the number of bits selected to store the image, and so on. The quality of the scanned image depends on factors such as the quality of the image on the paper, and the scanner and attributes set during scanning. Figure 13.1 shows the bitmap image of an Arabic word.

In order to find the boundary of a bitmap image, first its chain code is extracted [7, 8]. Chain codes are a notation for recording the list of edge points along a contour. The chain code specifies the direction of a contour at each edge in the edge. From the chain-coded curve, boundary of the image is found [9]. The selection of boundary points is based on their corner strength and contour fluctuations. The input to boundary detection algorithm is a bitmap image. The algorithm returns number of pieces in the image. And for each piece, number and values of these boundary points:

$$p_i = (x_i, y_i), i = 1, 2, \ldots, N, \tag{13.1}$$

are determined. For example, Figure 13.2 shows the detected boundary of the image of Figure 13.1.

13.3   Detecting Corner Points

In the next important step of algorithm design, corner points are detected from the boundary points. The corner points are those points that partition the boundary into various segments. A number of approaches have been proposed by researchers for corner detection [3, 4, 10–12]. The details of various algorithms were provided in Chapter 11. The reader should refer to Chapter 11 for the choice of algorithm. The SAM06 algorithm in Section 11.5 has been selected for the purpose of this chapter.

The demonstration of the SAM06 algorithm is made in Figure 13.3, which shows detected corner points obtained from boundary of Figure 13.2. Similarly, Figure 13.4(b) is representing the outline together with the detection of corner points of the image in Figure 13.4(a). Figure 13.5(b) represents the outline together with the detection of corner points of the image in Figure 13.5(a).

FIGURE 13.3. Corner points shown with circles.

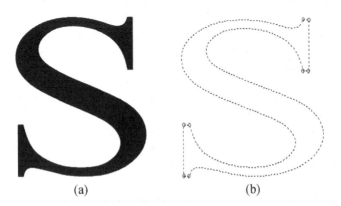

(a)   (b)

FIGURE 13.4. (a) Bitmap image of character "S." (b) Outline of the image "S" together with corner points shown with circles.

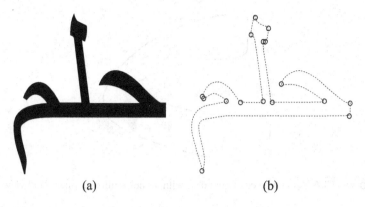

(a)   (b)

FIGURE 13.5. (a) Bitmap image of an Arabic word. (b) Outline of the image together with corner points shown with circles.

13.4   Filtering Noise

The points obtained by extracting the boundary of the bitmap image may have noise (due to jagged edges). There are many sophisticated techniques [13, 14] to filter out the noise from the image/contour. The technique adopted here is known as an approximation to a *Gaussian filter*, which is simple and computationally efficient. Sample data of boundary (except corner points) is passed through the filter to remove noise. Mathematically, one can express the Gaussian filter as follows:

$$x_i = 0.5x_i + 0.25x_{i+1} + 0.25x_{i-1}, \quad y_i = 0.5y_i + 0.25y_{i+1} + 0.25y_{i-1}. \quad (13.2)$$

The filter spreads out the local variation by replacing each point with a half-weighted average of its own value and a quarter-weighted averages of its immediate neighbor point values. The filtering process is repeated a number of times. By experimentation, it has been found that six to ten iterations are enough to filter noise. One can argue that noise can be filtered before detection of the corner points and then detecting corner points from filtered data. But, by experiments, it has been found more suitable to detect the corner points first and then filter the noise from points other than the corner points. Due to this strategy, corner points are detected more accurately and the overall shape of character is more intact.

The system, presented in this chapter, works quite well even without filtering any noise from the sample data. Filtering improves the performance of the system by needing a smaller number of significant points. Figure 13.6 shows the second piece of boundary without applying noise filtering. Figure 13.7 shows the second piece of boundary after applying noise filtering up to six iterations.

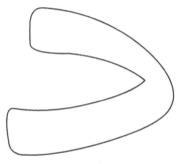

FIGURE 13.6. Second piece of boundary without noise filtering (magnified view).

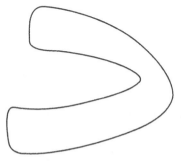

FIGURE 13.7. Second piece of boundary with noise filtering (magnified view).

13.5   Curve Fitting with Cubic Bézier

Curve fitting is a well-studied area in computer graphics and mathematics. Different types of curves and techniques have been proposed by various authors. For example, the details of curve fitting with splines are given in [15] and the use of piecewise parametric cubics is made in [16]. A recursive algebraic curve-fitting method is proposed in [17]. In this chapter, Bézier cubics have been used for curve fitting. This is because they are computationally efficient and have a high level of accuracy when approximating character shapes.

The boundary points of each piece are divided into groups, called segments, and fit a cubic Bézier curve to each segment. The division is based on corner points. It means that if there are m corner points $cp_1, \ldots, cp_m$, then there will be m segments $seg_1, \ldots, seg_m$. For example, the first segment has all the boundary points between the corner point cp_1 and the corner point cp_2, inclusive. The second segment has all the boundary points between the corner point cp_2 and the corner point cp_3 inclusive. Likewise, the last segment has all the boundary points between the corner point cp_m and the corner point cp_1 inclusive. Of course, corner points obey the order of boundary points. The situation is illustrated in Figure 13.8 for the second piece of Figure 13.2. If boundary points of the kth segment are $p_u, \ldots, p_w$,

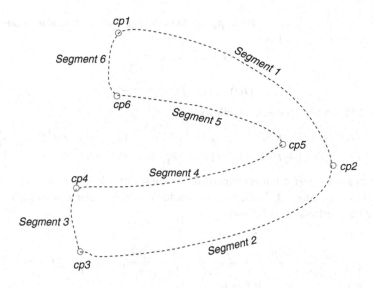

FIGURE 13.8. Division of the boundary into segments based on corner points.

then (13.3) describes the relationship between the boundary points and the corner points, and (13.4) is used to count the number of points in the kth segment:

$$p_u = cp_k \quad \text{for } 1 \le k < m;$$
$$p_w = \begin{cases} cp_{k+1} & \text{for } 1 \le k < m; \\ cp_1 & \text{if } k = m. \end{cases} \quad (13.3)$$

$$n_k = \begin{cases} w - u + 1 & \text{if } w \ge u; \\ N - u + 1 + w & \text{if } w < u. \end{cases} \quad (13.4)$$

The process of fitting a cubic Bézier curve is similar to all the segments. More explanations of how to process for the kth segment, are given in the following sections.

13.5.1 *Finding Intermediate Control Points*

The Bézier form of a cubic polynomial curve has four control points P_0, P_1, P_2 and P_3. The Bézier curve interpolates the two end control points P_0 and P_3, and approximates the two intermediate points, P_1 and P_2. The two end control points are the two corner points of the curve segment. But, the two intermediate control points of the fitted Bézier cubic curve need some processing to be manipulated. Mathematically, a Bézier cubic curve can by written as follows:

$$Q(t) = \sum_{k=0}^{3} P_k B_k = (1 - t^3)P_0 + 3t(1 - t^2)P_1 + 3t^2(1 - t)P_2 + t^3 P_3, \quad (13.5)$$

where $0 \leq t \leq 1$, $P_0 = p_u$, $P_3 = p_w$ for the kth segment, the boundary points of which are $p_u, \ldots, p_w$. Let

$$P_i = (P_{x_i}, P_{y_i}),$$

and

$$Q(t) = (Q_x(t), Q_y(t)),$$

then (13.5) can be expressed as follows:

$$Q_x(t) = (1 - t^3)P_{x_0} + 3t(1 - t^2)P_{x_1} + 3t^2(1 - t)P_{x_2} + t^3 P_{x_3}, \quad (13.6)$$
$$Q_y(t) = (1 - t^3)P_{y_0} + 3t(1 - t^2)P_{y_1} + 3t^2(1 - t)P_{y_2} + t^3 P_{y_3}. \quad (13.7)$$

As far as *parameterization* is concerned, the choice of *chord-length parameterization* has been adopted. Thus, the parametric value t, associated with each point p_i, can be to estimated as follows:

$$t_i = \begin{cases} 0, & \text{if } i = u; \\ \dfrac{|p_u p_{u+1}| + |p_{u+1} p_{u+2}| + \cdots + |p_{i-1} p_i|}{|p_u p_{u+1}| + |p_{u+1} p_{u+2}| + \cdots + |p_{w-1} p_w|}, & \text{for } u + 1 \leq i \leq w - 1; \\ 1, & \text{if } i = w. \end{cases}$$

(13.8)

It is obvious that the number of points in the kth segment (i.e., n_k) and the number of t values associated with them are same.

The goal here is to approximate the boundary of the original image by a parametric curve in an *optimal way*. To achieve this goal, one needs to find the values of P_1 and P_2 that minimize the distance between the boundary and parametric curve. For this purpose, the least square method has been used. That is, one can define the sum of squared distances S from the boundary to the parametric curve. Mathematically, it can be expressed as follows:

$$S = \sum_{i=u}^{w} [Q_i(t) - p_i]^2,$$

(13.9)

$$= \sum_{i=u}^{w} [Q_{x_i}(t) - p_{x_i}]^2 + \sum_{i=u}^{w} [Q_{y_i}(t) - p_{y_i}]^2.$$

The goal is to minimize S. It is required to find partial derivatives of (13.9) with respect to P_1 and P_2 and equate them to zero as follows:

$$\frac{\partial S}{\partial P_1} = 0, \quad (13.10)$$

$$\frac{\partial S}{\partial P_2} = 0. \quad (13.11)$$

The solution will provide the values of P_1 and P_2 that approximate the boundary by a parametric curve in the best way for given values of t. Now, manipulating Equation (13.15) yields the following:

$$\frac{\partial S}{\partial P_1} = 2 \sum_{i=u}^{w} \frac{\partial Q(t_i)}{\partial P_1} [Q(t_i) - p_i] = 0,$$

which implies

$$\sum_{i=u}^{w} B_1(t_i)[Q(t_i) - p_i] = 0. \tag{13.12}$$

Manipulating Equation (13.16) yields following:

$$\frac{\partial S}{\partial P_2} = 2 \sum_{i=u}^{w} \frac{\partial Q(t_i)}{\partial P_2}[Q(t_i) - p_i] = 0,$$

which implies

$$\sum_{i=u}^{w} B_2(t_i)[Q(t_i) - p_i] = 0. \tag{13.13}$$

Let

$$A_k = \sum_{i=u}^{w} [B_k(t_i)]^2,$$

$$A_{1,2} = \sum_{i=u}^{w} [B_1(t_i)B_2(t_i)],$$

$$C_{x_k} = \sum_{i=u}^{w} [B_k(t_i)[p_{x_i} - B_0(t_i)P_{x_0} - B_3(t_i)P_{x_3}], C_{y_k}$$

$$= \sum_{i=u}^{w} [B_k(t_i)[p_{y_i} - B_0(t_i)P_{y_0} - B_3(t_i)P_{y_3}].$$

Then, solving (13.13) and (13.13) for P_1 and P_2 gives the following:

$$\begin{bmatrix} A_1 & A_{1,2} \\ A_{1,2} & A_2 \end{bmatrix} \begin{bmatrix} P_{x_1} \\ P_{x_2} \end{bmatrix} = \begin{bmatrix} C_{x_1} \\ C_{x_2} \end{bmatrix}, \tag{13.14}$$

$$\begin{bmatrix} A_1 & A_{1,2} \\ A_{1,2} & A_2 \end{bmatrix} \begin{bmatrix} P_{y_1} \\ P_{y_2} \end{bmatrix} = \begin{bmatrix} C_{y_1} \\ C_{y_2} \end{bmatrix}. \tag{13.15}$$

Solving (13.14) and (13.15), one will achieve the following:

$$P_{x_1} = \frac{A_2 C_{x_1} - A_{1,2} C_{x_2}}{A_1 A_2 - A_{1,2}^2}, \quad P_{y_1} = \frac{A_2 C_{y_1} - A_{1,2} C_{y_2}}{A_1 A_2 - A_{1,2}^2}, \tag{13.16}$$

$$P_{x_2} = \frac{A_1 C_{x2} - A_{1,2} C_{x_1}}{A_1 A_2 - A_{1,2}^2}, \quad P_{y_2} = \frac{A_1 C_{y2} - A_{1,2} C_{y1}}{A_1 A_2 - A_{1,2}^2}. \tag{13.17}$$

Now, all the four control points P_0, P_1, P_2, P_3 and t values are in hand. Using these, one can fit the cubic Bézier to the segment. The demonstration of fitted Bézier cubic curves (solid line) over boundary (dotted line) is shown in Figure 13.9.

FIGURE 13.9. Fitted cubic Bézier (solid line) over the boundary (dotted line).

13.5.2 *Comparing the Boundary and Parametric Curve*

We estimate the accuracy of our fit, for the segment under process, by computing the *squared distance*[1] between each of the points p_i on boundary and its corresponding points $Q(t_i)$ on the parametric curve:

$$
\begin{aligned}
d_i^2 &= |p_i - Q(t_i)|, \\
&= \left[p_{x_i} - Q_x(t_i)\right]^2 + \left[p_{y_i} - Q_y(t_i)\right]^2.
\end{aligned}
\tag{13.18}
$$

Among all the computed distances computed by Equation (13.23), we find maximum squared distance:

$$
d_{\max}^2 = \text{Max}(d_u^2, d_{u+1}^2, \ldots, d_w^2).
$$

If $d_{\max}^2$ exceeds the predefined error tolerance limit $d_{\text{tolerance}}^2$, then we apply reparameterization on the segment. The reparameterization process is explained in the following section.

13.6   Reparameterization

Reparameterization means finding new and better values of the t parameter so that we might not have to break a segment into two or more segments, and hence we would need a lesser number of Bézier curves. Reparameterization is explained as follows: Given a parametric curve $Q(t)$ and a point p on the boundary, we need to find a corresponding point on the parametric curve closest to p. In other words, we need to find the parameter value t such that the distance from p to $Q(t)$

---

[1] Computing the *squared distance* is computationally more efficient than simply computing *distance*; otherwise their semantic is the same.

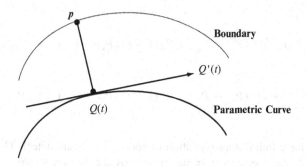

FIGURE 13.10. Distance between p and $Q(t)$.

is minimum. This situation is illustrated in Figure 13.10. Note that distance p to $Q(t)$ is perpendicular to the tangent, that is, $Q'(t)$ of the curve at $Q(t)$ We can write the reparameterization equation as follows:

$$[Q(t) - p] . Q'(t) = 0. \tag{13.19}$$

This is a quintic equation (There is dot the product of $[Q(t) - p]$ and $Q'(t)$) in t and can be solved by *Newton-Raphson's* method. $[Q(t) - p]$ is a polynomial of degree three and $Q'(t)$ is of degree two. So Equation (13.24) is a polynomial of degree five. Let

$$Q_1(t) = Q(t) - p, \tag{13.20}$$
$$Q_2(t) = Q'(t). \tag{13.21}$$

Now, we can write Equation (13.24) as follows:

$$Q_1(t).Q_2(t) = 0. \tag{13.22}$$

Writing Equation (13.25) in Cartesian form as follows:

$$Q_1(t) = [Q_x(t) - p_x]i + [Q_y(t) - p_y]j. \tag{13.23}$$

Let

$$Q_{1x}(t) = Q_x(t) - p_x, \tag{13.24}$$
$$Q_{1y}(t) = Q_y(t) - p_y. \tag{13.25}$$

Then we can write (13.23) as follows:

$$Q_1(t) = Q_{1x}(t)i + Q_{1y}(t)j. \tag{13.26}$$

Similarly, one can write Equation (13.26) in Cartesian form as follows:

$$Q_2(t) = Q'_x(t)i + Q'_y(t)j, \tag{13.27}$$

where

$$Q'_x(t) = 3\left[(1-t)^2\,(P_{x_1} - P_{x_0}) + 2t\,(1-t)\,(P_{x_2} - P_{x_1}) + t^2(P_{x_3} - P_{x_2})\right],$$
(13.28)

$$Q'_y(t) = 3\left[(1-t)^2\,(P_{y_1} - P_{y_0}) + 2t\,(1-t)\,(P_{y_2} - P_{y_1}) + t^2(P_{y_3} - P_{y_2})\right].$$
(13.29)

We already have initial approximation of roots (i.e., t parameter). The new and better value of parameter t can be determined by the *Newton-Raphson* method as follows:

$$t_{new} \leftarrow t_{old} - \frac{f(t)}{f'(t)}.$$
(13.30)

In the present scenario,

$$f(t) = Q_1(t).Q_2(t)$$
$$= \left[Q_{1x}(t)i + Q_{1y}(t)j\right].\left[Q'_x(t)i + Q'_y(t)j\right].$$
(13.31)

Dot product yields the following result:

$$f(t) = Q_{1x}(t)Q'_x(t) + Q_{1y}(t)Q'_y(t).$$
(13.32)

Now Equation (13.35) can be solved by substituting the initial approximation of parameter t, $f(t)$ and $f'(t)$. This will give the new value of t. Using new values of parameter t, we find new control points and apply the fitting process as usual. We do reparameterization of the segments not fulfilling the threshold tolerance limit. Since reparameterization is an expensive process, one can fix a maximum limit on the number of times a segment can go for reparameterization.

Table 13.1 gives details of how the reparameterization step improves the performance of the algorithm by reducing number of break points required in fitting a cubic Bézier. The first column is without reparameterization and the last column is with reparameterization.

TABLE 13.1. Effect of reparameterization on the fitting process.

Number of times reparameterization applied	Number of break points required
0	16
2	10
4	10
6	9
10	8
12	8

13.7 Breaking Segment

If either the maximum limit of reparameterization exceeds or reparameterization increases the square distance between the digitized curve and the parametric curve rather than decreasing it (in some cases it is possible), then we can break the segment into two segments at the point of maximum distance. Then the point corresponding to the maximum distance is added to list of significant points. The number of segments and number of significant points are increased by one. This process is repeated for each segment until all the segments of all the pieces meet the threshold tolerance limit. Figure 13.11 shows the fitted Bézier curve using significant points over the boundary. Corner points are shown by "o" and break points are shown by "◇".

When all the segments meet the square distance threshold limit, then there is no need to keep the specific t values. The use of specific t values has been made to find the best possible intermediate control points and provide an initial estimate for finding new t values in the Newton-Raphson method. After having all the control points for all the segments, there is no more need of specific t values. One can write a general expression for finding t values. By this general expression, one can find t values on the fly (i.e., during fitting Bézier to a segment). If we fit a cubic Bézier to a segment using n points then the expression of t can be written as follows:

$$t_i = \begin{cases} 0 & \text{if } i = 1, \\ t_{i-1} + 1/(n-1) & \text{for } 2 \leq i \leq n-1, \\ 1 & \text{if } i = n. \end{cases} \qquad (13.33)$$

Figure 13.12 shows the final fitted outline (parametric representation) of the contour of Figure 13.1 (bitmap character). Figure 13.14 shows the parametric representation of a Kanji (Japanese language) character in Figure 13.13.

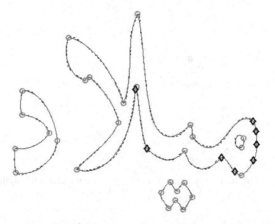

FIGURE 13.11. Fitted cubic Bézier (solid line) over boundary (dotted line). *Corner points* are shown by a circle "o"; break points are shown by a diamond "◇".

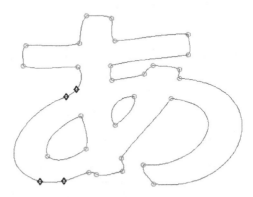

FIGURE 13.12. Final outline (parametric representation of bitmap character of Figure 13.1).

FIGURE 13.13. A Kanji character.

FIGURE 13.14. Parametric representation of a Kanji character with significant points.

Figure 13.15 (a)-(f) shows various phases of the process from a bitmap image (Figure 13.15(a) to the outline (Figure 13.15(f)) achieved for an English character

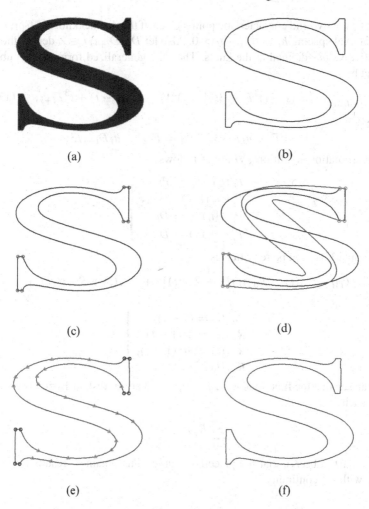

FIGURE 13.15. (a) Bitmap image. (b) Contour/boundary of digitized image. (c) Contour/boundary with corner points. (d) Bézier outline fitted to corner points. (e) Bézier outline fitted to significant points "Δ." (f) Final outline.

"S." Figure 13.15(b) is the contour/boundary of a digitized image, Figure 13.15(c) is the contour/boundary with corner points. Figure 13.15(d) shows the Bézier outline fitted to the corner points. Figure 13.15(e) is the Bézier outline fitted to significant points.

13.8   Alternate Method Using Hermite Cubic

This section describes an alternative way of manipulating the cubic curve. This is achieved by using an alternative form, namely, the Hermite cubic. Let F_i, F_{i+1},

$i \in Z$, be the two end characteristic points given at the distinct knots $t_i, t_{i+1}, i \in Z$ with interval spacing $h_i = t_{i+1} - t_i > 0$. Also let $D_i, D_{i+1}, i \in Z$ denote the first derivative values defined at the knots. Then the generalized form of the cubic is defined by:

$$P_i|_{(t_i, t_{i+1})}(t) = (1 - t)^3 F_i + 3t(1 - t)^2 V_i + 3t^2(1 - t) + t^3 F_{i+1}, \qquad (13.34)$$

where

$$V_i = F_i + h_i D_i/3, \quad W_i = F_{i+1} - h_i D_{i+1}/3,$$

The interpolation conditions, $\forall i$ are as follows:

$$\left.\begin{array}{ll} P_i(t_i) & = F_i, \\ P_i(t_{i+1}) & = F_{i+1}, \\ P_i^{(1)}(t_i) & = D_i, \\ P_i^{(1)}(t_{i+1}) & = D_{i+1}. \end{array}\right\}$$

Equation (13.34) can be rewritten as

$$P_i|_{(t_i, t_{i+1})}(t) = R_{0,i}(t) F_i + R_{1,i}(t) V_i + R_{2,i}(t) + R_{3,i}(t) F_{i+1},$$

where

$$\left.\begin{array}{l} R_{0,i}(t) = (1 - t)^3, \\ R_{1,i}(t) = 3t(1 - t)^2, \\ R_{2,i}(t) = 3t^2(1 - t), \\ R_{3,i}(t) = t^3. \end{array}\right\}$$

One can see that the functions $R_{j,i}, j = 0, 1, 2, 3$ are Bernstein-Bézier basis functions, such that

$$\sum_{j=0}^{3} R_{j,i}(t) = 1.$$

One can also observe that the piecewise curve, thus obtained, results to a cubic spline with C^1 continuity.

13.8.1   Estimation of Tangent Vectors

We define a distance-based choice for tangent vectors D_i's at F_i's as follows. For open curves, the tangents are defined as follows:

$$\left.\begin{array}{l} D_0 = 2(F_1 - F_0) - (F_2 - F_0)/2, \\ D_n = 2(F_n - F_{n-1}) - (F_n - F_{n-2})/2, \\ D_i = a_i(F_i - F_{i-1}) + (1 - a_i)(F_{i+1} - F_i), i = 1, \ldots, n - 1. \end{array}\right\}$$

For close curves, the tangents are described as follows:

$$\left.\begin{array}{l} F_{-1} = F_{n-1}, \quad F_{n+1} = F_1, \\ D_i = a_i(F_i - F_{i-1}) + (1 - a_i)(F_{i+1} - F_i), i = 0, \ldots, n, \end{array}\right\}$$

where

$$a_i = \frac{|F_{i+1} - F_i|}{|F_{i+1} - F_i| + |F_i - F_{i-1}|}, \quad i = 0, \ldots, n.$$

13.8.2 *Optimal Design Curve*

The case, when tangents are estimated as described in Section 13.8.1, is a C^1 Hermite spline curve and will be treated as a default design curve here. This is a simplest case to consider and requires less computation initially. We can assume all h_i are equal to 1, which yields:

$$V_i = F_i + D_i/3 \quad \text{and} \quad W_i = F_{i+1} - D_{i+1}/3.$$

Suppose, for $i = 0, 1, 2, \ldots, n - 1$, the data segments

$$\{P_{i,j} = (x_{i,j}, y_{i,j}), j = 1, 2, \ldots, m_i\}$$

are given as the ordered sets of the universal set of the data points. Then the square roots $S_{i,j}$'s of distances between $P_{i,j}$'s and their corresponding parametric points $P_i(t_j)$'s on the curve are computed as:

$$S_i = \sqrt{|P_i(u_{i,j}) - P_{i,j}|}, \quad i = 0, 1, 2, \ldots, n - 1,$$

where the parameterization over u's is in accordance with the chord length parameterization.

For the best fitting of the curve to the given data, we have to find out the spline curve so that the $S_{i,j}$'s are minimal in each segment. This can be done by breaking the curve pieces at those points, where the square roots of distances are highest. Thus, the curve fitted using this way will be a candidate of best fit.

For the practical demonstration of this alternate scheme, consider the bitmap character in Figure 13.16(a). Its outline has been achieved in Figure 13.16(b). Instead of SAM06, the corner detection algorithm applied is CS99 of Section 11.4. Therefore, some visually incorrect corners can be seen in Figure 13.16(c) when they are detected. Figure 13.16(d) is the Hermite cubic spline fitted to the corner points thus detected. Figure 13.17 also presents a similar scenario when repeated for another bitmap character.

A fitted Hermite spline curve may not satisfy the threshold tolerance limit as can be seen in Figures 13.16 and 13.17. The curve is then subdivided at the point of worst error —the point where the fitted spline is farthest from the digitized curve. The new break point will be considered as a significant point, and the curve is again fitted to these corner and break points obtained so far. This process of inserting break points is repeated unless a threshold value is not violated.

Figures 13.18 and 13.19 demonstrate the scheme. In the matrices of Figure 13.18, the first (from left to right) is for the bitmapped image of the font; the second is for the outline of the font the third is showing the corner points; the fourth is the Hermite spline curve fit; and the from the fifth to the ninth is the insertion of break points against the threshold value three.

The matrix of Figure 13.19 follows in the same way against the threshold value two. One can observe that lesser threshold value gives rise to more break points, hence more accuracy costs in terms of break points.

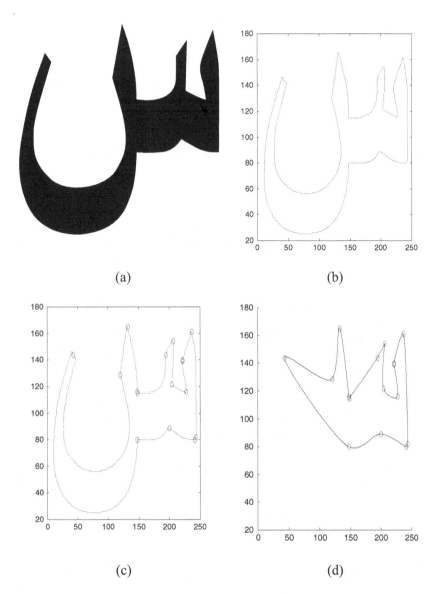

FIGURE 13.16. (a) A bitmap character. (b) Outline of the bitmap character. (c) CS99 corner detection algorithm of Section 11.4 is applied. (d) Hermite cubic spline fitted to the corner points.

Remark 13.1. One can devise the whole algorithm based on the Hermite spline curve model to capture the outline of any planar bitmap image in such a way that the tangents are calculated using the least square method. This way of manipulating the scheme will enhance the power of the algorithm.

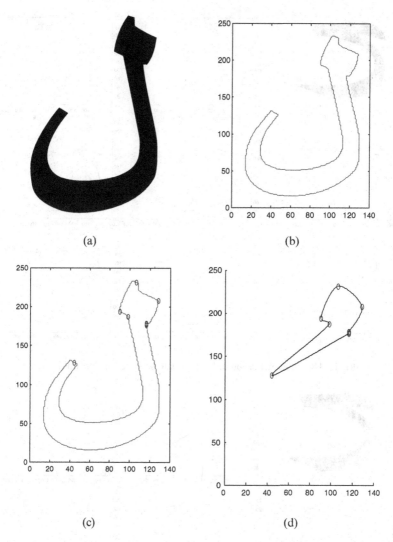

FIGURE 13.17. (a) A bitmap character. (b) Outline of the bitmap character. (c) CS99 corner detection algorithm of Section 11.4 is applied. (d) Hermite cubic spline fitted to the corner points.

13.9   Transformations and Mapping

This chapter deals with producing various sizes and shapes of fonts using transformations and mapping. As we described earlier, outline fonts have many advantages over bitmap fonts. By manipulation of a small number of points, various sizes and shapes of the same character can be obtained very efficiently. Section 13.9.1 describes transformations while Section 13.9.2 is related to mapping.

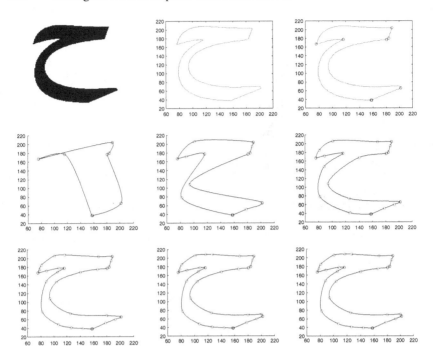

FIGURE 13.18. Implementation of the alternate scheme for threshold value 3.

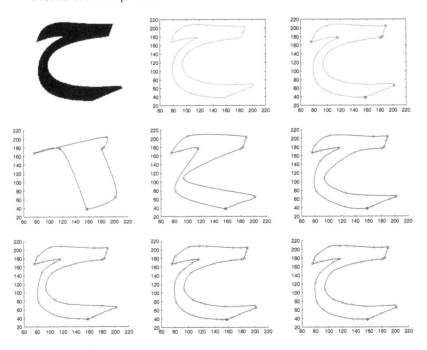

FIGURE 13.19. Implementation of the alternate scheme for threshold value 2.

13.9.1   *Transformations*

A *scaling* transformation alters the size of an object. This operation can be carried out for polygons by multiplying the coordinate values (x, y) of each vertex by *scaling factors* s_x, s_y to produce the transformed coordinates (x', y'):

$$x' = x.s_x, \quad y' = y.s_y.$$

- Scaling factor s_x scales objects in the x-direction.
- Scaling factor s_y scales objects in the y-direction.

The scaling transformation equations can be rewritten in the matrix form as follows:

$$\begin{bmatrix} x' \\ y' \end{bmatrix} = \begin{bmatrix} s_x & 0 \\ 0 & s_y \end{bmatrix} . \begin{bmatrix} x \\ y \end{bmatrix}. \tag{13.35}$$

Or

$$P' = S.P,$$

where S is the 2×2 scaling matrix.

If we do not want to scale along an axis, then its scaling factor (s_x or s_y) is set to 1. Figure 13.20 shows the character "Allah" before scaling. Figure 13.21 shows scaling along the x-axis ($s_x = 1/2, s_y = 1$). Figure 13.23 shows scaling along the y-axis ($s_x = 1, s_y = 1/2$) for the image in Figure 13.22. Similarly, Figure 13.25 shows scaling along both x-axis and y-axis ($s_x = 1/2, s_y = 1/2$) for Figure 13.24.

It should be noted that to do scaling we multiply scaling factors (i.e., s_x or s_y) with only control points and then fit the cubic Bézier to new set of points.

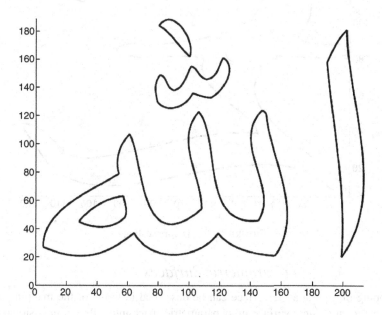

FIGURE 13.20. Before scaling.

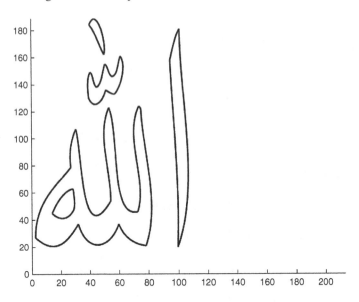

FIGURE 13.21. Scaling along the x-axis $s_x = 1/2$; $s_y = 1$.

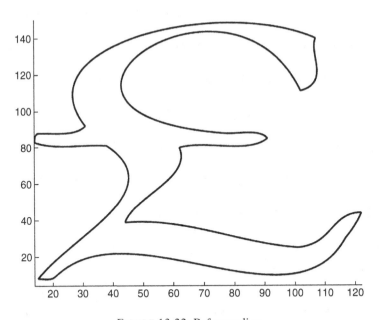

FIGURE 13.22. Before scaling.

13.9.2 Mapping Parametric Surfaces

Mapping of a parametric surface can be described in terms of the mapping of a two-parameter planar surface in uv parametric space into a three-dimensional xyz object space. A surface in object space is represented by the functions that map

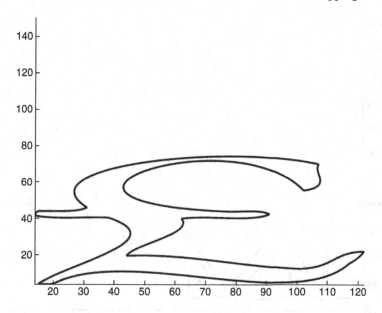

FIGURE 13.23. Scaling along the y-axis $s_x = 1$; $s_y = 1/2$.

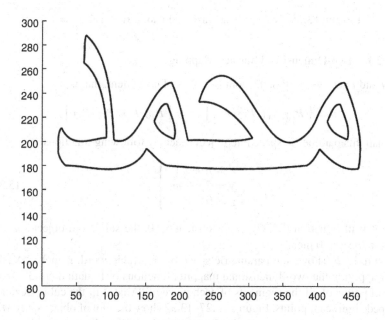

FIGURE 13.24. Before scaling.

the parametric surface into the xyz object space, that is,

$$\left.\begin{array}{l} x = x(u, w), \\ y = y(u, w), \\ z = z(u, w). \end{array}\right\} \tag{13.36}$$

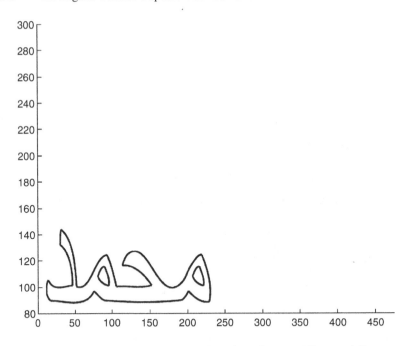

FIGURE 13.25. Scaling along x-axis and y-axis, $s_x = 1/2$, $s_y = 1/2$.

13.9.2.1 Two-Dimensional Surface Mapping

Let u and w arrays contain the control points of a segment, that is,

$$u = \begin{bmatrix} P_{x0} & P_{x1} & P_{x2} & P_{x3} \end{bmatrix}; v = \begin{bmatrix} P_{y0} & P_{y1} & P_{y2} & P_{y3} \end{bmatrix}.$$

We map this parametric space into object space by following functions:

$$\left. \begin{aligned} x &= u - w, \\ y &= 2u + w, \\ z &= 0. \end{aligned} \right\} \tag{13.37}$$

Note that in Equation (13.37), $z = \text{constant} = 0$, the surface in object space is lying in the $z = 0$ plane.

Figure 13.26 shows the parametric space of an Arabic word, namely, "Allah." After applying the two-dimensional mapping functions of Equation (13.37) to all control points of all the segments of each piece of "Allah." fit the cubic Bézier to mapped significant points. Figures 13.27–13.32 show the plot of object space with various elevation (El) and azimuth (Az) angles (the angle orientation with respect to the $z = 0$ plane is called elevation and the angle with respect to the $x = 0$ plane is called azimuth). The examples of two-dimensional surface mapping show that holding a single parametric value constant (i.e., z), yields a curve on the surface of object space. The curve is called isoparametric.

FIGURE 13.26. Parametric space.

FIGURE 13.27. 2-D Surface mapping. Object space. Az = 30°, El = 30°.

FIGURE 13.28. 2-D Surface mapping. Object space. Az = 45°, El = 45°.

FIGURE 13.29. 2-D Surface mapping. Object space. Az = 160°, El = 160°.

FIGURE 13.30. 2-D surface mapping. Object space. Az = 210°, El = 210°.

FIGURE 13.31. 2-D Surface mapping. Object space. Az = 330°, El = 330°.

FIGURE 13.32. 2-D Surface mapping. Object space (mirrored view). Az = −120°, El = −60°.

FIGURE 13.33. 3-D Surface mapping. Object space. Az = 0°, El = 55°.

FIGURE 13.34. 3-D Surface mapping. Object space. Az = −40°, El = 45°.

13.9.2.2 Three-Dimensional Surface Mapping

Similarly, as in the previous section, one can apply three-dimensional mapping to map parametric space into object space. In this case, mapping functions may be the following:

$$\left.\begin{array}{l} x = u, \\ y = w, \\ z = (u - w)^2. \end{array}\right\} \qquad (13.38)$$

This selection of mapping functions is based on following criteria:

- The legibility of the character should be preserved.
- A continuous segment must not map to a discontinuous segment.

13.10 Summary

We have presented an efficient algorithm for approximation of the boundary of digital character images. The algorithm is particularly suitable for languages that are highly curvilinear in nature, such as Arabic, Japanese, Urdu, and so on. In addition to the detection of *corner points*, a strategy to detect a set of *break points* has also also been explained to optimize the outline. Parametric cubic Bézier curves are used for fitting. Filtering noise and reparameterization steps are added to improve the performance of the algorithm. The proposed approach eliminates the human interaction in obtaining the outline of the original character [18].

13.11 Exercises

1. Using a Gaussian filter, write a program to filter the outlines of images.
2. Repeat the filtering process in Exercise 1 a number of times and explain the difference you observe.
3. Repeat the filtering process in Exercise 1 a number of times and explain the difference you observe when

   a. the corner points are included,
   b. the corner points are excluded.

4. Write a program to detect corner points using the SAM06 corner detection algorithm and then filter the noise in such a way that the corner points remain included. Do you think the claim in the book is justified, that, due to this strategy, corner points are detected more accurately and the overall shape of character is more intact?
5. Write a program using chord length parameterization to plot a Bézier cubic curve with given four input control points.
6. Write a program using unit length parameterization to plot a Bézier cubic curve with given four input control points.

7. How different would the two Bézier cubic curves, in Exercises 5 and 6, look when fitted to the following control points:

   a. $P_0 = (0, 0)$, $P_1 = (5, 10)$, $P_2 = (15, 15)$, $P_3 = (25, 5)$,
   b. $P_0 = (0, 0)$, $P_1 = (5, 10)$, $P_2 = (-10, 15)$, $P_3 = (5, 5)$,
   c. $P_0 = (0, 0)$, $P_1 = (5, 10)$, $P_2 = (15, -15)$, $P_3 = (25, 5)$,
   d. $P_0 = (0, 0)$, $P_1 = (5, 10)$, $P_2 = (15, 15)$, $P_3 = (0, 0)$.

8. Find the intermediate control points for the following data (read from left to right in order) when a Bézier cubic is fitted as in Section 13.4.1:

   a. (0, 0), (5, 10), (15, 15), (25, 5), (30, 20), (30, 30), (35, 40),
   b. (0, 0), (1, 10), (2, 11), (3, 12), (4, 13), (5, 15), (6, 17), (7, 17),

9. Write a program using chord length parameterization to plot a Hermite cubic curve with given input data points as given in Exercises 7 and 8.
10. Write a program using unit length parameterization to plot a Hermite cubic curve with given input data points as in Exercises 7 and 8.
11. Write a program to implement the whole algorithm based on the Bézier curve model to capture the outline of any planar bitmap image.
12. How different would the two Hermite cubic curves in Exercises 10 and 11 look when fitted?
13. Write a program to implement the whole algorithm based on the Hermite spline curve model to capture the outline of any planar bitmap image.
14. Devise the whole algorithm based on the Hermite spline curve model to capture the outline of any planar bitmap image in such a way that the tangents are calculated using the least square method.

References

1. Karow, P. (1994), *Digital Typefaces: Description and Formats*. Springer-Verlag, Berlin.
2. Karow, P. (1994), *Font Technology: Methods and Tools*. Springer-Verlag, Berlin.
3. Beus, H.L. (1987), An improved corner detection algorithm based on chain-coded plane curves. *Pattern Recognition* 20(3):291–296.
4. Liu, H.C., and Srinath, M.D. (1990), Corner detection from chain-code. *Pattern Recognition*, 51–68.
5. Sarfraz, M., and Khan, M.A. (2003), An automatic outline-fitting algorithm for Arabic characters. *Lecture Notes in Computer Sciences* (LNCS) 2669, 589–598\.
6. Sarfraz, M., and Khan. M.A. (2002), Automatic outline capture of Arabic fonts. *Information Sciences*, 269–281.
7. Avrahami, G., and Pratt, V. (1991), Subpixel edge detection in character digitization. *Raster Imaging and Digital Typography II*, 54–64.
8. Hou. Z.J., and Wei, G.W. (2002), A new approach to edge detection, *Pattern Recognition* 35, 1559–1570.
9. Richard, N., and Gilbert, T. (2002), Extraction of dominant points by estimation of the contour fluctuations, *Pattern Recognition* (35), 1447–1462.

10. Pei, S. (1994), Corner detection using nest moving average. *Pattern Recognition*, 27(11):1533–1537.
11. Chetrikov, D., and Zsabo, S. (1999), A simple and efficient algorithm for detection of high curvature points in planar curves, *Proc. 23rd Workshop of the Australian Pattern Recognition Group*, 1751–184.
12. Davis, L. (1979), Shape matching using relaxation techniques. *IEEE Trans. PAMI.* 60–72.
13. Braquelaire, J.P., and Vialard, A. (1997), A new anti-aliasing approach for image compositing. *The Visual Computer*, 13(5), 218–227.
14. Fabris, A.E., and A.R. Forrest. (1997), Anti-aliasing of curves by discrete prefiltering. *SIGGRAPH 1997 Proceedings*, pp. 317–326.
15. Cox, M.G. (1971), Curve fitting with piecewise polynomials. *J. Inst. Math Appl.* 8, 36–52.
16. Plass, M., and Stone, M. (1983), Curve-fitting with piecewise parametric cubics. *Computer Graphics* 17(3), 229–239.
17. Zhang, S., Li, L., Seah, H.S. (1998), Recursive curve fitting and rendering. *The Visual Computer*, 69–82.
18. Sarfraz, M., and Khan, M.A. (2004), An automatic algorithm for approximating boundary of bitmap characters. In: *Future Generation Computer Systems*, Elsevier Science, Vol. 20, pp. 1327–1336.
19. Sarfraz, M. (2004), Some algorithms for curve design and automatic outline capturing of images, *Int J Image Graphics*, World Scientific Publisher, 4(2), 301–324.
20. Sarfraz, M. (2003), Curve fitting for large data using rational cubic splines, *Int J Comput Their Appl* 10(4), 233–246.
21. Sarfraz, M., and Khan, M.A. (2003), An automatic outline fitting algorithm for Arabic characters, *Lecture Notes in Computer Science*, Vol. 2669: *Computational Science and Its Applications*, Eds.: V. Kumar, M.L. Gavrilova, C.J.K. Tan, and P.L'Ecuyer, Springer-Verlag, New York, pp. 589–598.
22. Sarfraz, M. (2003), Optimal curve fitting to digital data, *Int J WSCG* 11(1), 128–135.
23. Sarfraz, M., and Razzak, M.F.A. (2003), A web-based system to capture outlines of Arabic fonts, *Int J Infor Sci.* Elsevier Science, 150(3–4), 177–193.
24. Sarfraz, M., and Razzak, M.F.A. (2002), An algorithm for automatic capturing of font outlines, *Int J Comput Graphics*, Elsevier Science, 26(5), 795–804.
25. Sarfraz, M., and Khan, M.A. (2002), Automatic outline capture of Arabic fonts, *Int J Infor Sci*, Elsevier Science, 140(3–4), 269–281.
26. Sarfraz, M., Riyazuddin, M. and Baig, M.H. (2006), Capturing planar shapes by approximating their outlines, *Int J Computational Appl Math*, Elsevier Science, 189 (1–2), 494–512.
27. Sarfraz, M. (2004), Representing shapes by fitting data using an evolutionary approach, *Int J Comput Aided Design Appl* 1(1–4), 179–186.
28. Sarfraz, M., and Raza, A. (2002), Towards automatic recognition of fonts using genetic approach, *Recent Advances in Computers, Computing, and Communications*, Eds.: N. Mastorakis and V. Mladenov, WSEAS Press, 290–295.
29. Sarfraz, M. (2003), Outline representation of fonts using genetic approach, *Advances in Soft Computing: Engineering Design and Manufacturing*, Eds.: Benitez, J.M., Cordon, O., Hoffmann, F., and Roy, R., Springer-Verlag, New York, pp. 109–118.

14
Computer-Aided Reverse Engineering Using Evolutionary Heuristics on NURBS

Abstract. *This chapter is related to the issue of computer-aided reverse engineering. Although the proposed techniques have been presented for image-based planar objects, it is extendable to the objects in 3D with some modifications. Two nondeterministic evolutionary approaches have been presented. Nonuniform rational B-splines (NURBS) have been utilized as an underlying approximation curve scheme. Simulated annealing and simulated evolution heuristics are used as evolutionary methodologies. The optimized NURBS models have been fitted over the contour data of the planar shapes for the ultimate and automatic output. The output results are visually pleasing with respect to the threshold provided by the user.*

14.1 Introduction

Computer-aided reverse engineering (CARE) is an important area of study in the modern age of computers. Many solutions in modern industry are provided for design and manufacturing [12–16, 19]. In modern design, scanned digital data leads to using contour styling [9, 10] which helps to guide visual acceptance after adopting some curve or surface approximation scheme [3, 5, 7]. Various objects including manufactured parts or human body parts are designed and redesigned with complex free-form geometry. This trend can be found in recent years in various applications such as vehicle body design. The wide acceptance of free-form curves and surfaces for component design can also be attributed to advances in curve and surface modelling and their implementations in CAD/CAM/CAE/CARE systems.

Although the techniques of using curve and surface models for representing complex geometries have become quite mature and stable, people still debate using an appropriate model for a specific application. From the perspective of reverse engineering, nonuniform rational B-spline (NURBS) curves and surfaces can approximate complex geometry more accurately and effectively. However, curve or surface approximation using NURBS has not been found in many practical applications in recent years. One of the reasons is that methods for computing the best rational approximation are in general nonlinear [17]. With large amounts of digitized data and heavy computations in the case of multivariable nonlinear equations, the amount of computation time is too expensive and is almost not affordable in most of the CARE practices. This is one of the reasons that most of the designers frequently use a B-spline curve or surface approximation. But it is a fact that the accuracy requirement in curve and surface approximation is continuously increasing due to very complex models being faced in the industry.

Although increasing the number of control points of B-splines can, in general, improve the curve or surface-fitting accuracy, it is basically against the data reduction principle and will increase the burden of the database [15]. Thus, under the circumstances when the factors of accuracy and model size are important, the NURBS curve and surface approximation can prove to be a useful solution. However, efficient fitting algorithms are required to be developed and used for NURBS applications.

This study is related to the NURBS curve and surface approximation using efficient fitting algorithms. In shape design problems, the main objective is to achieve an optimized curve or surface with the least possible computation cost. For complicated shapes with large measurement data, the problem depends on the selection of appropriate parameters in the description of the curve or surface model. Algorithms based on heuristic techniques such as genetic algorithms (GA), simulated annealing (SimE), simulated evolution (SimE), and so on, can provide us with an approach to finding optimal parameters with reasonable cost. Since the data in such problems cannot be approximated with a single polynomial, the application of splines, Bézier curves, and so on, are utilized. NURBS [4], which provide more local control on the shape of the curve, give a better approximation of the underlying data in shape design problems.

When using NURBS for curve and surface approximation of digitized data, it can be shown [18] that in the context of optimization the objective function to be set up is the sum of the squared errors. Since the NURBS consist of multiparameters, knots, control points, and weights, the rational format of the objective function makes the fitting task a multivariable nonlinear optimization problem. Although there exist various algorithms for nonlinear optimization problems, they are typically computationally expensive and time-consuming. Furthermore, when faced with a problem that involves many variables, the initial values become very difficult to predict. This chapter concentrates only on weight parameters to be optimized so that an optimal curve or surface model can be achieved efficiently.

Since SimE and SimA are heuristics, the problem of initial values will also be resolved by assuming their random values. Thus, the optimization problem in this chapter becomes a univariate optimization problem, which is easy to manage. This problem was solved in [12, 13, 19] and is different from other techniques in [9, 10, 12, 14]. In [9], knots corresponding to the control points have been optimized using a genetic algorithm. An approach based on a Tabu search has been applied in [14]. An algorithm proposed in [12] discusses optimization of knots and weights using simulated annealing. In [10], a novel approach was proposed for optimization of NURBS control points using SimE. The main objective of this chapter is to describe curve or surface-fitting algorithms based on SimE using NURBS. Here, the shape parameters in the description of the NURBS have been selected to be computed such that the computed curve or surface provides a best fit to the original data raised from the geometric models after the scanning process.

The chapter is divided into various sections. The following section deals with preprocessing issues such as image contour extraction and detection of corner points. Section 14.3 gives a brief description of NURBS whereas the SimE algorithm is discussed in Section 14.4. The approach, with details of the evolutionary optimization curve technique, SimE, is described and demonstrated in Section 14.5. The two approaches are demonstrated for surfaces in Section 14.6. The chapter is summarized in Section 14.7.

14.2 Preprocessing

This section is devoted to preprocessing issues such as image contour extraction and detection of corner points.

14.2.1 *Image Contour Extraction*

A digitized image is obtained from an electronic device or by scanning. For the planar objects, the quality of a digitized scanned image depends on various factors such as the image on paper, scanner type and the attributes set during scanning. The contour of the digitized image is extracted using the boundary detection algorithms. There are numerous algorithms for detecting the boundary. In this study, the algorithm used is one proposed by Quddus [8]. The input to this algorithm is a bitmap file and the output is the number of boundary points and their values. The algorithm returns a number of boundary points and their values. As a demonstration, one can see the output in Figures 14.1(b) for the BMP image in Figures 14.1(a). It should be noted that, to acquire 3D data from 3D models, some sophisticated 3D scanners can be used with an appropriate technique.

14.2.2 *Detection of Corner Points*

Detection of corner points is the next step after finding out contours. The corner points are those points that partition the outline into various segments. A number of approaches have been proposed by researchers; the reader is referred to Chapter 11 for details. In this chapter, two different corner detectors, namely CS99 (see Section 11.4) and SAM06 (see Section 11.5), have been used. The reverse engineering technique based on the SimE approach in Section 4.4 uses CS99, whereas SAM06 is used for the technique based on SimA in Section 14.5.

Detection of corner points using CS99 with different settings of parameters is made for Figure 14.1(b). Figure 14.2(a) demonstrates the corner points detected

(a)   (b)

FIGURE 14.1. Extracting a digital outline contour of the model: (a) bitmap image, (b) the digital contours of the model in (a).

(a)   (b)

FIGURE 14.2. Detection of corner points using CS99 with different settings of parameters: (a) detecting corner points for Figure 14.1(b) against choice I of parameters in Table 14.1; (b) detecting corner points for Figure 14.1(b) against choice II of parameters in Table 14.1.

TABLE 14.1. Different settings of parameters for the detection of corner points.

Image Name	Choice I				Choice II			
	d_{min}	d_{max}	K	α_{max}	d_{min}	d_{max}	K	α_{max}
Fork.bmp	4	6	4	150	4	6	4	155

against choice I in Table 14.1. Choice II, in Table 14.1, produces the corner points as in Figure 14.2 (b). One can observe that choice II has produced more corner points as compared to choice I.

Table 14.2 provides a detailed study of the digital contours and their corner points. One can see that the plane figure consists of three contours having $1250(= 1106 + 61 + 83)$ contour points. It has 13 and 18 corner points corresponding to choices I and II, respectively. Similarly, fork figure consists of one contour having 693 contour points. It has 8 and 10 corner points corresponding to choices I and II, respectively.

Detection of corner points using SAM06 is made for Figure 14.3(a). Clearly, the detected points are more precise and more appealing to the eye.

TABLE 14.2. Different settings of parameters for the detection of corner points.

Image	# of Contours	# of Contour Points	# of Corner Points with Choice I	# of Corner Points with Choice II
Fork.bmp	1	[693]	10	12

FIGURE 14.3. Detection of corner points using SAM06.

14.3 NURBS

A unified mathematical formulation of NURBS provides free-form curves and surfaces. NURBS contains a large number of control variables; because of those variables it is flexible and powerful. NURBS is a rational combination of a set piecewise rational polynomial of basis functions of the form:

$$S(t) = \frac{\sum_{i=1}^{n} w_i P_i N_{i,k}(t)}{\sum_{i=1}^{n} w_i N_{i,k}(t)}, \tag{14.1}$$

where P_i are the control points and w_i represent the associated weights. The value t is the parametric variable and $N_{i,k}(t)$ is the B-spline basis function [6]. Assuming a basis function of order k (degree $k-1$), a NURBS curve has $n+k$ knots and the number of control points equals to weights. The knot set $\{t_i\}$ is a nondecreasing sequence: $t_1 \leq t_2 \leq \ldots \leq t_{n+k-1} \leq t_{n+k}$. The parametric domain for each piece of curve is $t_i \leq t \leq t_{i+1}$. NURBS include weights as extra degrees of freedom, which are used for geometric design [5–7]. NURBS are attracted toward a control point if the corresponding weight is increased and it is pushed away from a control point if the weight is decreased. If a weight is zero, the corresponding rational basis function is also zero and its control points do not affect the NURBS shape.

NURBS generalize polynomial-based parametric representations for shape modeling. Analogous to B-splines, the rational basis functions of NURBS sum to unity; they are infinitely smooth in the interior of a knot interval provided that the denominator is not zero, and at a knot they are at least C^{k-1-r} continuous with knot multiplicity r. They inherit many properties from B-splines, such as the strong convex hull property, variation diminishing property, local support, and invariance under affine geometric transformations. Moreover, NURBS have additional properties. NURBS offer a unified mathematical framework for both implicit and parametric polynomial forms. In principle, they can represent analytic functions such as conics and quadrics precisely, as well as free-form shapes.

NURBS surfaces are the extended version of the curve case, as defined here:

$$S(u,v) = \frac{\sum_{i=1}^{n} \sum_{j=1}^{m} P_{i,j} w_{i,j} N_{i,k}(u) N_{j,k}(v)}{\sum_{i=1}^{n} \sum_{j=1}^{m} w_{i,j} N_{i,k}(u) N_{j,k}(v)}, \tag{14.2}$$

where $w_{i,j}$ and $P_{i,j}$ are weights and control points, respectively. The knot sets $\{u_j\}$ and $\{v_j\}$ is a nondecreasing sequence as $u_1 \leq u_2 \leq \ldots \leq u_{m+k-1} \leq u_{m+k}$ and $v_1 \leq v_2 \leq \ldots \leq v_{m+k-1} \leq v_{m+k}$, respectively. The parametric domain for each piece of the surface is $[u_i, u_{i+1}] \times [v_j, v_{j+1}]$.

14.3.1 Data Fitting Using NURBS Curves

Given a set of data points F in the plane, we compute a planar NURBS curve to approximate the points. The given data is assumed to represent the shape of a known curve, which can be open or closed but not be self-intersecting. This curve is called the target curve or the target shape. For generalization, let us assume that ε is the measurement error between the fitted curve and the target curve. So, we can write

$$F(t) = f(t) + \varepsilon(t) \tag{14.3}$$

where t represents the parameter. In the above equation, $f(t)$ is the underlying function that is to be approximated using NURBS, and $\varepsilon(t)$ represents the measurement error at the particular value of t at that data point.

Let $\xi_i (i = 1, 2 \ldots, n + m)$ be knots for data fitting, where n is the number of control points and m is the order (degree + 1) of NURBS. In this study, we have used *centripetal parameterization* for the parameter t. At the end of the interval [a, b], we set,

$$\left. \begin{array}{l} a = \xi_{1-m} = \ldots = \xi_0, \\ b = \xi_{n+1} = \ldots = \xi_{n+m} \end{array} \right\} \tag{14.4}$$

There are three commonly used methods to parameterize the value of t. These methods are: (i) equally spaced parameterization, (ii) chord length parameterization and (iii) centripetal parameterization. In this chapter, we use *centripetal parameterization* to estimate the parametric value t associated with each data point P_i. After having the t value associated with each point, we fit NURBS curve to the set of data points of each segment:

14.3.2 Generation of Control Points for Curves

We optimize the NURBS curve for the given digital data, and the proposed method is based on optimizing with respect to weights of the NURBS curve using SimE. But, for simplicity and economical reasons, the computation of control points to be used in NURBS will be computed through nonuniform B-spline (NUBS) which is the nonrational counterpart of the NURBS. Determining control points that generate a NUBS curve for a set of known digitized data points is as follows:

The equation for the NUBS curve is:

$$D(t) = \sum_{i=1}^{n+1} P_i N_{i,k}(t) \tag{14.5}$$

If the data points lie on the curve. then it must satisfy Equation (14.5). Rewriting Equation (14.5) for each of j data points yields the following:

$$D(t_1) = N_{1,k}(t_1)P_1 + N_{2,k}(t_1)P_2 + \ldots + N_{n+1,k}(t_1)P_{n+1}$$
$$D(t_2) = N_{1,k}(t_2)P_1 + N_{2,k}(t_2)P_2 + \ldots + N_{n+1,k}(t_2)P_{n+1}$$

$$\tag{14.6}$$

$$D(t_j) = N_{1,k}(t_j)P_1 + N_{2,k}(t_j)P_2 + \ldots + N_{n+1,k}(t_j)P_{n+1}$$

where $2 \le k \le n+1 \le j$ (k is order of the basis and n is the number of control points). This system of equations is written more compactly as

$$[D] = [N][P] \tag{14.7}$$

where

$$[D]^T = \begin{bmatrix} D(t_1) & D(t_2) & \ldots & D(t_j) \end{bmatrix},$$
$$[P]^T = [P_1 P_2 \ldots P_{n+1}],$$
$$[N] = \begin{bmatrix} N_{1,k}(t_1) & \ldots & \ldots & N_{n+1,k}(t_1) \\ \vdots & \ldots & & \ldots \\ & \ldots & & \ldots \\ N_{1,k}(t_j) & \ldots & \ldots & N_{n+1,k}(t_j) \end{bmatrix}.$$

The value of the parameter t for each data point is measured using centripetal parameterization as discussed earlier. If $2 \le k \le n+1 = j$ then the matrix N is a squared matrix and the control points can be obtained directly by matrix inversion as follows:

$$[P] = [N]^{-1}[D] \quad 2 \le k \le n+1 = j.$$

In this case, the resulting curve passes through each data point and hence a curve fit is obtained. A fairer or smoother curve is obtained by specifying fewer control points than data points, that is, $2 \le k \le n+1 < j$. Here in this case, matrix N

is no longer a squared matrix. Recalling that a matrix times its transpose is always square, the control polygon for a curve that fairs or smoothens the data is given by:

$$[D] = [N][P],$$

or

$$[N]^T[D] = [N]^T[N][P],$$

or

$$[P] = \left[[N]^T[N]\right]^{-1}[N]^T[D]. \qquad (14.8)$$

Solving Equation (14.8) will give the control point matrix for the curves.

14.3.3 Generation of Control Points for Surfaces

A similar treatment, as mentioned in the previous subsection, can be extended for the generation of control points for surfaces. Because they are out of the scope of this book, the details are omitted here.

14.4 Approach Using SimE

14.4.1 Outline of SimE

SimE is a powerful general iterative heuristic for solving combinatorial optimization problems [11, 13]. The algorithm consists of three basic steps: evaluation, selection and allocation. These three steps are executed sequentially for a prefixed number of iterations or until a desired improvement in goodness is observed. The SimE algorithm starts with an initial assignment, and then seeks to reach better assignments from one generation to the next. SimE assumes that there exists a population P of a set M of n elements. A cost function is used to associate with each assignment of element m a cost C_m. The cost C_m is used to compute the goodness g_m of element m for each $m \in M$.

The selection step partitions the elements into two disjoint sets P_s and P_r based on their goodness. The elements with bad goodness are selected in the set P_s and the rest of the elements are in the set P_r. The nondeterministic selection operator takes as input the goodness of each element and a parameter B, a selection bias. Hence, the element with the high goodness still has a nonzero probability of being assigned to the selected set P_s. The value of the bias is application-dependent.

The allocation step takes P_s and P_r and generates a new solution P', which contains all the members of the previous population P. The members of P_s are then worked on so that their goodness can be enhanced in the subsequent iterations. The choice of a suitable allocation function is problem-dependent [13].

14.4.2 Problem Mapping SimE

The approach to the curve problem is described here in detail. However, the surface problem is not explained here, since it is beyond the scope of this book. This section describes the SimE formulation of the current problem in detail. In curve-fitting problems, the solution space consists of the number of data points on the image boundary.

14.4.2.1   Initialization

Initialization is the first step in SimE. It consists of selecting a starting solution for the problem under consideration. This solution can be generated randomly or the output of any constructive heuristic. In our case from the boundary points, the initial solution is created using the corner detection algorithm.

The corner detection algorithm divides the given image into segments. The corner points are the only end points of the segment (S). For example if there is n number of corner points, we have $n - 1$ segments. For each segment we need to calculate the parameters t, control points, knot vector and the weight of NURBS. The initial solution of the weight vector is randomly selected from the range $[0, 1]$. The number of elements in the weight vector corresponds to the number of control points. The values of the parameters t for each segment are calculated using the centripetal method. The number of control points of the segment are always equals to the order of the NURBS curve.

In our proposed approach we have included the two corner points of the segment as the control points, and the remaining control points are determined using the least square method. The weight corresponding to each control point of a segment is taken randomly between 0 and 1. After calculating the required parameters for each segment, the curve is fitted using NURBS. This fitted curve for each segment is considered to be the initial solution for SimE. The other important parameters that are initialized in this step are a stopping condition and selection bias (B). We have taken the selection bias (B) in the range of $[-1, 1]$ and fixed number of iterations.

14.4.2.2   Evaluation

In this step, each individual segment of the curve is evaluated on the basis of goodness. The goodness g_i of each segment S_i is determined by:

$$g_i = \frac{\varepsilon}{Q_i + \varepsilon}, \varepsilon \geq 1. \tag{14.9}$$

This criterion is different than that discussed in [10]. In this research, we have taken $\varepsilon = (l_i + k)$ where l_i is the length of the knot vector for each segment, k is the order of the curve and Q_i is sum square error between the target and the fitted curve. Q_i can be defined as:

$$Q_i = \sum_{1}^{N} \{(S(t_i) - F_i)^2\}. \tag{14.10}$$

Here $S(t_i)$ is the approximated curve and $\{F_i\}$ is the target curve data. N is the total number of data points in each segment. The goodness g_i represents a measure of how near each segment is the optimum curve fit. As is obvious from Equation (14.9), the goodness of an element is between 0 and 1. The value of goodness g_i nearer to 1 means that the segment i is nearer to its optimum curve fitting.

14.4.2.3 Selection

The goodness g_i is used to probabilistically select segments (S_i) in the selection step. On the basis of the goodness g_i, the selection function partitions the segments into two sets, P_r and P_s, probabilistically. The selection function is defined as follows:

If (Random $[0, 1] \leq 1 - g_i + B$) then
$$P_s = P_s \cup \{S_i\}$$
Else
$$P_r = P_r \cup \{S_i\}$$

Set P_s contain the segments with low or bad goodness and the set P_r contains the rest of the segments.

14.4.2.4 Allocation and Weight Optimization for Curves

The purpose of the allocation is to perturb the current solution in such a way that it reaches the optimum solution. In our case, the optimum solution achieves a smooth curve with least error. After fitting the initial curve, further refinement of curve have to be done to achieve better fitting accuracy. For this purpose, different NURBS parameters have to be changed.

The allocation step for optimizing weights is to perturb the current solution of weights by assigning the selected segments in P_s to new values. In our case we perturb the weights in neighborhood of $[w_i^{\text{cur}}, w_i^{\text{cur}} + 0.5]$, where w_i^{cur} is the current weight corresponding to the control point i. For each segment, 10 to 15 trail allocations for the weight vector are made, and for each trail error between the fitted curve and target is calculated. After performing all trails of the perturbing weight vector, the trail with the least error is made permanent and the corresponding segment is removed from P_s. This process is repeated until all the segments in P_s are perturbed. The flowchart for weight optimization process using SimE is given in Figure 14.4.

14.4.3 Algorithm Outline for Curves

We can summarize all the phases from digitization to optimization discussed in the previous sections. The algorithm of the proposed scheme is contained on various steps as follows:

Begin
   Input the digitized image.
          Step 1:   Find the image contour.
          Step 2:   Find the corner points

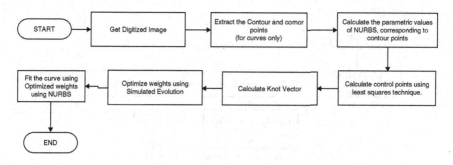

FIGURE 14.4. Flowchart for the weight optimization of curves using SimE.

Step 3:   For each segment S_i
(a) Find control points from data points using the method of least square.
(b) Find the knot vector.
(c) Find the weight vector corresponding to the control points.
(d) Fit the curve with NURBS
End for
Step 4:   Initialize population (Weights generated at step 4(c)) Pi, Bias value and number of iterations for SimE
Step 5:   for $j = 1$ to number of iterations (say 100)
(a) Evaluation
    For each segment S_i
        Find goodness (g_i)
    End for
(b) Selection
    For each segment S_i
        If (Random $[0, 1] \leq 1 - g_i + B$) then
            $P_s = P_s \cup \{S_i\}$
        Else
            $P_r = P_r \cup \{S_i\}$
    End for
(c) Allocation
    For each segment S_i in P_s.
        Perturb the weight vector for 10–15 trails and choose the best one.
    End for
        $P = P_r \cup P_s$
    end for j
Step 6:   Return the final fitted curve with NURBS
End

Figure 14.5 depicts the flowchart for the optimization of the weight vector using SimE for NURBS. The data for different digitized images (objects) were used

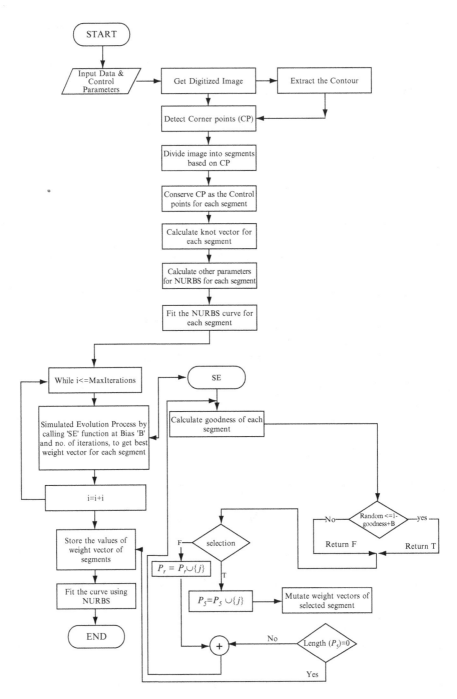

FIGURE 14.5. Flowchart for weight optimization using SimE for NURBS.

to test the weight optimization of the NURBS curve using the SimE technique. Digitized image data is segmented using corner points. Each segment has its own weight vector for fitting NURBS. The length of the weight vector equals the number of control points generated using the least square technique for that segment. Experience has shown that using the fewest number of control points yields the fairest curve. Keeping this in mind for each segment, the number of control points taken is equal to the order of the curve. Table 14.3 shows the various parameters used and generated in the optimization of weight using SimE.

14.4.4   Demonstration

Figure 14.5 depicts the flowchart for the optimization of weight vector using SimE for NURBS. The data for different digitized images (objects) were used to test the weight optimization of NURBS curve using SimE technique. Digitized image data is segmented using corner points. Each segment has its own weight vector for fitting NURBS. The length of the weight vector equals the number of control points generated using the least square technique for that segment. Experience has shown that using the fewest number of control points yields the fairest curve. Keeping this in mind for each segment, the number of control points taken is equal to the order of the curve. Table 14.3 shows various parameters used and generated in the optimization of weight using SimE.

Figure 14.6 demonstrates the optimization results for the object "fork" in Figure 14.1(b) when a smaller set of corner points is achieved; see Figure 14.2(a), for the setting of parameter choice I in Table 14.1. Figure 14.6(a) represents the default curve. Figures 14.6(b) and 14.6(c) demonstrate the intermediate results for SimE curve fitting obtained for the object "fork" at iterations 1 and 40. respectively. The final NURBS fitted image for object fork, after 60 iterations, is shown in Figure 14.6(d). The algorithm converged at the 60th iteration for the object "fork." The sum square error (SSE) between the boundary of the image object "fork" and the NURBS fitted curve with respect to the number of iterations is as shown in Figure 14.7. Average goodness of the fitted curve is shown in Figure 14.8. The number of segments selected for each iteration is plotted in Figure 14.9. The results obtained using the proposed algorithm are found to be better compared to the results obtained using the genetic algorithm discussed in [9].

Figure 14.10 demonstrates the optimization results for the object "fork" in Figure 14.1(b) when a bigger set of corner points was achieved, see Figure 14.2(b), for the setting of parameter choice II in Table 14.1. Figure 14.10(a) represents the default curve. Figures 14.10(b) and 14.10(c) demonstrate the intermediate results

TABLE 14.3. Parameters used for weight optimization.

Image	Order of NURBS	No. of control points (for each segment)	Bias value (B)
Fork	4	4	−0.5

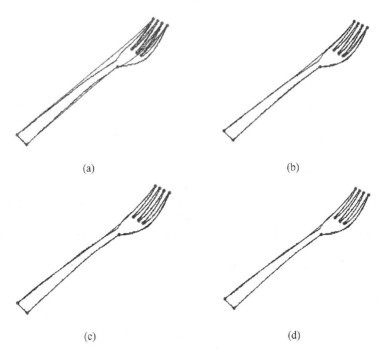

(a)   (b)

(c)   (d)

FIGURE 14.6. Curve fitting on the set of corner points extracted (as shown in Figures 14.3(a) and 14.33(c)) : (a) using default values of shape parameters as 1; (b) after first iteration of SimE; (c) after the fifth iteration of SimE; (d) after final iteration of SimE.

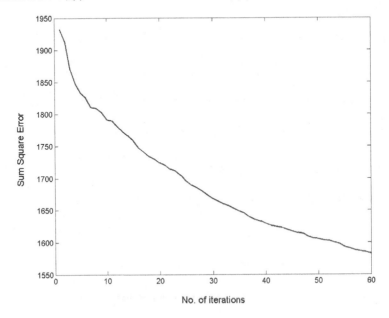

FIGURE 14.7. Sum square error (SSE) plotted against number of iterations for the object "fork."

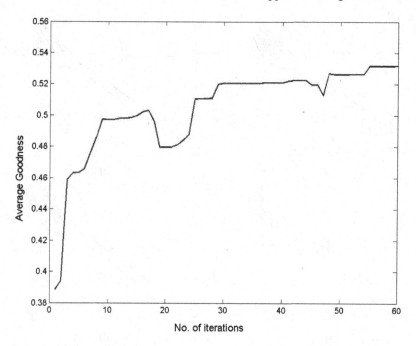

FIGURE 14.8. Average goodness plotted against number of iterations.

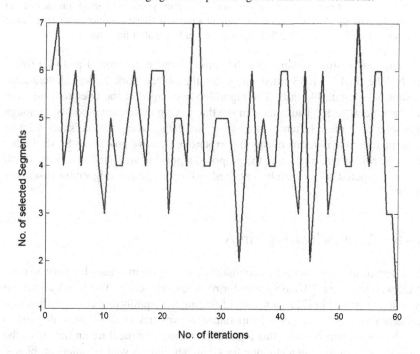

FIGURE 14.9. Number of segments selected for SimE plotted against number of iterations for object "fork."

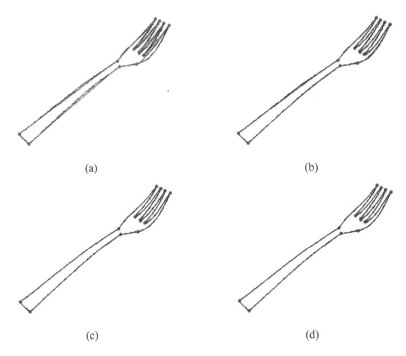

(a)   (b)

(c)   (d)

FIGURE 14.10. Curve fitting on the set of corner points extracted (as shown in Figures 14.2(b) and 14.2(d)): (a) using default values of shape parameters as 1; (b) after first iteration of SimE; (c) after fifth iteration of SimE; (d) after final iteration of SimE.

for SimE curve fitting obtained for the object "fork" at iterations 1 and 10, respectively. The final NURBS fitted image for the object "fork," after 20 iterations, is shown in Figure 14.10(d). The algorithm converged at the twentieth iteration for the object "fork." Thus, one can see that having more corner points, although it costs a little more in terms of memory and hence computation, saves a lot of computation time in terms of running expensive iterative process of SimE. In this case, the results obtained using the proposed algorithm are found to be even much better compared to the results obtained using the genetic algorithm discussed in [9].

14.5   Approach Using SimA

This section also represents the simulated annealing optimization heuristic to optimize weights of the NURBS curve for reverse engineering. The SimA algorithm was first proposed in [7] as a means of finding the equilibrium configuration of a collection of atoms at a given temperature. Kirkpatrick et al. [4] were the first to use the connection between this algorithm and mathematical minimization as the basis of an optimization technique for combinatorial (as well as other) problems. It is derived from the analogy of the physical annealing process of metals.

14.5.1   *Outline of SimE*

SimA's major advantage over other methods is its ability to avoid being trapped in local minima. The algorithm employs a random search, which not only accepts changes that decrease the objective function E, but also some changes that would increase it. The latter are accepted with a probability

$$\text{Prob(accept)} = \exp(-\Delta E/T),$$

where ΔE is the increase in E and T is a control parameter, which by analogy with the original application is known as the system "temperature," irrespective of the objective function involved.

SimA can be briefly described as follows: Given a function to optimize, and some initial values for the variables (initial solution), SimA starts initially with a high temperature and a solution (or state). Based on the actual solution, it selects a new random tentative solution in the neighborhood of the actual solution. The tentative solution is generated by a small perturbation of the actual solution. If the tentative solution has lower objective function value, then it is accepted as the new solution. On the other hand, if the objective function value is high, it might still be accepted based on certain probability depending on the change in the value of the objective function and the temperature. This process is repeated slowly by decreasing the temperature until the optimized solution is reached. More details of SimA are given in Section 14.5.1 and can also be found in [19].

In order to implement simulated annealing, we need to formulate a suitable cost function for the problem being solved. In addition, as in the case of local search techniques, we assume the existence of a neighborhood structure, and need the neighbor function to generate new states (neighborhood states) from current states. And, finally, we need a cooling schedule that describes the temperature parameter T and gives rules for lowering it.

14.5.2   *Problem Mapping*

This section focuses on the organization of all the phases toward the achievement of outline capture of planar images. In particular, a detailed study is made to discuss how the weights and knots, in the description of NURBS, can be optimized in an independent manner. We start with the digitized image obtained from an electronic device or scanner. The contour of the digitized image is extracted using the boundary detection algorithm [8], discussed in Section 14.3. This algorithm returns a number of segments and, for each segment, a number of boundary points (data points) and their values.

14.5.2.1   Weight Optimization Using SimA

There are three commonly used methods to parameterize knots (the equally spaced method, the chord length method and the centripetal method), which can be utilized to identify knots. In this research, we use the chord length method. Assume that the parameter value t lies between zero and one. For the set of the available data points, the maximum value of the knot vector, say at the ℓ th data point, is denoted by t_{max}.

$$\left.\begin{aligned} t_1 &= 0, \\ \frac{t_\ell}{t_{max}} &= \frac{\displaystyle\sum_{s=2}^{\ell} |D_s - D_{s-1}|}{\displaystyle\sum_{s=2}^{j} |D_s - D_{s-1}|}, \ell \geq 2. \end{aligned}\right\}$$

(14.11)

The control points are calculated using the least squares technique as the next step. A fairer or smoother curve is obtained by specifying fewer control polygon points than data points, that is, $2 \leq k \leq n < j$. Recalling that a matrix times its transpose is always square, the control polygon for a curve that fairs or smoothens the data is given by

$$[D] = [B][P],$$

which implies

$$[B]^T [D] = [B]^T [B][P].$$

Hence

$$[P] = \left[[B]^T [B]\right]^{-1} [B]^T [D],$$

where

$$[D]^T = \left[D_1 (t_1) \ D_2 (t_2) \ \ldots \ D_j (t_j)\right],$$

are data points, and

$$[P]^T = \left[P_1 \ P_2 \ \ldots \ P_{n+1}\right],$$

are the control points and $[B]$ is the set of B-spline basis functions.

The evaluation of the control points, by least squares approximation, can be viewed as an initial estimation of the fitted curve. Further refinement can be obtained by optimizing the different NURBS parameters, such as the knot values and the weights in order to achieve better fitting accuracy. The error function (or cost function) between the measured points and the fitted curve is generally given by the following equation:

$$E = \left(\sum_{i=0}^{s} |Q_i - S(\alpha_1, \ldots, \alpha_n)|^r / s\right)^{1/r},$$

(14.12)

where Q represents the set of measured points of the target curve. S $(\alpha_1 \ldots \alpha_n)$ is the geometric model of the fitted curve, where $(\alpha_1, \ldots, \alpha_n)$ are the parameters of the fitted curve; s is the number of measured points and r is an exponent ranging from 1 to infinity. The fitting task can then be viewed as the optimization of the curve parameters $(\alpha_1, \ldots, \alpha_n)$ to minimize the error (or cost) E. In case the exponent r is equal to 2, the above equation reduces to the least squares function. It is to be noted that the weights present a large number of independent variables (equaling the number of control points) to the optimization problem, which may lead to a large search space. Therefore, global optimization techniques are needed for optimizing such problems.

We describe, in this section, the use of SimE optimization heuristic to optimize weights of the NURBS curve. The initial solution S_0 of weight vector is randomly selected from the range [0, 0.5]. The number of elements in the weight vector corresponds to the number of control points. The cooling schedule used here is presented similar to the one in [4]. It is based on the idea that the initial temperature T_0 must be large to virtually accept all transitions and that the changes in the temperature at each invocation of the Metropolis loop are small. The scheme provides guidelines to the choice of T_0, the rate of decrements of T, the termination criterion and the length of the Markov chain (M).

14.5.2.2   Initial Temperature T_0

The initial temperature must be chosen so that almost all transitions are accepted initially. That is, the initial acceptance ratio $\chi(T_0)$ must be close to unity where

$$\chi(T_0) = \frac{\text{Number of moves accepted at } T_0}{\text{Total number of moves attempted at } T_0}.$$

To determine T_0, we start off with a small value of initial temperature given by T_0', in the Metropolis function. Then $\chi(T_0')$ is computed. If $\chi(T_0')$ is not close to unity, then T_0' is increased by multiplying it by a constant factor larger than one. The above procedure is repeated until the value of $\chi(T_0')$ approaches unity. The value of T_0' is then the required value of T_0.

14.5.2.3   Decrement of T

A decrement function is used to reduce the temperature in a geometric progression, and is given by

$$T_{k+1} = \alpha T_k, k = 0, 1, \ldots,$$

where α is a positive constant less than one, since successive temperatures are decreasing. Further, since small changes are desired, the value of α is chosen very close to unity, typically $0.8 \leq \alpha \leq 0.99$.

14.5.2.4   Length of Markov Chain M

The length of Markov chain M is equivalent to the number of times the Metropolis loop is executed at a given temperature. If the optimization process begins with a high value of T_0, the distribution of relative frequencies of states will be very close to the stationary distribution. In such a case, the process is said to be in quasi-equilibrium. The number M is based on the requirement that at each value of T_k quasi-equilibrium is restored.

Since at decreasing temperatures uphill transitions are accepted with decreasing probabilities, one has to increase the number of iterations of the Metropolis loop with decreasing T (so that the Markov chain at that particular temperature will remain irreducible and with all states being non null). A factor β is used ($\beta > 1$) which, in a geometric progression, increases the value of M. That is, each time the Metropolis loop is called, T is reduced to αT and M is increased to βM.

14.5.2.5   Weight Seclection

The neighborhood of each element of the weight vector is randomly selected within a range of [weight_element_value, weight_element_value + 1]. Since the number of elements of the weight vector equals the number of control points, this range is selected in order to optimize the locality of the search. The details of the implementation are as follows:

First of all, construct an initial NURBS curve using the weights, knots and the measured control points. The initial solution S_0 (NewS) of weight vector is currently assigned to the best solution (BestS). In the next step, we call Metropolis iteration. In this step, we measure the value of cost function E (CurCost) and assign a new cost. After perturbing the elements of the weight vector in a small neighborhood ($[w_i^{cur}, w_i^{cur} + 1]$ where w_i^{cur} is the current weight corresponding to the control point i), we calculate again the cost function E for the newly fitted curve as NewCost. If the value of CurCost is less than NewCost, we assign the current cost value as the new cost and weight vector corresponding to this cost as the best solution (BestS). If the CurCost value is higher than in the comparison with NewCost, that means the perturb solution is worse than the original one. In this case, we accept the new solution only on probability basis, that is, a random number is generated between 0 and 1. If the generated random number is smaller than $e^{\frac{CurCost-NewCost}{T}}$, where T is the current temperature, then we keep the new settings. Otherwise, we neglect the perturb solution. This process is repeated slowly by decreasing the temperature until the optimized solution is reached. The flowchart for the NURBS curve approximation, based on simulated annealing, is shown in Figure 14.11.

14.5.3 *Demonstration*

This section is meant for the demonstration of results achieved during the implementation of the SimA scheme. Some discussion is also made on the merits and demerits of the schemes. We used the bitmap images as the input to the algorithm for weight optimization of NURBS for curves. The general parameters taken for curves are described as follows: While cooling, since small changes in temperatures are desired, we have chosen the value of α as 0.99, which is close to unity. Since the value of β should be greater than 1, a value of 1.5 is chosen. The algorithm executes the Metropole function, based on Maxtime, which is set to 250. The order k is chosen to be 4. The number of control points have been taken as 70. These are the default settings and hence can be changed by the users when desired.

Figure 14.18 shows the calculation of the best cost by the SimA heuristic when approximated the outline in Figure 14.13 of the pound image in Figure 14.12. Figures 14.14–14.17 depict the intermediate fittings of the "pound" symbol for weight optimization at various iterations. A gradual decrease in the (current) cost function can be viewed in Figure 14.18. Figure 14.18 also shows that (current) costs are selected for the next iteration, even if previous (current) costs were better, to avoid getting trapped in the local minimum.

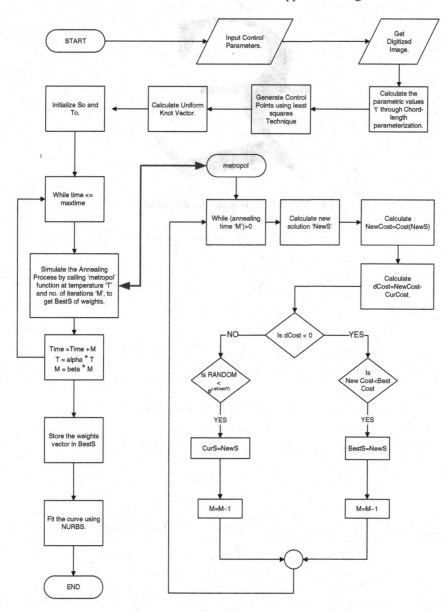

FIGURE 14.11. Flowchart for weight optimization of NURBS using simulated annealing.

Table 14.4 shows that he Metropole function executes time + M, that is, 238.5 + 168.75, which is equal to 407 number of times, which is correctly shown in Figure 14.17. The BestCost (leasterror) is found to be 3.378 units and the execution time is found to be 530.859 seconds.

FIGURE 14.12. Bitmap image "Pound."

FIGURE 14.13. Outline of the image "Pound."

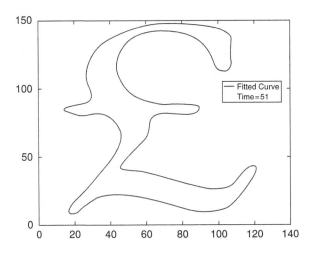

FIGURE 14.14. SimA based NURBS approximated image at 51st iteration.

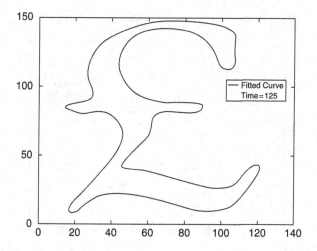

FIGURE 14.15. SimA based NURBS approximated image at 126th iteration.

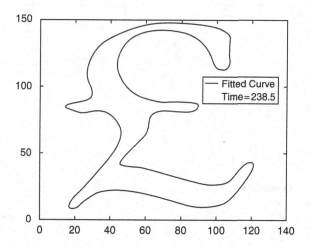

FIGURE 14.16. SA-based NURBS approximated image at 238th iteration.

The experimental results using the bitmap image "Pound" have shown that the performance of the method is not very pleasing since the corner points of the image do not appear in the resulting curves. However, this deficiency can be removed when the idea of a corner point is incorporated into the algorithm. In this way, one can break the overall boundary at the corner points. Breaking the overall boundary at the corner points may definitely help to achieve better results, but it can open

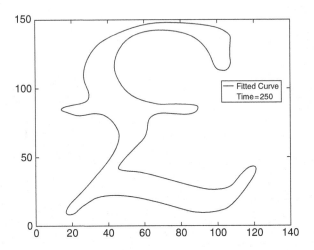

FIGURE 14.17. SA-based NURBS approximated image at 256th iteration.

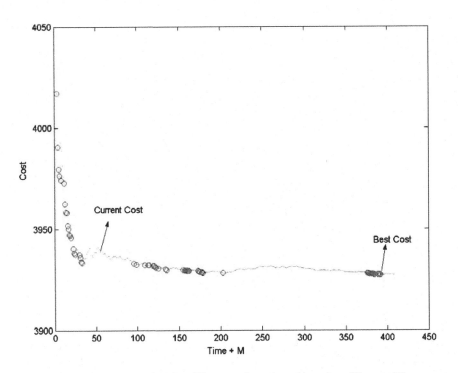

FIGURE 14.18. Error function (E) vs. total number of iterations (Time $+ M$).

up with a huge computation cost due to repetition of the algorithm in a number of divided segments. Therefore, we propose the scheme to be used for images without corner points.

TABLE 14.4. Weight optimization parameters for "Pound."

Name	POUND
dpts (# of data points)	688
k (order of NURBS)	4
npts (# of control points)	70
α (cooling rate)	0.99
β (constant)	1.5
M (Annealing time)	50
MaxTime	250
BestCost (least error)	3.378
Execution time (sec)	530.859

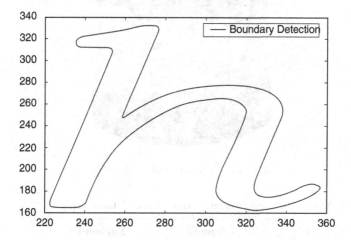

FIGURE 14.19. Outline image for the character "h."

FIGURE 14.20. NURBS approximation at final (256th) iteration.

Figure 14.20 shows the result of an another outline image in Figure 14.19 for the character "h." Some analysis, in terms of time and sum square error, is given in Table 14.5.

TABLE 14.5. Weight optimization results summary, for the the algorithm, using SimA.

Shapes	Data points	SimA weight optimization	
		Time	Least error
Pound	688	530.859	3.378
Aich	787	625.406	14.332

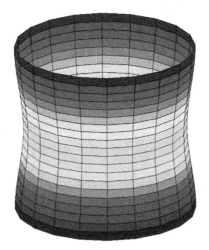

FIGURE 14.21. Original "surface 1."

TABLE 14.6. Input parameters for "surface1" fitting using SimE.

Name	Surface1
Mesh size	21×21
Order in u direction	4
Order in v direction	4
Control points in u direction	10
Control points in v direction	10
Bias value	-0.5
Maximum no. of iterations	100

14.6 Surfaces

The two schemes SimE and SimA have also been tested for the surface data. The input "Surface1" for weight optimization of the NURBS surface using SimE is shown in Figure 14.21. The control parameters used for the surface are given in Table 14.6. Figures 14.22 and 14.23 depict fitting at 10th and 50th iterations. The final NURBS approximated surface is shown in Figure 14.24 at the 100th iteration.

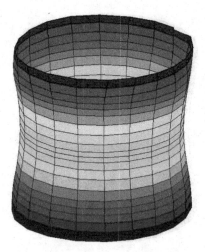

FIGURE 14.22. Approximated NURBS Surface at 10th iteration.

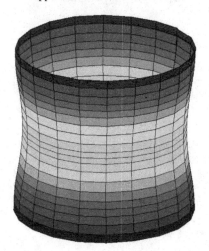

FIGURE 14.23. Approximated NURBS surface at 50th iteration.

We can observe an increase in fitting accuracy from Figure 14.25 as the number of iterations increased. Figure 14.26 depicts the actual reduction in the cost as the number of iterations increase. From this it is clear that by mutating weight vector of the patches there is a development in the smoothness of the surface.

The input "surface2" for weight optimization of the NURBS surface using SimA is shown in Figure 14.27. Table 14.7 shows the various parameters used and generated in the weight optimization of "surface 2." The *BestCost* (least error) is found to be 0.1925 units and the execution time is found to be 117.016 seconds.

Figures 14.28 and 14.29 depict the intermediate fittings of the "surface 2" at iterations (Time$+i$) $= 51$ and 126, respectively, and Figure 14.30 shows the fitting

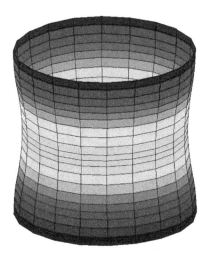

FIGURE 14.24. Approximated NURBS surface at 100th iteration.

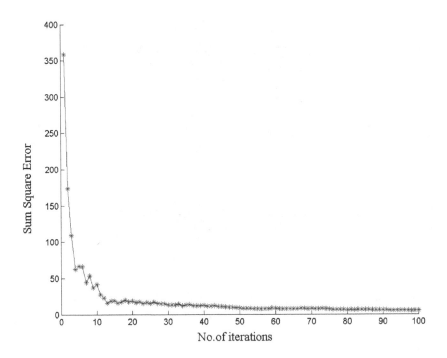

FIGURE 14.25. Sum square error versus number of iterations for "surface1" using SimE.

for the actual iteration of 250 (*Maxtime*), where "*I*" iterates over annealing time "*M*." Figure 14.31 depicts the actual reduction in the costs (error) as the number of iterations increase.

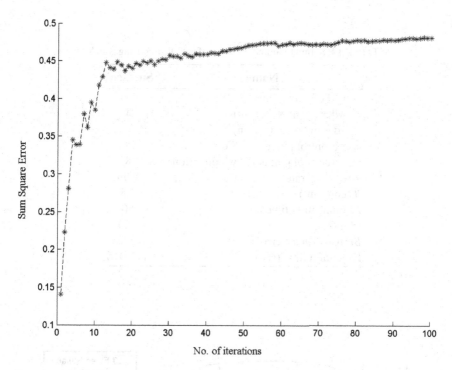

FIGURE 14.26. Average goodness plotted against number of iterations for "surface1" using SimE.

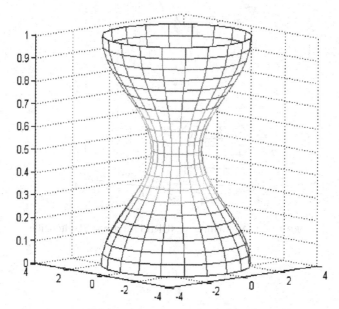

FIGURE 14.27. Original "surface 2."

TABLE 14.7. Input parameters for surface2 fitting using SimA.

Name	Surface2
dpts (# of data points)	441
k (order in "u" direction)	4
l (order in "w" direction)	4
npts (control points in "u"direction)	8
mpts (control points in "w" direction)	8
α (cooling rate)	0.99
β (constant)	1.5
M (annealing time)	50
MaxTime	250
BestCost (least error)	0.1925
Execution time (sec)	117.016

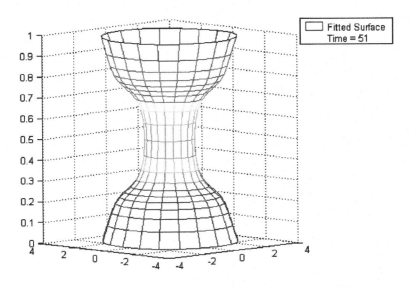

FIGURE 14.28. Approximated NURBS surface at 51st iteration.

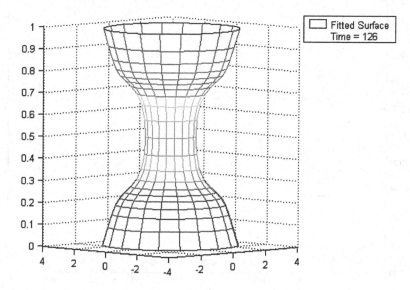

FIGURE 14.29. Approximated NURBS surface at the 126th iteration.

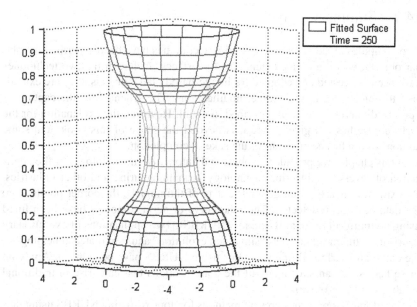

FIGURE 14.30. Approximated NURBS Surface at the 250th iteration.

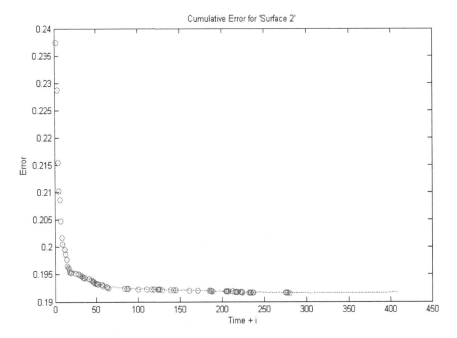

FIGURE 14.31. Demonstration of reduction in the costs (error) as the number of iterations increase for "surface2" using SimA.

14.7   Summary

Two computer-aided reverse engineering techniques have been described for planar objects, which are also extendable to surfaces. Although the two techniques have been suggested and adopted for image-based planar objects, they are extendable to objects in 3D with some modifications. The schemes for the capture of optimized curves have been described in detail. However, the explanation for the surface case has not given since it is beyond the scope of this book, and some demonstration has been given for the sake of completion.

In this chapter we provided a robust and automated methodology for the application of reverse engineering technology in manufacturing and other industries. By extracting nearly exact geometric data of the models, the corner points from the data have been detected. Then the curve or surface models have been fitted using nonuniform rational B-splines (NURBS). Two applications of evolutionary heuristic techniques known as "simulated evolution" and "simulated annealing" to the curve and surface-fitting problems using NURBS have been given. Applying these heuristics can save many of the complications that can arise in traditional solutions of the problem.

The adopted approaches present methods for approximating NURBS using digitized data. The shape parameters, in the description of NURBS, have been targeted to be optimized in the best possible way. The overall algorithms have been

devised to combine various faces including scanning and obtaining a digital outline, acquiring data, detecting corner points, generating control points, and computing optimized curves or surfaces by optimizing the shape parameters in the
description of the NURBS using simulated evolution and simulated annealing
heuristics. Demonstration of the two schemes has been made by implementing
them in practical examples. Both curve and surface fittings have been made with
many interesting results obtained.

14.8   Exercises

1. Write a program, using chord length parameterization, to plot a NURBS cubic
   curve with the given input control points. The program should also assume user
   input for the weight parameters.
2. Repeat Exercise 1 using unit length parameterization.
3. Implement the SimE-based methodology for the reverse engineering purpose
   for planar images using NURBS.
4. Implement the SimA-based methodology for the reverse engineering purpose
   for planar images using NURBS.
5. Design and implement the SimE-based methodology for the reverse engineering purpose for planar images using the weighted Nu-spline of Chapter 2.
6. Design and implement the SimA-based methodology for the reverse engineering purpose for planar images using the weighted Nu-spline of Chapter 2.
7. Compare the results of Exercises 3 and 4 with respect to time and number of
   iterations for the same image, same degree of NURBS and same error threshold.
8. Compare the results of Exercises 5 and 6 with respect to time and number of
   iterations for the same image, same degree of NURBS and same error threshold.
9. What is your conclusion after making analysis in Exercises 7 and 8?

References

1. Akaike, H. (1974), A new look at the statistical model identification, *IEEE Trans Auto Control*, 716–723
2. Chetverikov, D., and Szabo, Z. (1999), Simple and efficient algorithm for detection of high curvature points in planar curves. *Proc. 23rd Workshop of the Australian Pattern Recognition Group*, pp. 175–184
3. Dierckx, P. (1993), *Curve and Surface Fitting with Splines*. Clarendon Press.
4. Farin, G. (1992), From conic to NURBS: a tutorial and survey. *IEEE Comput Graphics Appl* 12(5), 78–86
5. Farin, G. (1989), Trends in curves and surface design. *Comput Aided Des* 21(5), 293–296
6. Piegl, L., and Tiller, W. (1997), *The NURBS Book*. Springer-Verlag, New York.
7. Piegl, L., and Tiller, W. (1991), Curve and surface reconstruction using rational B-splines. *Comput Aided Des* 19(9), 485–498.

8. Quddus, A., (1998), *Curvature Analysis Using Multi-resolution Techniques.* PhD Thesis. Department of Electrical Engineering, King Fahd University of Petroleum & Minerals, Dhahran, Saudi Arabia.

9. Sarfraz, M., and Raza, S.A. (2001), Capturing outline of fonts using genetic algorithm and splines. *The Proceedings of IEEE International Conference on Information Visualization-IV'2001-UK*, IEEE Computer Society Press, 738–743.

10. Sarfraz, M., Raza, S.A. and Baig, M.H. (2005), *Computing Optimized Curves with NURBS Using Evolutionary Intelligence*, Lecture Notes in Computer Science, Vol. 3480: Computational Science and Its Applications. Gervasi, O., Gavrilova, M.L., Kumar, V., Laganà, A., Lee, H.P., Mun, Y., and Taniar, D., eds., Springer-Verlag, New York, pp. 806–815.

11. Kling, R.M., and Benerjee, P. (1991), Empirical and theoretical studies of simulated evolution method applied to standard cell placement. *IEEE Trans Comput Aided Design* 10(10).

12. Sarfraz, M., Riyazuddin, M., and Baig, M.H. (2005), Capturing planar shapes by approximating their outlines, *Int J Computational Appl Math,* Elsevier Science.

13. Sarfraz, M., Sait, Sadiq, M., Balah, M., and Baig, M.H. (2006), Computing optimized NURBS curves using simulated evolution on control parameters, applications of soft computing: recent trends. In: *Advances in Soft Computing,* Tiwari, A., Knowles, J., Avineri, E., Dahal, K., and Roy, R., eds., Springer-Verlag New York, pp. 35–44.

14. Youssef, M. (2001), *Reverse Engineering of Geometric Surfaces Using Tabu Search Optimization Technique.* Master Thesis, Cairo University, Egypt.

15. Yau, H.-T., and Chen, J.-S., (1997), Reverse engineering of complex geometry using rational B-splines, *Int J Adv Manufacturing Technol* 13(8), 548–555.

16. Cho, M.-W., Seo, T.-I., Kim, J.-D., and Kwon, O.-Y. (2000), Reverse engineering of compound surfaces using boundary detection method, *Korean Soc Mech Eng Int J* 14(10), 1104–1113.

17. Pratt, M.J., Goult, R.J., and Ye, L. (1993), On rational parametric curve approximation, *Comput Aided Geom Des* 10, 363–377.

18. Laurent-Gengoux, P., and Mekhilef, M. (1993), Optimization of a NURBS representation, *Comput Aided Des* 25(11), 699–710.

19. Sarfraz, M. (2006), Computer-aided reverse engineering using simulated evolution on NURBS, *Int J Virtual Phys Prototyping*, Taylor & Francis, 1(4), 494–512.

15

Multiresolution Framework
for B-Splines

Abstract. *The piecewise polynomial B-spline representation is a flexible tool in CAGD for representing and designing geometric objects. In the field of computer graphics (CG), computer-aided design (CAD), or computer-aided engineering (CAE), a very useful property for a given spline model is to have locally supported basis functions. This allows localized modification of the shape. Unfortunately this property can also become a serious disadvantage when the user wishes to edit the global shape of a complex object. Multiresolution representation is proposed as a solution to alleviate this problem. Various multiresolution methods are described for different B-spline models.*

15.1 Introduction

In the field of geometric modeling, the construction of efficient, intuitive and interactive editors for geometric objects is a fundamental objective, but it is still a difficult challenge. In many freeform geometric modeling systems the users are allowed to work in the framework of a specific data model such as Bézier or nonuniform rational B-splines [6]. This imposes constraints on the set of geometric manipulation operations that can be performed, the man-machine interface and the type of objects that can be modeled.

There are various curve manipulation techniques proposed in the current literature [1–21]. The Euclidean distances between the point of modification and the control points of a B-spline curve were used as weights to affect the control points in [4]. The difficulty with this approach appears when the two separate portions of the curve are close. To alleviate the difficulty in editing freeform shapes while matching engineering specifications, constraint-based approaches have been proposed in [2, 22]. Direct and interactive manipulation tools of freeform curves and surfaces are investigated in [5].

In the field of computer graphics or computer-aided design, a very useful property for a given spline model is to have locally supported basis functions. This property allows localized modifications of the shape. Unfortunately this property can also become a serious disadvantage when the user wishes to edit the global shape of a complex object. Piecewise polynomial B-spline representation is common in many contemporary geometric modeling systems. While this is a powerful tool with many desirable properties, the same properties impose some undesirable constraints on the user. For example, the most attractive property, *locality*, restricts the user to perform global operations on the object being modeled. To perform a global operation, it has to be transformed into a series of local operations affecting only a small portion of the curve, which makes the process time a waste and precision hazardous [12]. The ability to simultaneously perform both local and global operations at will would add significant functionality to any modeling system.

Multiresolution representation is a possible solution that addresses this problem, because it allows the user to edit objects at different resolution levels. Both local and global operations can be performed on curves by representing them using multiresolution decomposition. Several approaches have been proposed for multiresolution representation of splines, mostly based on wavelets. All these approaches involve expensive precalculations in the case of curves and surfaces. It often requires specific treatment of boundary control points. Moreover, these approaches depend on the given spline model they manipulate. The whole scheme has to be redefined when it comes to manipulating other spline models; only the philosophy of the calculus can potentially be reused [12].

All the approaches presented are either for the uniform B-splines or nonuniform B-splines (NUBS). NUBS are useful because:

- By manipulating the control points, knot vector and weights, NUBS provides the facility to design a large variety of shapes.
- They offer a common mathematical form for representing and designing both standard analytic shapes (conics, quadrics) and freeform curves and surfaces.
- Evaluation is reasonably fast and computationally stable.
- NUBS have clear geometric tool kit (knot insertion/deletion, degree elevation, etc.), which can be used to design, analyze, process and interrogate objects.

In this chapter, Section 15.2 describes the general theory of B-splines. In Section 15.3, we discuss two of the multiresolution representations presented for B-splines. Section 15.4 is about another method for multiresolution representation for NUBS; it is based on control point decimation. This method, in Section 15.5, is demonstrated by means of graphics.

15.2   Theory of NUBS

The general expression for the calculation of coordinate positions along a B-spline curve in a blending function formulation is of the form:

$$P(t) = \sum_{i=0}^{n} P_i B_{i,p}(t), \quad t_{\min} \leq t < t_{\max}, 2 \leq p \leq n+1,$$

where P_i is an input set of $n+1$ control points and the B-spline blending functions $B_{i,p}$ are polynomials of degree p. The Cox Deboor [7, 13] recursive formula for the B-spline basis can be defined as:

$$B_{i,1}(t) = \begin{cases} 1, & if\ t_i \leq t \leq t_{i+1} \\ 0, & \text{otherwise.} \end{cases}$$

and

$$B_{i,p}(t) = \frac{(t - t_i)B_{i,p-1}(t)}{t_{i+p-1} - t_i} + \frac{(t_{i+p} - t)B_{i+1,p-1}(t)}{t_{i+p} - t_{i+1}},$$

where a knot vector $t = \{t_0, t_1, \ldots, t_m\}$ of $m + 1$ knots is assumed. NUBS are nonuniform B-splines and is the term given to curves that are defined on a knot vector where the interior knot spans are not equal. As an example, we may have interior knots with spans of zero. Some common curves require this type of nonuniform knot spacing. The use of this option allows better shape control and the ability to model a larger class of shapes.

15.3   Multiresolution Representation of B-Splines

In the fields of computer graphics or computer-aided design, a very useful property for a given spline model is to have locally supported basis functions in order to allow localized modifications of the shape. Unfortunately, this property can also become a serious disadvantage when the user wishes to edit the global shape of a complex object. Piecewise polynomial B-spline representation is common in many contemporary geometric modeling systems. While this is a powerful tool with many desirable properties, the same properties impose some undesirable constraints on the user. For example, the most attractive property, *locality*, restricts the user to perform global operations on the object being modeled. To perform a global operation, it has to be transformed into a series of local operations affecting only a small portion of the curve, which makes the process a waste of and precision hazardous [12]. The ability to simultaneously perform both local and global operations at will would add significant functionality to any modeling system.

Multiresolution representation is a possible solution that addresses this problem, because it allows the user to edit objects at different resolution levels. Both local and global operations can be performed on curves by representing them using multiresolution decomposition. Multiresolution analysis can be defined as an ability to simultaneously perform both local and global operations on the analyzed object [6]. Several approaches have been proposed for multiresolution representation of splines, mostly based on wavelets. All these approaches involve expensive precalculations and in the case of open curves and surfaces, often require specific treatment of boundary control points. Moreover, these approaches depend on the given spline model they manipulate; the whole scheme has to be redefined when it comes to manipulating other spline models, only the philosophy of the calculus can potentially be reused [12].

For the sake of completeness, two of the existing approaches for the multiresolution representation of B-splines are briefly presented. One uses B-spline wavelets for endpoint interpolating B-splines. Another deals with multiresolution control for nonuniform B-splines, which uses the knot decimation and least squares approximation.

15.3.1 Multiresolution Representation of B-Splines Using Wavelets

To understand the basic ideas behind wavelets and multiresolution analysis, consider a discrete signal C^n, expressed as column vector of samples. The samples can be the control points of the curve if we want to create a low-resolution version C^{n-1} of C^n with a fewer number of samples m'. The approach is to use some form of filtering and downsampling on m samples of C^n. This process can be expressed as the matrix equation:

$$C^{n-1} = A^n C^n, \tag{15.1}$$

where A^n is $m' \times m$ matrix.

Since C^{n-1} contains fewer samples than C^n, it is clear that some amount of detail is lost in the filtering process. If A^n is appropriately chosen, it is possible to capture the lost details as another signal D^{n-1}, given as:

$$D^{n-1} = B^n C^n, \tag{15.2}$$

where B^n is $(m - m') \times m$ matrix, which is related to matrix A^n. The matrices A^n and B^n are called *analysis filters*. The process of splitting C^n into low-resolution version C^{n-1} and detail D^{n-1} is called *decomposition*.

If A^n and B^n are chosen correctly, the original signal C^n can be recovered from C^{n-1} and D^{n-1} by using another pair of matrices P^n and Q^n as

$$C^n = P^n C^{n-1} + Q^n D^{n-1}, \tag{15.3}$$

The recovery process of C^n from C^{n-1} and D^{n-1} is called *reconstruction*, and the pair of matrices P^n and Q^n are called *synthesis filters*. The procedure of splitting C^n into a low-resolution part C^{n-1} and a detail part D^{n-1} can be applied recursively to the new signal C^{n-1}. Thus, the original signal can be decomposed as a hierarchy of low-resolution signals $C^0, \ldots, C^{n-1}$ and details $D^0, \ldots, D^{n-1}$. This recursive process is known as a *filter bank*.

Since the original signal C^n can be recovered from the sequence $C^0, D^0, D^1, \ldots, D^{n-1}$, this sequence can be thought of as a transform of the original signal, known as *wavelet transform*. The total size of the transform $C^0, D^0, D^1, \ldots, D^{n-1}$ is the same as that of the original signal C^n, that is, no extra storage is required. For the detailed description, refer to [19–21].

For performing the wavelet transform, all that is needed is an appropriate set of analysis and synthesis filters A^j, B^j, P^j, and Q^j. To construct these filters, each signal C^n is associated with a function $f^n(u)$ with $u \in [0, 1]$ given by:

$$f^n(u) = \Phi^n(u) C^n, \tag{15.4}$$

where $\Phi^n(u)$ is a row matrix of basis functions $\left[\phi_1^n(u), \ldots, \phi_1^n(u)\right]$ called *scaling functions*.

The scaling functions are required to be refinable; that is, for all j in $[1, n]$ a matrix P^j must exist such that

$$\Phi^{j-1} = \Phi^j P^j. \tag{15.5}$$

Each scaling function at level $j - 1$ must be expressible as a linear combination of *finer* scaling functions at level j.

Next, let V^j be the linear space spanned by the set of scaling functions Φ^j. From Equation (15.5), it is implied that these spaces are nested, that is, $V^0 \subset V^1 \subset \ldots \subset V^n$. Choosing an inner product for the basis functions in V^j allows us to define W^j as the orthogonal complement of V^j in V^{j+1}, that is, the space W^j whose basis functions $\Psi^j = \left[\psi_1^n(u), \ldots, \psi_{m-m'}^n(u)\right]$ are such that Φ^j and Ψ^j together form a basis for V^{j+1}, and every $\psi_i^j(u)$ is orthogonal to every $\phi_i^j(u)$ under the chosen inner product. The basis functions $\psi_i^j(u)$ are called *wavelets*.

The synthesis filter Q^j can be constructed as the matrix that satisfies

$$\Psi^{j-1} = \Phi^j Q^j. \tag{15.6}$$

The above two equations can be expressed as a single equation by concatenating the matrices together:

$$[\Phi^{j-1}|\Psi^{j-1}] = \Phi^j[P^j|Q^j]. \tag{15.7}$$

The analysis filters A^j and B^j are formed by the matrices satisfying the inverse relation:

The matrices $[P^j|Q^j]$ and $[A^j|B^j]^T$ are both square matrices. Therefore, we have the following:

$$[\Phi^{j-1}|\Psi^{j-1}]\begin{bmatrix} A^j \\ \hline B^j \end{bmatrix} = \Phi^j,$$

$$\begin{bmatrix} A^j \\ \hline B^j \end{bmatrix} = \left[P^j|Q^j\right]^{-1}.$$

15.3.2 Multiresolution of NUBS Using Knot Decimation

Another method described is for the multiresolution representation of nonuniform B-splines (NUBS) as presented in [6]. The multiresolution decomposition of the freeform NUBS curve is computed using the least-squares approximation based on existing data-reduction techniques. The least-squares decomposition allows the support of NUBS curves, but it also imposes some processing penalties in both time and space compared to techniques for multiresolution uniform B-spline curves [6].

Let $C_k(t)$ be a B-spline curve of order n and l_k control points, defined over the knot vector τ_k, where $k \in Z^+$. Let V_k be the space induced by τ_k, and let $\tau_{k-1} \subset \tau_k$. The new space induced by τ_{k-1}, denoted by V_{k-1} is clearly a strict subspace of V_k. Now, suppose $C_{k-1}(t) (\in V_{k1})$ is the least-squares approximation of $C_k(t)$ in the space V_{k-1}, and their difference is the *detail* $D_{k-1}(t) \in V_k$, given by:

$$D_{k-1}(t) = C_k(t) - C_{k-1}(t). \tag{15.8}$$

This process of decomposing a curve into two parts, one a low-resolution approximation and one a high-resolution detail can be applied recursively. The value of $C_k(t)$ can then be expressed as:

$$C_k(t) C_0(t) + \sum_{i=0}^{k-1} D_i(t), \tag{15.9}$$

where $C_0(t) \in V_0$ and $D_i(t) \in V_{i+1}$. In order to construct a multiresolution decomposition of a NUBS curve, as in the above equation, the knot sequence τ_i, inducing the subspaces V_i must first be defined. The value of τ_k is the knot vector of the original curve; the subsequent knot vectors $\tau_i, 0 \le i < k$, can be constructed such that $\tau_i \subset \tau_{i+1}$ and $2|\tau_i| \approx |\tau_{i+1}|$, where $||$ denotes the size of the knot vector. The end conditions of the original curve must be preserved; hence the knots $\tau_j \in \tau_i, 0 \le j < n$ and $l_i \le j < l_i + n, \forall 0 \le i < k$ are unmodified, where l_i denotes the number of control points defining $C_i(t)$ over τ_i. In general, $l_i = |\tau_i| + n$. This knot decimation process defines the function space hierarchy and is independent of the specific curve being decomposed.

For a B-spline curve with knot vector τ_k of size 2^k, k subspaces will be constructed; each induced by approximately half the knots of the previous level. The lowest resolution approximation $C_0(t)$ will a single polynomial curve, that is, the knot vector τ_0 has no interior knots ($\tau_0 = 2n$). Least-squares techniques are employed to find the curve $C_i(t) \in V_i$, defined over τ_i, best approximating $C_k(t)$.

Knots are selected so as to minimize the local effect on the curve due to removals from level i to level $I + 1$. Hence, consecutive knots should not be removed in one step. Removing every nth knot, where n is the order of the curve that will cause the least change from one level to the next, yet affect the entire curve. As the degree of a Bézier or B-spline curve is increased, the curve becomes smoother due to the low-pass property of the basis functions of the representation. Therefore, as n increases, by selecting every nth knot for removal, the knots are removed at larger intervals, yet the curve becomes smoother. In practice, it is found that removing every alternate knot still retains a sufficient number of resolution levels to enable an effective multiresolution control. Moreover, the computational overhead required for the algebraic summation is kept at interactive speeds.

15.4 Multiresolution of NUBS Using Control Point Decimation

In this section, we present a model based on control point decimation for multiresolution representation of NUBS. By using the ability to control a B-spline curve by changing the position and order of the control points, we can come up with a multiresolution representation for NUBS.

Let $C_k(t)$ be a NUBS curve, defined over the set of polygon vertices or control points P_k, containing l_k points. Let the curve uses the knot vector T_k, where k is a positive integer, greater than zero. There are various methods proposed for the calculation of nonuniform knots. A popular method is to calculate the knot vector proportional to the chord lengths between the defining polygon vertices. We use the same knot calculation method. The NUBS curve $C_k(t)$ is calculated from the control points P_k as described in detail in Section 15.2.

Let V_k be the space of all the curves that can be defined using control points P_k. Now, we find a subset P_{k-1} of $P_k (P_{k-1} \subset P_k)$; clearly the space V_{k-1} induced by P_{k-1} is a subset of V_k. Let $C_{k-1}(t) \in V_{k-1}$ be a curve defined over the control points P_{k-1}. We find that it is the approximation to the higher-resolution curve $C_k(t)$. To find P_{k-1} from P_k, we use the process of decimation.

Let a unary operator $\mathbf{d}_j$ be defined for decimation, where j denotes the interval that is used to decimate the control points. If j is 2 then every second (alternate) control point is decimated; if j is 3 then select every third control point (i.e., control points numbered 3, 6, 9, etc.) for removal. Similarly, if j is i then decimate every ith control point. Mathematically, control point decimation is given by:

$$P_{k-1} = \mathbf{d}_j(P_k). \tag{15.10}$$

To minimize the local effect on the resulting curve $C_{k-1}(t)$, consecutive control points from P_k should not be removed to obtain P_{k-1}. It is observed that removing every alternate point causes the acceptable amount of local effect and still retains a sufficient number of resolution levels to enable an effective multiresolution control. The lost control points can be captured as Q_{k-1}.

Let another unary operator $\mathbf{c}_j$ be defined to capture the decimated control points. Here also j denotes the interval used to decimate the points. Mathematically Q_{k-1} can be computed as:

$$Q_{k-1} = \mathbf{c}_j(P_k). \tag{15.11}$$

The process of decomposition can be applied recursively until P_0, which contains only n control points where n is the order of the B-spline curve. The following algorithm summarizes the multiresolution decomposition process, and the flow chart in Figure 15.1 shows it pictorially.

INPUT:
$C_k(t)$, a NUBS curve.

OUTPUT:
$P_0, Q_i, 0 \leq i < k$, the multiresolution decomposition of $C_k(t)$.
ALGORITHM:
- $P_k \Leftarrow$ control points of $C_k(t)$;
- for $i = k - 1$ to 0 step -1 do
begin
$$P_i = \mathbf{d}_j(P_{i+1});$$
$$Q_i = \mathbf{c}_j(P_{i+1});$$
end;

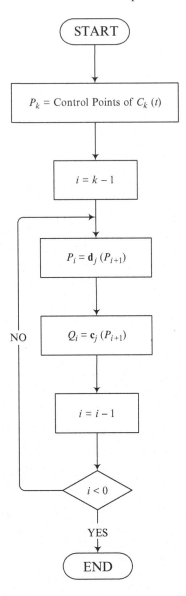

FIGURE 15.1. Flow chart of the multiresolution decomposition process.

The reconstruction of P_i from P_{i-1} and Q_{i-1} is carried out by merging the sets P_{i-1} and Q_{i-1}. Let a binary operator $\mathbf{r}_j$ be defined for the process of reconstruction of P_i from P_{i-1} and Q_{i-1}. The reconstruction is mathematically represented as:

$$P_i = \mathbf{r}_j(P_{i-1}, Q_{i-1}). \qquad (15.12)$$

While reconstructing, the criteria used for the decomposition should be followed. For example, if every jth point is decimated during decomposition, then the reconstruction of P_i is obtained by rearranging P_{i-1} and Q_{i-1} as; place $(j-1)$ points from P_{i-1} and one point from Q_{i-1} in the same order and so on.

By means of recursively applying the reconstruction operator, the original set of control points can be represented in terms of its multiresolution components as:

$$P_k = \mathbf{r}_j(P_0, Q_0, Q_1, Q_2, \ldots, Q_{k-1}). \qquad (15.13)$$

The recursion in Equation (15.13) can be expanded as follows:

$$
\begin{aligned}
P_k &= \mathbf{r}_j(\mathbf{r}_j(P_0, Q_0), Q_1, Q_2, \ldots, Q_{k-1}) \\
&= \mathbf{r}_j(P_1, Q_1, Q_2, \ldots, Q_{k-1}) \\
&= \mathbf{r}_j(\mathbf{r}_j(P_1, Q_1), Q_2, \ldots, Q_{k-1}) \\
&\quad \ldots \\
&= \mathbf{r}_j(P_{k-1}, Q_{k-1})
\end{aligned}
$$

15.5 Demonstration

In this section, the multiresolution representation of Section 15.5 is demonstrated by applying it to NUBS curves. This scheme is also demonstrated for surfaces as an extension. Figure 15.2 shows a NURBS curve of degree 3 consisting of 319 control points with default weight values. In total, six multiresolution levels are obtained for this curve, as shown in Figure 15.3. The original curve is shown in thin lines and the curves in thick lines are the decomposed versions at each level of multiresolution. We assume that the original curve is at *level* 6; the curve in Figure 35.3(a) consists of 159 control points and is at *level* 5. Similarly, the curves in Figure 15.3(b)–(f) contain 80, 40, 20, 10 and 5 control points and are at decomposition level 4, 3, 2, 1, and 0, respectively.

Figure 15.4 shows another NUBS curve drawn with 259 control points. After applying the multiresolution decomposition, the decomposed curves are obtained

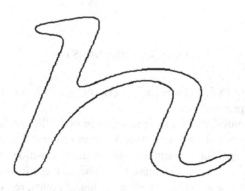

FIGURE 15.2. A NUBS curve.

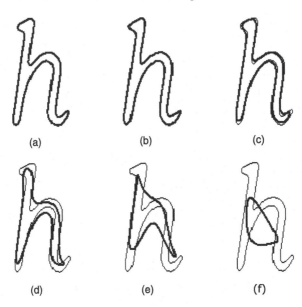

(a)   (b)   (c)

(d)   (e)   (f)

FIGURE 15.3. Multiresolution decomposition of the NUBS curve in Figure 15.2.

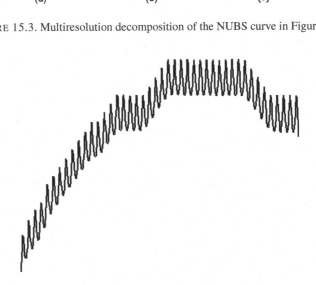

FIGURE 15.4. Another NUBS curve.

as shown in Figure 15.5. Figures 15.5(a)–(f) contain 130, 66, 34, 18, 10 and 6 control points, respectively.

As part of the muiltiresolution representation of NUBS surfaces, Figure 15.6 shows a NUBS surface drawn with 30×30 mesh of control points. This surface is decomposed by applying the multiresolution decomposition to obtain the low-resolution versions as shown in Figure 15.7. The surfaces in Figures 15.7(a)–(c) consist of 15×15, 8×8, and 4×4 mesh of control points, respectively.

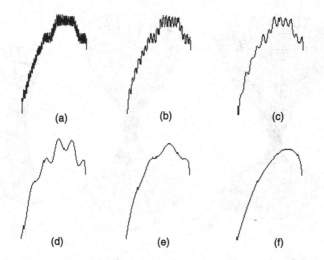

FIGURE 15.5. Multiresolution decomposition of the curve in Figure 15.4.

FIGURE 15.6. A NUBS surface.

Figure 15.8 shows another NUBS surface with 33×33 mesh of control points, its decomposed version of the surfaces are shown in Figures 15.9(a)–(c), consisting of 17×17, 9×9, and 5×5 mesh of control points, respectively.

15.6 Summary

A framework for multiresolution representation of NUBS is developed for use in various computer graphics applications that require both local and global operations to be performed on B-splines. The developed method of multiresolution can

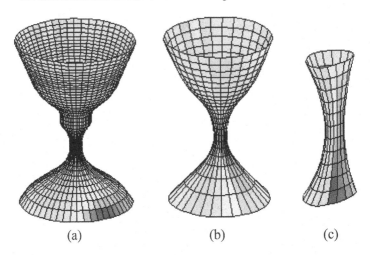

(a)   (b)   (c)

FIGURE 15.7. Multiresolution decomposition levels of the surface in Figure 15.6.

FIGURE 15.8. Another NUBS surface.

be used for the purpose of performing editing on the B-splines. The idea of multiresolution representation of NUBS curves is extended to achieve multiresolution control for surfaces as well. The method is very efficient with respect to execution time as it uses a very simple technique for the decomposition, which does not require extensive calculations. The method presented is not capable of providing a continuous resolution control, that is, the decomposition at fraction levels.

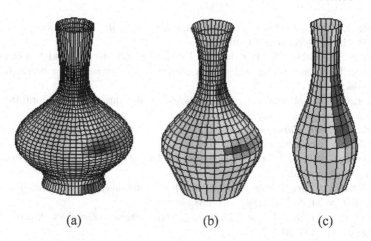

(a)   (b)   (c)

FIGURE 15.9. Multiresolution decomposition of the surface in Figure 15.8.

15.7   Exercises

1. Implement the multiresolution method of Section 15.3.1.
2. Implement the multiresolution method of Section 15.3.2.
3. Implement the multiresolution method of Section 15.4.
4. Make a comparative study of the three schemes in Exercises 15.6.1–15.6.3 with respect to time.
5. Make a critical thinking on a possible extension to the scheme in Section 15.4 so that it has the ability to have a continuous multiresolution control. This would add a significant functionality to this method.
6. Extend the method in Section 15.4 to the weighted Nu-splines of Chapter 2 that has the similar properties as those of NUBS but with extra freedom of shape parameters. (*Hint*: Sometimes we encounter curves and surfaces in which some control points are significant. Decimation of these control points may drastically change the shape of the object. In view of this, there should be an intelligent technique that can check these significant points at the time of decimation. This can be achieved by assigning a weight value for each point based on its significance.)

References

1. Bartels, R.H., and Samavati, F.F. (2000), Reversing subdivision rules: local linear conditions and observations on inner products, *J Computational Appl Math* 119(1–2), 29–67.
2. Celniker, G., and Gossard, D. (1991), Deformable curve and surface finite elements for freeform shape design, *Comput Graphics* 25(4).
3. Chughtai, M.S.A. (1999), *ANURBS: An Alternative to the NURBS of Degree Three*, MS Thesis, King Fahd University of Petroleum & Minerals, Dhahran Saudi Arabia.

4. Cobb, E. (1984), *Design of Sculptured Surfaces Using the B-spline Representation*, Ph.D. Thesis, University of Utah, Utah.

5. Conner, D., Snibble, S., Herndon, K., Robins, D., Zeleznic, R., and Van-Dam, A. (1992), Three-dimensional widgets, *Proceeding of the Symposium on Interactive 3D Graphics*.

6. Elber, G., and Gotsman, C. (1995), Multiresolution control for nonuniform B-spline curve editing, *Pacific Graphics '95*.

7. Farin, G. (1990), *Curves and Surfaces for Computer-Aided Geometric Design: A Practical Guide*, Academic Press, New York.

8. Farin, G. (1992), *NURB Curves and Surfaces: From Projective Geometry to Practical Use*, AK Peters Ltd.

9. Finkelstein, A., and Salesin, D.H. (1994), Multiresolution curves, *Proceedings of SIGGRAPH*, ACM, New York, pp. 261–268,

10. Foley, V.D., Feiner, H., and Phillips. (1994), *Computer Graphics*, Prentice-Hall, Englewood Cliffs, NJ.

11. Gregory, J.A., Sarfraz, M., and Yuen, P.K. (1994), Interactive curve design using C^2 rational splines, *Comput Graphics* 18(2), 153–159.

12. Grisoni L., Schlick C., and Blanc, C. (1997), *An Hermitian Approach for Multiresolution Splines*, Technical Report no. 1192–97, LaBRI.

13. Rogers, D.F., and Adams A.J., (1990), *Mathematical Elements for Computer Graphics*, 2nd Edition, McGraw-Hill, New York.

14. Sarfraz, M., and Raheem A. (2000), Curve designing using a rational cubic spline with point and interval shape control, *The Proceedings of IEEE International Conference on Information Visualization-IV*, IEEE Computer Society Press, pp. 63–68

15. Sarfraz, M. (1999), Designing of objects using rational quadratic spline with interval shape control, *Proc. International Conference on Imaging Science, Systems, and Technology (CISST'99)*, Las Vegas, NV, CSREA Press, pp. 558–564.

16. Sarfraz, M. (1995), Curves and surfaces for CAD using C^2 rational cubic splines, *Eng Comput* 11(2), 94–102.

17. Sarfraz, M (1994), Cubic spline curves with shape control, *Comput Graphics* 18(5), 707–713.

18. Sarfraz, M. (1994), Generalized geometric interpolation for rational cubic splines, *Comput Graphics* 18(1), 61–72.

19. Stollnitz, E.J., DeRose T.D., and Salesin D.H. (1995), Wavelets for computer graphics: a primer, part-1, *IEEE Comput Graphics Appl* 15(3), 76–84.

20. Stollnitz, E.J., DeRose T.D., and Salesin D.H. (1995), Wavelets for computer graphics: a primer, part-2, *IEEE Comput Graphics Appl* 15(4), 75–85.

21. Stollnitz, E.J., DeRose, T.D., and Salesin, D.H. (1996), *Wavelets for Computer Graphics: Theory and Applications*, Morgan Kaufman Publishers, San Francisco, CA.

22. Welch, W., and Witkin, A. (1992), Variational surface modeling, *Comput Graphics* 26(2).

Index